PUBLIC OPINION

THIRD EDITION

PUBLIC OPINION

THIRD EDITION

Carroll J. Glynn
THE OHIO STATE UNIVERSITY

Susan Herbst
UNIVERSITY OF CONNECTICUT

Mark Lindeman
VASSAR COLLEGE

Garrett J. O'Keefe
COLORADO STATE UNIVERSITY

Robert Y. Shapiro
COLUMBIA UNIVERSITY

WESTVIEW
PRESS
A Member of the Perseus Books Group

WESTVIEW PRESS was founded in 1975 in Boulder, Colorado,
by notable publisher and intellectual Fred Praeger.
Westview Press continues to publish scholarly titles and
high-quality undergraduate- and graduate-level textbooks in core
social science disciplines. With books developed, written, and edited with the needs
of serious nonfiction readers, professors, and students in mind, Westview Press
honors its long history of publishing books that matter.

Copyright © 2016 by Westview Press
Published by Westview Press,
A Member of the Perseus Books Group
2465 Central Avenue
Boulder, CO 80301
www.westviewpress.com

Westview Press books are available at special discounts for bulk purchases
in the United States by corporations, institutions, and other organizations.
For more information, please contact the Special Markets Department at the
Perseus Books Group, 2300 Chestnut Street, Suite 200, Philadelphia, PA 19103,
or call (800) 810-4145, ext. 5000,
or e-mail special.markets@perseusbooks.com.

Designed by Cynthia Young

A CIP catalog record for the print version of this book is available from
the Library of Congress
PB ISBN: 978-0-8133-4940-4
EBOOK ISBN: 978-0-8133-4941-1
10 9 8 7 6 5 4 3 2 1

CONTENTS

LIST OF ILLUSTRATIONS AND BOXES

TABLES

FIGURES

BOXES

PREFACE

This book began many years ago as a collaborative project among several scholars, all interested in the essential nature of public opinion. We all believe that public opinion is a vital component in the democratic process, and we were drawn to the topic long ago as students. Now, as researchers and teachers, we still think that students of politics and communication should understand how people form opinions, how public opinion is measured, and how the data of public opinion are used in American policymaking and journalism. Without public opinion, we do not have much of a democracy, so how public sentiments are expressed and evaluated is crucial for scholars, students, and citizens alike to understand.

The authors of this volume come from the diverse fields of political science, communications, and journalism; therefore we bring with us a large arsenal of ideas and perspectives. We take an open, interdisciplinary approach to the topic, unlike that applied in most public opinion textbooks. We look at public opinion on the macrohistorical level, the institutional level, the level of small group interaction, and the micropsychological level. We are interested in how Americans come to have opinions in the first place, how the media enable or prevent the formation of certain attitudes, and how our leaders acknowledge or fail to acknowledge the public mood regarding various policies. There are a great many moments when public opinion matters, so we study public opinion dynamics during campaigns and between them. Public opinion generally is most obvious during election campaigns or national crises, but here we pay close attention to day-to-day attitude formation with regard to issues on the contemporary scene. You will find, as you read through this wide-ranging book, that Americans' attitudes are sometimes stable and at other times malleable, sometimes liberal and at other times conservative. We hope that you come away from this book with a new appreciation for the complexities of public opinion.

This book was an enormous, although also very gratifying, undertaking. We have many people to thank, although a few stand out for their relentless and good-natured support. We would like to thank Jill Edy and Bruce Williams for their contributions to the first edition, many of which remain in this edition. The discussion of policymaking in Chapter 10 still heavily depends on the contributions of Larry Jacobs, who coauthored this chapter in the second edition. Michael Huge and Andrea Dixon contributed extensive research to help us update Chapters 5, 6, 7, and 11. We thank the many people who have commented extensively on the manuscript at various stages, including: Barbara Bardes, Charles Cameron, Jack Citrin, Rosalee Clawson, Serban Iorga, Ted Jelen, Noah Kaplan, Martha Kayler, Franco Mattei, David Park, Greg Shaw, and Oscar Torres-Reyna. At Westview Press, we are grateful for Ada Fung's guidance and yeoman editorial efforts and for Amber Morris's expert attention to manuscript preparation.

Once again, we celebrate the families who have sustained us and enriched our lives through the years and editions of this project. Many thanks to our significant others: Thomas Conrad, Doug Hughes, Nancy B. Rubenstein, the late Mary Lucy DeFlorio, Jane Viste, and Lucy Miller. And to all of our children: Biru, Patric, Ryan, Daniel, Becky, Margaret, and Harriet.

INTRODUCING PUBLIC OPINION | 1

1

The Meanings of Public Opinion

Public opinion is endlessly discussed in American politics and culture. The president, members of Congress, candidates for public office, interest group leaders, journalists, and corporate executives, as well as ordinary citizens, routinely ask: "What does the public think?" Political leaders need to know what sorts of policies and initiatives voters support, but other groups and individuals also need a working knowledge of public opinion. Interest group leaders must decide which battles to wage and how best to mobilize potential supporters. Journalists, who are key players in measuring and communicating public opinion, strive both to inform those of us who are curious about our fellow citizens' attitudes and to understand what their audience wants. Corporate executives must pay attention to trends in American culture—what consumers think about, what they purchase, and generally, how they choose to live.

How can all these parties—and the rest of us—obtain information about American public opinion? There are many sources. Perhaps the most obvious indicator of public opinion is the sample survey or opinion poll. Quantitative data from surveys can often give us a sense of how Americans feel about policy issues, social practices, or lifestyle issues. The results of elections and referenda sometimes reveal citizens' preferences in very dramatic ways; it is often said that an election is the only poll that matters. Yet students of American politics must go beyond these obvious techniques and consider all of the "places" that people's opinions can be found: in the scripts of television programs; at political rallies, town meetings, or city council hearings; in the rhetoric of journalism; in the dialogue among friends who frequent a coffeehouse or neighborhood bar; in the political discussions one sees on the Internet and on social media or hears on talk radio. This book takes a broad view of what the phrase "public opinion" really means. To focus on survey results alone is to miss most of the story.

Three key terms summarize the concerns of this text: politics, communication, and social process. What do we mean by these words? *Politics*, in the context of this book, refers to the ways Americans govern ourselves and implement public policy. Our discussions of public opinion in politics go far beyond campaigns. Political campaigns do often attract close attention to—if not obsession with—every shift in the "horse race" for public support. The role of public opinion in policy debates receives less (although still considerable) media coverage, but may be even more important. Even politicians who claim not to care much about public opinion often watch closely for insight into how to present their policy proposals or which proposals are better not presented at all.

Although the connections between public opinion and politics are widely studied, *communication* issues have received far less scholarly attention than they deserve. How is public opinion expressed in America? How do the media influence the ways opinions are communicated and even the substance of those opinions? It is widely said that we live in an "information age," but how have new communication technologies influenced public opinion? This book explores how both mass media and interpersonal forms of communication shape public sentiment. Since the diffusion of film in the early twentieth century, communication researchers have studied how mass media both reflect and shape people's preferences and models of the political world. Social psychology provides insights into how a human tendency toward conformity often affects how people talk, behave, and vote.

Finally, public opinion is the result of *social processes*. That is, it is intertwined with various societal forces and institutions, such as the changing American demographic profile, the problems of inner cities, and the state of family life. Public opinion is embedded in culture and should always be considered in its social context.

WHY STUDY PUBLIC OPINION?

Public opinion research is a very broad field, because scholars in many disciplines need to understand how attitudes about public affairs are formed, communicated, and measured. As we will see in Chapter 2, public opinion study is as old as democracy itself: the ancient Greek philosophers believed that democratic institutions, to be effective, had to be grounded in a solid analysis of popular sentiments. Here we consider four broad reasons why so many scholars and public officials study and care about public opinion.

1. The Legitimacy and Stability of Governments Depends on Public Support

The US Declaration of Independence states that governments "deriv[e] their just powers from the consent of the governed." That assertion implies that if citizens withdraw their consent, the government has no legitimate powers. "Democracy" may entail much more than public consent, but democratic theorists generally agree that it involves at least that much. Note that the declaration makes a claim about justice. Here, legitimacy is a *normative* concept—that is, an opinion (or a debate) about how things ought to be.

Normative issues aside, we might wonder: If citizens don't support a government, is it likely to collapse? How public attitudes affect government stability is an *empirical* question, or a matter of fact. Perhaps widespread public dissatisfaction with government and lack of commitment to democratic values put democratic states at risk. Many observers believe that one or both of these factors helped Germany's Nazi Party gain power in the 1930s and may explain the demise or fragility of democratic governments today. Others think that public opinion makes relatively little difference in whether democracies survive.

Public opinion researchers have investigated Americans' attitudes toward government and political arrangements for many years. How much do members of the public trust their political leaders? Do they believe that Congress is responsive to their needs? Do they believe that political campaigns help them choose the best candidates? Do they yearn for a powerful leader who can "get things done," essentially a dictator? Questions like these continue to inform—and at times to inflame—debates about legitimacy, stability, and other issues.

2. Public Opinion Constrains (or Should Constrain) Political Leaders

People's opinions about policy issues, like their opinions about government and democratic values, engage both normative and empirical questions. Normatively, how should public opinion influence policy? Should governments do whatever citizens want them to do? Does the answer depend on the issue, or on exactly what citizens want? Empirically, how does public opinion influence policy? To what extent, and under what circumstances, does public opinion cause political leaders to do things they would not otherwise do or prevent them from doing what they want? What are people's opinions about policy issues, anyway? Questions such as these inspire much research, debate, and armchair speculation.

FIGURE 1.1 **Public Opinion Demonstration during the Vietnam War Years.**
SOURCE: Courtesy of the Library of Congress.

Chapter 10 explores the links between public opinion and public policy in depth, and that linkage is among the most important reasons we study popular attitudes. Presidents, members of Congress, state legislators, and even local city council members must always be aware of public opinion. Sometimes leaders promote a policy and the public quickly supports their ideas, such as when the public "rallies around the flag" in the early days of a military conflict. At other times a groundswell of public opinion comes first, and leaders respond with action (see Figure 1.1). For the most part, however, the interaction between leaders and the public is far more complex, because communication is so imperfect. Journalists, for example, can knowingly or unknowingly distort public opinion; policymakers can confuse the "voice of the people" with the voices of media professionals. Or journalists may affect public opinion by misrepresenting or ignoring aspects of a policy debate.

3. Public Opinion Provides Clues about Culture

Public opinion on policy and social issues can offer crucial insights into larger currents in American culture. Since it is difficult for social scientists to study the many dimensions of American culture, we often draw inferences about that larger culture from narrower studies of public attitudes.

For example, researchers have researched public attitudes about welfare programs to study broader cultural attitudes. Since the 1960s, when the US government initiated several large antipoverty programs, public opinion researchers have asked Americans how they feel about such programs. The results of these studies tell us a lot about American norms and values. (Of course, varying descriptions of the programs can elicit very different answers—and those differences can contribute to our knowledge.) If, over the course of several years, survey respondents increasingly support the idea that welfare recipients should be required to work, we learn something about changing values: the trend may indicate a growing impatience with the poor, a renewal of the work ethic, or a general resurgence of conservative political ideology. All of these hypotheses need more rigorous study, but social scientists are often "tipped off" about larger cultural trends by survey results or other evidence about public opinion.

One might argue that public opinion and culture are so intertwined as to be inseparable. In addition to being the source of aesthetic "products" (e.g., art, music, dance, and the like), culture is a sum of people's norms, values, and sentiments—common subjects of public opinion research (see Box 1.1). In this text we do not assume that any part of popular culture is inherently outside the bounds of public opinion, but neither do we argue that public opinion subsumes everything worth knowing about culture.

4. Political Leaders Seek to Change or Mobilize Public Opinion

While political leaders may be constrained by public opinion, they also try to influence it. The most obvious circumstance is wartime, when presidents typically urge citizens to make large sacrifices: to send their sons and daughters off to war, to conserve scarce resources, and to contribute in other ways. During World War II this sort of mobilization was not particularly difficult. That war was widely perceived as, to use Studs Terkel's phrase, a "good war," in which we were fighting for freedom for ourselves and others. Other mobilizations for war have been more difficult or more complicated. A vocal and intelligent antiwar sentiment existed in the days before our entry into World War I, for example, as a variety of writers and artists attempted to persuade Americans that the United States should stay out of European affairs (see Figure 1.2). And in the 1960s President Lyndon B. Johnson attempted to convince an increasingly resistant

BOX 1.1
Culture, Art, and Public Opinion

History often provides excellent examples of how culture and public opinion are interwoven. Let us take one interesting historical case of this relationship—the popularity of Shakespearean drama in nineteenth-century America—to illustrate that nexus. Our example comes from historian Lawrence Levine's *Highbrow, Lowbrow: The Emergence of Cultural Hierarchy in America.* Today Shakespeare is generally considered "highbrow" entertainment with limited appeal, but in the nineteenth century his plays were vastly popular across class lines.

Levine argues that Shakespeare's drama was so popular because it appealed to some basic beliefs among Americans at the time. In particular, Shakespearean drama emphasized the struggle of the individual: "His plays had meaning to a nation that placed the individual at the center of the universe and personalized the large questions of the day."[1]

Levine gives an example of how popular political feeling of the period manifested itself in May 1849, when two leading Shakespearean actors (the American Edwin Forrest and the British star William Charles Macready) were giving competing performances in two different New York theaters:

Forrest's vigorous acting style, his militant love of his country, his outspoken belief in its citizenry, and his frequent articulation of the possibilities of self-improvement and social mobility endeared him to the American people, while Macready's cerebral acting style, his aristocratic demeanor, and his identification with the wealthy gentry made him appear Forrest's diametric opposite. On May 7, Macready and Forrest appeared against one another in separate productions of *Macbeth.* Forrest's performance, at the Broadway Theater, was a triumph both dramatically and politically. When Forrest spoke Macbeth's lines, "What rhubarb, senna or what purgative drug will scour these English hence?" the entire audience, according to the actor Lester Wallack, "rose and cheered for many minutes." Macready's performance, at the Astor Place Opera House, was never heard—he was silenced by a storm of boos and cries of "Three groans for the codfish aristocracy," which drowned out appeals for order from those in the boxes, and by an avalanche of eggs, apples, potatoes, lemons, and ultimately, chairs hurled from the gallery, which forced him to leave the stage in the third act.[2]

(continues)

WHY STUDY PUBLIC OPINION? 9

(continued)   BOX 1.1
                        Culture, Art, and Public Opinion

The next evening 1,800 people gathered at the Opera House to shout Macready down. A riot ensued, and when it was over, 22 people were dead and more than 150 injured.

For our purposes, this colorful yet tragic incident in American theatrical history has a variety of implications. To begin with, it demonstrates how the performing arts rest on ideology: Americans of the mid-nineteenth century, as well as those living in the early twenty-first century, have often been hostile toward art and artists who somehow reflect unpopular beliefs. This example also underscores the fact that public opinion and culture are inextricably intertwined: Americans have never drawn a sharp dividing line between politics and art. Finally, the riot illustrates how political expression (violent expression, in this instance) manifests itself in a variety of forms. In this case, a dramatic performance served as a trigger for public discourse and action, but often speeches, telecasts, and actions of our leaders serve as catalysts for the display of pent-up ideological feeling.

---
[1]Lawrence W. Levine, Highbrow, *Lowbrow: The Emergence of Cultural Hierarchy in America* (Cambridge, MA: Harvard University Press, 1988), 63.
[2]Ibid.

public that US military action in Vietnam was proper and morally sound. Often, of course, political leaders do not agree about what should happen, and then they may engage in a struggle to win public opinion over to their respective sides.

A political leader who needs to mobilize public opinion must first understand its nature. The same holds true for students of politics, who try to make sense of government-inspired collective action. Under what circumstances do people support the president with patriotic fervor, and why? How should military leaders present the nature of a conflict to the public to make the cause a popular one? Having an understanding of public attitudes, beliefs, and values is important if leaders are to persuade us with their rhetoric, but they must also have a good grasp of public opinion dynamics: the interaction of media and

FIGURE 1.2. **"Having Their Fling."** This cartoon, drawn by artist Art Young in 1917, depicts a variety of parties who supported US participation in World War I, which Young opposed. The drawing eventually was used in a landmark sedition case against Young and several other writers and artists who produced the antiwar, socialist magazine called *The Masses*. A jury found the group not guilty, although *The Masses* eventually folded due to a variety of other financial and political problems.

SOURCE: www.archive.org.

public opinion, the concept that different channels of communication have different effects on audiences, and the like.

THE MEANING OF PUBLIC OPINION

Although "public opinion" is an essential concept in democratic theory, it eludes a simple and agreed upon definition. Researchers and theorists from many disciplines, applying disparate assumptions and methodologies, often use distinct definitions. This diversity reflects the inherent complexity and ambiguity of the subject. Also, the meaning of public opinion is tied to changing historical circumstances: the sort of political culture that exists, the nature of communication technology, and the importance of public participation in the everyday workings of government.

A good place to begin our discussion of how to define "public opinion" is to consider what constitutes a "public." The concept of a public grew out of Enlightenment democratic ideals and the many important social transformations that took place in the late nineteenth and early twentieth centuries in Europe. A working definition of a public grew from its contrasts to other kinds of social formations, most prominently crowds and masses.

The Crowd

In the early twentieth century the new science of "crowd psychology" (a forerunner of social psychology) developed to explain how individuals could be caught up in mass behavior and transformed. How was it that people were collectively enticed to do things they would never dream of doing alone? For example, how can cheerleaders at a football game get people in the stands to jump, shout, yell, and carry on in ways they normally would not? During the early twentieth century societies were becoming more urban, and the labor and socialist movements were beginning to assert themselves. There were strikes, riots, and other instances of collective behavior that many elites feared signaled impending disaster.

The most prominent of the crowd psychology scholars was Gustave Le Bon, whose famous study *The Crowd* appeared in 1895. Le Bon believed that crowd behavior resulted from (1) the anonymity of crowd members, resulting in a perception of "invincibility" and lack of personal responsibility; (2) the contagion of ideas and feelings in the crowd, producing rapid shifts in behavior; and (3) the suggestibility of the crowd, enabling people to hold ideas and behave in ways they normally would not behave.[1] In fact, William Trotter likened crowds to animal herds—with the actions of the "lead" individuals transmitting to the others by "suggestion."[2]

A crowd is commonly defined by its "unity of emotional experience."[3] According to contemporary opinion researcher Vincent Price, "The crowd develops in response to shared emotions."[4] The study of crowds has expanded to consider fads, crazes, and social movements, and some scholars believe that crowd-like phenomena could be central to the early formation and expression of public opinion.[5]

The Mass

Crowds are defined by their shared emotional experiences, but masses are defined by their interpersonal isolation. Sociologist Herbert Blumer, writing in the 1940s, states that a mass is composed of anonymous individuals who engage in very little interaction or communication.[6] Price notes that a mass is extremely heterogeneous, including people from all strata of society and all walks of life.[7] A mass "merely consists of an aggregation of individuals who are separate, detached, anonymous," reacting in response to their own needs, Blumer argues.[8]

This concept of a mass, like the "crowd" concept, grew out of the social transformations occurring around the turn of the century. People became more mobile. Many moved to the cities and became disconnected from their roots in family and village life. They worked long hours and returned home to anonymous neighborhoods. This disconnection tended to remove the checks on antisocial behavior and the pressures of conformity that are possible in families and villages where everyone knows everyone else. Yet masses are not asocial; instead, they have distinct social dynamics. Blumer suggests that what binds a mass together is a common focus of interest or attention. As examples of masses, Blumer mentions individuals "who are excited by some national event, those who share in a land boom, those who are interested in a murder trial which is reported in the press, or those who participate in some large migration."[9] Members of a mass have an experience or an idea in common, but they may be unaware of this fact because they are unaware of each other. Despite this lack of awareness, mass behavior can have social consequences, such as when the individual buying decisions of millions of people turn an unknown recording artist into a star. Similarly, individual voting decisions can elect a new and largely unknown political candidate to office.

The Public

A public, as commonly defined, is sharply distinct from a crowd or a mass. Blumer defines a public as "a group of people (a) who are confronted by an issue, (b) who are divided in the ideas as to how to meet the issue, and (c) who engage in discussion over the issue."[10] Thus, a public emerges and is sustained through discourse over a controversy. Entering a crowd requires only "the ability to feel and empathize"—to share an emotion—whereas joining the public requires also, in Robert Parks's words, "the ability to think and reason with others." A public may be influenced by a shared emotional drive, but "when the public ceases to be critical, it dissolves or is transformed into a crowd," which according to Blumer creates "public sentiment" rather than public opinion.[11] Unlike a mass, a public is self-aware and interactive.

How realistic is this definition? Perhaps the citizens in a small town can form a public, but can the hundreds of millions of people in the United States really be said to "engage in discussion"? Many, including sociologist C. Wright Mills, doubt it. Mills argues that Americans are better construed as a mass than as a public: many more people receive opinions from the media than express opinions to each other.[12] Others argue that although the "American public" is far-flung and diverse, most people do somehow participate in a sort of national conversation. For some observers, the definition of public becomes a standard for evaluating political and social institutions: What do Americans need to function as a public?

Defining Public Opinion

Despite a chronic definitional problem, public opinion research is still a field with boundaries. Not all studies of American culture are studies of public opinion, because the study of public opinion does concern the formation, communication, and measurement of citizens' attitudes toward public affairs. We believe that there are five reasonable definitions of public opinion that are distinct but that also overlap to some extent. The differences among these definitions reflect ongoing debates in the field. While you are likely to prefer some of these definitions to others, they all merit your consideration.

Category 1: Public Opinion Is an Aggregation of Individual Opinions. Many researchers, journalists, policymakers, and citizens think of public opinion as the simple sum of many individual opinions. This is the most common definition of public opinion in contemporary American politics, and it serves as the justification for using surveys and polls to measure public opinion. By using the process of random selection, opinion polls enable an efficient aggregation of individual opinions. Because professionally conducted polls interview people across social groups, the results can be used to make general claims about the entire population. (We discuss this process at length in Chapter 3.)

This definition is widely accepted in public life today, for several reasons. First, it provides a straightforward prescription for measuring the public mood: if public opinion is the aggregation of individual opinions, it is clear that we must interview individuals and add their opinions together to ascertain it. Moreover, polling methodology has become routinized, so any trained researcher with resources can conduct a competent survey of the public. Second, this definition of public opinion resonates with the structure of the democratic elections. Surveys are like elections in the way they tally "votes" (opinions), so they seem to fit our particular system of governance. Third, this sort of quantitative approach to understanding public opinion enables researchers, journalists, and others to engage in complex causal analyses. If an analyst polls a sample of American citizens about welfare reform, for example, that makes it possible to test hypotheses about the relationship between support for reform and one's race, class, gender, political affiliation, or religion, as well as other attitudes and values.

Polling is used by legislators, presidents, and journalists to explore how people feel about various policy issues, but surveys also provide insight into more general attitudes about social life. The mass media regularly conduct and report on surveys of public attitudes on race relations, gender roles, religious values, and the like. Sometimes these polls shed light on policy debates, but more often they are interesting notes on culture in and of themselves.

Category 2: Public Opinion Is a Reflection of Majority Beliefs. Several theorists argue that we need to think of public opinion as the equivalent of social norms: that majority values and beliefs are the true basis of public opinion. Here "majority" is defined not as "greater than 50 percent," as in many elections, but as "dominant"—that is, so widely and/or intensely held that to challenge those norms is to stand apart in a way that most people would rather avoid. Theorists who use this definition are not making a judgment about the majority being right or wrong on a particular subject; they are simply arguing that people do pay close attention to the opinions of friends, coworkers, and neighbors and tend to conform to majority opinion.

One researcher who supports this definition of public opinion is Elisabeth Noelle-Neumann, whose work we discuss in greater depth in Chapter 7. Noelle-Neumann argues that public opinion is best defined as the "opinions on controversial issues that one can express in public without isolating oneself."[13] She believes that citizens do a surveillance of their environment, try to get a sense of what majority opinion is like on a particular topic, and then either express themselves or keep quiet on the subject. If people determine that they hold a minority opinion, they often remain silent, contributing to what Noelle-Neumann calls a "spiral of silence" in which others likewise withhold their opinions, thus making that view seem even rarer than it is.

There is considerable debate about Noelle-Neumann's hypothesis. First, various researchers have challenged her methodology, that is, how she tries to measure conformity dynamics. (How *does* one measure opinions that people decline to express?) Second, the term "majority" implies that people are equally likely to conform on any issue about which they are outnumbered. This seems unlikely—but if people feel more pressure to conform on some issues than on others, the theory doesn't explain why. Noelle-Neumann's theory raises many unanswered questions, which is not a bad thing. However, some researchers find her emphasis on conformity fundamentally misguided, given all the issues on which people freely and openly disagree.

Despite these reservations, Noelle-Neumann's definition of public opinion (among similar definitions) exposes limitations in construing public opinion as whatever surveys measure. One is that if we do not always honestly and fully express our opinions to each other, we probably don't do so to pollsters, either. So researchers need more sophisticated methods to explore what people really think. But there are other questions. If people are willing to say things to pollsters that they do not tell each other, does it make sense to think of their survey responses as "real" public opinion? Doesn't people's day-to-day behavior matter more than what they might tell an unknown interviewer? No matter how you answer these questions, you can see how survey results alone do not paint the entire picture.

Category 3: Public Opinion Is Found in the Clash of Group Interests. Some scholars believe that public opinion is not so much a function of what individuals think as a reflection of how their opinions are cultivated, crystallized, and eventually communicated by interest groups. These interest groups include political parties, trade organizations, corporations, and activist groups like the Sierra Club or the Christian Coalition. The strength of this definition is that it underscores power dynamics: in political reality, organized groups are those that lobby for legislation, have spokespeople who influence journalists, and mobilize votes during election campaigns. Under this definition, then, public opinion is the result of public debate among groups.

This definition of public opinion assumes that conflict is pervasive in social and political life, that groups are constantly engaged in a struggle to define social problems and provide solutions to them. People who subscribe to this definition do not discount the opinions of individuals but are most interested in how those opinions are translated into interest group behavior: policymakers and journalists are more likely to be attentive to what interest groups say and do than to what individual citizens think.

One theorist advocating this definition is Herbert Blumer, mentioned previously in our discussion of masses and publics. In a famous article published in 1948, Blumer argues that public opinion should be construed as the pattern of views "that come to the individuals who have to act in response to [the public opinion]."[14] (See Box 1.2.) He critiques the common assumption of survey research that every respondent's opinion should be treated as equally important. However democratic that might seem, Blumer says that it is fundamentally misleading, because all citizens are not equal; some are far more influential than others. Surveys are not well suited for measuring those differences in influence, and most do not even attempt to do so.

Category 4: Public Opinion Reflects Media and Elite Influence. Some political observers have suggested that public opinion is best understood as the product—or even, at times, a projection—of what journalists, politicians, pollsters, and other influential "elites" believe. This notion—that public opinion is a creation of social leaders—may sound cynical, but it has many adherents. The most famous is probably Walter Lippmann, a journalist and political philosopher who was prominent from World War I through the early years of the Vietnam War. Lippmann argued that the common citizen could not possibly stay informed on all public issues and therefore could hardly produce meaningful opinions on them. At most, then, public opinion consists of people's simplistic reactions to what they learn from the media and relatively few opinion leaders.

One can find a large number of policy matters about which the American public knows very little (see Box 1.3). Lippmann emphasized that the public's inability to opine on all issues was not a matter of laziness, but stemmed from inherent human limitations. He wrote in 1925:

> My sympathies are with [the private citizen], for I believe that he has been saddled with an impossible task and that he is asked to practice an unattainable

ideal. . . . I have not happened to meet anybody, from a President of the United States to a professor of political science, who came anywhere near to embodying the accepted ideal of the sovereign and omnicompetent citizen.[15]

Lippmann's book *Public Opinion* (1922) focuses not on what Americans think about various political issues, but on *how* Americans typically think—for instance, by relying on broad "stereotypes" and yes-or-no reactions to positions formulated by others—and on how opinion leaders' rhetorical choices and media reporting influence that thinking. Lippmann argues that political parties and newspapers often state symbolic principles on which many people can

---

BOX 1.2
Do Groups Matter More Than Individuals,
When It Comes to Public Opinion?

In his 1948 essay on opinion polling, sociologist Herbert Blumer tried to take the perspective of a legislator or executive. What kind of public opinion data would be important to them? Blumer argued that public opinion polls are practically irrelevant to a policymaker, who must "view society in terms of groups of divergent influence; in terms of organizations with different degrees of power; in terms of individuals with followings; in terms of indifferent people—all, in other words, in terms of what and who counts in his part of the social world." According to Blumer, polls:

> are unable to answer such questions as the following: . . . who are these people who have the opinion; whom do they represent; how well organized are they; what groups do they belong to that are stirring around on the scene and that are likely to continue to do so; are [they] . . . very much concerned about their opinion; are they going to get busy and do something about it; are they going to get vociferous, militant, and troublesome; . . . does the opinion represent a studied policy of significant organizations which will persist and who are likely to remember; is the opinion an ephemeral or momentary view which people will quickly forget?

SOURCE: "Public Opinion and Public Opinion Polling," *American Sociological Review* 13 (1948): 547.

BOX 1.3

An Ignorant Public?

L evels of civic knowledge among Americans, as measured by surveys, have always been lower than political scientists would like. In 2011 the Annenberg Public Policy Center conducted a study to measure knowledge about basic constitutional issues and contemporary politics. Some of the results are recorded below. Do you think Americans should be able to answer these questions correctly?

Question	% of Respondents Giving Correct Answer
What is the highest court in the United States?	91
What do we call the first ten amendments to the US Constitution?	78
How much of a majority is required for the US Senate and the House of Representatives to override a presidential veto: 51 percent, two-thirds, three-quarters, 90 percent, or are you not sure?	51
Do you happen to know which party has the most members in the US Senate?	42
Do you happen to know any of the three branches of government? Would you mind naming any of them? [% named all three]	38
If a person disagrees with a ruling by the Supreme Court, can he or she appeal the ruling to the Federal Court of Appeals or not, or are you not sure?	37
Do you happen to know who the Chief Justice of the US Supreme Court is?	15

SOURCE: Annenberg Public Policy Center, "New Annenberg Survey Asks: 'How Well Do Americans Understand the Constitution?'" Press release, September 16, 2011. http://www.annenbergpublicpolicycenter.org/Downloads/Releases/Civics%20Knowledge/Final%20CIVICS%20knowledge%20release%20corrected2.pdf

agree—such as "Americanism," "law and order," or "justice"—instead of specific policies on which people would sharply disagree. Lippmann concludes that advances in communications and psychological research have given political leaders an unprecedented capacity for "the manufacture of consent."[16] We can only imagine what Lippmann would think more than eighty years later.

While most scholars agree that elites wield great influence over public opinion, to define public opinion in terms of that influence goes further. It implies that for most purposes, at least, we can understand public opinion better by studying what leaders and the media say about issues than by studying what most people think about them. The next definition of public opinion has even less to do with "the public."

Category 5: Public Opinion Is a Fiction. Some theorists argue that public opinion is a phantom, a rhetorical construction that has no real connection to "the public" as a group of citizens. These theorists argue, for example, that journalists and politicians often make claims about public opinion on some issue without any evidence whatsoever. If people can invoke public opinion so indiscriminately, does the phrase have any objective meaning? Even if a political leader can cite a survey that indicates public support for his or her position, how solid are the opinions measured, and how consequential are they? And would citizens act on those opinions? If politicians or pundits make contradictory claims about public opinion, are some of these claims more correct than others, and does it really matter if they are? Theorists in this category consider "public opinion" fundamentally a mystification that puts words and ideas in the public's collective mouth. Crucially, they choose to study this fiction: public opinion is what leaders say it is, because any alternative "real" public opinion is unknown (perhaps even unknowable) and not practically relevant.

Scholars in this category focus on the rhetoric of public opinion: how speakers essentially manufacture a public (and its opinions) to suit their needs. Sometimes carefully worded polls are used to produce the desired results. At other times, speakers simply assert that their positions represent what "we Americans believe," "who Americans are," or "American values." Public opinion can also be manufactured through sophisticated public relations efforts intended to create the impression of widespread public support.

Critics in this category underscore the difficulty, if not futility, of trying to adjudicate competing claims to represent "real" public opinion. For example, scholars have noted that citizens think about politics using different terminology than do pollsters and policymakers. Some doubt that average citizens and political elites even recognize the same problems as being political in nature. Pierre

Bourdieu, a French sociologist, comments on the propensity of journalists to "further simplify the already simplified [polling] data." Bourdieu argues that a close analysis of multiple polling questions and answers would be "the only way to know what were the questions the people really thought they were answering."[17] Bourdieu does believe that academics, with great care, can occasionally conduct useful surveys, but he does not think that these surveys necessarily measure "public opinion." As a practical matter, "public opinion" is whatever people say it is, however fanciful and mutually inconsistent their statements may be.

Table 1.1 takes up the policy debate over health care reform and discusses how theorists from each category might explore the role of public opinion in this debate.

TABLE 1.1. **Thinking About and Measuring Public Opinion: American Health Care**

Definition of Public Opinion	*In the Context of Health Care Reform*
Category 1 (aggregation)	Researchers would construe public opinion as what most private citizens would say when questioned on the subject. These scholars would use sophisticated survey methods to explore Americans' opinions: Do they approve or disapprove of the Affordable Care Act ("Obamacare")? Which specific provisions do they support or oppose? What do they think of other proposals? Focus groups also might be used to collect more data in a more conversational forum.
Category 2 (majority opinion)	Scholars would construe public opinion as the opinion(s) that people feel comfortable expressing in public. They would ask: What are people saying about Obamacare and health care? Because it is difficult to observe people's speech directly, researchers might use special surveys or focus groups to explore this broad question. Or they might conduct a content analysis of social media to judge what opinions dominate public discourse.
Category 3 (clash of groups)	This approach would focus most rigorously on the "interests" and coalitions in the debate, such as the insurance industry, lobbying groups such as the

(continues)

(continued)

TABLE 1.1. Thinking About and Measuring Public Opinion: American Health Care

Category 3	older-American group AARP, and the president and political party leaders. How do the leaders of these groups characterize the opinions of their constituencies on Obamacare? Researchers would study public statements and would also conduct interviews with group leaders and members. Crucially, they would attempt to understand the way groups clash, by examining points of contention, areas of common ground, and the evolution of groups' strategies and approaches.
Definition of Public Opinion	*In the Context of Health Care Reform*
Category 4 (media/elite opinion)	Researchers in this tradition would focus on media and elite expressions of opinion on Obamacare and health care reform. Typically, they would perform content analyses of selected media sources—perhaps television news, major newspapers, and/or Internet news sites—to evaluate the range of opinions and information available to the public. The results may substantially diverge from other methods. For example, these sources may tend to convey positive or negative messages about Obamacare (such as families' successes or difficulties in obtaining affordable coverage), which may not match people's perceptions as reported in surveys.
Category 5 (public opinion as fiction)	Scholars in this category would argue that although people may have some latent opinions about Obamacare and how to improve health care, the expression of these opinions is entirely constructed by interest groups, public officials, and media. These parties are exaggerating actual opinion at times, but often they are constructing "public opinion" out of nothing at all. Researchers in this tradition often emphasize the failings and limitations of the methods used by other researchers, which may provide much insight into the fiction of public opinion, but far less into the reality.

DIMENSIONS OF PUBLIC OPINION

Regardless of their favored definitions of public opinion, most scholars agree that average citizens have opinions and attitudes that are at least potentially relevant to various policy issues. In general, when we refer to "public opinion" without specifying a definition, we refer to people's policy-relevant opinions and attitudes. Researchers' knowledge of public opinion in this sense is usually very limited. As Bourdieu pointed out, one or two survey questions and answers barely begin to reveal what people think. Public opinion has multiple, interdependent dimensions that are important to bear in mind.

First, consider the *direction* of public opinion. Simply put, it matters where people stand on issues: what they favor, oppose, or are uncertain about. People's opinions may often be more complicated than a simple "pro" or "con." For example, while people's opinions on abortion are often characterized as either favoring or opposing legal abortion rights—"pro-choice" or "pro-life"—many people believe that abortion should be legal in some circumstances but not in others, though they may not necessarily have thought through exactly what those circumstances are.

Second, the *intensity* of opinion can be critical. How strongly do people feel about an issue? Where an issue has intense advocates on both sides, as the abortion issue does, the result can indicate deep social divisions. If an intense minority confronts a relatively apathetic majority, majority public opinion may be ignored by policymakers seeking to appease the vocal minority. One of the unresolved problems of democracy is balancing majority and minority opinion. When a minority of people feels strongly on an issue, should its opinion outweigh that of the more apathetic majority? If neither side is particularly intense, policymakers may view the public opinion environment as permissive and enact the policies they themselves favor. Alternatively, if an issue draws an intense majority, policymakers may feel compelled to respond to the demands of public opinion.

Third, the *stability* of public opinion can affect scholars' and leaders' evaluation of the issue. Stability refers to the consistency of people's opinions over time. If public opinion on an issue is stable, leaders may be more likely to pay attention to it than if it changes frequently. This situation occurs because stable public opinion is believed to reflect true public desires, whereas unstable public opinion is perceived as capricious and uninformed. However, just because public opinion changes over time does not mean that those changes are not heeded by leaders. Political scientist Michael Corbett points out that "in 1953, 68 percent of Americans favored capital punishment for convicted murderers; then the proportion favoring capital punishment declined until it reached 42 percent in 1966; but then the proportion rose again until it reached 72 percent in 1985."[18] During this span of time, the death penalty was abolished, then reinstated.

The stability of public opinion can be affected by many things. One factor is intensity, already discussed. But stability is also affected by the *informational content* of the opinion. Informational content is the fourth quality of public opinion that scholars frequently explore. There is much evidence to suggest that people do not know very much about public issues. Some of this evidence we have already seen in Box 1.3, and a more complete discussion appears in Chapter 9. For now, it may be enough to say that scholars are unsure about exactly how much information the public needs to form "rational" opinions about public issues. However, it seems unlikely that uninformed public opinion will have as much impact on political leaders as will informed public opinion.

WHICH MEANING OF PUBLIC OPINION IS BEST?

It is difficult to say which definition of public opinion is "best." In contemporary American life, all the definitions are used, depending on the circumstances in which the public mood is being discussed. Scholars certainly use all five categories in their work, as do journalists and public officials. Some might argue that because of the popularity of polling, the first category (public opinion as an aggregation of individual opinions) is most common, but journalists and our leaders often gain knowledge of public opinion by speaking with interest group leaders. And almost all reporters and policymakers have, either knowingly or unknowingly, manufactured notions of public opinion through their spoken and written rhetoric.

The definition one chooses depends on several factors, including the following:

1. The type of research one is conducting matters. For example, if one is exploring how American women of the late nineteenth century viewed suffrage (the right to vote), they might look for evidence of public opinion in the letters of suffragettes or in the documents of women's rights organizations. This research assumes that public opinion is the product of interaction between individuals and organized interest groups. Since the question is a historical one, a researcher cannot define public opinion as the opinions of an aggregation of individuals. That would demand a survey, and in this case, the respondents died long ago.

2. Historical conditions often dictate the definition of public opinion one uses. We will see in the next chapter, for example, how the form of government can influence the ways leaders and citizens think about the public. In a dictatorship, public opinion is often used rhetorically (category 5) to manipulate the populace and make people think that leaders are acting in the interests of the citizenry. In a situation like this, public opinion really is a phantom, manufactured to make people feel as though they are listened to (even if that is not the case).

3. The kind of technology that exists in a particular society at a certain point in time may determine which meaning of public opinion is used. Take opinion polling as an example of technology. Today, computers are used extensively in the interviewing process and in analysis of survey data. Although opinion polling was developed to aggregate individual opinions (category 1), the technology for conducting a scientific poll has become so easy to use that people employ the aggregation approach because they can do surveys so quickly. This is not to say that the availability of technology always determines how we see the political and social world, but it is the case that we are attracted to techniques that enable us to understand the world in what seems an efficient manner.

As students of public opinion and political processes, we must live with ambiguity when it comes to defining public opinion. The fact that we cannot define the term with precision does not mean that the field has no boundaries, as we will see in subsequent chapters. The intellectual debates, political phenomena, and theories that are described in this book will give you a firm understanding of what the field of public opinion is about—what is included under the general heading of "public opinion studies" and what is not.

NOTES

1. Gustave Le Bon, *The Crowd: A Study of the Popular Mind* (London: Unwin, 1948), 27–38.

2. William Trotter, *Instincts of the Herd in Peace and War* (London: Oxford University Press, 1919).

3. Vincent Price, *Public Opinion* (Newbury Park, CA: Sage Publications, 1992).

4. Ibid., 26.

5. Nelson N. Foote and Clyde W. Hart, "Public Opinion and Collective Behavior," in Muzafir Sherif and Milbourne O. Wilson, eds., *Group Relations at the Crossroads* (New York: Harper and Bros., 1953), 308–331.

6. Herbert Blumer, *Collective Behavior* (New York: Barnes and Noble, 1946).

7. Price, *Public Opinion*.

8. Blumer, *Collective Behavior*.

9. Ibid., 185.

10. Ibid., 189.

11. Price, *Public Opinion*, 26; quotes from Robert E. Park, *The Crowd and the Public and Other Essays* (Chicago: University of Chicago Press, 1904), 80.

12. C. Wright Mills, *The Power Elite* (New York: Oxford University Press, 1956).

13. Elisabeth Noelle-Neumann, *The Spiral of Silence: Public Opinion—Our Social Skin* (Chicago: University of Chicago Press, 1984).

14. Herbert Blumer, "Public Opinion and Public Opinion Polling," *American Sociological Review* 13(1948): 545.

15. Walter Lippmann, *The Phantom Public* (New York: Harcourt, Brace, 1925).

16. Walter Lippmann, *Public Opinion* (New York: Harcourt, Brace, 1922).

17. Pierre Bourdieu, "Public Opinion Does Not Exist," in Armand Mattelart and Seth Siegelaub, eds., *Communication and Class Struggle* (New York: International General, 1979), 124–130.

18. Michael Corbett, *American Public Opinion Trends* (New York: Longman, 1991), 24.

2

The History of Public Opinion

In the previous chapter we discussed the various possible routes to understanding and measuring public opinion, but we only briefly considered its historical development. This chapter explores the history of public opinion: the ways that intellectuals, citizens, and leaders have thought about that concept through the ages and the ways that they have communicated and evaluated the popular sentiment.

There are two approaches to investigating the history of public opinion. One focuses on intellectual history: how philosophers and theorists in various epochs have thought about public opinion. Alternately, we can focus on sociocultural history, that is, the means people have used to communicate their opinions and the techniques leaders have employed to assess those expressed beliefs. In this chapter we explore both sorts of history so that you will understand the philosophical development of public opinion and the "nuts and bolts" of how it has been expressed and measured in different places and times. We begin with the intellectual history of the concept of public opinion and then move to social history.

A few prefatory comments are in order. First, since the history of public opinion—intellectual and social—is so lengthy, we cannot explore all topics, debates, events, or theories in great depth. Here we provide a schematic map of the history, not a definitive reference. Second, this chapter focuses on the ways that public opinion has been discussed, expressed, and assessed in the West—primarily in the United States, the United Kingdom, and European nations. This geographical exclusiveness is unfortunate, but contemporary notions of public opinion in the United States draw most heavily on Western intellectual traditions. Through the ages, individuals in many South American, African, and

Asian cultures have undoubtedly thought about the idea of public opinion, but not much of this thinking has been integrated into American political culture and institutions. Finally, just as different definitions of public opinion exist today, philosophers and citizens in different eras have understood the phrase (or similar phrases) differently, depending on their political, technological, and cultural circumstances (see Box 2.1). If the meaning of public opinion seems difficult to pin down, that is exactly our point: the meaning is always in flux, depending on the context in which the term is used.

BOX 2.1
One Philosopher's View

Jürgen Habermas is one of the most important and prolific philosophers of our time. Fortunately for us, he has focused his immense talents on the history and meaning of public opinion in a variety of books and journal articles. This chapter owes much to Habermas, a German scholar whose work has been enormously influential in almost all academic disciplines, among them political science, communications, sociology, philosophy, literature, anthropology, and history. Habermas believes that the meaning of public opinion shifts in each era and that this meaning is always tied to the nature of the broader political and social arena that he calls the "public sphere."

The public sphere is the forum for discussion of politics outside of our homes but also outside of governmental circles. In other words, talk about family matters or discussion of politics within a household is not part of public sphere discourse, nor is talk among congressional representatives or between the president and his advisers. Public sphere talk is what one hears in a neighborhood bar or on talk radio. One can also find public sphere discussions in the editorial pages of newspapers, both regional and national, or in the large number of American current affairs magazines.

For Habermas, the meaning of public opinion and the ways we express it are always changing because the nature of public life itself is always shifting. In mid-nineteenth-century America, for example, women were typically not part of the public sphere. Middle-class women ruled the *domestic* sphere—caring for children and for their homes—but played only social roles in public (e.g., as hostesses, entertainers, or supporting players to husbands and fathers). Since women were largely absent from the *public sphere* in any serious sense, their voices were not considered part of

(continues)

(continued)   BOX 2.1
                              One Philosopher's View

public opinion. As a result, they could not vote and tended not to write letters to editors or vigorously campaign for political candidates. "Public opinion" in mid-nineteenth-century America meant the opinions of certain classes of men.

Habermas summarizes the connection between public opinion and public life in this way: "A concept of public opinion that is historically meaningful, that normatively meets the requirements of the constitution of a social-welfare state [such as our own], and that is theoretically clear and empirically identifiable can be grounded only in the structural transformation of the public sphere itself and in the dimension of its development."

SOURCES: Jürgen Habermas, *The Structural Transformation of the Public Sphere: An Inquiry into a Category of Bourgeois Society*, trans. Thomas Burger (Cambridge, MA: MIT Press, 1989), quoted passage on p. 244. An application of Habermas's ideas to the analysis of women in the nineteenth century is given in Mary Ryan's *Women in Public* (Baltimore, MD: Johns Hopkins University Press, 1990).

WHY DOES HISTORY MATTER?

There are many compelling questions about current public opinion: how Americans feel about US intervention in foreign conflicts, how we evaluate the president and other political leaders, how opinions differ across various social groups, and so forth. Given all these questions, why should we be concerned about past notions of public opinion or the ways people expressed themselves centuries ago?

History matters for two major reasons. First, and most obvious, an understanding of history enables us to understand the present: how things got the way they are. Here is an analogy from social life. If we want to fully understand why a friend acts the way she does, we need to understand her life experiences: her family background, where she grew up, the sorts of schools she attended, and so on. Similarly, to understand the political culture of contemporary America, we need to know about the past: how political parties evolved, how the Constitution has been amended, how social movements have changed the practice of politics, and the like. In the narrower area of public opinion, historical context also matters. For example, opinion polling became very popular in America largely as a reaction to dictators, such as Adolf Hitler, who attempted to speak for the people instead of letting them express their own opinions. After two bloody world wars and the rise of various totalitarian regimes, polling seemed like a very democratic way to communicate public opinion.

Second, history gives us a sense of possibility. We have become accustomed to polls and the statements of interest groups being indicators of public opinion, but history provides examples of many other ways in which people have expressed themselves. When we recognize just how many options exist for communicating beliefs, we can become more creative in expressing and evaluating public opinion. For example, later in this chapter we discuss the creative rituals of eighteenth-century Europeans and how those rituals expressed public sentiment about certain institutions. If we think about rituals in general as a means for expressing public opinion, we can recognize that some of our contemporary rituals are also expressions of public opinion. Rituals such as Memorial Day parades or commemorations of the Hiroshima and Nagasaki bombings at the end of World War II enable citizens to express both love of country and critical attitudes toward government.

As we turn to the intellectual history of public opinion in ancient Greece, both these points are underscored. We begin with ancient Greece because the written history of democracy (public self-rule, or participation in politics and government) begins there. How early Greek philosophers debated democracy—and how Greek citizens practiced it—have influenced discussions of governance, representation, political participation, and human nature ever since.

PRE-ENLIGHTENMENT PHILOSOPHIES OF PUBLIC OPINION

The phrase "public opinion" was not used widely before the nineteenth century, but many political philosophers of the ancient period used similar phrases to speak about popular sentiment. Plato, a Greek philosopher of the fourth century BCE, acknowledged public opinion as a central force in political affairs, but he doubted that people could realize their own best interests or work on their own to create a morally sound state. Plato thought that the just state should be governed by philosopher kings, and that members of the public should be educated to appreciate how these leaders act on behalf of the common good in order to understand and appreciate their government and the laws they lived under. Early twentieth-century scholar Ernest Barker put it this way: "The Greeks believed in the need of education to tune and harmonise social opinion to the spirit and tone of a fixed and fundamental sovereign law. The modern belief is in the need of representation to adjust and harmonise a fluid and subordinate law to the movement of a sovereign public opinion or general will."[1] That is, the modern view puts the public first: public opinion should be the basis of all law, and laws should be altered as the public mood shifts.

Other Greek philosophers writing in the same period disagreed with Plato's negative assessment of the public's capabilities, although they did not hold the modern view. In particular, Aristotle argued most eloquently for the voice of the public, defending the wisdom of the common citizen. As scholar Robert Minar puts it: "Aristotelian political theory seems to suggest that public opinion may be regarded as the vehicle of the spirit and continuity of the life of the organic community. It carries the enduring wisdom of the social organism and reflects that wisdom on the particular, immediate actions of government."[2]

Aristotle did not see public opinion as the sentiments people held toward particular issues of the day, although he saw those attitudes as important and worth articulating. Instead, he emphasized the prevailing values, norms, and tastes of the citizenry—what sociologist Robert Merton much later called the "climate of opinion." This broad opinion is then funneled through institutions (such as courts and schools), which serve as moderating influences. In other words, institutions take "raw" opinion from communities, organize it, eliminate irrationalities, and make it coherent. Aristotle was undoubtedly more optimistic about the role and nature of public opinion than were many of his predecessors, who advocated for democracy but still did not really trust the people (see Box 2.2).

BOX 2.2

Aristotle Versus Plato: The Value of Public Opinion

Since Plato and Aristotle wrote about public opinion in the fourth century BCE, thousands of scholars of political theory have debated and reinterpreted their ideas. Even today, because those ancient texts were so immensely thoughtful and complex, a large number of thinkers scrutinize them, looking for cues about how democracy might work. Perhaps the best way to evaluate the argumentation of Plato and Aristotle is to turn to their original statements. These quotes are removed from their original contexts, but they will give you some idea of how these philosophers conceptualized the public will.

In *The Republic*, Plato explicates his famous analogy of "the cave" and writes on a variety of other topics, from mathematics to child rearing. He argues that democracy produces a sort of chaos that makes its citizens

(continues)

(continued)   BOX 2.2
                           Aristotle Versus Plato:
                        The Value of Public Opinion

lose sight of right and wrong, of beauty, and of all that is "good." Not all
men have good character:

> In a democracy you must have seen how men condemned to death or exile
> stay on and go about in public, and no one takes any more notice than he
> would of a spirit that walked invisible. There is so much tolerance and superior-
> ity to petty considerations; such a contempt for all those fine principles we laid
> down in founding our commonwealth, as when we said that only a very excep-
> tional nature could turn out a good man, if he had not played as a child among
> things of beauty and given himself only to creditable pursuits. A democracy
> tramples all such notions under foot; with a magnificent indifference to the sort
> of life a man has led before he enters politics, it will promote to honour anyone
> who merely calls himself the people's friend. . . . These then, and such as these,
> are the features of democracy, an agreeable form of anarchy with plenty of va-
> riety and an equality of a peculiar kind for equals and unequals alike.

Thus, Plato is concerned about the "side effects" of democracy: neglect of social values, lack of enforcement of societal norms, and an unde-
served sort of equality. Citizens are far from equal in their intelligence,
education, aesthetic sense, or integrity. Democracy, Plato argues, demands more from the public than it is capable of giving.

In contrast, Aristotle sees wisdom in the ideas and expressions of citizens acting in public. He glories in the diversity and the very inequalities
underscored by Plato. He notes in *The Politics*:

> It is possible that the many, no one of whom taken singly is a good man, may
> yet taken all together be better than the few, not individually but collectively,
> in the same way that a feast to which all contribute is better than one given at
> one man's expense. For where there are many people, each has some share
> of goodness and intelligence, and when these are brought together, they
> become as it were one multiple man with many pairs of feet and hands and
> many minds. So too in regard to character and the powers of perception.
> That is why the general public is a better judge of works of music and poetry;
> some judge some parts, some others, but their joint pronouncement is a ver-
> dict upon the whole. And it is this assembling in one what was before sepa-
> rate that gives the good man his superiority over any individual man from the
> masses.

(continues)

(continued)

BOX 2.2
Aristotle Versus Plato:
The Value of Public Opinion

The arguments between Plato and Aristotle about the value of public opinion continue today, although in a somewhat different form. As we discuss in Chapter 4, some observers believe that public opinion should play a minimal role in policymaking because of its many defects. Others agree with Aristotle that, at least in some circumstances, the opinions of the public at large are more trustworthy than those of any one person.

SOURCES: Plato, *The Republic*, ed. and trans. Francis MacDonald Cornford (New York: Oxford University Press, 1956), quoted passage on p. 283; Aristotle, *The Politics*, ed. and trans. T. A. Sinclair (Baltimore, MD: Penguin Books, 1962), quoted passage on p. 132.

The great philosophers of ancient Rome, like Plato before them, generally were skeptical of the common people and their desires. Cicero, the renowned statesman and orator, claimed, "Sic est vulgus: ex veritate pauce, ex opinione multa aestimat," which can be translated as "This is the common crowd: judging few matters according to truth, many according to opinion." The Romans did not dismiss public opinion completely, but they believed that it mattered most in regard to leadership. Were statesmen honored by the people? Were they popular? Much discussion of public opinion in Roman times was oriented around this narrow dimension of politics.[3]

For our purposes we can leap forward from the ancient Romans to Niccolò Machiavelli, the Italian statesman and writer, who began to write at the start of the sixteenth century (see Figure 2.1). Machiavelli is best known for his book on political strategy, *The Prince*, written as an advisory tract for potential rulers. In it he discusses such questions as how a prince should act ("bear himself") in public, whether he needs to build fortresses, and whether it is better to be feared or loved by the people. Machiavelli writes at length, and with derision, about the nature of the people:

For of men it may generally be affirmed that they are thankless, fickle, false, studious to avoid danger, greedy of gain, devoted to you while you are able to confer benefits upon them, and ready, as I said before, while danger is distant, to shed their blood, and sacrifice their property, their lives, and their children

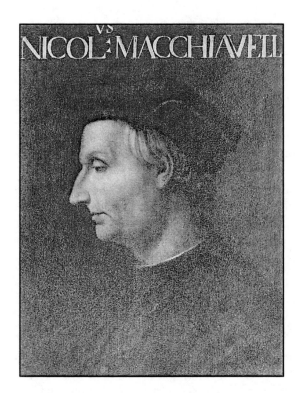

FIGURE 2.1.
Niccolò Machiavelli.
Political adviser and
author of *The Prince*.
SOURCE: Courtesy of the
Library of Congress.

for you; but in the hour of need they turn against you. . . . Men are so simple, and governed so absolutely by their present needs, that he who wishes to deceive will never fail in finding willing dupes.[4]

From Machiavelli we see how closely early theorizing about public opinion and governance was tied to observations about human nature. Before the twentieth century, it was conventional for philosophers to speculate about the essence of human nature so that they could provide a holistic picture of man as political animal: Machiavelli believed that humans are so obsessed with their immediate desires and comforts that they cannot rule themselves, thus leading to his political theory that the people must be governed by a benevolent dictator.

He respected public opinion as a political force that could harm the prince and the state, but not because he thought it had any inherent virtue, as Aristotle did. Machiavelli's perspective may seem antithetical to democratic theory and irrelevant in the US context. Yet similar thoughts about the citizenry are sometimes held today by journalists, policymakers, and citizens alike, whether or not this cynicism is openly expressed.

Machiavelli is best described as a *conflict theorist*, one who believes that underlying even the most peaceful society are conflicting values, unfulfilled needs, and animosities. He perceives a fundamental conflict in society between ruler and ruled. These two parties are always suspicious of each other, although the prince always has the upper hand. Machiavelli warns leaders to emphasize their superior strength, but also to be seen as acting with kindness and grace in the best interests of the people. In summary, for Machiavelli, public opinion was volatile, irrational, and potentially explosive. Leaders must be vigilant to ensure that their people continue to hold them in high regard.

Following Machiavelli in the seventeenth century were Thomas Hobbes and John Locke, two English philosophers who also had a great interest in the relationship between the people and the state. Hobbes, like Machiavelli, had a negative view of human nature, believing that people live in constant competition as they vie for property, reputation, and personal safety; he wrote in *The Leviathan* that life is "solitary, poor, nasty, brutish, and short." Hobbes's works are interesting from our perspective because he is an early *contract theorist*, believing that public opinion is crucial to the formation of the state. In Machiavelli's philosophical world, statesmen design society; the public plays no positive role. For Hobbes, on the contrary, people agree to the fundamental rules that establish government. Hobbes sees little role for public participation once the state is established and supports the notion of a benevolent dictator. Yet he argues that the state is created through a contract between the public and its leadership. If the state were to crumble—due to internal or external pressure—the citizenry would create a new governmental system.

John Locke, a contemporary of Hobbes, shared his belief in the contract, the agreement among people and leaders about how their community is to be governed. Yet Locke is far more optimistic about human nature and about the value of public participation in politics. Locke's theory of government greatly influenced our own Founding Fathers, who drew upon Lockean political theory in their plans for uniting the American colonies. He devoted considerable energy to arguing for his theory of inalienable natural rights that should be protected by the state. Like many philosophers of his day, he was somewhat skeptical about popular opinion, though he believed fiercely in the articulation of public opinion as a critical part of politics.

It may seem strange that Aristotle's relatively high view of public opinion was largely abandoned until Locke wrote in the 1600s. Yet democracy itself, as we understand it, has had a fairly short history, given the length of human existence. Even the ancient Greeks, who often are said to have invented the idea of democracy, were not quite democrats in the contemporary sense: in ancient Greece women, foreigners, and slaves had no voice in politics whatsoever.

PUBLIC OPINION IN THE AGE OF REVOLUTION

The eighteenth century was a time of immense political and social change. It was the century of the French and American Revolutions, and both were grounded in political philosophy. The most important discussions of democracy and public opinion occurred in Europe. Some leading early American statesmen, such as Thomas Jefferson and Benjamin Franklin, often participated in these debates during the considerable time they spent in France and Great Britain. Many other American leaders paid close attention to European thinkers of their day, particularly the French philosophers. This loose network of French philosophers produced some of the most original and compelling tracts on public opinion in the years before the French Revolution. This is a period often referred to as the Enlightenment, since there was great emphasis on the development of the human mind and spirit through science, the arts, and participation in political discourse.

Perhaps the most important work on public opinion was produced by Jean-Jacques Rousseau, a brilliant and unruly Enlightenment thinker who challenged a variety of social norms and existing theoretical paradigms (see Figure 2.2). The young Rousseau, who appeared on the Parisian philosophical scene from a rather humble background, developed an elegant theory of the state, with public opinion occupying a central role. Again, like philosophers before him, he was somewhat suspicious of the commoner. But more than any thinker to date, Rousseau thought it necessary to place considerable power in the hands of the public.

Like John Locke, Rousseau was very concerned with the rights of individuals. Yet he also placed great value on community and the need for people to respect and listen to each other. The state, Rousseau believed, was based on the *general will*: what citizens want when they think about the whole of the community. In other words, the general will is our most empathetic set of attitudes, or what we believe is the best course of action to promote the general welfare of the populace. Rousseau's discussion of the general will is somewhat complex and even confusing at times. He argues that public opinion is both an aggregation of individual opinions and a more organic force rooted in shared values and attitudes. For Rousseau, then, citizens think about themselves and their needs but are also capable of thinking about the general good of society (see Box 2.3).

FIGURE 2.2.
Jean-Jacques Rousseau.
SOURCE: Courtesy of the
Library of Congress.

We cannot leave the era of the French Revolution without mentioning Jacques Necker, finance minister to Louis XVI, widely believed to have popularized the phrase "public opinion." Necker recognized that political discourse and the nature of politics had changed dramatically in the eighteenth century. For the first time, a bourgeoisie had emerged to gather and discuss politics through interpersonal dialogue and the press. At the time, public opinion meant the opinion of the middle classes. Even in a monarchy, Necker recognized just how much of the institutional structure of the state rested on the benevolence of public opinion. He noted that most foreigners "have difficulty in forming a just idea of the authority exercised in France by public opinion; they have difficulty in understanding the nature of an invisible power which, without treasures, without a bodyguard, and without an army gives laws to the city, to the court, and even to the palaces of kings."[5]

In the nineteenth century various political philosophers tackled the problem of public opinion. Among them were the English scholars known as the Utilitarians. Jeremy Bentham was the first of the Utilitarians to write extensively about public opinion, and he was most interested in how public opinion acts as a sanction or constraint. Bentham believed that public opinion keeps society in equilibrium by preventing people from engaging in non-normative behavior. People are afraid of public opinion, so they dare not step outside the bounds of what is "acceptable" to most other people. This view of human society may seem bleak,

BOX 2.3
Rousseau on the General Will

In *The Social Contract* (1762), Jean-Jacques Rousseau explicated the notion of a "general will," a broad form of public opinion. He believed, unlike so many philosophers before him, that people were difficult to manipulate. People, Rousseau argued, are basically honest and expect honesty from others, including their leaders. In the chapter "That the General Will Is Indestructible," he discusses human nature and its relationship to the general will:

> As long as several men united together regard themselves as a single body, they have only a single will which relates to their common preservation and to the general welfare. Then all the mainsprings of the state are vigorous and simple, its maxims are clear and luminous, there are no tangled, contradictory interests, the common good is everywhere clearly evident and requires only good sense to be perceived. Peace, union, equality are enemies of political subtleties. Upright and simple men are difficult to deceive due to their simplicity: traps, sophisticated pretests do not deceive them. They are not even sharp enough to be duped. When, among the happiest people in the world, one sees bands of peasants settling affairs of state beneath an oak and always acting wisely, how can one help but scorn the sophistication of other nations which make themselves illustrious and miserable with so much art and mystery?

This passage may strike you as strangely naïve. How many people can gather with a "single will" and spontaneously agree on the common good? Yet Rousseau's view that ordinary people have a clearer sense of the common good than political leaders vying for advantage is one that is widely shared.

SOURCE: *The Major Political Writings of Jean-Jacques Rousseau: The Two Discourses and The Social Contract*, translated and edited by John T. Scott (Chicago: University of Chicago Press, 2012), quoted passage on p. 295.

but Bentham and other Utilitarians were most concerned about maximizing happiness among the populace through maintaining social harmony, preferably without resort to state violence. Bentham and John Stuart Mill, another writer in this British philosophical circle, supported democracy but emphasized the importance of majority opinion. In fact, they thought that laws are only needed where the "law of opinion" is not working effectively.

Similar views of public opinion as a force of social control were held by Alexis de Tocqueville, the French observer of nineteenth-century American politics. In his landmark study *Democracy in America*, still considered a seminal work of political theory, Tocqueville stated this about the way public opinion affects writers and artists:

In America the majority has enclosed throughout within a formidable fence. A writer is free inside that area, but woe to the man who goes beyond it. Not that he stands in fear of an auto-da-fé [style of public sentencing from the Inquisition], but he must face all kinds of unpleasantness and everyday persecution. A career in politics is closed to him, for he has offended the only power that holds the keys. He is denied everything, including renown. Before he goes into print, he believes he has supporters; but he feels that he has them no more once he stands revealed to all, for those who condemn him express their views loudly, while those who think as he does, but without his courage, retreat into silence as if ashamed of having told the truth.[6]

In the same work, Tocqueville made his famous argument about political equality and its relationship to mass opinion. He noted that in societies with extreme inequality—in an aristocracy, for example—public opinion is not viewed as particularly important. He argued that disadvantaged people in such societies generally recognize that others are better educated and more worldly than they are and therefore have more informed opinions. Yet as citizens achieve greater equality, they are less likely to defer to their supposed betters and are more respectful of majority opinion:

The nearer men are to a common level of uniformity, the less they are inclined to believe blindly in any man or any class. But they are readier to trust the mass, and public opinion becomes more and more mistress of the world. . . . In times of equality men, being so like each other, have no confidence in others, but this same likeness leads them to place almost unlimited confidence in the judgment of the public. For they think it not unreasonable that, all having the same means of knowledge, truth will be found on the side of the majority.[7]

This insight is particularly relevant in an age of mass communication, in which citizens potentially can gather extensive information about public affairs as a basis for their opinions. Although Americans are far from equal in wealth or education, most do have some access to news sources, particularly since the advent and growth of the Internet. We tend to think that we and everyone else are entitled to an opinion—and, accordingly, we tend to value majority opinion.

At the same time that Tocqueville was writing about American politics, Karl Marx was studying political and social life from an entirely different standpoint (see Figure 2.3). In Tocqueville we see a celebration of some aspects of democracy and deep concerns about others. In Marx we see a man who was completely dissatisfied with the status quo and believed that democracy (like other forms of government) was subject to corruption by the forces of capitalism. To this day, many scholars argue that democratic ideals have been co-opted or even crushed by capitalism and consumer culture. The argument is complex, but simple examples of this conflation between democracy and capitalism abound. Contemporary neo-Marxists argue that Americans (and citizens of young Eastern European democracies) tend to think of freedom as consumer choice: the right to choose among a variety of products and lifestyles. Social choices such as regulations imposed on business are more likely to be construed as restrictions on freedom than as the free choices of a free people.

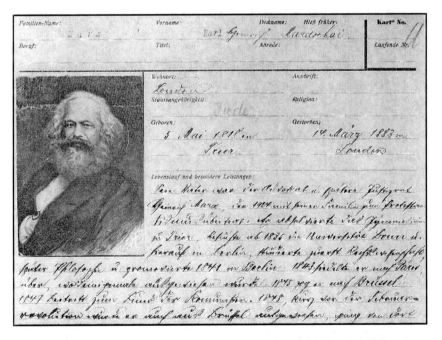

FIGURE 2.3. **Karl Marx's Identity Card.** Marx wrote about public opinion, although he used the language of class oppression to discuss formation of public attitudes. SOURCE: Courtesy of the Library of Congress.

Marx did not often use the phrase "public opinion," in part because it was not commonly used in German philosophical thought until later in the nineteenth century. Yet he and Friedrich Engels, his collaborator and patron, did argue strongly that organic, grassroots public opinion is rare. In *The German Ideology*, for example, Marx and Engels argue that common citizens tend to mimic the opinions of those in the ruling class—people with great wealth and power—even though these attitudes are often not in their best self-interest. As a result, Marx and Engels assert, the working class does not wield much political power. It is unable to realize its interests because its members have come to believe that the ruling class knows what is best. This process, in which the ideas of an elite class become widely held, is often called *hegemony* in the academic literature. Marx and Engels made the initial statement about this phenomenon, although since 1846 much more has been written on the subject:

> The ideas of the ruling class are in every epoch the ruling ideas, i.e. the class which is the ruling material force in society, is at the same time its ruling intellectual force. . . . For each new class which puts itself in the place of one ruling before it, is compelled, merely in order to carry through its aim, to represent its interest as the common interest of all the members of society, that is, expressed in ideal form: it has to give its ideas the form of universality, and represent them as the only rational, universally valid ones.[8]

PUBLIC OPINION THEORIES: THE LATE NINETEENTH AND EARLY TWENTIETH CENTURIES

Late in the nineteenth century a British statesman named James Bryce traveled widely in the United States, observing the political scene. He devoted long chapters in his two-volume masterwork *The American Commonwealth* to examining public opinion, in an attempt to understand how the concept fit into the constellation of American institutions. Bryce was interested in how the expression and measurement of public opinion were related to party activity, to legislatures, and to the mass media (newspapers, during this period). He is often cited as the first "modern" theorist of public opinion, because his work was sociological and empirical. Instead of speculating on the grand nature of public opinion, he looked for its manifestations in political culture. In fact, some critics would prefer that Bryce had spent less time reporting his observations and more time developing a philosophical or social psychological framework for them.

Despite such reservations about his work, Bryce is celebrated for foregrounding the crucial role of newspapers in the communication of public opinion. Tocqueville certainly recognized the value of newspapers, but Bryce explicated their role in far more detail. He believed that the mass media were astonishingly powerful in fin de siècle America and should hold a place among our other institutions (Congress, the courts) as a molder of public opinion. He noted in 1891, during an age when newspapers were far more obviously partisan than they are today: "It is chiefly in its . . . capacity as an index and mirror of public opinion that the press is looked to. This is the function it chiefly aims at discharging; and public men feel that in showing deference to it they are propitiating, and inviting the commands of, public opinion itself. In worshipping the deity you learn to conciliate the priest."[9]

For Bryce, newspapers both reflect and direct public opinion, so the place of this medium in the political process is crucial. Bryce's emphasis on the role of mass media feels contemporary, although other forms of media are increasingly important. Because contemporary journalists generally value objectivity as a goal far more than did journalists of Bryce's time, the role of the media in advocacy has changed somewhat, but they remain powerful movers of public opinion. Newspapers endorse candidates at election time and, more important, value investigative reporting that can greatly change the course of public policy.

Bryce also recognized that the American newspaper contained multiple forms of public opinion, not only news stories and editorials, but letters from citizens as well. Letters to the editor had long been overlooked by theorists as a source of public opinion data, but Bryce underscored their role in the communication of popular sentiment. Near the end of his discussion of newspapers, however, Bryce made it clear that no one—politicians included—can depend entirely on newspapers to gain a comprehensive view of public opinion. As he noted:

> Every prudent man keeps a circle of [four or five discerning friends of different types of thought] . . . by whom he can test and correct his own impressions better than by the almost official utterances of the party journals [newspapers]. So in America there is much to be learnt—even a stranger can perceive it—from conversation with judicious observers outside politics and typical representatives of political sections and social classes, which the most diligent study of the press will not give.[10]

The French sociologist Gabriel Tarde had even more to say on the relationship between newspapers and interpersonal discussion. Tarde noted in his 1898 essay "Opinion and Conversation" that "conversation at all times, and the press, which at present is the principal source of conversation, are the major factors in opinion."[11] Tarde described a unidirectional model of opinion formation that can be depicted graphically (see Box 2.4).

After Tarde, various other political theorists tackled the fundamental questions about public opinion: what it means, how it operates, and how it relates to political institutions and culture. And more recent twentieth-century discussions of public opinion, particularly those based on empirical research, are covered in some of the following chapters. Yet a scholarly discussion from 1924 deserves mention here. In that year a group of prominent scholars of politics met

---

BOX 2.4
Gabriel Tarde's Model of Public Opinion[1]

Media ⟶ Conversation ⟶ Opinion ⟶ Action

This is one model to use when thinking about the relationship of media to political action. Gabriel Tarde firmly believed that news media (in his era, primarily newspapers) are a national springboard for political discussion. Conversation about politics, in turn, enables people to clarify their opinions about various political and social policies so that they can act accordingly by voting, volunteering for a campaign, attending a demonstration, and the like.

One might take issue with Tarde's model on several counts. For example, is it possible that conversation and discussion cause journalists to write particular articles? If that is the case, we need to put some sort of conversational variable in this equation before the element "media." And we might question whether exposure to the media commonly leads to political action. Some researchers have argued that media are more likely to debilitate or dissuade us from political action than they are to prompt us toward political participation.

---

[1]There is growing interest in Tarde, thanks in large part to Elihu Katz. See Elihu Katz, "Press–Conversation–Opinion–Action: Gabriel Tarde's Public Sphere" (Annenberg School for Communication at the University of Pennsylvania, 1997). On the question of whether media dissuade or encourage political activity, the classic discussion can be found in Paul Lazarsfeld and Robert Merton's "Mass Communication, Popular Taste and Organized Social Action," in Lyman Bryson, ed., *The Communication of Ideas* (New York: Harper and Brothers, 1948). The diagram above is Katz's interpretation of Tarde.

at their yearly convention for a roundtable discussion of how to measure public opinion. According to the formal report, the roundtable began with an attempt to define terms:

> Some members of the round table believed that there is no such thing as public opinion; others believed in its existence but doubted their ability to define it with sufficient precision for scientific purposes. Others again . . . believed that the term could be defined, but were of different minds concerning the kind of definition that should be adopted. [After extensive discussion,] it was agreed that an exact definition of public opinion might not be needed until after the technical problem of measuring the opinions of the individual members of the public had been disposed of. It was decided therefore that the round table might well proceed to consider the problem of measuring opinion, especially that related to political matters, and *avoid the use of the term public opinion if possible* (emphasis added).[12]

By now you may appreciate the appeal of this choice. Like those scholars, we have not settled on a single definition of public opinion. However, we strongly disagree that measuring opinions is a mere technical problem that can be "disposed of" before grappling with definitional questions. Neither do we endorse simply avoiding the term "public opinion." We do not suppose that political observers can stop caring about the concept of public opinion any more than they can abandon the concept of democracy. Both these concepts are contested, often in similar ways, because they matter. Rather than eschewing the complexity of public opinion, we prefer to use it as a gateway for exploring the challenges of democratic theory and practice.

THE SOCIAL HISTORY OF PUBLIC OPINION: EXPRESSION AND MEASUREMENT

Intellectual histories of public opinion such as the brief one provided above are crucial to understanding the philosophical development of the concept in political theory. Yet the social history of public opinion—how popular sentiment has been communicated and measured over time—is equally important and interesting. When we explore how public opinion has been expressed and assessed in previous eras, we gain much insight into the advantages and disadvantages of our own techniques for communicating popular attitudes.

In this section we often refer to methods of public opinion communication as public opinion *technologies*. That is, citizens and leaders alike use a variety of tools both to express opinions and to evaluate them. In contemporary American politics, the public opinion poll or survey is one of the premier technologies for expression and measurement of opinion. Newspapers remain important for communicating popular sentiment, as in Bryce's day, although they are being superseded by new media.

Often the same tools can be used to express public opinion and to measure it. Consider political demonstrations. When thousands of people gather in Washington, DC, to protest a government policy or to show that a large number of Americans support a particular cause, identity, or political agenda, the marchers are expressing their opinions. At the same time, however, others are measuring those opinions. Journalists and policymakers can assess the size of the crowd as well as the rhetoric of the speeches and the intensity of feeling among rally participants. Thus, the political demonstration, as a technology of public opinion, enables both the expression and the evaluation of public feeling.

Before we begin our review of the more important technologies used throughout history to communicate people's attitudes about public affairs, let us call out some broad trends in public opinion technologies. Three forces have altered these technologies through the ages:

1. An increasing emphasis on order and routinization.
2. Movement toward private and anonymous means for communicating opinion.
3. A shift from local to national and even global opinion expression and assessment.

Techniques for communicating attitudes have become increasingly standardized and routinized. That is, people have developed more rigorous schemes for quantifying and aggregating public opinion so that it can be more easily understood. Furthermore, in capitalist societies public opinion data are a valuable commodity, so it is important to develop standard methods of opinion measurement that are valued by consumers, be they citizens, legislators, or media outlets. Random sampling techniques that enable a researcher to poll a small number of citizens and then generalize to all Americans are a relatively new set of tools, developed in the mid-twentieth century. The representative public opinion poll uses a much more standardized methodology than other technologies (such as counting the crowd members at a demonstration). This is not to say that opinion polls have superseded other techniques. All methods of communicating public opinion have positive and negative aspects, as we shall see in the following discussion.

The increased *privacy* of opinion expression is closely connected with the development of two opinion technologies in the nineteenth and twentieth centuries: the secret ballot for elections and the straw poll (which evolved into the sample survey). Before the widespread diffusion of these methods, in which one's identity is concealed, technologies of public opinion demanded that citizens either sign their names or show their faces; one had to sign a petition, for example, or appear at a political demonstration. There is no protection of a citizen's identity in these cases.[13] The rise of social media may have altered the trend toward privacy, but social media users do have some control over how widely they share opinions and whether their real identities are attached to them.

Another important trend is the increasing emphasis on national—as opposed to local—opinion. The historian Charles Tilly has eloquently characterized this shift. Tilly argues that expressions of opinion were largely local before the mid-nineteenth century:

> Broadly speaking, the repertoire [of opinion techniques] of the seventeenth to nineteenth centuries held to a *parochial* scope: It addressed local actors or the local representatives of national actors. It also relied heavily on *patronage*— appealing to immediately available power holders to convey grievances or settle disputes. . . . The repertoire that crystallized in the nineteenth century and prevails today is, in general, more national in scope: Although available for local issues and enemies, it lends itself easily to coordination among many localities. As compared with the older repertoire, its actions are relatively *autonomous*: instead of staying in the shadow of existing power holders and adapting routines sanctioned by those power holders, users of the new repertoire tend to initiate their own statements of grievances and demands. Strikes, demonstrations, electoral rallies, and similar actions build, in general, on much more deliberately constructed organization than used to be the case (emphasis in original).[14]

This shift from local to national expression of opinion was facilitated by the development of mass media, particularly the newspaper. Other factors contributed as well: the increasing importance of the nation-state as global actor, improvements in transportation infrastructure (roads, trains, etc.), and the greater size and scope of many national governments.

PRE-NINETEENTH-CENTURY OPINION COMMUNICATION TECHNIQUES

The number and variety of methods people have used to communicate and assess public opinion over time are extraordinarily large. Here we discuss some of the major techniques, those that scholars of public opinion have focused on most closely.

Among the most enduring public opinion techniques—which you might not immediately consider as such—is the art of rhetoric and oratory. As described by Aristotle, rhetoric is "the faculty of discovering the possible means of persuasion in reference to any subject whatever," that is, the art of persuasive writing and speaking.[15] (The related term *oratory*—derived from the Latin "oratorio"—usually refers to public speaking.) Of course the ancient Greeks did not invent persuasion, but their extensive discussions of the relationship between rhetoric and democratic politics has had enduring influence. For Aristotle, the value of rhetoric was to give a forceful accounting of true arguments so they may win out over false ones. From at least the fifth century BCE on, citizens and leaders of Greek city-states consciously employed rhetoric to argue for their preferred policies. Ancient Rome had its own vibrant practice of political oratory.

In many respects Greek and Roman citizens were sophisticated consumers of all this rhetoric. Kathleen Hall Jamieson, a contemporary scholar of rhetoric, notes:

> Ancient oratory was considered a fine art, an art regarded by its cultivators, and by the public, as analogous to sculpture, to poetry, to painting, to music and to acting. This character is common to Greek and Roman oratory. So, for example, Isocrates [a Greek orator] notes that listeners broke into loud applause when antitheses, symmetrical clauses, or other striking rhetorical figures were skillfully presented. . . . When the world of entertainment, persuasion and politics was in the main an oral one, listeners were drawn together in large numbers to experience a piece of communication.[16]

Regardless of what Aristotle's intentions were, persuasion always poses dangers. In the words of German historian Wilhelm Bauer, "oratory rapidly developed as the technique best suited to the manipulation of public opinion and continued throughout later Greek and Roman times as the most powerful instrument of political propaganda and agitation."[17] The word *demagogue* (in Greek, *dēmagōgos*), literally just "leader of the people," came to connote a politician who led the people astray to serve his own interests. Even the word "rhetoric" often implies empty or misleading words.

In ancient times rhetoric occurred in unmediated forums. Speakers addressed crowds in arenas and marketplaces, at festivals and public meetings of all sorts. Such direct address still occurs today, such as when legislators speak from the floor or when political candidates give speeches to gathered supporters. Yet these days much of the public speaking in political life is mediated by television, and that technology has changed the nature of rhetoric itself. About oratory over the airwaves, Jamieson notes:

> Television invites a personal, self-disclosing style that draws public discourse out of a private self and comfortably reduces the complex world to dramatic narratives. Because it encompasses these characteristics, the once spurned womanly style is now the style of preference. The same characteristics comprise a mode of discourse well suited to television and much needed in times of social stress or in the aftermath of divisive events. By revivifying social values and ennobling the shared past, epideictic or ceremonial discourse helps sustain the state.[18]

The first technological breakthrough in the mediation and distribution of rhetoric occurred almost 2,000 years after Aristotle: the invention of the modern printing press (see Figure 2.4). Introduced in the later fifteenth century, the printing press enabled the formation of modern publics. That is, the publication of newspapers, books, and pamphlets made it possible for large numbers of dispersed people to communicate with each other. Before printing, most people could only communicate with neighbors and anyone they met while traveling (which was uncommon among ordinary citizens). With the introduction of printed materials about public affairs, however, people could ally themselves with causes, ideas, and organizations. The invention of printing was revolutionary in many respects, but its importance to the expression of public opinion is unmatched.

Printing made possible the mass distribution of knowledge itself. Common citizens, especially those in rural areas, could gain access to ideas about politics, religion, and the arts. The availability of inexpensive pamphlets, newspapers, and books boosted literacy rates in European nations, creating pressures for political reform. The explosion of printed materials was not accompanied by freedom of the press, of course, since monarchs could and did shut down newspapers when such publications threatened their rule. Indeed, some printers were tortured and executed for publishing newspapers that criticized the state.

FIGURE 2.4. **"A True Representation of a Printing House with the Men at Work."**
The printing press enabled the development of modern "publics"—geographically
dispersed people who shared the same interests or points of view.
SOURCE: Courtesy of The Lewis Walpole Library, Yale University.

Printing served as a catalyst for the development of other public opinion
communication techniques. The newspapers themselves carried opinions and
letters to the editor, but they also served as a starting point for discussion among
citizens. In the seventeenth and eighteenth centuries, for example, newspapers
and books were vital to the evolution of two important opinion technologies: the
coffeehouse and the salon.

Coffeehouses were popular places in England during the centuries following
the introduction of printing (see Figure 2.5). Admission to these forums was
cheap, and one could spend hours in coffeehouses reading newspapers and political tracts and arguing about ideas with other patrons. Eighteenth-century descriptions of coffeehouses noted that the mix of individuals in attendance varied
greatly, with judges, journalists, and lawyers sharing tables with tradesmen,
workers, and even the occasional thief or pickpocket. Perhaps the sociologist

FIGURE 2.5. **Lloyd's Coffeehouse in London, 1978.** Coffeehouses and taverns served as forums for political debate in the seventeenth and eighteenth centuries. During this period, people went to coffeehouses for the express purpose of learning and talking about public affairs.
SOURCE: © Hulton-Deutsch Collection/CORBIS.

Lewis Coser best describes the importance of the coffeehouses as a technology of public opinion:

> A common opinion cannot be developed before people have an occasion to discuss with one another, before they have been drawn from the isolation of lonely thought into a public world in which individual opinion can be sharpened and tested in discussion with others. The coffeehouse helped to crystallize a common opinion from a multitude of individual opinions and to give it form and stability. What the newspaper had not yet been able to accomplish was achieved to a large degree by the coffeehouse.[19]

Meanwhile, another forum for discussion and debate about public affairs became popular in France. Salons—gatherings of intellectuals, statesmen, and artists—were crucial to the development of political discourse in seventeenth-and eighteenth-century France. Salons were in many ways less "democratic" than coffeehouses, which were open to all for a tiny entrance fee. The salons were run with an iron hand by bourgeois women, who decided who should be invited and what topics should be discussed. Despite this relative exclusivity, the effects of the conversations within these gatherings were tremendous. It was in the salons of Paris that Rousseau developed the ideas for his *Social Contract*, an essay often cited as laying the philosophical groundwork for the French Revolution. Many writers and artists refined their ideas in the salons before they wrote books for mass distribution. But salons, like all public opinion technologies, were also technologies for public opinion measurement. Kings and their courtiers regularly visited the salons to gather "data" about public opinion. These data reflected only a small, elite sampling of French opinion, yet since the ideas generated in salons were destined for diffusion throughout France and the world, such information was extraordinarily valuable to those interested in public opinion.[20]

At this point we should revisit one of the issues raised in Chapter 1: the changing and contested meaning of the "public." For the king of France in the eighteenth century to develop economic policy, for example, it was less important to gather public opinion from the French countryside than to monitor the way influential bankers and businessmen talked in the salons. Construing "public opinion" as the discourse of exclusive salon meetings may seem elitist, but in that context, salon discourse was the public opinion that mattered. In other settings, the scope of public opinion was disputed. For example, writing a bit later (in 1828), the English author William A. Mackinnon asserted that public opinion was "that sentiment . . . maintained by the best informed, most intelligent, and most moral persons in the community, which is gradually spread and adopted by nearly all persons of any education, or proper feeling."[21] Whatever else one thinks of it, this definition can reasonably be termed elitist; many observers did not agree that public opinion was the sole preserve of the best and brightest plus whoever happened to agree with them.

The seventeenth and eighteenth centuries witnessed the evolution of other interesting techniques for communication of public opinion. Two closely related ones are the petition and the public rally. Beginning as early as 1640, citizens of England petitioned Parliament about a number of public affairs, from taxes and monopolies to social issues and peace. Petitions were a very effective means of focusing legislators' attention on topics of importance to common people. Petitions were presented peaceably at times, but very often an angry mob delivered its petition to Parliament in person. In a colorful description of violent petitioning during the first English civil war (1642–1646), a British writer noted how women—who were often the leaders in petitioning for peace—presented their demands. The women:

> kepte knockinge and beatinge of the outwarde dore before the parliament house, and would have violently forced the same open, and required Mr Pym, Mr Strode, and some other members . . . and threatened to take the rounde heades of the parliament whome they saide they would caste into the Thames [River]. . . . These women were not any whit scared or ashamed of their incivilities, but cryed out so much the more, even at the doore of the house of Commons, Give us these Traytors that are against peace, that we may teare them in pieces, Give us Pym.[22]

Not all petitioners were angry mobs, but so much violence accompanied the presentation of petitions to Parliament that in 1648 legislators passed a bill against unruly petitioning. This law was ineffective, so Parliament then limited the number of people who could present a petition to twenty. Even this did not deter violence, so in 1699, all petitioners were required to give their petition to their representative so that he could present it for them in parliamentary debate.

This series of incidents in British history could be interpreted in several ways. One might argue that the petitioners were too unruly to engage in the sort of rational political dialogue necessary for the construction of public policy. Mackinnon, if he had discussed these petitions, probably would have characterized them as "popular clamour," the low-quality antithesis of public opinion. Alternately, we can read Parliament's response as an attempt to dilute public opinion by preventing citizens from presenting their demands directly and jointly. Historians' interpretations of these events, as well as other acts by citizens during the English civil wars, are interesting and varied.[23]

Rioting and demonstrations can be seen as relatively new opinion technologies. Although crowds gathered in the ancient city-states of Greece and throughout the ages, rioting escalated as a form of public opinion expression in seventeenth-century England. Most of these "popular disturbances" (as they were called at the time) centered on economics: rioters protested fiscal policies of the Parliament as well as the food shortages and food price hikes resulting from those policies. In early twenty-first-century America, we are not accustomed to food rioting, but such demonstrations were common during this period. In a 1938 book, British scholar Max Beloff reports on his archival research concerning the food riots of the late seventeenth and early eighteenth centuries, for example in 1708:

The steepness of the rise in [grain] prices was indeed sharper in these years than at any other time in the period under discussion. . . . The populace was not slow to react. In May of 1709 it was reported from Essex that mobs of women amounting to hundreds were on the move and had threatened to '[set on] fire divers houses, and shoot several persons, by reason they have been dealers in corn to London, on pretense they make the same dear [i.e., expensive].'[24]

Rioting is quintessentially public among public opinion technologies: the people involved expect to be heard. In contemporary American politics, we often witness demonstrations, strikes, and marches, as we did in 2014 in Ferguson, Missouri, and all around the country, after the shooting of Michael Brown and the grand jury decision not to indict the policeman involved. Yet the intensity of these gatherings pales in comparison to the violent protests over government economic policy in seventeenth- and eighteenth-century England.

The general election is an even younger opinion technology. In modern democratic states, typically all legislators—and often other political leaders, such as the US president—are chosen through general elections, in which most adult citizens are eligible to participate. (While elections date back at least to the ancient Greek democracies, most officials in those city-states were not elected.) Many people consider general elections the most important mechanism by which public opinion influences policy in these countries, not only by selecting political leaders, but also by indirectly providing information about voters' priorities. Unlike most previous means of expressing public opinion, votes cast in modern general elections are anonymous. The spread of the secret ballot in the latter half of the nineteenth century thus marked a turning point in public opinion: people could express their opinions without their neighbors (or even their families) knowing about them.

The spread of general elections in the United States in the early nineteenth century (although many adults could not vote) encouraged the rise of straw polling. Straw polling is "nonscientific" polling conducted with pen and paper, over the telephone, or by less formal means such as a "show of hands." In the early nineteenth century journalists, party operatives, and citizens polled people in their communities about upcoming elections. Major newspapers, such as the *New York Times* and the *Chicago Tribune*, often published polls conducted by their reporters, who traveled around the country covering political rallies and speeches. For example, many journalists conducted straw polls on long train or boat rides to get a sense of public opinion in the local community.

Were these straw polls accurate? Probably not, but it is difficult to tell in retrospect. In 1932 sociologist Claude Robinson published an analysis of straw polling that found much variability. Straw polls conducted in person tended to be more accurate than the sort that asked readers to cut a ballot from the newspaper and mail it in. Yet even the in-person interviews did not always yield accurate forecasts of upcoming elections.[25]

Regardless of their accuracy, straw polls were important in the nineteenth and early twentieth centuries because they were a vehicle for getting citizens involved in politics. First, straw polls made elections seem like "horse races." This comparison may sound pejorative (and often it is), but news articles that emphasize a contest—who is ahead, by how much—may encourage voters to pay attention to the campaign. Second, people often conducted their own straw polls instead of waiting for journalists to poll them or their neighbors. Finally, historical accounts show that straw polling accompanied political discussion; the polling usually followed or preceded a debate about the issues and the campaign. Thus, straw polling prompted people to engage their neighbors and coworkers in discussions of public affairs. Do today's scientific polls equally serve this function of inspiring public discourse? The answer is unclear, but the question merits consideration.

Regardless of the benefits of straw polling, more systematic and accurate approaches to opinion measurement were bound to emerge. The most famous pioneer of scientific polling, George Gallup, bolstered his reputation by showing up a straw poll. In 1936 a massive mail-in straw poll conducted by the *Literary Digest*, a popular magazine, mistakenly predicted that Alf Landon would easily defeat Franklin Roosevelt in the presidential election. Gallup, using a new technique called random sampling, did not determine the election outcome perfectly (he was off by 7 percentage points), but his result was far closer than the *Digest*'s.

The key to Gallup's success was sampling theory, which dictates that one use methods of *random selection* to choose respondents for a poll (see Box 2.5). If one selects a survey sample at random from the population to be studied and response rates are reasonably high, the sample should "simulate" the opinions of the population. The *Literary Digest* did not use sampling methods; it simply relied on various lists of citizens (gathered, for example, from phone directories and auto registration records) and sent out millions of ballots, asking citizens to mark their preference for the upcoming election. The *Digest* had used this approach with considerable success since 1916, but in 1936, the people on its lists apparently were far less favorable to Roosevelt than the actual electorate was.

At this time, scientific surveys mark the last revolutionary change in how Americans think about and measure public opinion. (The Internet could provide the next major changes, as we discuss later in the book.) Petitions, rioting, and

---

BOX 2.5
George Gallup on Polling in a Democracy

George Gallup's success as a pollster was primarily attributable to his early use of random sampling. Gallup had an almost religious belief that polling could strengthen democracy in America and beyond. In 1940 he and Saul Rae wrote:

> The kind of public opinion implied in the democratic ideal is tangible and dynamic. It springs from many sources deep in the day-to-day experience of individuals who constitute the political public, and who formulate these opinions as working guides for their political representatives. This public opinion listens to many propagandas, most of them contradictory. It tries in the clash and conflict of argument and debate to separate the true from the false. It needs criticism for its very existence, and through criticism it is constantly being modified and molded. It acts and learns by action. Its truths are relative and contingent upon the results which its action achieves. Its chief faith is a faith in experiment. It believes in the value of every individual's contribution to political life, and in the right of ordinary human beings to have a voice in deciding their fate. Public opinion, in this sense, is the pulse of democracy.

SOURCE: George Gallup and Saul Forbes Rae, *The Pulse of Democracy: The Public-Opinion Poll and How It Works* (New York: Simon and Schuster, 1940), quoted passage on p. 8.

---

demonstrations are still influential means of expressing and assessing public opinion, but scientific polling is now the preeminent tool for communicating opinion. Since Gallup's earliest polls, a variety of technical improvements in the collection and analysis of survey data have made preelection polling much more accurate. Polling on issues—how people feel about health care reform, foreign policy, and other current affairs—is still extraordinarily difficult and complicated. We discuss many aspects of sampling and survey design in Chapter 3, as well as several other methods of assessing public opinion.

As we have seen, the story of public opinion is long and varied. How a society thinks about public opinion depends on, among other things, the technologies available for expressing and communicating it, as well as the form of government in place. As governments change and new controversies arise, the same broad questions recur: Who composes the public? And how might we know its desires? As we saw in Chapter 1, these questions are difficult to answer. Yet no democratic state can evolve if its leaders and citizens fail to grapple with these fundamental theoretical and practical concerns.

NOTES

1. Ernest Barker, *Greek Political Theory: Plato and His Predecessors* (London: Methuen 1918), 38–39, cited in Paul Palmer, "The Concept of Public Opinion in Political Theory," in C. Wittke, ed., *Essays in History and Political Theory in Honour of Charles Howard McIlwain* (New York: Russell and Russell, 1964).

2. Robert Minar, "Public Opinion in the Perspective of Political Theory," *Western Political Quarterly* 13 (1960): 31–44.

3. Thanks to Professor Jean Goodwin of Northwestern University for her translation and insights.

4. Niccolò Machiavelli, *The Prince*, trans. and ed. N. H. Thompson (Buffalo, NY: Prometheus Books, 1986), 57–58.

5. Quoted in Palmer, "The Concept of Public Opinion in Political Theory," 239.

6. Alexis de Tocqueville, *Democracy in America*, ed. and trans. J. P. Mayer (New York: Anchor Books, 1969), 255.

7. Ibid., 435

8. C. J. Arthur, ed., *The German Ideology* (New York: International Publishers, 1984), 65–66.

9. James Bryce, *The American Commonwealth* (London: Macmillan, 1891), 265.

10. Ibid., 267.

11. Terry N. Clark, ed., *Gabriel Tarde: On Communication and Social Influence* (Chicago: University of Chicago Press, 1969).

12. Arthur N. Holcombe, "Roundtable on Political Statistics," *American Political Science Review* 19 (February 1925): 123–124.

13. For a more detailed discussion of these trends in the history of public expression, see Susan Herbst, *Numbered Voices: How Opinion Polling Has Shaped American Politics* (Chicago: University of Chicago Press, 1995).

14. Charles Tilly, "Speaking Your Mind Without Elections, Surveys, or Social Movements," *Public Opinion Quarterly* 47 (1983): 465.

15. Aristotle, Rhetoric 1.2.1, *Aristotle in 23 Volumes*, vol. 22, trans. J. H. Freese (Cambridge, MA: Harvard University Press; London: William Heinemann Ltd., 1926).

16. Kathleen Hall Jamieson, *Eloquence in an Electronic Age: The Transformation of Political Speechmaking* (New York: Oxford University Press, 1988), 5.

17. Wilhelm Bauer, "Public Opinion," in Edwin Seligman, ed., *Encyclopaedia of the Social Sciences* (New York: Macmillan, 1930), 671.

18. Jamieson, *Eloquence in an Electronic Age*, 84.

19. Lewis Coser, *Men of Ideas: A Sociologist's View* (New York: Free Press, 1970), 20.

20. On salons and their place in political history, see Susan Herbst, *Politics at the Margin: Historical Perspectives on Public Expression Outside the Mainstream* (New York: Cambridge University Press, 1995).

21. William Alexander Mackinnon, *On the Rise, Progress, and Present State of Public Opinion in Great Britain and Other Parts of the World* (London: Saunders and Otley, 1828), 15.

22. Quoted in Patricia Higgins, "The Reaction of Women, with Special Reference to Women Petitioners," in Brian Manning, ed., *Politics, Religion, and the English Civil War* (London: Edward Arnold, 1973), 190–191.

23. See Manning, *Politics, Religion, and the English Civil War*, or Maurice Ashley, *England in the Seventeenth Century* (Baltimore, MD: Penguin Books, 1968). On petitioning and political meetings in British history, see Cecil Emden, *The People and the Constitution* (London: Oxford University Press, 1956).

24. Max Beloff, *Public Order and Popular Disturbances 1660–1714* (London: Oxford University Press, 1938), 68.

25. Claude Robinson, *Straw Votes* (New York: Columbia University Press, 1932).

Methods for Studying Public Opinion

From the variety of definitions, dimensions, and theories of public opinion discussed in Chapters 1 and 2, you might have guessed that public opinion is difficult to measure and study. Researchers have puzzled over the best way to measure it since the early decades of the twentieth century. Despite this, some methods of studying public opinion stand out as most important. Researchers can use many techniques to assess the public mood, including election returns, consumer behavior, stock market fluctuations, public meetings and demonstrations, and other such behavioral indicators. But political leaders and journalists seeking insight into public opinion often turn to four formal methods: survey research or polling, focus groups, experimental research, and the analysis of mass media content. In this chapter we provide a general overview of these methods.

SURVEY RESEARCH: AGGREGATING INDIVIDUAL OPINIONS

Survey research has significantly shaped contemporary views of publics and their opinions. As we have seen, in the early twentieth century social theory grew more concerned with the concept of mass publics. How could researchers rigorously study the ideas and behaviors of large, dynamic groups? Sociologists were accustomed to carefully interviewing people in smaller group situations, such as the workplace or particular neighborhoods. They could not conduct enough interviews in enough places to support broad generalizations about mass publics. Journalists often employed informal preelection straw polls and "person-in-the-street" interviews, which were more entertaining than reliable.

Considerable data existed on mass publics, but they were fragmentary and frustrating. Every ten years the US census attempted to provide an actual head count and some basic demographic information. The best measures of public opinion were election results. Obviously, neither indicator could reveal much about what people were thinking about public issues, much less explain why they thought as they did.

A major impetus for better public opinion measures was the growth of broadcast radio in the 1920s and 1930s. Advertisers wanted to know how many people were listening; broadcasters needed ways to find out. Statistical sampling offered the key. *Probability samples*, or random samples, of perhaps a few thousand people—even several hundred—can offer reasonably accurate insights into a much larger population.

In those early years, door-to-door interviewing was required to obtain a roughly fair sample of a population, and that process was—and remains—exorbitantly expensive and time-consuming. Polling by telephone tended mainly to reach the wealthier, who could afford telephones, and mail surveys suffered from lack of valid address lists. Nonetheless, early survey efforts yielded at least some representative indications of early radio audiences. Preelection polls also became more formal, although still primitive by today's standards.

In the late 1930s and into the 1940s, many elements came together to make large-scale opinion surveys the more reliable tool they are today. For one thing, people became easier to find, with increased telephone ownership and better phone networks, more accurate mailing lists, and population movement to urban areas. Also important were advances in statistical theory and, later, the application of computers to statistical modeling. Computerizing both survey sampling and analytic techniques made surveys far more efficient and cost-effective.

Moreover, the birth of academic survey research centers at such places as the University of Chicago and the University of Michigan spawned many innovations in survey procedures and greatly improved their validity. Survey research today is a multibillion-dollar industry, with studies of nearly every type imaginable being conducted by academicians, market researchers, mass media, governmental agencies, and political pollsters. Without survey research, most of this book could not have been written.

Despite the long history of survey research, many people have misconceptions about what surveys can and cannot show and about how their results can be interpreted. We outline some basic principles below, with particular attention to survey applications in public opinion research. Several excellent handbooks provide detailed information and guidance for conducting surveys. *Internet, Phone, Mail and Mixed-Mode Surveys: The Tailored Design Method* by sociologist Don Dillman and his colleagues is a standard in the field.[1]

Elements of Survey Design

A *survey* is a research technique for measuring characteristics of a particular population of individuals. Every survey depends on several interrelated design decisions. Following are the most important:

1. The population that the survey is to provide information about.
2. The kind of sample of individuals that will be chosen from that population.
3. The method of data gathering to be used, usually involving in-person, phone, mail, or Internet interviews.
4. The kind of questionnaire or interviewing instrument used.
5. The kinds of analyses done and inferences drawn.

The choice of population to study influences many other survey design decisions. Strategies for sampling and interviewing differ according to whether the population includes, for example, all US adults, Democrats likely to vote in Ohio, chief executive officers of biotechnology companies, or first-year students at a midwestern state university.

The purpose of the survey obviously influences the kinds of analyses to be done and the inferences drawn. If our purpose is preliminary and exploratory—perhaps to get some broad ideas about how the Internet and social media might affect college students' political views—we may begin with a rather small sample of students we know in one dormitory at a large university just to try out some questions. We might also use focus groups, described later in this chapter, to get more insight. If, however, we are conducting a preelection poll of who is ahead in a governor's race and why, our sampling needs to be larger and more representative of likely voters, and our questions should be clear and precise. Or if our purpose is to test the hypothesis that watching television leads to less public social interaction, we need several well-validated measures of television viewership, social interaction, and any other variables we intend to study. Depending on our specific hypothesis, we may not need a representative sample of the US population as a whole; we might want to focus on young adults, for instance.

Types of Surveys

Some surveys are essentially descriptive: they primarily measure characteristics such as how widespread a particular opinion or vote intention is. Such simple descriptive surveys are sometimes called *polls*. Other surveys, more ambitiously, investigate relationships among these characteristics, such as exploring why people support the candidates they do. For example, CNN might do a preelection poll to see who is ahead in a presidential contest, whereas during the same time period, the American National Election Study at the University of Michigan would be doing more extensive surveys with hundreds of questions that can shed light on people's political reasoning and behavior.

Most surveys are *cross-sectional*, meaning that they are done at one point in time to provide a "snapshot" of public views at that particular time. In contrast, *panel surveys* reinterview the same people over time to get a better picture of how opinions may change over months or even years. Surveys are often a main element in *field experiments*, in which groups within the sample are subjected to different "treatments." For example, one community may receive a particular public health information campaign, while another does not. Then a survey can be used to determine how much difference the campaign made. In this example, the second community serves as a *control*: even if some news event creates learning in both communities, the difference between the two communities may be attributable to the campaign (although other possibilities should be considered).

Survey Sampling

So far we have emphasized *probability* samples, commonly called *random* samples, which can be used to generalize about the populations from which they are drawn. *Nonprobability* samples are not representative of the larger population, but they can still be very useful. For example, as mentioned previously, small informal samples can help us investigate social concepts and processes that larger studies could overlook and try out questions that can be used as measures in later studies. Marketing researchers sometimes use "person-in-the-street" or "mall-intercept" samples. Interviewers position themselves in a shopping mall or other well-traveled location and try to interview people in selected age, gender, or other categories. The researchers cannot know whether the resulting sample is representative of the broader community—or even other shoppers at the mall— but they may nonetheless glean some useful marketing insights.

In probability sampling, each person in a given population is assumed to have a certain known chance of being included in the sample. In the case of simple random sampling, every person in the population has an equal chance of being sampled, and that chance is independent of the selection of any other person into the sample. Note that this definition of "random" is far more demanding than its everyday usage, in which the term usually implies doing things "unsystematically" or "without thought or planning." Probability sampling, on the contrary, requires careful planning. Sophisticated random number tables are often used to try to ensure that the selection of each person for a sample is independent of the selection of every other person. The analogy often used is continuously shaking a bin of numbered balls, as in lottery drawings, between selection of the numbered balls.

For example, suppose that a news story reports that according to a probability sample survey of US adults, 57 percent support an immigration reform proposal, 36 percent do not, and 7 percent are undecided. The story also reports that the sample size was 1,000 and that the margin of error for the findings is plus or minus 3 percent. This *margin of error* means that in 95 percent of all possible samples of that population, the results should be within plus or minus 3 percentage points of the results for the entire population if everyone in the population had been interviewed. So, if the sample is accurately drawn, it offers good (though not decisive) evidence that somewhere between 54 and 60 percent of the adult population supports the proposal—or at least would say they did if asked.

Note that this method cannot reveal what the true population value is, that is, exactly what percentage of US adults supports the proposal. To find that out, we really would have to ask every adult in the United States. Being unable or unwilling to do that, the survey researchers hedged their bets, conducting enough interviews to reduce the likely magnitude of error to an acceptable level and reporting how much error was likely. Most researchers (as in this example) report the margin of error for a "95 percent confidence level," meaning that if they could draw one hundred separate samples, they would expect ninety-five of those samples to produce results within that margin of error. Increasing the confidence level entails either widening the margin of error or increasing the sample size: it is more difficult to be 99 percent confident than to be 95 percent confident.

In general, increasing the sample size reduces the margin of error for a given confidence level. For a 95 percent confidence level, a simple random sample of 100 people has a margin of error of plus or minus 10 percent; a sample of 10,000 people has a margin of error of plus or minus 1 percent. Many people are surprised that the margin of error depends heavily on the sample size but very little on the *population* size, unless a large fraction of the population is sampled. Conducting 1,000 interviews works about as well for the entire US population as it does for a city of 100,000 people. The key is the sampling. If you want to know how salty some soup is, tasting a spoonful can suffice whether it is drawn from a bowl or a huge vat—but only if the soup is well mixed. A simple random sample has the effect of effectively "mixing" the population.

Unfortunately, simple random sampling is not always "simple" or ideal in practice. Consider a national survey conducted in person. To interview a simple random sample of a few thousand people, researchers might have to send interviewers to many hundreds of cities and towns all over the country. More practical is a *multistage* sample, in which researchers (for example) select certain municipalities to interview, then conduct several interviews in each city or town. A multistage sample is not as accurate as a simple random sample of the same size; some kinds of people may be overrepresented or underrepresented based on where they live. However, it may be much more economical. In some circumstances, researchers may deliberately "oversample" some kinds of respondents and then adjust the results accordingly. For example, if a study is designed to compare the opinions of black versus white Americans, researchers might interview 500 black respondents and 500 white respondents—far from a simple random sample—to attain a reasonably small margin of error for each group. To obtain estimates for the entire population, the various responses would have to be "weighted" so that blacks and whites were proportionately represented according to their actual proportions in the overall population.

The Problem of Survey Participation

A key problem in survey research is that some people statistically chosen to be included in a sample are more difficult to reach than others, and some are more willing to cooperate than others. In 2012 the Pew Research Center reported that its response rate—the percentage of households sampled in which an interview was completed—had slumped to just 9 percent, down from 36 percent as recently as 1997.[2] Not only do such lower response rates increase the expense of completing the needed number of interviews, but they raise doubts about whether those who do participate are a representative random sample of the entire population.

Many researchers argue that as long as it can be shown that those not participating in the survey are similar to those who are, the problem is minimal. Most opinion surveys are able to compare the demographics of their respondents with US census demographics (gender, age, race/ethnicity, and so on) of the populations of interest. Often the demographics are highly similar. When they are not, the results can be weighted in an effort to better represent the population.

Other researchers argue, however, that even if demographics are similar, we can never really know how closely the interviewed respondents compare to the general population in their opinions and behaviors. For example, people who agree to be interviewed may be somewhat more interested in public affairs, more knowledgeable, and more active. So samples may be unrepresentative due to *nonresponse bias*—the differences between respondents and nonrespondents— and weighting based on demographics may not solve the problem.

What can be done to maximize response rates and/or minimize bias? It is clear that people are more willing to participate when they sense the study is legitimate (e.g., not a sales promotion), when they are interested in the subject area, and when they are given additional inducements, such as payment for their time. However, paying respondents raises concerns that people who need money may be overrepresented, and that paid respondents may be more likely to give answers that they believe will please the interviewer. Evidence suggests that many (probably most) surveys are reasonably accurate. Nevertheless, bear in mind that a poll's reported margin of error refers only to random sampling error, not to nonresponse bias or any other possible source of error.

Methods of Gathering Survey Data

The most common methods of getting survey data from respondents are in person, by telephone, by mail, and over the Internet. Each has advantages and disadvantages; again, the choice of method may depend on how well it fits with other components of the survey.

In-Person Interviews. Most researchers would ideally prefer to do in-person, face-to-face interviews for nearly all surveys. Personal interaction makes it easier for interviewers to build rapport with respondents. Better rapport can lead to more accurate and complete answers, especially in studies that deal with sensitive issues. Greater rapport can also permit longer, more detailed interviews. Interviewers are also able to note more emotive aspects of responses through facial expressions and body language. Another advantage over phone and mail interviews is the ability to use visual aids and other explanatory tools. Questions about campaign advertising, for example, can be asked by showing the actual ads on a portable device.

Unfortunately, in-person interviews are far more expensive than other options, and for this reason they are used quite sparingly Much of this expense is from interviewer time—not just conducting the interviews, but tracking down and recruiting the prospective respondents. Sampling costs also are higher, given the need to use physical addresses or similar locators. (No researcher has a "master list" of every American's address; approximating a fair sample becomes a daunting challenge, even before interviewers are sent into the field.)

Telephone Interviews. Telephone interviewing remains by far the most-used public opinion survey technique and is far cheaper than in-person interviewing. With the advent of Voice over Internet Protocol (VoIP) telephone services like Skype, a nationwide telephone survey may cost little more than a survey of the same size in one city, in sharp contrast to in-person interviews.

Most general population telephone samples use *random digit dialing*. Telephone numbers to be called are probability-sampled from computerized lists of all possible telephone exchanges in the population area. As calls are made, nonworking numbers and business and other nonhousehold numbers are systematically excluded, leaving what is usually an excellent representation of all private household telephones within the specified geographic area, including unlisted numbers. Software "auto-dialers" reduce the time and effort of reaching these numbers. However, the rapid spread of cell phones and cell-phone-only households has complicated research, as we elaborate upon below.

Telephone surveys are fast and flexible, so they are widely used for quick-reaction opinion polls on major news events, candidate debates, and the like. A news organization such as CNN can commission a national poll on reactions to a major presidential speech and air the results within a few hours of the speech. Computer-assisted telephone interviewing (CATI) techniques allow interviewers to enter answers instantly and can customize what questions are asked or the order in which they are asked. Some surveys go one step further and do not use interviewers at all: the questions are prerecorded, and respondents give their answers via the telephone keys or through automated voice recognition. These "robopolls" tend to have lower response rates because respondents find it easier to hang up on a prerecorded interviewer than a live one. But at least some of them have been found to be reasonably accurate.

Although telephone surveys do not allow the rapport of personal interviews, they do far better than the more impersonal methods discussed below. The telephone questionnaire format does need to be relatively simple, however, with questions and response categories that are easy to read and comprehend. The most effective maximum length for telephone surveys is about fifteen minutes; anything over twenty minutes can be quite wearing on respondents, risking lower quality data (as respondents lose interest) and the respondents hanging up before completing the survey.

Interviewer training is a critical ingredient for both in-person and telephone surveys. Most reputable survey organizations maintain permanent staffs of experienced interviewers who are expert at eliciting answers that are as honest and unbiased as possible. The best interviewers act as professional communicators between researcher and respondent, not as persuaders, helpers, teachers, or confidants. Good interviewers are alert, interested, and appreciative of the respondent's time but do not approve or disapprove of answers or prompt or imply what answers are expected.

Mail-Administered Surveys. Collecting public opinion data by mail surveys has been widely derided as a last resort, often not worth the trouble. Although costs can be low—printing, postage, and data entry for the returned surveys—response rates can border on the horrific. General population mail surveys sometimes have response rates of less than 5 percent, raising grave doubts about their representativeness. (The *Columbus Dispatch*'s final 2012 preelection mail poll reported a "respectable" 15 percent response rate.) Indeed, some mail "surveys" are promotional gimmicks, such as the questionnaires sent out by special interest groups supposedly to solicit opinions but actually to raise money.

Nonetheless, mail surveys have retained a role in collecting data from smaller, more specialized population groups. One such group has been college faculty, who routinely receive polls regarding their own areas of interest, academic policy, and student interests. Faculty typically respond in respectable numbers to these polls, whether out of altruism, curiosity, compulsiveness, or self-interest in expressing their views. Physicians, civil servants, business executives, and other groups have been successfully polled by mail. However, such surveys increasingly are conducted over the Internet, with recruitment via e-mail.

Internet Surveys. Not long ago, "Internet surveys" generally referred to voluntary "polls" on news Web sites. Such "polls" can provide some oblique insights into people's opinions, but the results are not representative of any population beyond the individuals who happened to click on them. However, that has changed in recent years, and Internet surveys that do attempt to use rigorous sampling techniques are becoming more common. One of the best-known Internet pollsters, YouGov, uses a combination of recruitment methods to build a large and diverse panel of respondents who are available to participate in various surveys. Then, for any particular study, YouGov randomly draws a sample from its panel and sends e-mail invitations to complete the survey on a special Web page. Because panel members already have expressed interest in participating, YouGov and other pollsters who use this method can attain relatively high response rates.

Critics of Internet surveys have argued that they are unlikely to be representative because people who volunteer for such surveys are likely to be more technologically savvy and/or politically engaged than people who do not volunteer. In the early days of Internet surveys, users tended to be younger and more prosperous than nonusers. They still are, but this gap seems to have narrowed over time.[3] Moreover, some pollsters have provided Internet access to panel recruits who would not have it otherwise—a practice that has become more viable as Internet use has increased throughout US society and as equipment has become cheaper.

Questions about Internet surveys persist. For example, even if the panels are in principle representative of the public at large, do they remain representative after being repeatedly asked their opinions on a wide range of topics? During the 2012 presidential campaign, many news organizations refused to report results of Internet polls. However, several of these polls performed reasonably well, and if telephone survey response rates continue to decline, it seems likely that Internet surveys will continue to emerge as a valid complement to if not a replacement for other surveys.

Questionnaire Design

Anyone can ask a question, but asking a good question can be difficult, especially in survey research. Writing good questionnaire items requires a solid understanding of the topic matter and of the people being interviewed. The average US adult has had about a year of college beyond high school and has not paid close attention to most of the issues and events that surveys typically ask about. Survey designers need to pose their questions and response options clearly, in everyday language—neither too technical nor too vague. Often researchers include some background information as part of the question.

For example, in June 2013 controversy erupted about the National Security Agency's access to cell phone "telephony metadata": certain information about telephone calls, such as the phone numbers involved and the time and duration of each call. A poll question that asked, "Under what circumstances do you think the National Security Agency should be permitted to collect telephony metadata?" would have been incomprehensible to many if not most respondents, even at the height of news coverage. At the other extreme, asking "Do you think the National Security Agency should collect information about phone calls?"

would not help much: "information about phone calls" may be *simpler* than "telephony metadata," but it is far from *clear*. Even if respondents are knowledgeable about the topic—which should not be taken for granted—there is no way to know which "information" their responses refer to. More detailed questions can benefit both respondents and researchers.

But providing details in survey questions poses at least three problems. First, respondents have limited time and patience to attend to details—especially if a telephone survey has interrupted something they would rather be doing instead. Second, each detail may tend to influence respondents in one direction or another, and there is no objective way of deciding which details are most important or fair to include. Third, when a survey tells people things they did not know (or did not pay much attention to), it seems to be not just measuring public opinion, but *creating* it or at least evoking it. Is public opinion an illusion after all? Most public opinion researchers would say that good survey questions at least resemble thoughts and conversations that people are already having and therefore offer some insight into public opinion as it exists independent of the survey. But researchers can disagree sharply about the merits of particular questions. (See Box 3.1.)

If respondents often struggle with opinion questions, they especially struggle with hypotheticals. A researcher might ask, "What would you think if the United States invaded Ireland tomorrow?," but how could a respondent possibly know what to answer? On the other hand, respondents often give more consistent answers to factual questions about their actions and behaviors. Even "factual" questions are not necessarily simple, however. People often have trouble answering questions about "how many hours a day you spend watching television" or "how many times in the last year you have gone to the movies," facts that most of us do not systematically keep track of.

Researchers also must contend with respondents' reluctance to give answers that might make a bad impression on the interviewers—what is known as the *social desirability* effect. For example, the reported voter turnout among survey respondents tends to be several percentage points above actual turnout. Researchers have confirmed that, in fact, some people report having voted although public records prove otherwise. Also, people are less likely to "fudge" about their voting behavior if the question is worded to make not voting seem socially acceptable, such as stating that "a lot of people weren't able to vote." (Most of the American National Election Studies have used that approach.)

Survey results can be prone to *question order effects*. As all of us who ever persuaded our parents to let us do something know from personal experience, what one says first can make a big difference. Here is a classic example. In 1948,

BOX 3.1
Questionnaire Wording and the
Holocaust Denial Controversy

In 1992 a well-respected survey research firm, the Roper Organization, fielded a national survey on attitudes of Americans toward the Holocaust and its impact on Jews and on the subject of intolerance more generally. To assess knowledge of the Holocaust, or more precisely, belief that the German government under the Nazis had purposely killed several million Jews in the 1940s, Roper asked the following question: "The term Holocaust usually refers to the killing of millions of Jews in Nazi death camps during World War II. Does it seem possible or does it seem impossible to you that the Nazi extermination of the Jews never happened?"

The findings appeared surprising, if not shocking, to many: 22 percent of the respondents said it was "possible" the mass killings had not happened, 12 percent said they "didn't know," and 65 percent said it was "impossible" that the event had not happened. That nearly one-fourth of US adults denied that the Holocaust had happened and that nearly one-third either denied it or did not know whether it had happened or not raised serious questions about the quality of knowledge about recent history. It also raised concerns about an anti-Semitic undercurrent involving rumors being spread at the time by white supremacist and other extremist groups that the Holocaust had indeed been a hoax, perpetrated by Jewish groups to gain sympathy and political favor.

Although news of the findings made headlines and focused on the denial and ignorance of much of the public, other survey researchers keyed in on the confusing, double-negative wording of the question and its possible impact on the responses. Criticisms included that the question was misleading and too hypothetical or that some people might have been led to respond that "anything's possible" and that technically, the Jews had not been fully "exterminated," as the question may have implied.[1]

The Roper Organization immediately admitted these possible problems and worked with a larger research team to do a more definitive study of the issue. (In fact, the question that was asked had replaced an earlier version that was recognized as even more biased: "Does it seem possible to you that the Holocaust never happened?") The new study—and a number of others that followed up on the topic—demonstrated the way in which minor wording changes can influence responses to questionnaire items. The new items also restored some faith in the knowledge and values of the American public. A few examples follow, drawn from a detailed

(continues)

(continued)   BOX 3.1
Questionnaire Wording and the
Holocaust Denial Controversy

account of the controversy by Tom W. Smith.[2] In each case, the question is introduced by this sentence: "The Holocaust is a term used to describe the extermination of the Jews in World War II."

"Some people have said it is possible it never actually happened. In your own mind, are you certain that the Nazi extermination of the Jews happened, or does it seem possible to you that it never happened?" (93 percent "certain it happened"; 4 percent "possible it never happened"; 4 percent "don't know").[3]

"Do you think the Nazi extermination of millions of Jews actually took place, or not?" (90 percent "yes, took place"; 4 percent mixed, maybe (volunteered); 3 percent "no, did not take place"; 5 percent "don't know").[4]

"Do you doubt that the Holocaust actually happened, or not?" (9 percent "yes, doubt it"; 87 percent "no, don't doubt it"; 4 percent unsure, etc.).[5]

---

[1]Tom W. Smith, "Review: The Holocaust Denial Controversy," *Public Opinion Quarterly* 59 (1995): 269–295.

[2]Ibid.

[3]May 1993 Bruskin polling organization telephone survey; see Smith, "Review."

[4]January 1994 CBS telephone survey; see Smith, "Review."

[5]January 1994 Gallup telephone survey; see Smith, "Review."

---

as the Cold War between the United States and the Soviet Union was intensifying, a survey asked respondents whether Soviet reporters should be allowed to report freely about the United States. But half the respondents were first asked whether US reporters should be allowed to report freely about the Soviet Union. Fully 90 percent of that group answered yes, and 73 percent went on to say that Soviet reporters should have the same freedom, compared to less than half as many (36 percent) among the other respondents. Schuman and Presser, who found similar (but smaller) effects in a 1980 survey, speculated that the results could be explained by a norm of reciprocity—roughly, the idea that we should treat others as well as they treat us. More subtly, respondents are more likely to mention crime as one of the most important problems facing the country if they are first asked whether they have recently been victims of a crime—even if, like most people, they have not. This is called a *priming effect*, as in priming a fuse to help it catch fire.

These and other "effects" underscore that no matter how scientific the sampling technique and how careful the design, public opinion research has a crucial subjective element. Respondents do not simply report their preexisting opinions; they react to questions much as they might in an ordinary conversation, thinking as they go, reacting to context and their interviewer (if there is one). When asking questions that have a correct answer, researchers will seek the design that elicits the most accurate responses—but for matters of opinion, often there is no clear criterion of accuracy. The best possible design may try several approaches (e.g., alternative question wording) to see whether the results change.

Issues in Survey Research

Survey research can be useful to explore social processes and to describe public moods and behaviors on a wide range of topics. As with any technique, inappropriate uses of it, and overreliance on it, can cause problems.

A major complaint against political uses of surveys is that pollsters can ask questions in biased or distorted ways, or use inappropriate samples, to get the results they want. Sometimes, campaigns even employ "push polls," which, in the guise of asking people's opinions, convey misinformation about opposing candidates. Such uses of polls are difficult to track down, and candidates often deny any such doings. The use of push polls has declined because of pressure from professional organizations such as the American Association for Public Opinion Research, which upholds strict standards against such practices by its members. To avoid reporting on willfully biased polls, many news media will only report poll results if they consider the pollster reputable and if they can include the exact questions used and provide detail on how the survey was carried out.

A broader issue is whether policymakers and analysts may over-rely even on relatively good survey data. Critics charge that too much dependence on surveys results in a leadership vacuum: leaders may avoid policy actions that "don't poll well" or have never been polled about at all. Political candidates can use surveys for insight into how to tell voters what they want to hear, instead of revealing the truth about their views. On the other hand, it is not clear that citizens would be better off if polling did not exist and leaders heard almost exclusively from their own advisers, lobbyists, and a small fraction of the public.

As a social research tool, surveys can be faulted for focusing on public opinion in the aggregate, devoting too little attention to individual motivation and activity, especially to the dynamics of smaller group interactions. One method does not fit all research questions. Many valuable studies either eschew surveys or combine them with other methods such as focus groups, content analyses, participant observation, and in some cases even intensive clinical psychological examinations. By taking this wider view, findings from surveys can be more validly interpreted in the full context of social behavior and interaction.

FOCUS GROUPS: USING GROUP DYNAMICS TO MEASURE PUBLIC OPINION

Focus group interviewing is one popular method for examining interpersonal dynamics in public opinion.[4] They are "carefully planned discussion[s] designed to obtain perceptions on a defined area of interest in a permissive, nonthreatening environment."[5] The roots of this method can be traced to sociologist Robert Merton's examination of propaganda during World War II, but it was largely ignored in public opinion research for decades thereafter. However, focus groups have enjoyed a modest resurgence, most notably in market research and campaign consulting, but also in journalism and academia.

Unlike survey methods that typically ask individual subjects to answer a series of closed-ended questions, focus groups involve open discussion among a group of subjects. The typical focus group discussion includes between six and ten participants, give or take a few. Researchers may use one focus group, several, or even dozens, depending on their purposes and budget. The participants rarely are recruited as a true random sample of the target population; they may fit particular demographic targets, or various groups may include different kinds of participants. For example, in her analysis of attitudes toward gender roles, Roberta Sigel ran separate groups for men and women, also stratifying several groups further by age, class, and occupational status.[6] Stratifying groups by demographic characteristics or attitudes may help participants speak more freely. Most focus group projects include a conventional questionnaire, at least to collect basic demographic and attitudinal information.

Focus group moderators use a predetermined protocol to guide the discussions, although this "script" is seldom followed literally. Conversations often take an unexpected but potentially valuable turn, and the moderator may decide to deviate from the protocol to pursue new terrain. Usually the protocol serves as a checklist to ensure that by the discussion's end, all of the key points have been addressed. Researchers attempt to put participants at ease by making the setting as natural and informal as possible, sometimes even meeting in someone's home. The typical focus group discussion lasts from one to two hours.

Focus groups help to bridge the gap between large-sample survey analysis and more qualitative, interpretive methods such as in-depth interviews. Results can be analyzed both quantitatively (through systematic content analysis, described below) and qualitatively. Focus groups allow researchers to observe social dynamics that are invisible in many other methods: "The hallmark of focus groups is the explicit use of the group interaction to produce data and insights that would be less accessible" otherwise.[7] They balance the probing and flexibility of in-depth interviews with the ability to talk to a larger number of people. And they allow participants to say surprising things that lead to unanticipated insights.

These benefits do not come without costs. For example, precisely because focus groups allow complex social dynamics to play out, it is difficult to generalize from their results. No matter how many people participate in a particular focus group meeting, they only have one discussion, which may not even be very representative of those people, much less a broader population. (Some researchers call this the "n equals 1" problem, where n refers to the sample size. A "large-n" survey sample can support broader generalizations—but perhaps only about how people respond to surveys.)

Focus group research, despite much diversity, tends to support some broad conclusions about public opinion processes: that public opinion is exceptionally dynamic and complex; that opinions are constructed and reconstructed in particular social contexts; and that opinions emerge from a synthesis of personal, social, and mass media information. Perhaps most important, in contrast to much survey research, focus group research paints a picture of a thoughtful citizenry. When it comes to the formation of public opinion, focus groups indicate that citizens can be—with some prompting—active, critical, and reasonably sophisticated. Focus group research does not always challenge the conclusions drawn from survey methods, but it does illuminate and enrich them. Focus group methods have been used in two crucial ways: as a check on or supplement to traditional survey methods and as an independent method to explore phenomena that survey research ignores.

Supplementing Traditional Survey Methods
Roberta Sigel and Cliff Zukin's focus group study of gender relations helped to reignite political psychologists' interest in the method. Sigel and Zukin chose focus groups for two related purposes: to help in the construction of

closed-ended survey questions measuring attitudes about gender relations and gender roles and to generate hypotheses to be tested with more quantitative techniques. The six focus groups proved useful for these purposes, but Sigel also found them helpful in fleshing out the findings of subsequent quantitative analyses: "Notwithstanding their limitations, our focus group observations greatly enriched our understanding of men's and women's perceptions of gender relations. In fact, we found them to 'deliver' much more than we had anticipated."[8]

In another example of using focus groups to supplement quantitative projects, Pamela Conover and her colleagues, in their comparative study of citizenship in the United States and Great Britain, used focus groups as a "critical first step" in a larger survey research project.[9] They noted that this format ensures that "participants talk to one another in their own language, rather than simply reacting to the questions and language of an interviewer in a one-to-one situation."[10] This approach reduces the researchers' influence and allows more scope for unexpected conclusions.

The Independent Contributions of Focus Groups

Focus groups are especially helpful in investigating dynamics that survey research and other methods may miss entirely. As we noted in our discussion of survey questionnaire design, surveys do have some capacity to examine how people's expressed opinions are influenced by the course of "conversation"—for example, the order in which questions are asked. But even the most creative survey designs cannot fully capture the dynamism of opinion formation and expression. Closed-ended survey questions inherently force respondents to reply as if they had fixed, preexisting opinions. Interviewers are trained to disregard "thinking out loud," to politely rebuff attempts to rephrase the questions, and under no circumstances to hint at their own opinions (although participants may well guess at those opinions!). Focus groups, by contrast, can be "catalyst[s] for the individual expression of latent opinion . . . [and] for free-associating to life."[11] By essentially *forcing* people to think out loud in each other's presence, focus groups become windows through which to observe the process of opinion formation.

For example, Tamar Liebes and Elihu Katz consider the conversational and social nature of focus groups their greatest asset. Liebes and Katz used focus groups to study the reactions of viewers in Israel, Japan, and the United States to the then-popular television program *Dallas* and other shows. In their study, they argue that focus groups are effective in illustrating "the processes of collective meaning-making," because they permit tentative interpretations to be floated by someone and shot down by someone else, because they permit bullies to try to impose their opinions, because people can seek or appeal to expert opinion (e.g., about how rich Americans really live), and because participants' interpretations can be influenced by their relationships with each other. (Many of the participants in these focus groups already knew each other.) All these things happen in life. In short, focus groups succeed because they replicate the kinds of exchanges that citizens actually have. Because people do watch television programs together—albeit not in focus groups—and often discuss the programs socially, Liebes and Katz saw focus group discussion following a program broadcast as "a key to understanding the mediating process via which a program . . . enters into the culture."[12]

As focus group participants "think out loud"—constructing, not just reporting, their opinions—their statements may be inconsistent or even contradictory. Consider these comments excerpted from a focus group study conducted by Michael Delli Carpini and Bruce Williams:

> I think it definitely is [possible to protect the environment in today's world]. I mean, to think there's all these big brains and all this big money for making things, surely they can come up with some way to make them in a safe manner, or to protect the public, or the land or animals.
>
> There's just a lot of other stuff you have to deal with. . . . I mean, you would just have to take over the world pretty much, it would have to be every person in the United States, every company, every—I just don't think it would be possible [to protect the environment in today's world]. . . . I hate to be Miss Negative, but I just don't think so.[13]

As you have probably guessed, the same participant (named Kara) made both comments. Which one expresses her real opinion? Delli Carpini and Williams argue that the question is misdirected: both statements reflect real aspects of how Kara thinks about environmental protection. In survey research, giving inconsistent or contradictory responses—when it is even possible—may be dismissed as carelessness, but Kara seems far from careless here. Instead, she seems to be visibly struggling with a large, complicated public question for which she does not have a pat, predetermined answer. Being able to observe participants arguing with themselves as well as with each other is an important benefit of focus group research.

Admittedly, as real life goes, focus groups are not all that real. As William Gamson notes, "Most people do not spontaneously sit down with their friends and acquaintances and have a serious discussion for more than an hour on different issues in the news."[14] Gamson compares the exchanges that occur in focus groups with two other forms of discourse. *Public discourse* involves "speaking to the gallery," proclaiming one's views to a wide audience, whereas *sociable interaction* is the informal, private conversation that occurs among friends, family members, and the like. Focus groups in academic research typically combine these two types of communication. On the one hand, participants know that their comments are being recorded and interpreted for an academic "gallery." On the other hand, the conversational format, the relaxed setting, and (often) participants' familiarity with each other give the discussions elements of sociable interaction as well. Gamson labels this blend of public and private exchange "sociable public discourse."

Does focus groups' hybridization of public and private discursive forms make them irrelevant to how people really (or usually) think? Arguably they are more relevant than the dominant survey methods. Consider, for example, the dynamics of a telephone interview. One minute you are sitting at dinner or watching TV with family or friends, when a telephone interviewer calls. The next minute you are engaged in a formal interview with a stranger, answering questions about a variety of political issues with no time to think about them. Your answers may not necessarily reflect how you really think or feel. Also, how people usually talk about politics may actually be closer to sociable public discourse than either of the alternatives that it combines. Surely many more people talk with each other about politics than would be willing to speak at a public hearing. Very likely, too, people typically talk differently about politics than about many other topics. Politics is widely considered controversial and consequential; people "talking politics" may choose their words more carefully, perhaps anticipating disagreement from the people they are talking with or thinking about the broader public implications of their opinions. Focus groups seem especially well-suited to capturing this aspect of public opinion. (See Box 3.2.)

EXPERIMENTAL METHODS AND OPINION RESEARCH

Some public opinion research is explicitly experimental: it investigates how people respond to particular information, situations, or other treatments. Here is an early example. During World War II the US Army commissioned a team of psychologists to study the effectiveness of some training films. These films—the *Why We Fight* series, mostly directed by Frank Capra of *Mr. Smith Goes to Washington* and *It's a Wonderful Life* fame—were intended to boost soldiers'

BOX 3.2
An Illustration of Focus Group Research

Like many other researchers, William Gamson uses focus groups as a method for studying the interplay of mass-mediated and interpersonal communications. Gamson argues that despite survey results documenting low levels of political knowledge, people are neither "passive" nor "dumb." Rather, they "read media messages in complicated and sometimes unpredictable ways, and draw heavily on other resources as well in constructing meaning."[1] To demonstrate this active negotiation process and explore implications, Gamson conducted thirty-seven "peer group conversations." He was interested in the way "working people"—a term that emerged from the participants' own self-references—talk about politics and how talk is translated into the potential for collective political action. The 188 individuals who participated in his peer group discussions were about equally split between men and women and between whites and blacks.

Drawing on social movement theory, Gamson argues that for citizens to turn "talk into action," they need "collective action frames."[2] These frames allow groups to see that an injustice has occurred; that they have the power—the agency—to address the injustice; and that they have a clear identity that distinguishes "us," the victims, from "them," the perpetrators. The mass media are obviously critical in determining how public issues are framed, and based on an extensive content analysis of several different news media, Gamson concludes that the extent to which the media use the frames of injustice, agency, and identity varies significantly from issue to issue. He also finds that the extent to which citizens use these frames in their own discourse is connected to the prevalence of these frames in the media.

Gamson concluded, however, that this connection between media coverage and citizens' opinions is much looser and more complex than a simple persuasion or agenda-setting model would anticipate. Although often unable to construct their own injustice frames, citizens were able to resist some of those constructed by the media. For example, Gamson found that the media often presented the Japanese as the source of injustice regarding America's industrial problems. However, citizens seldom followed this cue, tending instead to discuss the Japanese with great admiration.

(continues)

(continued)   **BOX 3.2**
An Illustration of Focus Group Research

Gamson, like others, supports his conclusions through a combination of tables, verbal summaries, and direct quotes from transcripts. Through a careful reading of the transcripts, Gamson has discovered that in discussing public issues, citizens draw on a much wider range of media discourses than the news and therefore have a somewhat wider range of frames upon which to draw. For example, in discussing affirmative action, individuals in several groups referred to public service advertisements they had seen (e.g., to the United Negro College Fund's slogan "A mind is a terrible thing to waste"). Similarly, in discussing nuclear power, the popular movies *Silkwood* and *The China Syndrome* were referenced to make points.

Besides the media, citizens drew upon two additional "conversational resources" for construction-shared frames: "experiential knowledge" and "popular wisdom." Experiential knowledge was based on personal experiences or the experiences of relatives, friends, coworkers, and so forth. Popular wisdom transcended personal experience and was based on cultural "truisms," to be accepted at face value. They were often introduced or concluded with phrases such as "As everyone knows" or "It's human nature." Establishing shared frames from discussing public issues allowed group members to find a common language, but it did not mean that the conversations were always consensual.

Gamson concludes that although the working people in his groups generally lacked political consciousness, they did have "the elements necessary to develop [it]." Further, the more participants could draw on integrated resources to frame their discussions, the better able they were to develop the collective action frames necessary for political consciousness. It is Gamson's reasonable suspicion that frames based on integrated strategies are also the most robust and are thus resistant to shifting media frames. And although the ability to employ an integrated strategy varies, Gamson argues that "media dependence . . . is only partial and is heavily influenced by the issue under discussion."[3]

---

[1] William Gamson, *Talking Politics* (Cambridge, UK: Cambridge University Press, 1992), 6.

[2] Ibid., 6–7.

[3] Ibid., 17.

morale and educate them about the political stakes of the war. Did they work? To find out, researchers divided soldier participants into two groups, as is done in many experimental studies: a "treatment group," which saw the films, and a "control group," which did not. Soldiers in both groups filled out a questionnaire both before and after the days on which the soldiers in the treatment group saw the films. The results were somewhat disappointing. The films were effective in teaching soldiers about the events leading up to the war, but apparently did not increase their motivation to fight.[15] This government-commissioned study inspired an enduring subfield of experimental research into the effects of mass media.

Political psychologists still use experiments to investigate how people form their opinions and how these opinions might be manipulated. These experiments have become far more sophisticated than the early wartime studies, as psychologists have encountered and (to some extent) overcome design pitfalls that weaken their experimental controls. Shanto Iyengar and Donald Kinder explain the basic logic:

> For us, the essence of the true experiment is control. Experiments of the sort we have undertaken here are distinguished from other systematic empirical methods in the special measure of control they give to the investigator. In the first place, the experimenter *creates* the conditions under investigation, rather than waiting for them to occur naturally. In the second place, the experimenter *randomly assigns* individuals to those conditions, thereby superseding natural processes of selection. By creating the conditions of interest, the experimenter holds extraneous factors constant and ensures that individuals will encounter conditions that differ only in theoretically decisive ways. By assigning individuals to conditions randomly, the experimenter can be confident that any resulting differences between individuals assigned to varying conditions must be caused by differences in the conditions themselves. (emphasis in original)[16]

Media effects cry out for experimental research, because people tend to be exposed to different media, for many reasons. For example, a series of surveys conducted soon after the Iraq War of 2003 found that Fox News Channel viewers were far more likely than National Public Radio (NPR) listeners to believe, wrongly, that the United States had found weapons of mass destruction in Iraq.[17] This gap may have reflected differences in the two networks' Iraq coverage, but it also, or instead, may have reflected differences between the networks' audiences.

Experimental studies cannot resolve this kind of question; we cannot go back in time and randomly assign people to one network or the other. Similar relationships have been found in the years since: audience members' political beliefs and attitudes tend to coincide with the political orientations of the media they consume, particularly as media have become more fragmented. However, experimental studies *can* explore how people with varied political predispositions react to particular news stories, thus illuminating the dynamics that play out over longer periods. (We discuss some of this research in Chapter 11.)

Conventional survey methods can incorporate complicated experimental designs, albeit with a limited variety of treatments, or the differences in experiences between experimental groups. We previously described a classic survey experiment that examined question order effects in opinions about press freedom. That experiment used a simple "half sample" design: half of respondents were assigned to each question order. With computer-assisted telephone interviewing (CATI) systems and similar technology, researchers can readily implement elaborate designs in which, for example, interviewers ask varying questions in varying orders, partly depending on answers that respondents have given so far.

The principles of control and randomization can be difficult to apply. Often the "treatment" goes beyond that intended by the researcher. In the *Why We Fight* study, for example, *any* difference between the activities of control and treatment groups could affect the outcome, such as what control group members did instead of watching the movies, or even whether and what refreshments were provided during the movies. (As far as we know, this example is hypothetical, and no "popcorn effect" distorted that study's results!) In a study on the effects of news stories, it may be very difficult to present stories that differ only in the way that researchers intend to study those effects. Random assignment poses its own problems. Sometimes researchers cannot randomly assign individuals; for example, if they are considering the impact of high school anti-drug strategies, they may have to assign entire schools to one treatment or another. Even when individuals are flawlessly randomly assigned, if some of them drop out of the study, the groups may vary in ways that obfuscate the treatment effect.

Experimental studies can be difficult to generalize to broader phenomena for other reasons. First, researchers often cannot administer the treatments that they might expect to have important effects in practice. A researcher might want to recruit 1,000 randomly selected people to watch Fox News regularly for several years, and another 1,000 to watch MSNBC, to measure the networks' long-term effects—but that will not work. It is far beyond what people will do voluntarily, and even if one could afford to pay people to do it, people who are paid to watch Fox News probably will not react in the same way as people who do so spontaneously. A related problem is that the more ambitious the experiment, the harder it may be to assess the treatment. If researchers did demonstrate that prolonged exposure to different networks has different effects, that result would raise a slew of questions about exactly what people had been exposed to and how it affected them. (As we have seen, even fairly simple experiments can raise such questions.) For these reasons, researchers generally study relatively simple treatments, and it may not be clear how these treatments apply to real life. Also, most post-treatment measurements happen right after the treatment, or perhaps at follow-up interviews a few weeks later. Do persuasive communications, new programs, or political advertisements have long-term effects that last for months or years? Most studies cannot tell us. Another problem is that often the appropriate population is difficult to study. Many academic studies investigate the opinions of college students because, simply put, such studies are cheap and easy compared to studies of the population at large. But while US college students have many virtues, they are not necessarily representative of all US adults.

A final quandary of experimental research has to do with "demand characteristics"—basically, people's propensity to adapt their behavior based on their perceptions of researchers' expectations. Some participants may (consciously or unconsciously) behave in ways that they expect to please the researchers; others may actually rebel against these perceived expectations or react in more subtle ways. Experimental researchers generally try to minimize demand characteristics by giving very vague descriptions of the purpose of the research that do not hint at researchers' expectations or hopes. However, researchers can hardly prevent participants from guessing, rightly or wrongly, what they are "supposed" to do. (Also, outright deception often is considered unethical, and some institutions may forbid it.)

All these difficulties of experimental studies do not argue against conducting experiments. Instead, they illustrate challenges to be borne in mind when designing experiments and interpreting their results. Despite their inevitable limitations, experimental studies have produced remarkable insights into public opinion, some of which we discuss throughout this book. A solid overview of experimental and experimental/survey research can be found in many textbooks.[18]

CONTENT ANALYSIS OF MASS MEDIA: "ARCHIVES" OF PUBLIC OPINION

A very different approach to measuring public opinion is *content analysis*: the systematic (and usually quantitative) assessment of media texts. Media researchers have performed such analyses on all sorts of mass communications over the years: magazine and newspaper articles, advertisements, television programming, comic strips, radio talk shows, company newsletters, and now Internet communications of various kinds. (Internet content analysis is not limited to media texts; it can study individuals' communications such as Facebook comments and Twitter "tweets.") Content analysis most obviously reveals something about what the producer of that content—such as a journalist or a screenwriter— thinks. Yet we believe that media content represents much more than one individual's view of the world. The content of the mass media can reveal valuable evidence about public opinion.

Popular texts are popular because they somehow resonate with cultural norms, values, or sentiments. In a capitalist economy such as ours, it is crucial that mass media products resonate with public opinion. If they fail to appeal, they will not survive in a highly competitive world of images and discourse. Thus it is informative to examine the mass media texts that citizens "consume" during a typical day. If we can figure out what people like to read, listen to, and watch, we will have a good sense of their attitudes and opinions on public affairs. Moreover, the content of media communications undoubtedly influences what people think about. For example, people's impressions about crime trends may be influenced more by media coverage—such as intensive coverage of a high-profile murder trial—than by facts about crime in general. So, media content both reflects and influences public opinion.

It may seem obvious that we immediately learn something about citizens by knowing their public affairs media habits. If I tell you that my aunt likes to watch Bill O'Reilly on Fox News while my daughter prefers *The Daily Show* on Comedy Central, you can guess that my aunt probably is more politically conservative than my daughter. Yet beyond media consumption that directly focuses on public affairs, it is also useful to study the more entertainment-oriented texts that citizens are drawn to. For example, if one compares the portrayals of gay men and lesbians in television programs from the 1970s and 1980s with more contemporary portrayals, some patterns emerge. In older programs, lesbians and gay men almost always appear in single episodes rather than as regular characters; their sexuality is a focus of the episode, not an incidental aspect of their character; they are "depicted in terms of their place in the lives of heterosexuals";

and their romantic relationships and desires—never mind their sex lives—are not depicted.[19] In more recent programs, lesbians and gay men have featured as regular, well-rounded characters, complete with romantic relationships, such as Mitch and Cam on *Modern Family*. The popularity of such programs hints at changing attitudes toward homosexuality.

For measuring public opinion, the strengths of content analysis are inextricable from its limitations. Content analysis is an "unobtrusive" or "nonreactive" way to measure public attitudes. That is, it does not involve a conversation with citizens and therefore does not "obtrude" on their time or space. Consequently, it is immune to demand characteristics and other problems that researchers face when interviewing human participants. However, because people can react to a communication in very different ways, it is risky to generalize about what people think from what they watch, hear, or read. Most researchers agree that despite the difficulties, content analysis offers important insights into public opinion.[20]

How Is Content Analysis Done?

This section concentrates on systematic, quantitative content analysis. There are other forms of textual analysis, which involve interpretive tools from the humanities—in particular, literary criticism and rhetoric. Here, however, we focus on methods most commonly used by public opinion researchers, including communication researchers, political scientists, and sociologists.

Generally the biggest challenge in quantitative content analysis is to state hypotheses that are specific and testable. Suppose you start with a general interest in how news stories about marijuana policy changed between 2000 and 2014. After reading several such stories, you might form two general hypotheses: that the coverage has become more favorable, and that the debate has broadened beyond medical marijuana (e.g., the use of marijuana for relief from the pain of cancer). What exactly do you mean by "broadened"? After some thought, you might form a more specific hypothesis: that *non*-medical marijuana users appear more often in later stories. Are these hypotheses testable? Not quite yet. How will you measure how "favorable" a particular story is? Perhaps your basic approach will be to count "positive," "negative," and "mixed or neutral" paragraphs in each story. Then you will need to create some coding rules that define what counts as "positive" or "negative." These rules should seem reasonable to skeptical observers, and various coders should be able to apply them consistently. Researchers increasingly often use content analysis software, which works very fast and is not susceptible to subjective differences of opinion, but has no inherent understanding of meaning or tone.

Also, instead of simply categorizing paragraphs as "positive" or "negative," you may want to collect additional data. For example, the first hypothesis raises the question of what kind of person is being cited or quoted: a medical marijuana user? a non-medical marijuana user? a police officer? a policy advocate on one side or the other? an academic or some other putatively objective expert? If you only cared about whether a non-medical user did or did not appear in each story, you would not need all these data, but gathering more complete data on sources may permit you to consider more hypotheses about how coverage has changed. You may also want to code for certain arguments and themes to see whether they have become more or less common over time.

Along with your hypotheses and coding rules, you must determine the population of sources you are studying and your sampling strategy, if any. Suppose you are studying stories in a group of ten major newspapers around the United States. If you are using content analysis software and you can access the full text of all the news stories, then you might as well analyze all the stories from 2000 through 2014. (This approach is not as easy as it may sound; you will probably spend considerable time checking how the software codes particular stories—and changing the rules accordingly—before you can run the full analysis. You may also manually code a sample of these stories to check the software or to collect additional data.) If your research uses manual coding, however, you probably will not have the time or budget to code every available story. Instead, you can draw a random sample, perhaps from the entire "population" of stories over this fifteen-year period or perhaps focused on certain years or time spans.

Manual coding itself may be straightforward—or not. At least some stories should be coded by two researchers as a check on the coding design. (Ideally, these researchers should not know what hypotheses you are testing.) If the researchers often disagree about how to code particular stories, you may need to revise the coding rules so that they can be applied more reliably. You should report the rate of agreement between the coders, often called the *inter-coder reliability*, and take it into account when extrapolating from the results.

Problems Associated with Content Analysis

Content analysis confers many benefits, but it has some pitfalls. Perhaps most obvious is that it can be difficult to choose appropriate sources. For example, in the past many studies of television news coverage focused on three major networks: ABC, NBC, and CBS. Today, depending on one's research question, it would generally be a mistake to disregard cable news networks such as CNN, Fox News, and MSNBC—and it might be crucial to include Comedy Central's news programs as well. If you intend to generalize about public opinion based on what people watch, you must work to fairly represent what they watch, not just what content it is most convenient to analyze.

Second, the researcher must guard against bias in the coding scheme. Researchers sometimes use rules that seem reasonable to them, but that in effect exaggerate the evidence for their hypotheses. Often it is not obvious what counts as a fair and objective approach. For example, in studying stories about marijuana legalization, one might reason that any paragraph that describes or quotes a marijuana user without criticism is implicitly favorable toward legalization, since it presents a pro-legalization point of view. That coding rule may be reasonable, provided that a similar rule applies to opponents of legalization—but the researcher should look carefully. Some descriptions and quotations are more flattering than others; the mere absence of explicit criticism sets a low standard for "favorable" content. On the other hand, the more subjective the standard for favorability, the less trustworthy the coding results will be.

Even the most careful content analysis typically focuses on *manifest* content—the surface meanings of the text. Many researchers believe that latent content, such as the visual images in a story, may be more important. It is not difficult to create coding rules for visual images, but it is far from obvious what rules will best capture the likely influence of those images on viewers. Or consider *The Colbert Report*, a Comedy Central show whose host, Stephen Colbert, routinely parodied the arguments and opinions of political conservatives (the show went off the air at the end of 2014). Presumably, for most Colbert viewers the show's meaning is the opposite of its manifest content. However, researchers have found that some people unfamiliar with the show miss the joke, construe Colbert as a true conservative, and in some cases agree with statements that most viewers consider self-evidently ridiculous.[21] The problem here is not only a coding problem, although finding an objective coding rule for irony may indeed be problematic: the bigger challenge is generalizing about what viewers perceive and how they react.

CONCLUSION

This chapter has explored four of the most common means for assessing public opinion, but there are others as well, such as analysis of election results or stock market trends. The student of public opinion must decide on the most effective means for understanding popular moods, and the tools chosen must fit the research question at hand. Various methods are better suited to various definitions or dimensions of public opinion. Survey research, obviously, fits well with an understanding of public opinion as the aggregation of individual opinions: "one person, one vote." Researchers who prefer a different understanding are likely to prefer other methods that may provide more insight into, for example, the social dynamics of opinion formation. We believe that all the approaches discussed in this chapter are valid, if used with care and rigor— and that combining these (and other) methods can provide the richest and best understanding of public opinion. Nevertheless, researchers have limited capacity to combine techniques in any single study; they must do the best they can given their resources, the available opportunities to collect data, and their particular interests and skills. Then it is up to each of us to decide how the disparate research results fit together.

NOTES

1. Don A. Dillman, Jolene D. Smith, and Leah Melani Christian, *Internet, Phone, Mail and Mixed-Mode Surveys: The Tailored Design Method*, 4th ed. (Hoboken, NJ: John Wiley & Sons, 2014).

2. Pew Research Center, "Assessing the Representativeness of Public Opinion Surveys," May 15, 2012, 1, http://www.people-press.org/files/legacy-pdf/Assessing%20the%20Representativeness%20of%20Public%20Opinion%20Surveys.pdf.

3. Susannah Fox and Lee Rainie, *The Web at 25 in the U.S.* (Washington, DC: Pew Research Center, 2014).

4. Much of this section is based on Michael X. Delli Carpini and Bruce A. Williams, "The Method Is the Message: Focus Groups as a Method of Social, Psychological, and Political Inquiry," in Michael X. Delli Carpini, Leonie Huddie, and Robert Shapiro, eds., *Research in Micropolitics* (Greenwich, CT: JAI Press, 1994), 57–85.

5. Richard A. Krueger and Mary Anne Casey, *Focus Groups: A Practical Guide for Applied Research*, 5th ed. (Thousand Oaks, CA: Sage Publications, 2014).

6. Roberta Sigel, *Caught Between Ambition and Accommodation: Ambivalence in the Perception of Gender Relations* (Chicago: University of Chicago Press, 1996).

7. Pamela Conover, Ivor Crewe, and Donald Searing, "The Nature of Citizenship in the United States and Great Britain: Empirical Comments on Theoretical Themes," *Journal of Politics* 53 (1991): 800–832.

8. Sigel, *Caught Between Ambition and Accommodation*, 34.

9. Conover, Crewe, and Searing, "The Nature of Citizenship in the United States and Great Britain," 800–832.

10. Ibid., 805.

11. Tamar Liebes and Elihu Katz, *The Export of Meaning* (Oxford: Oxford University Press, 1990), 28.

12. Ibid., 82.

13. Michael X. Delli Carpini and Bruce A. Williams, "Methods, Metaphors, and Media Research: The Uses of Television in Political Conversations," *Communication Research* 21 (1994): 801–802.

14. William Gamson, *Talking Politics* (Cambridge, UK: Cambridge University Press, 1992), 17.

15. Some of the now-classic experiments are recounted in Carl I. Hovland, Arthur A. Lumsdaine, and Fred D. Sheffield, *Experiments in Mass Communication* (Princeton, NJ: Princeton University Press, 1949).

16. Shanto Iyengar and Donald R. Kinder, *News That Matters: Television and American Opinion*, upd. ed. (Chicago: University of Chicago Press, 2010), 6.

17. Steven Kull, Clay Ramsey, and Evan Lewis, "Misperceptions, the Media, and the Iraq War," *Political Science Quarterly* 118 (2003): 569–598.

18. See, e.g., Jeffrey A. Gilner, George A. Morgan, and Nancy L. Leech, *Research Methods in Applied Settings: An Integrated Approach to Design and Analysis*, 2nd ed. (New York: Routledge, 2009).

19. This discussion draws on Bonnie J. Dow, "*Ellen*, Television, and the Politics of Gay and Lesbian Visibility," in Toby Miller, ed., *Television: Critical Concepts in Media and Cultural Studies* (New York: Routledge, 2003), 2:252–271, esp. 259–260, which in turn references Fred Fejes and Kevin Petrich, "Invisibility, Homophobia, and Heterosexism: Lesbians, Gays and the Media," *Critical Studies in Mass Communication* 10, no. 4 (1993): 396–422.

20. For more on content analysis, see Daniel Riffe, Stephen Lacy, and Frederick Fico, *Analyzing Media Messages: Using Quantitative Content Analysis in Research*, 3rd ed. (New York: Routledge, 2014).

21. Heather L. LaMarre, Kristen D. Landreville, and Michael A. Beam, "The Irony of Satire: Political Ideology and the Motivation to See What You Want to See in The Colbert Report," *International Journal of Press/Politics* 14 (2009): 212–231.

THEORIES OF PUBLIC OPINION

2

CHAPTERS

4

Public Opinion and Democratic Theory

Democracy is the theory that the common people know what they want, and deserve to get it *good and hard.*

H. L. MENCKEN

WHY THEORIES?

"Theory" can mean many different things. People variously allude to the theory of general relativity, the big bang theory, Freudian psychological theory, theories of democracy (such as Mencken's facetious definition), the theory that the Mafia assassinated John F. Kennedy, the theory that burgers are better than hot dogs, and the theory that it will rain tomorrow. Adding to the confusion, while empirical researchers try to build better theories that summarize and account for the knowledge in their fields, many people construe theory as a pejorative term, meaning not a distillation of knowledge, but a poor substitute for it. ("Oh, that's just your theory!")

In social science, *theory* typically refers to a set of explanatory generalizations intended to inform research, understanding, and action. Simply put, a theory offers a perspective on why certain things happen and may help us to predict— or perhaps to influence—what will happen in the future. Some theories try to illuminate a wide range of behavior; others focus on just one kind. In social science as in natural science, one way to assess a theory is to test *hypotheses* that should be true if the theory is true. In general, evidence in favor of such hypotheses tends to increase our confidence in the theory, and evidence against them compels us to disregard it.

For example, in international relations, *democratic peace theory* postulates that democratic nations are less likely to go to war with each other and tries to explain why this is so. This theory could have important implications for democratic nations' foreign policy (Should the United States try to "spread democracy"?) and self-understanding (How do democracies differ from non-democracies?). Democratic peace theory immediately implies an empirical hypothesis: that democratic nations really are less likely to war with each other. This hypothesis is supported by historical experience. If it is so, then why? Perhaps citizens in democratic countries tend to oppose wars generally. That explanation suggests the hypothesis that democracies are less likely to start wars (even with *non*-democracies) than are non-democracies—but that seems not to be true. The elaboration of theory and hypotheses goes on from there.[1] Some scholars suspect that the democratic peace has nothing to do with democracy, but rather is explained by other factors that many democracies have in common. Many hypotheses remain controversial, in part because of the inability to experiment: researchers cannot, say, create diplomatic crises between randomly selected pairs of countries to see how they react. Despite its relatively narrow scope, democratic peace theory has remained a topic of discussion, in part because it connects to perennial questions about democracy.

Most people pay no attention to social science theories as such, but it seems that we all have social theories, some of which we act on every day. For example, chances are that you expect most people you encounter to treat you reasonably well as long as you treat them that way. At the same time, you will be surprised and even suspicious if they treat you *too* well. You might object that these and other expectations are not based on "theory," but rather on experience. But how do you decide which of your experiences are relevant to any particular social encounter? Probably you rarely think about this, and arguably "theory" is too highfalutin a word for a largely unconscious process. Whatever we call them, your tacit assumptions about how people behave inform your social actions and your interpretations of other people's actions, as broadly and as thoroughly as any theory could do. Social scientists call such unsystematic assumptions about social behavior (and other topics) *lay theories*.

Many political debates hinge on differences in lay social theories at least as much as on ethical disagreements. Consider an example from US antipoverty policy. In a survey taken in June 2013 respondents were asked, "Which of the following reasons do you think is most responsible for the continuing problem of poverty?" The most popular response (chosen by 24 percent) was "too much government welfare that prevents initiative"; the second most popular response (18 percent) was "lack of job opportunities."[2] We should not overinterpret one poll question, but those responses suggest very different social theories, and probably very different political stances.

Empirical social theories about how people behave often connect to *normative* theories about how democratic governments ought to operate—in particular, how public opinion should fit in how government works. Like people's social theories, many normative theories of democracy are not fully elaborated. When people consider these questions, they may think in broad generalities, such as "the government should do what most people want it to do," or "elected officials should focus on solving the problems that we think are most important," or "frankly, a lot of people's opinions aren't worth listening to." Or they may tacitly apply similar generalities to a particular topic: "Most people want X, and policy-makers should listen!" In one sense, these normative assertions—these "shoulds"—are sharply distinct from empirical claims. People's ethical beliefs do not have to be based on arguments about facts. However, our normative views often do depend on our empirical assumptions, at least to some extent. For instance, someone who thinks that the government should usually follow majority opinion probably also thinks that its doing so will not cause widespread misery. Indeed, many disagreements about the proper *role* of public opinion seem to be rooted in factual disagreements about its nature and content. Learning about public opinion could actually change how you think democracy should work.

MEANINGS AND MECHANISMS OF DEMOCRACY

We have been discussing "democratic nations" and "how democracy should work" as if everyone agreed on the meaning of these terms, which of course isn't true. Defining "democracy" might even be more controversial than defining "public opinion," which can make for some muddled conversations about "the role of public opinion in a democracy." Let us briefly consider some of the widely varied institutions that are (sometimes) considered democratic.

The term *democracy* comes from the Greek words for "people" and "rule," but the authors of the US Constitution did not intend that the people would rule directly. James Madison, in the *Federalist Papers* Number 10, argued that "pure democracies," in which citizens "assemble and administer the government in person," are inevitably unstable and conflict ridden, as majority factions attempt to impose their will on minorities. The authors of the *Federalist Papers* referred to the new government as a *republic*, but over time it came to be known as a democracy—more specifically, as a *representative democracy*. The United States and every state within it (along with many smaller jurisdictions) are considered representative democracies, meaning that for the most part citizens influence policies indirectly by electing officials who represent them. We prefer to use the phrase "representative democracy" to describe a practice within a political system, not an entire political system. So we would say that the US government incorporates representative democracy because, for example, citizens choose the members of Congress.

Citizens face considerable constraints even on choosing who will represent them. In the United States most elected officials belong to one of the two major political parties, Republican and Democratic. (The Constitution says nothing about political parties, but parties emerged within a few years of its enactment.) Some party candidates are chosen in primary elections that are open to voters who belong to or support that party. Then, in the general election, voters can choose among the candidates—often just two, a Republican and a Democrat—for each office. Sometimes voters have even less choice than this. Often a candidate is nominated without a competitive primary; some candidates even run unopposed in the general election. Moreover, representative democracy is not the whole story; many policymaking officials are not elected by voters. The US president and vice president are elected not directly by voters, but by the members of the *electoral college*, called electors. Nowadays the electors are chosen by voters and are pledged to vote for particular candidates, but the Constitution allows each state legislature to decide how its electors are chosen. Until it was amended in 1913, the Constitution specified that US senators were to be chosen by state legislatures, not elected by voters. Federal judges are not elected at all; nor are the leaders and staff of federal departments and agencies, who play a large role in promulgating regulations and other aspects of policymaking.

To be sure, public influence in US federal policymaking is not limited to elections, although they arguably offer the most direct means of influence. As we will discuss at length, both elected and unelected officials often refer to survey research and other sources of information on public opinion. Citizens often are urged to "call your member of Congress" or "write the president," and officials may construe such communications as evidence about how many people are strongly engaged on each side of a policy issue. Campaign contributions—from individuals as well as political action committees (PACs), corporations, and other collective donors—can be considered a very important form of public influence that is unevenly distributed: some people wield far more influence than others. Rulemaking (the process by which formal regulations are written and adopted) usually incorporates a procedure for soliciting public comments, which regulators are supposed to take into consideration but are not required to follow. These and other mechanisms may give the public—or some part of the public— substantial influence on policy.

In *direct democracy*, all qualified citizens can participate directly in policy-making. Again, we think of direct democracy as a practice within a political system, not an entire system; it is difficult to imagine any government making all decisions by direct democracy. In a strong form of direct democracy, qualified citizens can participate in meetings at which all major policies are decided. (Of course, people can disagree about what counts as a "major" policy or decision.) In many small New England towns to this day, all registered voters can participate in an annual *town meeting*, which sets the town's budget, elects its officers, and may make other policy decisions.[3] Special town meetings may also be called. In principle, any number of people may participate in such decisionmaking meetings—as many as can fit in a room, or even more using teleconferencing technology. However, some forms of participation are more exclusive than others. Many people can vote in a short time, but how many people can speak on an issue to the extent of influencing the proposal being voted on or even other people's votes? Time is limited, and so are attention spans; some people tend to be more persuasive than others, even when they are wrong. Extending a meeting may increase the number of people who can speak, but it may also decrease the number who can stay to the end.

In more limited forms of direct democracy, qualified citizens vote occasionally on certain issues, not all major issues. Over half of US states have some form of *initiative* and/or *referendum*, through which citizens can vote on policy issues, usually at the same time as other elections. (Initiatives appear on the ballot when a large number of citizens sign petitions in support of them; referenda appear when legislatures vote to place them on the ballot.) Even where they are most common, initiatives and referenda only determine a small fraction of any state's policy decisions.

NORMATIVE THEORIES OF DEMOCRACY AND THE PROBLEM OF DEMOCRATIC COMPETENCE

You can see that these various democratic procedures differ widely both in how much power they give to the public and in the demands they place on citizens. They imply different normative theories about how much power citizens *should* have, about how democracy should be implemented. As a starting point, we can consider these theories as forming a continuum from minimalist to maximalist conceptions of democracy. At the *minimalist* end, democracy only entails being able to replace one set of rulers with another through elections. At the *maximalist* end, direct democracy applies to all policymaking, so citizens more or less govern themselves. Between these extremes fall distinctions not only of formal power but also of informal influence. People near the minimalist end believe that public opinion should have little influence on policy. Others believe that policymakers should take public opinion into account, to varying degrees (whose opinions, expressed how?), even when the public has no formal policymaking role.

To some extent, these various normative theories reflect differences in factual assumptions about citizens' *democratic competence*, their capacity to live up to the requirements of various democratic models. An especially vivid opinion on the minimalist side is attributed to former US secretary of state Dean Acheson, who stated: "If you truly had a democracy and did what people wanted, you'd go wrong every time."[4] Obviously, if the public has spectacularly poor policy judgment, its role in policymaking should be limited and indirect. Other observers are far more sanguine about democratic competence, although very few think that people are equipped for a maximalist ideal of complete direct democracy. For instance, Thomas Jefferson wrote in 1789 that "whenever the people are well informed, they can be trusted with their own government"—but the quotation does not end there. Jefferson clarifies "that whenever things get so far wrong as to attract their notice, they may be relied on to set them to rights."[5] Evidently Jefferson does not mean that "the people" can or should administer the government themselves. In fact, he is praising Americans for supporting the new Constitution, which creates central political institutions far from citizens' direct control. Yet Jefferson seems to think that people's values and judgment are basically sound, and that when they choose to weigh in, they will probably do so wisely.

Abraham Lincoln reportedly commented early in his presidency (before the Confederate states seceded): "What I want is to get done what the people desire to have done, and the question for me is how to find that out exactly."[6] Surely Lincoln was not calling for direct democracy, but he seems to have meant that the federal government's basic policy course should be consistent with public opinion. That was a normative judgment (or, a cynic might suspect, cheap talk), but much evidence indicates that it dovetailed with Lincoln's generally high regard for Americans' good judgment.

Crucially, even minimalist accounts of democracy require some degree of democratic competence. Consider Walter Lippmann's classic statement in 1925 that "the essence of popular government" is simply for the public to support and vote for "the Ins" (the political party in power) "when things are going well [and] to support the Outs when they seem to be going badly."[7] Deciding whether things are going "well" or "badly" cannot give citizens much influence over fine points of policy, but at least it provides some protection against blatant tyranny or mismanagement. Also, it does not require voters to know much or to think very hard. However, uninformed voters may punish or reward the in-party for circumstances beyond its control. (That may not be so harmful, as long as policymakers still have some incentive to govern well.) Worse, many voters may reward the in-party for repressing an unpopular minority or for pursuing a policy that sacrifices the long-run common good for temporary benefits or one that feels right although most people would oppose its actual consequences. So even if we agree that the public should play a minimal role, questions about democratic competence remain.

Although normative disagreements sometimes hinge on differing views of democratic competence, that is not the whole story. Normative democratic theories often attempt to design institutions and procedures that promote democratic values by drawing on knowledge about the limits of democratic competence. For example, many theorists argue that participating in democratic debate and decisionmaking helps to inculcate a variety of important skills, actually to make people more competent to govern themselves.[8] They reason that rather than moralizing about how much more people ought to participate, democratic societies should directly promote such participation. Bruce Ackerman and James Fishkin's proposal for a "deliberation day," discussed in Chapter 9, is one specific suggestion based on a normative argument for participation. Various proposals target particular democratic objectives. Robert Dahl (mentioned in this chapter as an empirical theorist) has offered five normative criteria for democracy: effective participation, voting equality, enlightened understanding, control of the agenda, and inclusiveness.[9] Even without further discussion of these criteria, you can readily imagine how (for example) proposals focused on effective participation may differ from those focused on enlightened understanding. (You can also imagine why we choose not to try to summarize all such proposals!)

EMPIRICAL THEORIES OF PUBLIC OPINION AND POLICY

Alongside wide-ranging arguments about how public opinion *should* influence what governments do, there are distinct debates about whether and how public opinion *does* influence policy. In Chapter 10 we consider a variety of evidence on this question. Here we focus on broad empirical theories. At first blush this approach may seem odd: Wouldn't it be better to set aside "theory" and turn straight to the evidence? But we think that in practice, most learning from evidence takes the form of theory testing. When people do not think closely about their theories, they may wrongly imagine that the evidence supports those theories—or they may not attend to evidence at all. For now, as you read about public opinion processes in the ensuing chapters, bear in mind these considerations about how public opinion may affect policy.

Theoretically, there is good reason to expect policymaking to be at least somewhat responsive to public opinion. We can identify specific political processes that should contribute to responsiveness. First and foremost among these is the periodic election of government officials. Because elected officials know that they (or, if they are not running for reelection, their party's candidate) will be held accountable at election time, they have incentives to act in accordance with public preferences and to avoid acting against those preferences. Some evidence suggests that policy responsiveness increases closer to elections, when the public may be paying most attention.[10] Even at other times, elected officials know that they or their party may be punished for their actions at the next election. Crudely, they face a choice: do (to some extent) what the public wants, or be replaced by other leaders who will. Either path leads to policy responsiveness.[11]

Another possible reason to expect policy responsiveness is that voters choose leaders from among themselves, who therefore tend to share their values and opinions. Elected officials from, say, New York City and rural Louisiana may vote differently not primarily because they are trying to win the support of different constituencies, but simply because they come from those different constituencies. This explanation is called the "sharing model."[12] It is not clear, however, how similar political leaders actually are, individually or as a group, to citizens in general. These leaders self-select to be very active in politics, and they are clearly of upper status in terms of education, income, and occupation (disproportionately lawyers). And though this has begun to change in recent years, for a long time women and members of minority groups rarely held important public offices. So the sharing model suggests that policy may be more responsive to some people's opinion than others'.

Policymakers may experience social and ethical pressures to comply with the public's wishes. Politicians often evince a strong desire to be liked, which presumably helps them develop the social skills that make them effective electoral candidates. They may therefore be reluctant to take actions that would anger their constituents. Moreover, some elected representatives may believe that they are generally obligated to do what their constituents or voters have delegated them to do. In fact, representatives who adopt this style of representation have been called "delegates." Other leaders—elected or appointed—believe that they have been chosen to act as their own consciences dictate, to do what they think is best for the public. These "trustees" may react to new information in much the same way that the public does, but they have no particular reason to consider public opinion itself. [13] Of course, leaders' style may depend on the issue or the circumstances. For example, a leader may generally act as a trustee but defer to the public when it expresses strong opinions on a particular issue. This hybrid approach has been called the "politico" style.

How do policymakers learn about the public opinion they are, perhaps, responding to? Contemporary politicians may have more access than ever to public opinion research: major campaigns can conduct opinion polls continuously and can also conduct focus groups to gain further insight into people's thinking and how voters might react to a new advertisement or issue position. With so much information available, including media polls, we might expect greater responsiveness to public opinion than ever before. To put it another way, in the past politicians may have known substantially less about public opinion; as a result, they may sometimes have adopted policies in part because they misjudged the likely political consequences. John Geer argues, for instance, that Abraham Lincoln's decision to issue the Emancipation Proclamation may have constituted "leadership by mistake"; he may have expected the action to be far more popular than it was.[14] But these differences should not be taken too far. There have long been many sources of information about public opinion available to politicians and government officials: constituency mail; various informants who report what they observe, including staff members, advisers, and even friends and acquaintances; information from political party leaders and others in the party; reports, editorials, and commentaries in the mass media; and the opinions and information conveyed by organized groups.

Political scientists have long thought that interest groups play a major, or even a central, role in the pathways between public opinion and policymaking. Groups have the capacity to, as political scientists say, "aggregate and articulate"—that is, to combine and widely communicate—opinions found among the public. Political scientists such as Arthur Bentley (in the early 1900s), David Truman (in the 1950s), and Robert Dahl (in the 1960s and after) offered theoretical accounts of "interest group pluralism," often just called *pluralism*. These theories generally depicted groups as an effective means of representing public opinion. In pluralist theory, as new issues arise or as segments of the public come to feel underrepresented, existing groups adapt or new groups form to represent the public's disparate viewpoints.[15] Political parties themselves also act as intermediaries between the public and policymaking, as we discuss further in Chapter 10.

Critics of pluralism challenge the view that interest groups represent public opinion in a fundamentally democratic way. (That view is not integral to pluralist theory, but many critics find pluralist accounts unduly cheerful about democratic representation.)[16] Critics argue that not all opinions have groups to represent them. Yes, new advocacy groups form all the time, but they tend to represent interests that are small and concentrated: relatively few people are involved, and they can readily find each other. Generally the most influential groups represent interests that have substantial wealth or other resources, giving them the means to organize, and have much to gain by doing so.[17] More diffuse and weaker interests are less likely to organize effective groups to represent their "latent" opinions.[18] As E. E. Schattschneider memorably put it, the flaw in the pluralist heaven is that the heavenly chorus sings with an upper-class accent.[19]

In contrast to pluralism—and even many of its critics—is elite theory. *Elite theory* holds that policymaking, both nationally and locally, is dominated by powerful elites: relatively few individuals or small groups, such as business leaders, military leaders, and specific political leaders, who have connections to each other. These individuals and groups have been given various political labels, such as "the power elite."[20] A variant analysis, Marxist or influenced by Marxism, holds that business interests dominate policymaking on behalf of largely shared support for policies that promote corporate economic growth.[21] Whereas many critics of pluralism accept that the political system represents a wide variety of opinions, even if not altogether equitably, elite theorists assert that a small number of interests hold all the real power.

A different theory maintains that American democracy is thwarted not by a single "power elite" but by various powerful groups that dominate the narrow, but important, policy areas that are of special interest to them. Thus, different groups control specific areas of policymaking, especially in different states and localities. For example, state farming organizations dominate farm policy in their various states, and a few groups dominate nationally; power and utility companies unduly influence how states and localities regulate their enterprises; and so on. As a result of this dominance by private centers of power, it is rare for public opinion to be very influential. We might think of this theory as pluralism (involving multiple interest groups) without representation of public opinion.[22]

One way in which elites or special interests can thwart public opinion is by keeping issues off the visible political agenda. If the public is unaware of what is happening or has no idea what to do about something it does know about, it cannot effectively mobilize against these groups or elites.[23] We return to the role of the mass media in setting the "issue agenda" in Chapter 11. Financial resources help special interests exercise agenda control in many ways: by (directly and indirectly) supporting the political campaigns of allies, by publicizing their views in advertisements, by funding think tanks to promote ostensibly expert arguments for their preferences, and even by directly funding media outlets.

In short, various political processes have different consequences for the public's influence on government. Electoral accountability, how political leaders see their roles, and group-based democratic pressures can help the public have substantial influence on policymaking. Conversely, other processes can sharply limit the public's ability to constrain or influence what government does. Therefore, without systematically examining evidence (as we begin to do in Chapter 10), we can reasonably surmise that public opinion has considerable policy influence but is far from all powerful. Thus, the public opinion processes we discuss in the following chapters are presumptively important, although just how important is not obvious.

ELEMENTS OF DEMOCRATIC COMPETENCE

We have noted that even minimalist (or "elite") normative theories of democracy entail some degree of democratic competence. What constitutes democratic competence? According to Walter Lippmann in 1922, although US political thinkers have disagreed about who is qualified to deal with political affairs, they generally have agreed on the basic qualifications, which they have construed as innate: "What counted was a good heart, a reasoning mind, a balanced judgment. These would ripen with age, but it was not necessary to consider how to inform the heart and feed the reason. Men took in their facts as they took in their breath."[24] (Whether women should be counted as "men" in this context has been a topic of debate.) Just what these traits mean is open to interpretation; let us consider a rough sketch.

Let us begin with "a good heart." Most conceptions of democratic government (and even of non-democratic government) assume the existence of a common good, or what the preamble to the US Constitution calls "the general welfare." Now, belief in "general welfare" need not be a matter of "heart" at all; in principle, people may cooperate to promote a shared interest even if they are utterly indifferent—or even hostile—to each other's welfare. Nevertheless, most conceptions of a well-ordered society assume that citizens generally respect and sympathize with each other's basic interests. For example, we typically are heartened, but not surprised, by reports of donations pouring in to help survivors of a natural disaster. People who seem to value no interests other than their own may be called "antisocial," or on a more extreme level, "sociopathic": hostile to society and everyone within it.

But the issue of "good-heartedness" is not a simple morality tale of human generosity and solidarity versus blinkered selfishness. One complication is that people tend to assess whether others are "antisocial" by whether they conform to social norms, some of which are widely shared, others of which are divergent or controversial. (We wrestle with how to define "norms" in the next chapter.) For instance, no one would argue that it is wrong to push children in front of speeding cars, but we have seen many angry disagreements about same-sex relationships and marriage. When almost everyone shares a social norm, it may seem that only a "bad heart" would violate it. But if the norm or its importance is disputed, then some people will consider any attempt to impose the norm far worse than a violation of it. Most people would agree that "good-heartedness" entails at least some tolerance for difference and disagreement, but there is no agreement on where to draw the line.

Moreover, people tend to identify with social groups, large and small. You might identify as an American, a Chicagoan, a Chicago Cubs fan, a woman, a dog lover, a feminist, a Republican, a Baptist, a vegetarian, or any of dozens of other social identities. Sometimes our identifications and how we think about them—and how we think about people in other social groups—can influence our attitudes and behaviors in ways that we may not even notice. People may think of each other as comrades, adversaries, or anything in between based on our perceptions of each other's group identities. As with social norms in general, there is no agreement on how to deal with our divergent group identities—and even if we agreed in the abstract, we would still be influenced by our often unconscious assumptions.

Because there is no normative consensus on the "right" way to handle social norms and group identity, there is unlikely to be agreement on how to measure the "good-hearted" dimension of democratic competence. Probably most people can agree on abstract, ambiguous criteria: people should have a reasonable regard for each other's individual interests; they should have a substantial sense of common interest, of shared fate; they should evince tolerance for diversity; and they should not be unduly swayed by group loyalties. None of these criteria is absolute; again, no one (to our knowledge) espouses "tolerance" for people who push children in front of moving cars. Interestingly, many people feel that they are not applying these criteria as well as they should be; perhaps they should be more generous, or more tolerant, or on the other hand, more willing to stand up for their own values in opposition to other people's. These are interesting, complicated, important problems that we revisit throughout this book.

Now we turn to "a reasoning mind." Probably most policy questions will not simply yield to benevolence, tolerance, and a willingness to transcend group loyalties, important as those may be. Policymakers should weigh relevant facts and consider the likely and possible consequences of their actions, resisting wishful thinking. Plato, in book 6 of *The Republic*, argued that government should only be entrusted to the sort of person "who has the gift of a good memory, and is quick to learn—noble, gracious, the friend of truth, justice, courage, temperance." Plato's ideal ruler (a "philosopher king") thus combines expert knowledge and intelligence with a range of noble virtues. Most citizens, however gracious and courageous they may be, may lack the time and motivation to learn and reason about policy issues. Thomas Jefferson, who is often considered a maximalist democrat, bluntly wrote in 1789 that "the people . . . are not qualified to exercise themselves the EXECUTIVE department . . . to LEGISLATE . . . [or] to JUDGE questions of law"—although, he said, they are qualified to choose the president and legislators and to serve as jurors deciding questions of fact.[25] Indeed, many people may not be well suited to reason about policy issues, regardless of time constraints. Most of us know people whose eyes seem to glaze over when a conversation turns to politics or policy, as well as others who are "often wrong but never in doubt."

Assuming that most people do not, and will not, know enough about policymaking to participate directly, the question remains whether their policy opinions are worth taking seriously, and if so, how. Again, this question breaks down into several complicated and interesting elements. Presumably people are better equipped to address some policy issues than others, because they know more about those issues or because the issues are easier to understand. Sometimes people can form reasonable opinions—at least, reasonable given their values—based on very little knowledge. Even opinions that aren't well informed or systematically reasoned may provide useful insights into people's underlying values and assumptions. Chapter 7 looks closely at the problems of interpreting public opinion on policy issues.

What is "balanced judgment," and how is it distinct from a "reasoning mind"? We cannot be sure what Lippmann meant, but we can consider at least two meanings, which both pertain to the previous points. Some people think of "judgment" as a sort of practical wisdom—a sense for how to listen to people who disagree with each other, when to postpone a decision and when to move ahead, how to avoid big mistakes, and how to identify the mistakes one has made—that reason alone cannot confer. Alternatively, but not incompatibly, one can think of judgment as a decisionmaking process that integrates Lippmann's other elements: a good heart and a reasoning mind. If our emotions (our "heart") and our reason seem to tug in opposite directions, reconciling the dispute may be a matter of judgment. Or if our emotions seem to sweep our reason along in their path—if our reason is providing *rationalizations* for conclusions we immediately jumped to—"balanced judgment" may be the mental attribute or process that tells us not to decide until we have really considered all sides as fairly as we can.

So democratic competence makes considerable demands, although observers will disagree about how large those demands are and how capable people are of fulfilling them. Those disagreements will depend in part on normative assumptions about the proper scope of democracy: minimalist definitions of democracy tend to demand less of citizens. Presumably, substantially less competence is required for most people to vote for reasonable candidates most of the time than, say, for people to reach some informed agreement on policy issues. But even someone with a relatively minimalist conception of democracy may in some cases wish that citizens were better equipped to play their parts.

CONCLUSION

Our discussion of both normative and empirical theories of democracy sets the stage for the wide array of empirical theories we consider in the following chapters. This is not to say that all theory and research about public opinion processes should be interpreted solely in terms of their implications for democratic theory and practice. But we do encourage you to ponder those implications, and we often touch upon them here. Whatever your normative predispositions are about how public opinion should—or should not—influence public policy, you should be wary of any impulse to trim the facts to suit your values. Frankly, we wish we didn't believe some of the results presented in this book, and we do not always agree about their implications. They are more interesting than that.

NOTES

1. The literature on democratic peace is enormous. One starting point is a forum in *American Political Science Review* 99 (August 2005): 3, including four articles presenting various viewpoints.

2. NBC News/Wall Street Journal Survey study number 13200, conducted by Hart /McInturff, May 30–June 2, 2013, with one thousand adult respondents, documented at http://msnbcmedia.msn.com/i/MSNBC/Sections/A_Politics/_Today_Stories_ Teases/May-June-NBC-WSJ-Filled-in.doc, p. 12 (accessed January 27, 2015).

3. Frank M. Bryan, *Real Democracy: The New England Town Meeting and How It Works* (Chicago: University of Chicago Press, 2003); Jane Mansbridge, *Beyond Adversary Democracy* (Chicago: University of Chicago Press, 1983), pt. II.

4. Quoted in Bruce Cumings, "Revising Postrevisionism, or the Poverty of Theory," *Diplomatic History* 17, no. 4 (1993): 557.

5. Thomas Jefferson to Richard Price, Paris, January 8, 1789, http://www.loc.gov /exhibits/jefferson/60.html.

6. Quoted in "The Diary of a Public Man," part IV, *North American Review* 129, no. 276 (November 1879): 494 (available at http://books.google.com/books?id=UV4CAA AAIAAJ).

7. Walter Lippmann, *The Phantom Public* (New York: Harcourt Brace, 1925), 126.

8. For example, Mark E. Warren, "Democratic Theory and Self-Transformation," *American Political Science Review* 86 (1992): 8–23; James Bohman, *Public Deliberation: Pluralism, Complexity, and Democracy* (Cambridge, MA: MIT Press, 2000); Amy Gutmann and Dennis Thompson, *Democracy and Disagreement* (Cambridge, MA: Harvard University Press, 1996).

9. Robert A. Dahl, *Democracy and Its Critics* (New Haven, CT: Yale University Press, 1989).

10. Classic examples are James H. Kuklinski, "Representation and Elections: A Policy Analysis," *American Political Science Review* 72 (1978): 165–177; and Edward R. Tufte, *Political Control of the Economy* (Princeton, NJ: Princeton University Press, 1978).

11. James A. Stimson, Michael B. MacKuen, and Robert S. Erikson, "Dynamic Representation," *American Political Science Review* 89 (1995): 543–565, esp. 544–545.

12. Norman R. Luttbeg, *Public Opinion and Public Policy: Models of Political Linkage* (Homewood, IL: Dorsey Press, 1968); Robert S. Erikson, Gerald C. Wright Jr., and John P. McIver, "Political Parties, Public Opinion, and State Policy in the United States," *American Political Science Review* 83 (1989): 736–737.

13. A classic exposition is John C. Wahlke, Heinz Eulau, William Buchanan, and Leroy C. Ferguson, *The Legislative System* (New York: Wiley, 1962).

14. John G. Geer, *From Tea Leaves to Opinion Polls: A Theory of Democratic Leadership* (New York: Columbia University Press, 1996).

15. See Arthur F. Bentley, *The Process of Government* (Chicago: University of Chicago Press, 1908); David B. Truman, *The Governmental Process: Political Interests and Public Opinion* (New York: Alfred A. Knopf, 1951; 2nd ed., 1971); and Robert A. Dahl, *Who Governs?: Democracy and Power in an American City* (New Haven, CT: Yale University Press, 1961).

16. A helpful discussion of pluralism and some of its critics is Donald R. Brand, "Three Generations of Pluralism: Continuity and Change," *Political Science Reviewer* 15 (1985): 109–141.

17. See Mancur Olson, *The Logic of Collective Action: Public Goods and the Theory of Groups* (Cambridge, MA: Harvard University Press, 1965).

18. On "latent opinion" or latent interests, see Truman, *Governmental Process*, and V. O. Key Jr., *Public Opinion and American Democracy* (New York: Alfred A. Knopf, 1961).

19. See E. E. Schattschneider, *The Semi-Sovereign People* (Hinsdale, IL: Dryden Press, 1960). Later works in this vein include Kay Lehman Schlozman and John T. Tierney, *Organized Interests and American Democracy* (New York: Harper and Row, 1986); Kay Lehman Schlozman, Sidney Verba, and Henry E. Brady, *The Unheavenly Chorus: Unequal Political Voice and the Broken Promise of American Democracy* (Princeton, NJ: Princeton University Press, 2012).

20. See C. Wright Mills, *The Power Elite* (New York: Oxford University Press, 1956); and Floyd Hunter, *Community Power Structure* (Chapel Hill: University of North Carolina Press, 1953).

21. For example, see Charles E. Lindblom, *Politics and Markets: The World's Political-Economic Systems* (New York: Basic Books, 1977).

22. See Grant McConnell, *Private Power and American Democracy* (New York: Random House, 1966).

23. See Schattschneider, *Semi-Sovereign People*; and Peter Bachrach and Morton S. Baratz, "Two Faces of Power," *American Political Science Review* 56 (1962): 947–952 and "Decisions and Nondecisions: An Analytical Framework," *American Political Science Review* 57 (1963): 632–642.

24. Lippmann, *Public Opinion*, 164.

25. Thomas Jefferson to the Abbé Arnoux, July 19, 1789, in Julian P. Boyd et al., eds., *The Papers of Thomas Jefferson* (Princeton, NJ: Princeton University Press, 1958), 15:282–283.

5

Psychological Perspectives on Public Opinion

Given how often opinion is construed as a matter of mind, it is no wonder that psychology—the study of mind—offers crucial insights into public opinion. Why do some people believe in global warming, while others do not? Why are some people convinced that the Affordable Care Act (Obamacare) is the answer to providing health care for millions of uninsured Americans, whereas others believe it represents the erosion of basic American values? Psychological concepts and research help us understand how people's mental makeup affects how we process events and new information: how our minds change, and why they often do not. Although much public opinion research relies on methods taken from psychology, researchers sometimes neglect psychological, sociological, and communication theories when they interpret their findings, perhaps because there are so many disparate theories. But even though these scholars do not agree on a master theory of mind, a grounding in psychology is relevant to many aspects of public opinion. In this chapter we focus on psychological processes at the individual level. In Chapter 7 we explore how social and psychological factors interact in the formation and expression of public opinion.

SPEAKING THE LANGUAGE: BELIEFS, VALUES, ATTITUDES, AND OPINIONS

Psychological research typically employs one or more of four basic concepts: *beliefs, values, attitudes,* and *opinions.* Scholars often have debated the definitions and even the merits of these concepts, but most contemporary discussions rely on definitions similar to the ones we present here. Statements about what and how people think are often bewilderingly vague; distinguishing among these concepts can help to bring clarity.

Beliefs

Beliefs are the cognitive components that make up our understanding of the way things are, that is, the information (true or false) that individuals have about objects and actions.[1] They are the building blocks of attitudes and opinions. Beliefs are often difficult to identify, especially when they are widely shared. Such beliefs are the assumptions by which we live our lives, and we generally presume that others think of the world the same way that we do. For example, most Americans hold the belief that people can change for the better or the worse, through their choices or because of circumstances beyond their control. (Some people place more emphasis on choice, others on circumstance.) In contrast, the caste system is based on the belief that people do not—and in fact cannot—rise above, or sink below, their origins.

Some beliefs stand on their own, but many are grouped together as belief systems. These systems may be quite simple, consisting of only a few items, or they may be enormously complex, involving hundreds of related beliefs. For example, belief in castes is often part of a Hindu religious belief system that integrates beliefs about reincarnation and karma.

Belief systems, to the extent that they are "systems" at all, tend to be thematically and psychologically consistent.[2] However, we often see conflicts between these belief systems. For example, in contemporary US politics, Republicans tend to hold various beliefs associated with distrust of big government—a basic premise of the Republican Party is that government regulations usually hurt the economy, that tax cuts usually help the economy, and so on—whereas Democrats tend to hold contradictory beliefs. Democrats often believe government regulations are necessary to curb the power that corporations have in a capitalist system. These clashing belief systems can often complicate or preclude compromise. Even within individuals, beliefs or belief systems can conflict, as we discuss below.

Values

Values are ideals. While beliefs represent our understanding of the way things are, values represent our understanding of the way things should be. Many researchers, following Milton Rokeach,[3] distinguish between terminal and instrumental values.[4] *Terminal* values are the ultimate social and individual goals we want to reach, like freedom or financial prosperity. *Instrumental* values are the constraints on the means we endorse to pursue our goals, such as honesty, responsibility, and loyalty.

Leaders of social movements often invoke values, sometimes incorporating them into a motto that describes the movement to others. Leaders of social movements often attempt to connect their activities to a desired goal. Mottoes like Patrick Henry's "Give me liberty or give me death" helped to frame the American Revolution in terms of the value of freedom. Individual liberties and personal accomplishment have been important characteristics of American culture. The French Revolution was built on a slightly different set of values: "Liberty, equality, fraternity." Note that supporters of both revolutions tended to share not only values but some beliefs—including, crucially, the belief that a revolution could bring about progress toward realizing their values.

Because values, like beliefs, tend to be taken for granted or treated as universal, people often are taken aback by value differences. One of the authors once taught at a university in another country in which collective and societal attainment is valued far more highly than individual accomplishment as generally construed in the United States. The professor confronted a student for cheating on an exam by getting answers from the person in front of her. The student said very little, except that she was "ashamed." The professor did not realize that this situation reflected a difference in values until she discussed the incident with another student. "Yes," the other student agreed. "I'd be ashamed as well. . . . Getting caught that easily is a very silly thing to do." The student explained, "It is not wrong to cheat, but it is very embarrassing not to cheat correctly." Many American students agree that it is not wrong to cheat,[5] but perhaps not many would have said so to a professor.

Attitudes

Attitudes have been defined as relatively stable and consistent positive or negative views about a person, place, or thing.[6] More often, attitudes are defined as *evaluations*—good or bad, likable or unlikable—that have both emotional (affective) and cognitive elements.[7] Naturally, attitudes can be mixed: you may find a person likable in some ways and unlikable in others.

The distinction between beliefs and attitudes is not always sharp. After all, some beliefs are evaluative. You may believe that Apple makes good smartphones—and if you do, you probably also have a positive attitude toward iPhones. Still, the belief is distinct from the attitude. To believe that iPhones are "good" is to think that they have some particular merits—perhaps that they are highly reliable, easy to use, or attractive. If you believe those evaluations (or some of them), then you construe them as inherent characteristics of iPhones, or at least as judgments that many other people would share. You might have a positive attitude toward iPhones—or anything else—without having particular beliefs about why they are good.

Although attitudes are distinct from beliefs, they are related to beliefs and values. For example, if you believe that marijuana is harmful, or if you hold the value that people should avoid mind-altering substances, then you are likely to have a more negative attitude toward marijuana. Some theories show that our attitudes are largely built on our beliefs and values, while others posit that our attitudes influence our beliefs and values, as we will see.[8]

Researchers disagree about the relationship between attitudes and behavior. For some researchers, behavior is actually a component of attitude structure,[9] and perhaps a particularly useful one: how people react to spiders may reveal quite a bit about their actual attitudes toward spiders. Using a more complex example, perhaps I have a friend whom I like very much. However, I may strenuously disapprove of people who live on welfare. If my friend goes on public assistance, I may decide that I no longer like him. or that people on public assistance are not so bad. Or I may just live with these conflicting feelings, retaining my beliefs while still liking my friend.

Regardless of whether or not there is overlap between attitudes and behaviors, public opinion researchers generally distinguish between the two. As scholar Bernard C. Hennessy puts it, attitudes create "predispositions to respond and/or react [and are] directive of behavior."[10] How directive? It depends. Changing people's attitudes does not always change their behavior. And in some circumstances, people's attitudes may not predict their behavior at all.

Opinions

Some researchers use "opinion" and "attitude" more or less interchangeably, but many make a distinction, as we do here. In Thurstone and Chave's classic definition from 1929, an opinion is "a verbal expression of attitude." They write that a man's attitude about pacifism means "all that he feels and thinks about peace and war," whereas if the man says that the United States was mistaken in entering World War I against Germany, that statement is an opinion.[11] Under some definitions, the man might hold that opinion even if he never expresses it—but to hold an opinion generally implies that someone *would* express it if asked. Thus, opinions tend to be narrower and more consciously held than attitudes, more like someone's answer to a simple question, rather than a mélange of thoughts and feelings. Indeed, for many researchers in the tradition of Thurstone and Chave, opinions primarily are the answers that people give to questions designed to investigate their underlying attitudes.

Opinions	I support equal rights for women. I wouldn't support a tax increase. I favor increased immigration.
Attitudes	I respect most people. I value public schools. I distrust censorship.
Values	We should respect diverse viewpoints. People should be free. Everyone should have the opportunity to succeed.
Beliefs	People are basically good. All people are created equal. Human beings can be perfected.

FIGURE 5.1. **Beliefs, Values, Attitudes, and Opinions: A Cognitive Hierarchy.** This figure depicts a model in which beliefs form the basis for values, values for attitudes, and attitudes for opinions.

Opinions may be less stable than attitudes or beliefs. Suppose that I am asked my opinion of the president's job performance. If I am like most people, I do not have a fixed belief about how well the president is doing; I have attitudes about various things the president has done. I might opine that I strongly approve, or that I somewhat disapprove, of his performance, depending on what attitude(s) come to mind when I am asked. Even the opinions I volunteer can be inconsistent: I might say that the president is doing a great job, or a terrible one, depending on the course of the conversation.

Figure 5.1 summarizes what we have been discussing in this section. Notice how attitudes are built on beliefs and values and are finally expressed as opinions. Notice, too, that the same beliefs and values may produce divergent opinions that may even seem contradictory.

EARLY THEORIES OF ATTITUDE FORMATION AND CHANGE: THE LEGACIES OF BEHAVIORISM

You may already have noticed a problem: psychologists cannot examine attitudes (much less beliefs and values) directly. Generally, researchers infer attitudes from people's answers to questions—their stated opinions—or from people's behavior in experimental settings. Even if people's opinions and actions provide accurate measures of their attitudes, often we cannot know whether those attitudes existed before they were measured, or if the research study brought them into being. Partly for this reason, researchers often use the term "attitude change" to include attitude *formation*. Presumably people form and change attitudes through similar processes.

Paradoxically, an enduring model of attitude change—behaviorism—originally disregards attitudes altogether. Behaviorism starts from the proposition that people, like many other animals, can be *conditioned* to respond in particular ways to specific "triggers," or stimuli.[12] In the early twentieth century Ivan Pavlov discovered that dogs could be conditioned to salivate in response to various sounds; "Pavlov's dogs" remain famous to this day. [13] Pavlov studied how dogs behaved, but said nothing about dogs' attitudes, if any, toward the sounds. However, psychologists discovered that people's expressed attitudes as well as their behaviors could be conditioned. Behaviorists in the middle of the twentieth century reasoned that conditioning might be the main process of attitude change.[14] If it was, then experimental research might lead to a comprehensive understanding of attitudes—and conditioning might make it possible to largely control people's attitudes and behaviors.

Two variants of conditioning theories have been of special interest to public opinion scholars: *classical conditioning* and *operant conditioning*.

Classical Conditioning

Classical conditioning theory depends on a *stimulus-response* model.[15] Take Pavlov's experiments as an example. Suppose that dogs naturally salivate when they get meat; in the language of this model, salivation is an unconditioned response (UCR) to the unconditioned stimulus (UCS) of getting meat. In classical conditioning, dogs are conditioned to associate an initially neutral stimulus such as the sound of a bell—the conditioned stimulus (CS)—with the unconditioned stimulus of getting meat. Pavlov found that if he rang a bell each time he gave a dog meat, *pairing* these stimuli, eventually the dog would salivate whenever the bell rang, presumably because the dog associates the sound (the CS) with getting meat (the UCS). Salivation became a conditioned response (CR). (See Figure 5.2.)

But do people have anything in common with Pavlov's dogs? Behaviorist researchers established that, yes, people also are amenable to classical conditioning. In one classic study, Arthur and Carolyn Staats presented research subjects with pairs of words: a national name projected on a screen and a word that was read to them. Supposedly, each subject's task was to learn both sets of words. But Staats and Staats repeatedly paired the name *Dutch* with positive words such as *gift* and

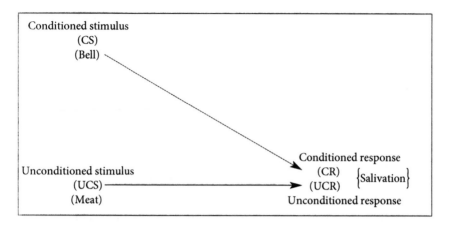

FIGURE 5.2. **An Example of Classsical Conditioning**.
SOURCE: Adapted from Richard E. Petty and John T. Cacioppo, *Attitudes and Persuasion: Classic and Contemporary Approaches* (Dubuque, IA: William C. Brown Company, 1981), p. 41.

happy. They paired *Swedish* with negative words such as *ugly* and *failure*. And they paired the other national names with neutral words such as *chair*. At the end, subjects were asked to rate how they felt about each of the national names, on a scale from pleasant to unpleasant. Sure enough, on average, they felt more warmly about "Dutch" than "Swedish."[16] In this experiment, the response is an emotion or feeling—an evocation of attitude—rather than a manifest behavior.

Conditioning surely occurs outside experimental settings. For example, as Alice Eagly and Shelly Chaiken[17] describe, a child eventually learns the evaluative meaning of the words "good" and "bad" if these conditioned stimuli are repeatedly paired with unconditioned stimuli such as food or physical punishment. Classical conditioning provides a mechanism for inculcating group prejudice.[18] Eagly and Chaiken describe how a child might acquire a negative attitude toward some minority group:

> Imagine that the child hears a number of negative adjectives (e.g., bad, dirty, stupid) paired with the name of a particular minority group (e.g., blacks, Jews). In this application, the minority group name is the CS, and the negative adjectives are the UCSs. The UCSs are assumed to regularly evoke UCRs—in this case implicit negative evaluative responses.... With repeated pairings of the CS and the various UCSs, the minority group name comes to elicit ... an implicit negative evaluative response, or negative attitude toward the minority group.[19]

Thus, there may be situations in which the Staats and Staats experiment could play out in real life, with potentially horrific consequences.

Operant Conditioning

Operant conditioning is based on the supposition that people act to maximize the positive and minimize the negative consequences of their behavior—and, by extension, their attitudes.[20] We may come to adhere to attitudes that yield rewards and to reject attitudes that result in punishments.[21] Figure 5.3 illustrates how such operant conditioning might work for individuals who are being indoctrinated into a cult.

In a classic example of operant conditioning from the 1950s, researcher Joel Greenspoon used verbal rewards to change what people would say.[22] Subjects were asked to "say all the words that you can think of." In one group, Greenspoon said "mmm-hmm" (a positive reinforcement) each time a subject used a plural noun; in a control group, Greenspoon said nothing. Subjects in the "mmm-hmm" group used about twice as many plural nouns as people in the control group—and almost all of them were unaware of what Greenspoon was doing. Many studies since then have used a similar approach.[23] Other studies indicate that verbal conditioning really can change people's attitudes, not just their word choice.[24] However, in some cases what looks like unconscious conditioning may be simple compliance, "going along" with the experimenter without an underlying change in attitude.

Operant conditioning may have been one among many factors at work in Nazi Germany during the 1930s. German citizens were heavily rewarded for

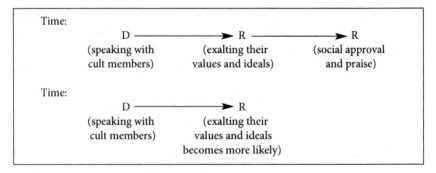

FIGURE 5.3. **An Example of Operant Conditioning.**
SOURCE: Adapted from Richard E. Petty and John T. Cacioppo, *Attitudes and Persuasion: Classic and Contemporary Approaches* (Dubuque, IA: William C. Brown Company, 1981), p. 48.

participating in activities deemed patriotic, such as saluting and attending Nazi rallies, and were severely punished for "incorrect" responses, particularly expressions of opposition to the Nazis. In the short run, these incentives tended to elicit compliance; over time, they may have led many people to feel real allegiance toward the Nazi regime.

In many contexts, conditioning (both classical and operant) sounds like dreadful manipulation—and if it works, it's terrible news for democratic competence. Are we simply at the mercy of how we have been conditioned to respond? It turns out that conditioning offers a limited and flawed explanation of human behavior. A central premise of behaviorism is that people confronted with the same stimulus tend to respond in the same way. But in real life, people often respond differently, and attributing all those differences to conditioning is not helpful, if it is even plausible. If we are studying how, say, Democrats and Republicans respond differently to a speech about global warming, we certainly can't explain these differences through conditioning alone, and in any event we don't know how these people have been conditioned. A more realistic perspective is that conditioning is one among many of the ways that human beings can learn. It is clear that different kinds of theories may be more useful for scholars as they attempt to understand public opinion.

COGNITIVE PROCESSING: WHAT HAPPENS WHEN PEOPLE THINK

In our daily lives we are bombarded with information from various sources. Cognitive processing models (as well as some other models) construe this information as *messages* that our brains actively process or filter out. These approaches reject behaviorism's model of unthinking response to a stimulus, but they also recognize that people do not pay equal attention to everything that happens around them.

The elaboration likelihood model (ELM) is a prominent example of cognitive processing approaches. Richard Petty and John Cacioppo[25] developed this model in reaction to earlier "cognitive response" models, which they felt were too narrow. The model considers how people process messages that pertain to controversial issues, especially to messages intended to be persuasive. Elaboration refers to "the extent to which a person thinks about the issue-relevant arguments contained in a message."[26] Elaboration ranges from low—unthinking acceptance or rejection of the arguments—to high—complex thought processes such as active counterargumentation.

Petty and Cacioppo argue that a recipient of a persuasive message analyzes and evaluates issue-relevant information, comparing it to information already available in memory. Sometimes the recipient scrutinizes the message closely—elaboration is high—and relatively enduring attitude change may result. At other times the recipient of the message lacks the motivation or ability to process it closely, and elaboration is low. In that case, the recipient may then rely on peripheral factors, such as the attractiveness of the source or emotional appeal, for a more temporary attitude change. Or the recipient may discount the message entirely.

Crucially, the model considers influences on recipients' motivation and ability. Motivation may be high when an issue seems directly relevant, when recipients feel a sense of personal responsibility, or when people are predisposed to think about such questions (called "need for cognition"). Ability may be high if a message is repeated, if it is readily comprehensible, if recipients have prior knowledge, and if they are relatively free from distractions. If either motivation or ability is low, then elaboration is unlikely. Figure 5.4 is a diagram of the elaboration likelihood model.

Consider the implications of this model for public opinion scholars and those who design persuasive messages. The ELM suggests that there are two ways to produce attitude change: (1) by encouraging people to do a great deal of thinking about the message (the central route) and (2) by encouraging people to focus on simple, compelling cues (the peripheral route), although the resulting change may be ephemeral. For example, in political campaigns, probably most voters will not be highly motivated to ponder the various candidates' arguments and positions; for them, peripheral appeals may be more effective than elaborate policy arguments. However, some voters will be highly motivated, and they are more likely to be persuaded by more detailed arguments. Accordingly, campaigns may run frankly superficial campaign advertisements while providing extensive information on their Web sites.

Notice that the ELM serves primarily as a descriptive rather than an explanatory model.[27] That is, the model does not explain "why certain arguments are strong or weak, why certain variables serve as (peripheral) cues, or why certain variables affect information processing."[28] Nevertheless, as Eagly and Chaiken note, "the model represents a powerful and integrative empirical framework for studying persuasion processes."[29]

A related theoretical framework describes mental heuristics.[30] Mental heuristics, essentially, are shortcuts for reaching a plausible (and perhaps sound) conclusion with far less effort than a complete cognitive analysis requires. For example, if I am deciding how to vote on a ballot issue, I may follow the opinion

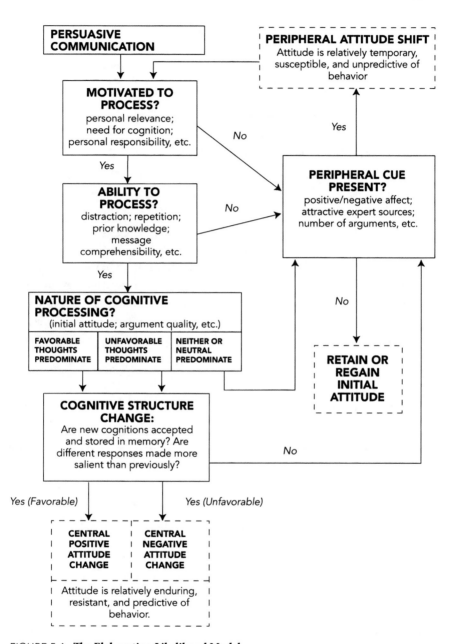

FIGURE 5.4. **The Elaboration Likelihood Model.**

SOURCE: Adapted from Richard E. Petty and John T. Cacioppo, "The Elaboration Likelihood Model of Persuasion," p. 126 in Leonard Berkowitz, ed., *Advances in Experimental Social Psychology* 19, 123–205. (San Diego, CA: Academic Press, 1986).

of a pundit I trust instead of doing my own research. Like the ELM and many other models, heuristic models assume that people think about their opinions, but also that they may not think very hard about those opinions. We say more about heuristics in later chapters.

CONSISTENCY AND JUDGMENTAL THEORIES: ATTITUDES COME IN PACKAGES

Attitudes are neither formed nor changed in a vacuum. The attitudes that we hold now affect the ways in which we process new information and assess persuasive messages. Existing attitudes form a frame of reference, a basis of comparison, for new ideas. Further, changing one attitude may result in changing a whole network of related attitudes. The models we have considered so far have relatively little to say about these interconnections; the theories we consider next place them front and center. *Consistency theories* describe how attitudes interact and how these attitudinal interactions are likely to affect opinion expression and attitude change. *Judgmental theories* emphasize how people's attitudes influence the ways in which they interpret new information. Let us consider each in turn.

Consistency Theories

All consistency theories describe cognitions (beliefs, attitudes, and so on) as being consistent, inconsistent, or irrelevant to one another. According to Leon Festinger,[31] two cognitions are consistent, or consonant, when one somehow "follows from" the other—perhaps according to logic, experience, or cultural norms. For example, "I love my children" is consonant with "I enjoy spending time with my children." Two cognitions are inconsistent when the opposite of one cognition follows from the other: "I take good care of myself" is dissonant with "I eat lots of unhealthy foods." Cognitions are mutually irrelevant when knowledge of one tells you nothing about what you might expect regarding the other—the belief that "the Dallas Cowboys are excellent" presumably has no bearing on whether "it will probably rain tomorrow," or vice versa. Consonance and dissonance are subjective judgments. To many people, "I love my children" seems dissonant with "I often don't enjoy my children at all," although these cognitions might not be at all contradictory.

Balance Theory. Balance theory, formulated by Fritz Heider,[32] applies consistency to triadic relationships among an observer and two other people or entities. Here is an informal, real-life example. One of our student advisees came to office hours to discuss a problem she was having with two of her roommates. She liked both roommates a great deal, and they liked her—but they disliked each other. As you would expect, this dynamic made everybody miserable. From the advisee's point of view, obviously her roommates "should" just get along. Heider would say that she was experiencing tension caused by imbalance. The advisee might have eliminated the imbalance by getting her roommates to like each other (if possible); by "choosing sides" and beginning to dislike one of them; or by moving out, escaping the situation—which is what she decided to do.

Heider[33] would present these relationships as shown in Figure 5.5. In Heider's figures, P represents the perceiver (in this case, the advisee), O is some other person or entity, and X is either a third person or some attribute of O. So, in this case, O and X are the two roommates. The plus and minus signs in the figure indicate an attitude or relationship. Thus, (P + O) indicates that P likes O; (O – X) indicates that O and X are in conflict. Balance exists if all three signs in a triad are positive or if exactly two are negative (e.g., "the enemy of my enemy is my friend"). Otherwise, there is imbalance, and probably discomfort.

If balance theory seems far too simple, of course it is. (To be fair, Heider's discussion is far more elaborate than our summary here.) Still, it is genuinely useful. Scholars have applied balance theory to phenomena such as how voters perceive candidates' issue positions. For example, Jon Krosnick found that voters tend to be biased toward perceiving that candidates they like agree with the voters' own positions on issues, and that disliked candidates disagree with those positions.[34] Thus, individual voters seem to be trying to maintain a balanced triad among themselves, their candidates, and their issue positions. More recent examples of balance theory in practice include an analysis of consumer reactions to a cause-related marketing campaign.[35]

Congruity Theory. One obvious limitation of Heider's balance theory is that it cannot distinguish degrees of liking or belonging among the elements. It does not "care" whether P is madly in love with O or faintly warm. Congruity theory, as presented first by Charles Osgood and Percy Tannenbaum,[36] extends balance theory by allowing for gradations of liking—shades of gray. Messages that conflict with our prior attitudes can case "incongruity," a state of cognitive imbalance. According to the model, people resolve these imbalances through what D. W. Rajecki describes as a compromise between the initial polarities. For example, "when a disliked person endorses a liked other, the resultant attitude will be the same toward both. By reason of association with each

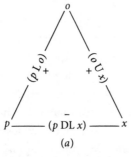

(a)

The given situation is unbalanced: two positive relations and one negative relation.

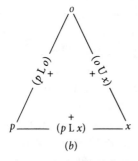

(b)

Change in sentiment relation resulting in a balance of three positive relations.

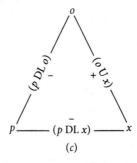

(c)

Change in sentiment relation resulting in a balance of two negative relations and one positive relation.

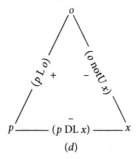

(d)

Change in unit relation resulting in a balance of two negative relations and one positive relation.

FIGURE 5.5. **An Illustration of Balance Theory.**

SOURCE: Adapted from F. Heider, *The Psychology of Interpersonal Relations* (New York: Wiley, 1958).

other, the person you initially disliked intensely will improve somewhat in your estimation."[37]

Congruity theory accommodates the fact that we sometimes disagree with our friends or our political leaders and yet continue to like and support them.[38] However, if our disagreements become more frequent or more important, we may decide to achieve balance by acquiring different friends, or supporting other political leaders, whose views are closer to our own.

Congruity theory has interesting applications in politics. Research has shown that not only do people tend to like politicians who agree with them on some issue, but they tend to move toward the issue positions of politicians they like. Eagly and Chaiken[39] discovered that American politicians behaved like congruity theorists. That is, politicians tended to (1) associate themselves with popular causes, (2) disassociate themselves from unpopular causes, and (3) avoid taking positions on issues on which voters are sharply divided. Politicians often behave in these ways toward issues that they cannot personally influence, and even on purely symbolic issues such as what baseball team they support.

Cognitive Dissonance Theory. Cognitive dissonance arises when an individual's beliefs, attitudes, and behaviors are not aligned. Since Festinger's book *A Theory of Cognitive Dissonance* was published in 1957, well over 1,000 studies of cognitive dissonance have been published. These studies have assessed various aspects of Festinger's theory, challenged hypotheses derived from the theory, and related it to different contexts, including marketing and religion.[40] As we have seen, Festinger argued that two cognitions could be dissonant, that is, mutually inconsistent. He further argued that cognitive dissonance— awareness that one's cognitions are at odds—causes discomfort, and so people act to reduce it. For example, I may feel that eating ice cream makes life worth living and also believe that it is bad for my health. Every time I see ice cream, or even think of it, I may feel conflicted: "I really want that! I really shouldn't have it!" If I can find a way to avoid that conflict, I will. Recent work has also looked at exercise motivation through the lens of cognitive dissonance.[41]

How people deal with cognitive dissonance will partly depend on the intensity of the cognitions and the value people attach to them. If I highly value eating ice cream and really don't think much about my health—or don't think that ice cream is very dangerous—then I will probably keep eating ice cream. Conversely, if I place a high value on "eating healthy," then I will probably stop. Dissonance is at its most powerful when the two cognitive elements are important and evenly valued—if I am really worried about my health but I really love ice cream.

Festinger describes three basic ways to reduce dissonance:

1. A person can change one of the cognitions so that the relationship becomes consonant. For example, I might convince myself that eating ice cream is safe after all—or, on the contrary, I might convince myself that, actually, apples are far tastier and more refreshing.
2. A person can "add" consonant cognitions to one side. For example, I may tell myself that when I eat ice cream, I am happier, more productive, maybe even more likely to exercise, *and* I get more calcium—so surely, overall, I am better off eating ice cream than not.
3. A person can alter the importance of the cognitions. For example, if I can avoid ice cream for a while, although I will not stop liking it, I may at least think less about how much I like it.

It is clear that cognitive dissonance is an important psychological state for researchers to study so they can determine how people react when faced with conflicting cognitive elements.[42] But how does cognitive dissonance apply specifically to public opinion research? Fundamentally, it is a deceptively simple idea that tends to complicate our assumptions about people's goals. As Festinger analogizes, cognitive dissonance leads one to actively reduce dissonance, as hunger inspires one to reduce hunger. This is a subtle yet powerful motivation, although it is difficult to tell just how powerful. Often we think of people as seeking safety, prosperity, love, and friendship; to think of them as trying to minimize internal conflict may shed a different light on many opinions and behaviors.[43] Also, we can consider cognitive dissonance as a potential cause of opinion change—not only within individuals, but in the wider public. Changing attitudes on various social issues can be considered instances of many individuals experiencing and working through cognitive dissonance.

Judgmental Theories: Adaptation Level Theory and Social Judgment Theory

The underlying principle of most judgmental theories is that all stimuli can be arranged in some meaningful order on a psychological dimension. That is, attitudes toward an object can be arranged from the most negative (unfavorable) to the most positive (favorable) in the same way people might be arranged from most attractive to least attractive, shortest to tallest, and so forth. How positive or negative something feels or how it is rated on an attitude scale depends on the frame of reference.[44] That is, our past experiences play an important role in the ways that we interpret new information.

In *adaptation level theory*, a person's adaptation level is that point on the dimension of judgment that corresponds to the psychological neutral point. As Petty and Cacioppo explain, "If you were to put your hand in a bucket of very cold water, eventually your hand would adapt to the water temperature so that the cold water would feel neutral or normal. Subsequent judgments of how cold or warm another bucket of water felt would be made relative to the water temperature to which your hand had previously adapted."[45] Adaptation level is important because other stimuli we experience are judged in relation to this level, which serves as an anchor or reference point.

Philip Brickman, Dan Coates, and Ronnie Janoff-Bulman conducted an interesting study on adaptation level theory, testing the proposition that extremely positive events do not increase one's overall level of happiness.[46] Brickman and associates asked people who had won from $50,000 to $1,000,000 in the Illinois state lottery how pleasant they found seven ordinary events like watching television and eating breakfast. People in a control group of nonwinners were asked the same questions. Brickman and associates suggested that this positive event—winning the lottery—should raise the winners' adaptation level so that more mundane events become less pleasurable than they used to be. Indeed, lottery winners rated these events as less pleasant than the controls, even though earlier studies had found no differences in overall pleasure ratings between the two groups.

The researchers speculated that the extra pleasure of winning the money is offset by the decline in pleasure from ordinary events. Indeed, we have a similar personal example to share. An accountant one of us knows won the state lottery—$18 million. And when the accountant-turned-millionaire, who is now able to enjoy the finer things of life, was asked if the pleasure of eating breakfast was reduced since winning the lottery, she answered, "Not on my [new] front porch!"

Social judgment theory assumes that people tend to arrange stimuli in a meaningful order; however, it posits that these stimuli are subject not only to contrast effects, but also to assimilation effects. That is, people interpret (and often distort) each other's attitudes, using their own attitudes as a reference point or anchor. Attitudes that are relatively close to one's own are assimilated (seen as closer than they actually are), but attitudes that are quite discrepant from one's own are contrasted (seen as further away than they actually are).[47]

How do we develop such misperceptions? Social judgment theory posits that people divide each attitudinal dimension—the spectrum of possible attitudes on some subject—into three "latitudes." The latitude of *acceptance* includes the range of attitudes that people find acceptable—attitudes not too far from their own. The latitude of *rejection* comprises the range of opinions that they find objectionable. Finally, the latitude of *noncommitment* comprises the remaining positions: attitudes that people do not find immediately acceptable or unacceptable.

If someone else's expressed attitude falls within my latitude of acceptance, I am likely to assimilate it as a reasonable position not far from my own. I also am more likely to change my own attitude, moving toward the other person's—splitting the difference, so to speak. On the other hand, if someone else's expressed attitude falls in my latitude of rejection, I am likely to contrast it, and my own attitude may move even further in the opposite direction. Attitudes in the latitude of noncommitment are most likely to be perceived accurately and least likely to produce attitude change in either direction. For example, say that you and a friend are discussing the issue of abortion. Assimilating your friend's attitude on abortion toward your own attitude would probably make you regard your friend's statements as "fair," "unbiased," and so forth, increasing the likelihood of attitude change. However, contrasting your friend's attitude on abortion would likely lead you to regard your friend's statements about abortion as "unfair" or "biased," reducing the likelihood that your attitude will change.

Of course, there are many theories from psychology that deal with how people process information to form their own attitudes and opinions. We have presented only a few to give you an idea of how the psychology of the individual can have a profound impact on the opinions of the whole. The fields of social psychology, sociology, and communication have provided even more rich theoretical perspectives to examine. While providing such a list of theories can seem overwhelming, each contributes to the understanding of public opinion in unique ways. We consider some of the more important contributions below.

MOTIVATIONAL THEORIES: SAME ATTITUDE, DIFFERENT REASON

Why do we hold the opinions we do? Consistency theories suggest one set of subtle reasons: for example, to minimize the discomfort caused by cognitive dissonance. But there are many reasons for holding opinions. In the 1950s two separate groups of investigators elaborated so-called functional theories about the diverse reasons behind human attitudes. Other theories describe and explain how our concerns about our own self-image affect the attitudes we hold and the opinions we express. One of these theories, impression management theory, is discussed here because of its close links to cognitive dissonance theory. Several related theories are discussed in the following chapters.

Functional Theories

Functional theories posit that people tend to form attitudes that serve various functions. These theories do not necessarily explain *how* people form functional attitudes; they do not assume that people consciously choose attitudes to be functional. For example, Daniel Katz's 1960 article "The Functional Approach to the Study of Attitudes"[48] describes four functions that attitudes might serve for a person:

1. *Adjustment* (utilitarian): People tend to form attitudes that help them to gain rewards and avoid penalties—stated in economic language, to maximize their net utility. If I burn myself on a hot stove once, I will probably henceforth be wary of hot stoves. If studying on a test helps me earn a high score—and if I value scoring highly on tests—I will probably have a warmer attitude toward studying. The adjustment function depends on *perceptions* of utility: I may come to love a "lucky shirt" if I believe it is possible for shirts to bring luck.

2. *Ego-defensive*: People can deploy attitudes to protect themselves from unflattering truths about themselves and "harsh realities in [their] external world."[49] For example, someone whose careless driving causes an accident may become angry at the car, the weather, the other driver—anything that helps deflect responsibility for driving badly. Or someone stuck in a bad job may blame "the welfare cheats," when in fact good jobs are scarce for reasons that have nothing to do with welfare programs.

3. *Value-expressive*: Sometimes people's attitudes express their values. A young person who values independence from adult conventions may prefer "edgy" clothes as an expression of that value. People who consider themselves environmentalists may be willing to pay extra for hybrid cars because they feel it is the green thing to do. (To an observer, a value-expressive attitude may seem completely reasonable or rather silly, but that is irrelevant to the theory. The theory considers how attitudes are functional, not whether they are rational.)

4. *Knowledge*: Katz writes that people "seek knowledge to give meaning to what would otherwise be an unorganized chaotic universe."[50] Knowledge in this sense may not be objectively true; its function is to help people feel that they understand their world, where they fit in it, and how they should behave in it. For example, people's attitudes about romantic relationships help them know how to behave—but what two people "know" about love may be sharply contradictory.

Functional theories such as Katz's imply that attempts at persuasion—changing other people's attitudes—should be informed by an understanding of what function(s) the attitudes serve. Consider a public health official who is designing a campaign to persuade smokers to quit. One obvious approach is to try to change their attitude that smoking is an acceptable choice by educating them about the dangers of smoking. That may work for smokers who know little or nothing about why smoking is dangerous; they may well be willing to learn (the knowledge function) and change their attitudes accordingly. However, most smokers already know that smoking is dangerous; an attempt to "educate" them is not likely to help. A smarter approach looks for deeper insights into smokers' attitudes and how they are functional.

For example, many smokers express the attitude that once you start smoking, there isn't much point in stopping—at least right now—because smoking isn't *that* dangerous, and smoking for one more day or week or month or year doesn't really matter. This attitude can serve an ego-defensive function: smoking is addictive, and many smokers have tried and failed to quit, so it is functional (in one sense) to believe that there is little point in trying again. Smokers who believe that may pooh-pooh an attempt to scare them or may simply feel worse about the long-term consequences of their behavior without seeing any reason to change now. Recent smoking cessation advertisements take a different approach. First, they state that in fact, people who stop smoking now can expect large health improvements fairly soon. Second, they reassure smokers that they really can quit, and that it doesn't matter how many times they have tried to quit in the past. Thus, the ads not only challenge a rationalization for continuing to smoke, but also address the fear behind the rationalization.

Critics of functional theories often complain that they are ad hoc. Who can determine which functions really matter, for which people, at which times? Scholars other than Katz have described functional approaches to the study of attitudes, including, among others, Herbert Kelman;[51] Mehta R. Grewal and F. R. Kardes;[52] and M. Brewster Smith, Jerome Bruner, and Robert White[53]—whose do you choose? These and related questions are fair ones, but we do not have to wrestle with them here. We believe that thinking of attitudes as (at least possibly) functional, rather than as personality quirks or straightforward reactions to information and experience, is worthwhile even if no one theory is entirely satisfactory.

Impression Management Theory

Impression management theory can be construed as a functional theory of attitude and behavior that posits one prime function: people present an image to others in order to achieve a particular goal—most often, to attain social approval.[54] Whereas cognitive consistency theories assume that people strive for internal consistency, impression management theory assumes that people strive to convey as positive and consistent an external image as possible, even if that image is inconsistent with their internal attitudes.

In fact, James Tedeschi, Barry Schlenker, and Thomas Bonoma[55] proposed impression management theory as an alternative to dissonance theory. As Schlenker states: "Irrespective of whether or not people have psychological needs to be consistent . . . there is little doubt that the appearance of consistency usually leads to social reward, while the appearance of inconsistency leads to social punishment."[56] Usually, if researchers can detect an instance of apparent cognitive dissonance, the people they are studying also realize that they appear inconsistent to others. People are likely to avoid such inconsistencies if they can or to work harder on impression management if they notice that they have slipped up.[57]

For example, if I say that people should always honor their civic obligations, I would probably also say that I would gladly serve jury duty if asked. Even if, in truth, I would try to avoid serving jury duty, or would complain bitterly about it, I am unlikely to say so in public—not because I would then wrestle with cognitive dissonance, but because I would look like a petty hypocrite. If I happen to blurt out something negative about jury duty, I would probably backtrack (perhaps by saying, "Still, someone has to do it")—again, not to restore "balance," but just to look better. Meanwhile, in another social setting I might sound a lot more cynical about civic obligations in general, and jury duty in particular, in order to fit in better.

Impression management theory provides one account of the obvious: participants in public opinion research may fudge, mislead, or even lie outright to appear more favorable in the eyes of the researcher. This phenomenon is known as *social desirability bias*. Even in an anonymous survey, people may all but swear that they will vote, when in fact the odds are against it. Or they may answer questions about racial attitudes in ways that they think will appeal to the interviewer. This behavior is not necessarily intended to be deceptive; all of us sometimes try to choose our words so as not to offend other people. Researchers always have to reckon with the possibility of social desirability bias.

LINKS BETWEEN ATTITUDES AND BEHAVIOR: WHAT PEOPLE THINK AND WHAT THEY DO

Social desirability bias frames a problem: What is the relationship between attitudes and behavior, between what people think—or, really, what they say they think—and what they do? As we mentioned, people often say they will vote, and then don't. But many questions about attitudes and behavior are more subtle. How well do Army recruits' statements about eagerness for combat predict their actual combat performance? If people say they intend to donate bone marrow, how likely are they to do so? When women are asked whether they want more children, how well do their answers predict whether they bear another child? Howard Schuman and Michael Johnson, summarizing the results of studies on these and other topics, say that the associations between attitudes and behaviors "seem to vary from small to moderate in size": strong enough to be worth considering, but far from strong enough to confidently predict individuals' behaviors. Some researchers have questioned whether there is much point in studying attitudes at all, if one wants to understand actual social behavior.[58] We think there is importance to this line of research. But why then are the relationships between attitudes and behaviors so intricate at best?

Measurement Issues

As we have already considered in Chapter 3, there are many methodological problems in public opinion research. Studies of the links between attitudes and behavior pose some special difficulties. One is that different research methods seem to produce contradictory evidence. Kelman notes that survey-based studies often indicate stronger relationships than experimental studies that examine people's actual behavior in research settings.[59] In general, many researchers give more credence to experimental studies than to survey studies in which people simply self-report their behaviors.[60] However, many topics are not amenable to experimental study. Eagly and Chaiken suggest that survey research often examines attitudes that "are more important and involving"—and therefore, perhaps, more influential—than in most experimental studies.[61]

Intuitively, some attitudes are better suited to predicting particular behaviors than others. Icek Ajzen formalized this intuition as the *principle of correspondence*: attitudes best predict behaviors when they correspond to the behaviors "in terms of action, target, context, and time elements."[62] For example, people's general attitude about environmental protection may not strongly predict their willingness to donate to an environmental group such as the Sierra Club. After all, giving money to the Sierra Club doesn't directly protect anything. People's attitudes about the effectiveness of the Sierra Club may better predict their willingness to donate to it.

Individual Differences

Individual differences can account for some inconsistencies in attitude–behavior relationships. You probably have some friends who exhibit high consistency between their attitudes and behaviors. If they tell you they think something, you can almost rest assured that their actions will be true to their words. However, you can probably think of just as many or more friends whose behaviors are much less consistent with their attitudes. They may say one thing and act in a completely different way.

As Perloff notes, your friends who fit the latter category may have a strong attitude about an issue, but they might withhold their opinion or may take the opposing viewpoint.[63] You may even know some habitual "devil's advocates" who wait to hear what other people say, then routinely disagree with the majority opinion. Perloff describes two key individual differences that influence this consistency (or lack thereof) between attitudes and behaviors: self-monitoring and direct experience.

Mark Snyder developed the *self-monitoring* concept, which he describes as "the extent to which people monitor (observe, regulate, and control) the public appearances of self they display in social situations and interpersonal relationships."[64] Snyder developed a scale that classifies people as high self-monitors or low self-monitors. As Perloff notes:

> High self-monitors are adept at controlling the images of self they present in interpersonal situations, and they are highly sensitive to the social cues that signify the appropriate behavior in a given situation. . . . Low self-monitors are less concerned with conveying an impression that is appropriate to the situation. Rather than relying on situational cues to help them decide how to act in a particular situation, low self-monitors consult their inner feelings and attitudes.[65]

Thus, high self-monitors are more likely to express public opinions that are different from their private opinions. Low self-monitors are likely to have private and public opinions that match, and so their attitudes may better predict their behaviors.[66]

Moreover, attitudes based on direct experience may predict behaviors better than other attitudes do. Russell Fazio and Mark Zanna assert that attitudes based on direct experience are "more clearly defined, held with greater certainty, more stable over time, and more resistant to counter influence."[67] For example, if a five-year-old says he is "never gonna do drugs," he is more likely basing this statement on television advertisements he has seen and on comments made by his teachers, rather than on having seen his friends "do drugs." Based on the research by Fazio and Zanna, the five-year-old's statement would be more meaningful and would be more likely to predict his behavior if he had actually witnessed a friend having a bad physical reaction to a drug.

Social and Situational Factors

Many social factors, such as cultural norms, may affect the linkages between attitudes and behavior. A classic study from 1934, explained in Box 5.1, demonstrates how social norms may affect attitude expression—in this case, how the norm of politeness may prevent people from acting on prejudiced attitudes.

When do attitudes predict behaviors? It is clear that there are a lot of cognitive and situational factors that must be considered in order to answer this question. One such concept related to the attitude–behavior relationship is *attitude accessibility*.[68] That is, attitudes are thought to guide behavior partially through the perception process. Attitudes that are highly accessible (i.e., that come to mind quickly) are thought to be more likely to guide perception and therefore behavior. Studies indicate that more accessible attitudes predict behavior better than less accessible ones, independent of the direction and intensity of attitude expression.[69] Thus, knowing how quickly someone can express an attitude or opinion can provide useful information about how that person is likely to behave.

Theory of Planned Behavior

Naturally some researchers have grappled with the attitude–behavior problem by developing more complex models. Icek Ajzen's theory of planned behavior, which is based on Martin Fishbein and Ajzen's theory of reasoned action, illustrates this general approach.

BOX 5.1

Traveling America: Weak Links Between
Prejudiced Attitudes and Prejudiced Behavior

In 1930 sociologist Richard LaPiere visited a hotel "in a small town known for its narrow and bigoted 'attitude'" toward Chinese people. LaPiere was traveling with a young Chinese student and his wife, whom he describes as "personable [and] charming." The hotel clerk accommodated them without hesitation. Two months later, he called the same hotel to ask if they could accommodate "an important Chinese gentleman." The response was "an unequivocal 'No.'"[1] Curious, LaPiere arranged with the student and his wife to conduct an extensive field study over the next two years. Of this study, LaPiere notes:

> In something like ten thousand miles of motor travel, twice across the United States, up and down the Pacific Coast, we met definite rejection . . . just once. We were received at 66 hotels, auto camps, and "Tourist Homes,' refused at one. We were served in 184 restaurants and cafes scattered throughout the country and treated with what I judged to be more than ordinary consideration in 72 of them.[2]

Six months after the trip, LaPiere sent each of these establishments a questionnaire that asked, "Will you accept members of the Chinese race as guests in your establishment?" Remarkably, 92 percent of the establishments that responded said that they would not accept Chinese. All but one of the rest said that it would depend on circumstances. Yet in fact, almost all these places had accepted Chinese guests—even in dozens of cases in which LaPiere sent the couple ahead, to ensure that proprietors were not simply deferring to him.

Strictly speaking, LaPiere's question did not measure an "attitude," but most people would agree that the responses evinced anti-Chinese prejudice. Why wasn't this prejudiced attitude manifest in proprietors' behavior? Donald T. Campbell suggests[3] that, face to face, the attitude was trumped by a prevailing social norm of politeness. Answering "no" to a written survey question hardly seems rude; telling particular people, to their faces, that they must leave is rude in the extreme. Thus, the subjective cost of expressing prejudice is much greater in person than in responding to the questionnaire. Campbell's explanation is both social and situational: it posits that how people act on their attitudes may crucially depend on the specific circumstances.

(continues)

(continued)   BOX 5.1

Traveling America: Weak Links Between
Prejudiced Attitudes and Prejudiced Behavior

Another possible explanation is that the Chinese couple did not trigger the negative attitude that the proprietors associated with the words "members of the Chinese race." Many Americans harbor negative attitudes toward various social groups in the abstract: "convicted criminals," "illegal immigrants," or "Tea Party supporters." Yet they may respond warmly to people who in fact belong to some group they disparage. To paraphrase LaPiere, people's reaction to a "symbolic social situation" may have little or no bearing on their reaction to "real social situations."[4]

SOURCES: Richard T. LaPiere, "Attitudes vs. Actions," *Social Forces* 13 (1934): 230–237; Donald T. Campbell, "Social Attitudes and Other Acquired Behavioral Dispositions," in *Psychology: A Study of Science*, ed. S. Koch (New York: McGraw-Hill, 1963), 94–172.

---

[1]Richard T. LaPiere, "Attitudes vs. Actions," *Social Forces* 13, no. 2 (December 1934): 231–232.

[2]Ibid., 232.

[3]Donald T. Campbell, "Social Attitudes and Other Acquired Behavioral Dispositions," in S. Koch, ed., *Psychology: A Study of Science* (New York: McGraw-Hill, 1963), 94–172.

[4]LaPiere, "Attitudes vs. Actions," 233.

First consider the theory of reasoned action, which attempts to explain voluntary behaviors. This theory assumes that people rationally calculate the costs and benefits of various actions. In evaluating a possible behavior, people consult their attitudes toward the behavior, including beliefs about its consequences. They also consult subjective norms: whether (they believe) other individuals and groups think the behavior should or should not be performed. These factors influence their behavioral intentions, and ultimately, their actual behavior.[70]

In general, the theory of reasoned action predicts that people will behave in ways that lead to favorable outcomes and that meet the expectations of others who are important to them. This makes sense; after all, most of us want to get along with others in this world and would also like social, financial, or other rewards. At the same time, the theory has obvious limitations. For example, it takes no account of situational characteristics such as people's access to information. Even so, it has been usefully applied to various topics, including voting and presidential elections,[71] family planning,[72] and consumer product preferences.[73]

Ajzen's theory of planned behavior (see Figure 5.6) was developed to help account for a wider range of behaviors, including those that are mandated or that may result from situations outside of the person's control. The theory posits that all behaviors can be regarded as goals, which may or may not be achieved. For example, you may have the goal of voting in an election, which may be frustrated if your car breaks down on the way to vote. One crux of this theory is the person's *perceived behavioral control*: one's perception of how easy or difficult it is to perform the action. As shown in Figure 5.6, perceived behavioral control affects behavior in two ways: it influences the intention to perform the behavior, and it may have a direct impact on the behavior.

Obviously the theory of planned behavior can be applied to many kinds of behaviors. People may vote, and express political opinions, very differently if they have subjective norms in mind than if they are simply speaking their minds.

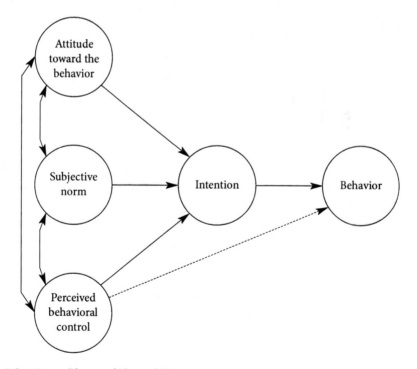

FIGURE 5.6. **Theory of Planned Behavior.**
SOURCE: Adapted from Icek Azjen, "The Theory of Planned Behavior," *Organizational Behavior and Human Decision Processes* 50 (1991):182.

EMOTIONS AND ATTITUDES

In most of the preceding discussion, attitudes and behaviors have appeared to be straightforward computations or even reflexes. While early psychology texts, such as William James's *The Principles of Psychology*,[74] devoted considerable attention to emotional processes, behavioralist theories had no use for them. When behavioralism began to wane in the 1950s, the attention turned to computer metaphors: information processing, logical consistency, decisionmaking algorithms.

However, more recently researchers have been studying mood and emotions from many different perspectives and backgrounds, including investigations of the role of emotions in approval of politicians and perspectives on social issues[75] They find that emotions play a crucial role in how we act, what we think, and who we are—and therefore, in every manifestation of public opinion. It is difficult to imagine an election cycle in American politics without also thinking of the constant barrage of negative—and often fear-inducing—messages that dominate media advertising. Rather than focus on the positive qualities of candidates or issues, much time and effort is spent painting the opposition—whether a candidate or those opposed to an issue—in the poorest light possible. While voters typically complain about such "gutter politics," these emotional appeals have proven effective and therefore remain a key component of many close political contests. We briefly consider two major efforts to integrate emotion: the cognitive and the social approaches.

Cognitive Approaches

Cognitive approaches to emotion seek to determine how emotions develop and how they interact with what we typically think of as cognition, or logical, conscious thought processes. Robert Zajonc, a leader in this area, focused on the relationship between thinking and feeling, or *affect*. Zajonc posited that information processing models in which cognition precedes affective evaluation were fundamentally wrong. He argued that affect is ubiquitous—the "major currency" of social interaction—and that it probably precedes cognition.[76] People have emotional reactions before they know why. Sometimes people never even consider why, and if they do, they may misunderstand the reasons. Public opinion polls that ask people's opinions on various issues, without tapping their feelings, may fundamentally misrepresent their views.

Researchers suggest that emotions and cognition work in tandem to motivate our attitudes and behavior. For example, Lyn Ragsdale has studied people's emotional reactions to presidents. Ragsdale found that people seem to weigh the emotional aspects of evaluation at least as strongly as the presidents' stands on issues or their economic situation—indeed, more strongly.[77] This result is alarming if we assume that people's emotions are contrary to reason. But emotions may convey information about other people—including presidents—that is valuable even if it isn't readily translated into dispassionate cognitions.[78]

Social Approaches

A very different perspective on emotions is provided by social psychologists who examine what are called *social emotions*, including embarrassment, pride, and shame. Over a century ago, Charles Cooley was among the first psychologists to describe the social role of emotions.[79] Cooley centered on pride and shame as managing devices that helped maintain a social bond and even hold the social system together. Writing in this tradition, Rowland Miller and Mark Leary[80] and Thomas Scheff[81] argue that many emotions are social emotions, as they usually arise from interactions with other people.[82]

These social emotions depend on the implied presence and attention of others. They depend on our concern about what others are thinking of us, and they would not occur if we were unaware of others' presence or did not care what others thought.[83] As such, these emotions surely lie at the root of the social comparison processes we discuss in Chapter 7, such as false consensus, although they are rarely considered as such. More recently, public opinion scholars have found other relationships between emotion and opinion outcomes.[84]

It is interesting to note that both social and cognitive perspectives suggest the important link between emotions and the separation of humans from other animals. It is no coincidence that one of the first scientists to describe the role of emotion in both cognitive and social perspectives was Charles Darwin, who devoted an entire book to the interplay of biology, emotion, and communication.[85] It is clear that emotion—whether approached from a cognitive or a social perspective—is increasingly playing an important role in public opinion research.

CONCLUSION

Beliefs and values generally affect the attitudes we hold, which are expressed as opinions. Much research has focused on how people form their attitudes. Early studies focused on the behaviorist views of classical and operant conditioning. More recent research has rejected conditioning's premise that all individuals will respond in the same way to the same stimulus and has developed several alternative explanations.

Cognitive response theories assume the brain is sorting through much information, ignoring or rejecting some and using the rest to derive opinions. The Elaboration Likelihood Model and the theory of heuristics attempt to describe this cognitive process by emphasizing the notion that we are constantly taking mental shortcuts to make decisions, form opinions, and process the vast amount of information that comes our way.

Attitudes are also studied in relationship to one another. Consistency and judgment theories focus on the interdependent relationship of attitudes. Cognitive dissonance and social judgment theories are among the most well known in this category. Researchers are also interested in functional aspects of opinion expression—determining what motivations are involved when forming and expressing opinions. Some hold that the individual's goal is to achieve consistency in attitudes held. Others argue that the individual goal is social approval, causing one to choose the position he or she considers most favored by an important social group.

Emotions also play a role in the development of public opinion. Zajonc's work in particular argues that affect has an influence on, and can be a precursor to, opinion. The study of emotion can have profound implications for the study of public opinion.

Individuals certainly have some similarities in how opinions are formed and maintained, but there are also key differences in how people collect information and choose which information and knowledge to value, as well as the role that emotions play in opinion formation. Public opinion can be thought of as an outcome of cognitions, emotions, and key social interactions. Though it makes analyzing the public opinion process more complicated, many who study public opinion now acknowledge that an "all of the above" approach is probably the most appropriate way to think of the entire system of opinion formation. While there are certainly individual and rational factors in play, the public opinion is heavily influenced by social factors and pressures. Perhaps it is best to think about public opinion arising at the intersection of cognitions, emotions, and social forces—a subject we cover in the next chapter.

NOTES

1. Richard M. Perloff, *The Dynamics of Persuasion: Communication and Attitudes in the 21st Century*, 4th ed. (New York: Lawrence Erlbaum, 2010), 46.

2. Philip E. Converse, "Information Flow and the Stability of Partisan Attitudes," *Public Opinion Quarterly* 26, no. 4 (1962): 578–599.

3. Milton Rokeach, *The Nature of Human Values* (New York: Free Press, 1973).

4. Ken-Ichi Ohbuchi, Osamu Fukushima, and James T. Tedeschi, "Cultural Values in Conflict Management—Goal Orientation, Goal Attainment, and Tactical Decision," *Journal of Cross-Cultural Psychology* 30 (1999): 51–71.

5. Stephen F. Davis, Patrick F. Drinan, and Tricia Bertram Gallup, *Cheating in School: What We Know and What We Can Do* (Malden, MA: Wiley-Blackwell, 2009).

6. Robert B. Cialdini, Richard E. Petty, and John T. Cacioppo, "Attitude and Attitude Change," *Annual Review of Psychology* 32 (1981): 357–404. See also Daryl J. Bem, *Beliefs, Attitudes, and Human Affairs* (Belmont, CA: Brooks/Cole, 1970); and Stuart Oskamp, *Attitudes and Opinions* (Englewood Cliffs, NJ: Prentice-Hall, 1977).

7. Alice H. Eagly and Shelly Chaiken, "Attitude Structure and Function," in D. T. Gilbert, Susan T. Fiske, and G. Lindzey, eds., *Handbook of Social Psychology* (New York: McGraw-Hill, 1998), 269–322.

8. Icek Ajzen, "Nature and Operation of Attitudes," *Annual Review of Psychology* 52 (2001): 27–58; Martin Fishbein, "An Investigation of the Relationships between Beliefs about an Object and the Attitude toward That Object," *Human Relations*, 16, no. 3 (1963): 233–239.

9. Perloff, *Dynamics of Persuasion*; Milton J. Rosenberg and Robert P. Abelson, "An Analysis of Cognitive Balancing," in Milton J. Rosenberg et al., eds., *Attitude Organization and Change* (New Haven, CT: Yale University Press, 1960), 112–163; Steven J. Breckler, "Empirical Validation of Affect, Behavior, and Cognition as Distinct Components of Attitude," *Journal of Personality and Social Psychology* 47, no. 6 (1984): 1191–1205.

10. Bernard C. Hennessy, *Public Opinion*, 5th ed. (Belmont, CA: Brooks/Cole, 1985).

11. Louis Leon Thurstone and E. U. Chave, *The Measurement of Attitude* (Chicago: University of Chicago, 1929), 7.

12. Clark L. Hull, *Principles of Behavior: An Introduction to Behavior Theory* (New York: Appleton-Century-Crofts, 1943); Edward L. Thorndike, *The Fundamentals of Learning* (New York: Teacher's College Press, 1932).

13. I. P. Pavlov, *Conditioned Reflexes* (New York: Dover Publications, 1927/2003).

14. B. F. Skinner, *The Behavior of Organisms* (New York: Appleton-Century-Crofts, 1938).

15. Jodene R. Baccus, Mark W. Baldwin, and Dominic J. Packer, "Increasing Implicit Self-esteem through Classical Conditioning," *Psychological Science* 15, no. 7 (2004): 498–502. See also Christina Dalla and Tracey J. Shors, "Sex Differences in Learning Processes of Classical and Operant Conditioning," *Physiology & Behavior* 97, no. 2 (2009): 229–238.

16. Arthur W. Staats and Carolyn K. Staats, "Attitudes Established by Classical Conditioning," *Journal of Abnormal and Social Psychology* 57 (1958): 37–40. See also Arthur W. Staats, "Paradigmatic Behaviorism: Unified Theory for Social-Personality

Psychology," in Leonard Berkowitz, ed., *Advances in Experimental Social Psychology* (San Diego: Academic Press, 1983), 125–179.

17. Alice H. Eagly and Shelly Chaiken, *The Psychology of Attitudes* (Orlando, FL: Harcourt Brace Jovanovich, 1993).

18. Shmuel Lissek, Alice S. Powers, Erin B. McClure, Elizabeth A. Phelps, Girma Woldehawariat, Christian Grillon, and Daniel Pine, "Classical Fear Conditioning in the Anxiety Disorders: A Meta-analysis," *Behaviour Research and Therapy* 43, no. 11 (2005): 1391–1424.

19. Eagly and Chaiken, *Psychology of Attitudes*, 400.

20. Skinner, *Behavior of Organisms*.

21. See, e.g., Richard E. Petty and John T. Cacioppo, *Attitudes and Persuasion: Classic and Contemporary Approaches* (Dubuque, IA: William C. Brown, 1981).

22. Joel Greenspoon, "The Reinforcing Effect of Two Spoken Sounds on the Frequency of Two Responses," *American Journal of Psychology* 68 (1955): 409–416.

23. For example, see Leonard Krasner, "Studies of the Conditioning of Verbal Behavior," *Psychological Bulletin* 55 (1958): 148–170; Leonard Krasner, "The Therapist as a Social Reinforcement Machine," in Hans H. Strupp and Lester Luborsky, eds., *Research in Psychotherapy* (Washington, DC: American Psychological Association, 1962), 61–94; Leon H. Levy, "Awareness, Learning, and the Beneficent Subject as Expert Witness," *Journal of Personality and Social Psychology* 6 (1967): 365–370; and Richard D. Singer, "Verbal Conditioning and Generalization of Prodemocratic Responses," *Journal of Abnormal and Social Psychology* 63 (1961): 43–46.

24. Some of these studies are described in Petty and Cacioppo, *Attitudes and Persuasion*.

25. Richard E. Petty and John T. Cacioppo, "The Elaboration Likelihood Model of Persuasion," in Leonard Berkowitz, ed., *Advances in Experimental Social Psychology* (New York: Academic Press, 1986), 19:123–205.

26. Ibid., 128.

27. Richard E. Petty, Pablo Briñol, and Joseph R. Priester, "Mass Media Attitude Change: Implications of the Elaboration Likelihood Model of Persuasion," in Jennings Bryant and Mary Beth Oliver, eds., *Media Effects: Advances in Theory and Research*, 3rd ed. (New York: Routledge, 2009), 125–164. See also Shu-Hui Chen and Kuan-Ping Lee, "The Role of Personality Traits and Perceived Values in Persuasion: An Elaboration Likelihood Model Perspective on Online Shopping," *Social Behavior and Personality* 36, no. 10 (2008): 1379–1399.

28. Petty and Cacioppo, "Elaboration Likelihood Model," 192.

29. Eagly and Chaiken, *Psychology of Attitudes*, 323.

30. A classic discussion is Shelly Chaiken, "The Heuristic Model of Persuasion," in Mark P. Zanna, James M. Olson, and C. Peter Herman, eds., *Social Influence: The Ontario Symposium* (Hillsdale, NJ: Lawrence Erlbaum, 1987), 3–39.

31. Leon Festinger, *A Theory of Cognitive Dissonance* (Evanston, IL: Row, Peterson, 1957), esp. 11–15.

32. Fritz Heider, "Attitudes and Cognitive Organization," *Journal of Psychology* 21 (1946): 107–112.

33. Fritz Heider, *The Psychology of Interpersonal Relations* (New York: Wiley, 1958).

34. Jon A. Krosnick, "Psychological Perspectives on Political Candidate Perception: A Review of Research on the Projection Hypothesis" (paper presented at the meeting of the Midwest Political Science Association, Chicago, 1988).

35. Debra Z. Basil and Paul M. Herr, "Attitudinal Balance and Cause-related Marketing: An Empirical Application of Balance Theory," *Journal of Consumer Psychology* 16, no. 4 (2006): 391–403. See also Christian S. Crandall, Paul J. Silvia, Ahogni N. N'Gbala, Jo-Ann Tsang, and Karen Dawson, "Balance Theory, Unit Relations, and Attribution: The Underlying Integrity of Heiderian Theory," *Review of General Psychology* 11 (2007): 12–30, doi: 10.1037/1089-2680.11.1.12.

36. Charles E. Osgood and Percy H. Tannenbaum, "The Principle of Congruity in the Prediction of Attitude Change," *Psychological Review* 62 (1955): 42–55.

37. D. W. Rajecki, *Attitudes*, 2nd ed. (Sunderland, MA: Sinauer, 1990), 64.

38. Ahmet Usakli and Seyhmus Baloglu, "Brand Personality of Tourist Destinations: An Application of Self-congruity Theory," *Tourism Management* 32, no. 1 (2011): 114–127.

39. Alice H. Eagly and Steven J. Karau, "Role Congruity Theory of Prejudice toward Female Leaders," *Psychological Review* 109, no. 3 (2002): 573–598.

40. Richard M. Perloff, *The Dynamics of Persuasion* (Hillsdale, NJ: Lawrence Erlbaum, 1993).

41. Nikos L. D. Chatzisarantis, Martin S. Hagger, and John C. K. Wang, "An Experimental Test of Cognitive Dissonance Theory in the Domain of Physical Exercise," *Journal of Applied Sport Psychology* 20 (2008): 97–115.

42. For a review of cognitive dissonance theory research see Eddie Harmon-Jones and Cindy Harmon-Jones, "Cognitive Dissonance Theory after 50 Years of Development," *Zeitschrift für Sozialpsychologie* 38 (2007): 7–16.

43. George A. Akerlof and William T. Dickens, "The Economic Consequences of Cognitive Dissonance," *American Economic Review* 72, no. 3 (1982): 307–319.

44. Joel Cooper, Russell H. Fazio, and Frederick Rhodewalt, "Dissonance and Humor: Evidence for the Undifferentiated Nature of Dissonance Arousal," *Journal of Personality and Social Psychology* 36 (1978): 280–285; Joel Cooper, Mark P. Zanna, and Peter A. Taves, "Arousal as a Necessary Condition for Attitude Change Following Induced Compliance," *Journal of Personality and Social Psychology* 36 (1978): 1101–1106.

45. Petty and Cacioppo, *Attitudes and Persuasion*.

46. Philip Brickman, Dan Coates, and Ronnie Janoff-Bulman, "Lottery Winners and Accident Victims: Is Happiness Relative?" *Journal of Personality and Social Psychology* 36 (1978): 917–927; Muzafer Sherif and Carl I. Hovland, *Social Judgment: Assimilation and Contrast Effects in Communication and Attitude Change* (New Haven, CT: Yale University Press, 1961).

47. Eagly and Chaiken, *Psychology of Attitudes*, 368; Muzafer Sherif and Carolyn W. Sherif, "Attitude as the Individual's Own Categories: The Social Judgment-Involvement Approach to Attitude and Attitude Change," in Carolyn W. Sherif and Muzafer Sherif, eds., *Attitude, Ego-Involvement, and Change* (New York: Wiley, 1967), 130.

48. Daniel Katz, "The Functional Approach to the Study of Attitudes," *Public Opinion Quarterly* 24 (1960): 163–204.

49. Ibid., 170.

50. Ibid., 175.

51. Herbert C. Kelman, "Compliance, Identification and Internalization: Three Processes of Attitude Change," *Journal of Conflict Resolution* 2 (1958): 51–60.

52. Rajdeep Grewal, Raj Mehta, and Frank R. Kardes, "The Timing of Repeat Purchases of Consumer Durable Goods: The Role of Functional Bases of Consumer Attitudes," *Journal of Marketing Research* 41 (2004): 101–115.

53. M. Brewster Smith, Jerome S. Bruner, and Robert W. White, *Opinions and Personality* (New York: Wiley, 1956).

54. Erving Goffman, *The Presentation of Self in Everyday Life* (New York: Anchor Books, 1959); Robert M. Arkin, "Self-Presentation Styles," in James T. Tedeschi, ed., *Impression Management Theory and Social Psychological Theory* (London: Academic Press, 1981), 311–333.

55. James T. Tedeschi, Barry R. Schlenker, and Thomas V. Bonoma, "Cognitive Dissonance: Private Ratiocination or Public Spectacle," *American Psychologist* 26 (1971): 685–695.

56. Barry R. Schlenker, *Impression Management: The Self-Concept, Social Identity, and Interpersonal Relations* (Monterey, CA: Brooks/Cole, 1980), 204.

57. V. M. Desai, "Does Disclosure Matter? Integrating Organizational Learning and Impression Management Theories to Examine the Impact of Public Disclosure Following Failures," *Strategic Organization* 12, no. 2 (2014): 85–108.

58. A classic expression of skepticism is Allan W. Wicker, "Attitudes versus Actions: The Relationship of Verbal and Overt Behavioral Responses to Attitude Objects," *Journal of Social Issues* 25, no. 4 (1969): 41–79.

59. Herbert C. Kelman, "Attitudes Are Alive and Well and Gainfully Employed in the Sphere of Action," *American Psychologist* 29 (1974): 312.

60. See Shirley S. Ho and Douglas M. McLeod, "Social-psychological Influences on Opinion Expression in Face-to-Face and Computer-Mediated Communication," *Communication Research* 35, no. 2 (2008): 190–207.

61. Eagly and Chaiken, *Psychology of Attitudes*, 157.

62. Icek Ajzen, "The Directive Influence of Attitudes on Behavior," in Peter M. Gollwitzer and John A. Bargh, eds., *The Psychology of Action: Linking Cognition and Motivation to Behavior* (Guilford Press, 1996), 385–403.

63. Perloff, *Dynamics of Persuasion*.

64. Mark Snyder, *Public Appearances/Private Realities: The Psychology of Self-Monitoring* (New York: Freeman, 1987).

65. Perloff, *Dynamics of Persuasion*, 85.

66. Clifton M. Oyamot Jr., Paul T. Fuglestad, and Mark Snyder, "Balance of Power and Influence in Relationships: The Role of Self-Monitoring," *Journal of Social and Personal Relationships* 27 (2010): 23–46.

67. Russell H. Fazio and Mark P. Zanna, "Direct Experience and Attitude–Behavior Consistency," in *Advances in Experimental Social Psychology*, ed. Berkowitz, 161–202.

68. Jon A. Krosnick, "Attitude Importance and Attitude Accessibility," *Personality and Social Psychology Bulletin* 15 (1989): 297–308.

69. Russell H. Fazio and Carol J. Williams, "Attitude Accessibility as a Moderator of the Attitude–Perception and Attitude–Behavior Relations: An Investigation of the 1984 Presidential Election," *Journal of Personality and Social Psychology* 51 (1986): 505–514.

70. Icek Ajzen and Martin Fishbein, eds., *Understanding Attitudes and Predicting Social Behavior* (Englewood Cliffs, NJ: Prentice-Hall, 1980), 6.

71. Martin Fishbein and Icek Ajzen, "Acceptance, Yielding and Impact: Cognitive Processes in Persuasion," in Richard E. Petty, Thomas M. Ostrom, and Timothy C. Brock, eds., *Cognitive Responses in Persuasion* (Hillsdale, NJ: Lawrence Erlbaum, 1981), 339–359.

72. Martin Fishbein et al., "Predicting and Understanding Family Planning Behaviors: Beliefs, Attitudes, and Intentions," in Ajzen and Fishbein, *Understanding Attitudes*, 130–147.

73. Martin Fishbein and Icek Ajzen, "Predicting and Understanding Consumer Behavior: Attitude-Behavior Correspondence," in Ajzen and Fishbein, *Understanding Attitudes*, 148–172.

74. William James, *The Principles of Psychology* (New York: Holt, Rinehart and Winston, 1890).

75. Sandra Gonzalez-Bailon, Rafael E. Banchs, and Andreas Kaltenbrunner, "Emotions, Public Opinion, and US Presidential Approval Rates: A 5-Year Analysis of Online Political Discussions," *Human Communication Research* 38, no. 2 (2012): 121–143. See also Michael B. Petersen, Daniel Sznycer, Leda Cosmides, and John Tooby, "Who Deserves Help? Evolutionary Psychology, Social Emotions, and Public Opinion about Welfare," *Political Psychology* 33, no. 3 (2012): 395–418.

76. Robert B. Zajonc, "Feeling and Thinking: Preferences Need No Inferences," *American Psychologist* 35, no. 2 (Feb. 1980): 151–175.

77. Lyn Ragsdale, "Strong Feelings: Emotional Responses to Presidents," *Political Behavior* 13 (1991): 33–65.

78. Gonzalez-Balion, Banchs, and Kaltenbrunner, "Emotions, Public Opinion, and US Presidential Approval Rates."

79. Charles H. Cooley, *Human Nature and the Social Order* (New York: Scribner, 1902).

80. Rowland S. Miller and Mark R. Leary, "Social Sources and Interactive Functions of Emotion: The Case of Embarrassment," in Margaret S. Clark, ed., *Review of Personality and Social Psychology* (Newbury Park, CA: Sage Publications, 1992), 202–221.

81. Thomas J. Scheff, *Microsociology: Discourse, Emotion and Social Structure* (Chicago: University of Chicago Press, 1990).

82. See also Paula M. Niedenthal, Lawrence W. Barsalou, Piotr Winkielman, Silvia Krauth-Gruber, and Francois Ric, "Embodiment in Attitudes, Social Perception, and Emotion," *Personality and Social Psychology Review* 9, no. 3 (2005): 184–211; and Perrine Ruby and Jean Decety, "How Would You Feel Versus How Do You Think She Would Feel? A Neuroimaging Study of Perspective-Taking with Social Emotions," *Journal of Cognitive Neuroscience* 16, no. 6 (2004): 988–999.

83. Rowland S. Miller and Mark R. Leary, "Social Sources and Interactive Functions of Emotion: The Case of Embarrassment," in Clark, ed., *Review of Personality and Social Psychology*, 202–221.

84. See Ted Brader, George E. Marcus, and Kristyn L. Miller, "Emotion and Public Opinion," in George C. Edwards III, Lawrence R. Jacobs, and Robert Y. Shapiro, eds., *The Oxford Handbook of American Public Opinion and the Media* (London: Oxford University Press, 2011), 384–401.

85. Charles R. Darwin, *The Expression of the Emotions in Man and Animals* (London: Murray, 1972).

6

Stereotyping, Social Norms, and Public Opinion

Most of the models and theories of mental processes we covered in Chapter 5 discuss what may be going on in the mind of the individual. In this chapter we focus on how social forces affect public opinion formation and expression.

Regardless of how public opinion is measured or expressed, it is not formed in a social vacuum. People interact with and acquire information from each other and influence each other; they are socialized into particular ways of thinking about social problems, and they often feel constrained by norms or standards of "correct" behavior in our society. In recent years it has become clear to social scientists that public opinion processes are complex and that they should include the understanding of social and group influences on the formation and expression of public opinion. Dozens of social influences impact the public opinion process: culture, political affiliation, and socialization, for a start. Rather than attempt an encyclopedic approach to this area of research, we focus on two important ways in which our own beliefs about others affect public opinion: attribution theory and stereotyping. Then we consider at length how social norms can also affect the opinions we form and the ways in which we express those opinions.

Group identity is a crucial theme of this chapter. You probably belong to many groups. You are a member of your family, of a racial or ethnic group, of a gender group, of a social class, of a neighborhood, of a larger community. You may belong to a sorority or fraternity and to any number of clubs. You may root for a favorite football or basketball team; you may belong to a group that supports a musician, television show, or actor. Many of these affiliations, and others like them, may never cross your mind; others may occur to you only in certain circumstances. But surely you think of yourself as belonging to some groups and

141

not belonging to others. These affiliations often have important consequences for public opinion. Even if people were oblivious to group identity, social dynamics would still pervade our opinions.

ATTRIBUTION THEORY

When you meet somebody, you may wonder: What is this person like? What does this person want? Or you may immediately form an impression: this person is nice, that one is trying to lie to me; this one is smart; that one . . . not so much; this person enjoys hearing other points of view; that one just hates to lose an argument. And so on. Human beings tend to make these *attributions* about other people's characteristics and motivations. Such attributions help people decide how to behave—for better or for worse, depending on how accurate the attributions are. Attributions also can influence our other attitudes. We tend to agree with people we trust and to disagree with people we distrust.

Attribution theories describe how people's inferences about the reasons behind others' behaviors or attitudes affect their own agreement with these behaviors or attitudes. Generally, attribution theories posit that people infer each other's underlying characteristics, including others' motivations and intentions, from the verbal and nonverbal behaviors they observe. Thus, "when there appears to be an obvious reason for some behavior, people confidently attribute that behavior to that cause."[1]

In Alice Eagly and Shelly Chaiken's account of attribution theory, people are likely to be persuaded by a message to the extent that they see it as conveying the "truth." They will discount the message if they attribute it "to factors that compromise truth value."[2] For example, most people are more likely to believe that aspirin may help prevent heart attacks if they see that information on a news program than if they see it in an aspirin advertisement. Loosely speaking, people often assume that advertisers have an interest in selling their product, not in telling the truth about it, whereas they may think that the news media are more likely to be interested in getting the story right. (However, in recent years confidence in the accuracy of the news media has waned considerably.)

Eagly and Chaiken point out that in evaluating messages, we may consider not only the identity of the speaker but also salient "contextual cues" such as the "communicator's personal circumstances and the audience the communicator is addressing."[3] Advertisers often pay popular celebrities to endorse various products. Attribution theory suggests that people may find these messages persuasive if they rely on their positive opinions of the celebrities, but are not likely to be persuaded if they consider that the celebrities are in fact being paid to sell the products. These ads also can be seen as persuasive if viewers think that the celebrities are sincere. (Or they may influence opinions through operant conditioning: people may "like" a product because they learn to associate it with a celebrity they like, regardless of what the celebrity thinks of the product.)

More recent work on attribution theory has focused on evaluating messages about health and safety. Rains, for example, investigated the impact of anonymity on the credibility of messages posted on a health information Web site.[4] Polk used attribution theory to better understand the communication patterns that emerge between health care providers and family members of a patient.[5] Other research demonstrates that support for same-sex marriage is more likely if homosexuality is deemed to be biological rather than controllable.[6]

In evaluating the truth value of a message we may try to ascertain the reason the communicator is conveying the information and why we are the targets of the message. For example, in the case of product advertising, we may believe that the company is communicating with us in order to encourage us to buy a product and that we are targets of the message because we have the resources (namely, money) that the company wants.

Research has found that people's attributions tend to be biased. One such bias is so ubiquitous that it is called the *fundamental attribution error*: people are too quick to attribute other people's behavior, both positive and negative, to personality rather than circumstances. For example, when people are told that someone donated blood, they tend to think of the donor as unusually generous. In reality, people's decisions to donate blood tend to have more to do with circumstance than with their character. For example, people are far more likely to donate blood if a blood drive is organized at their place of work or if somebody directly asks them to give.

We also tend to attribute others' negative behavior to personality traits. For example, when driving, if other drivers have wandered into your lane, you may have found yourself jumping to conclusions about their habitual carelessness, even if you have never seen them before. Those assumptions may be quite wrong, but probably harmlessly so; they may even lead you to drive more safely. However, jumping to invidious (or favorable) conclusions about strangers may not always be harmless. Faulty attributions can be especially problematic in the context of group-based stereotypes.

STEREOTYPING

Originally, around 1800, a stereotype was a metal plate used for printing. (The root "stereo" comes from the Greek word for "solid.") A stereotype, then, was a model used to produce many practically identical copies. Stereotypes were also called clichés, apparently in reference to a "click" as the plates were produced. The literal meaning of these words is almost forgotten, but they thrive as metaphors.

Walter Lippmann, in his 1922 book *Public Opinion*,[7] probably was the first to use *stereotype* in roughly its modern meaning: "a generalization based on category membership."[8] Lippmann, quoting the psychologist William James, argued that an "unfamiliar scene is like the baby's world, 'one great, blooming, buzzing confusion,'"[9] and that people generally make sense of what they see by relying on their previously existing categories. For example, he says, suppose that a man is unfamiliar with landscapes apart from paintings of rosy sunsets. When the man actually sees a rosy sunset, he will recognize it as a beautiful landscape. But when he thinks of it a few days later, he will mostly remember the paintings, not the sunset itself. "We do not so much see this man and that sunset; rather we notice that the thing is man or sunset, and then see chiefly what our mind is already full of on those subjects."

The very notion of stereotypes probably evokes a negative image in your mind. Typically we think of stereotypes as bad, and we fear that if we stereotype we are being narrow-minded or bigoted. In fact, this is not always the case. Stereotypes are very complex, often containing both positive and negative elements. Walter Lippmann argued that, in some sense, stereotyping is a necessary condition for functioning in the world:

> There is neither time nor opportunity for intimate acquaintance. Instead, we notice a trait which marks a well-known type, and fill in the rest of the picture by means of the stereotypes we carry about in our heads. He is an agitator. That much we notice, or are told. Well, an agitator is this sort of person, and so he is this sort of person. He is an intellectual. He is a plutocrat. He is a foreigner. He is a "South European." He is from Back Bay. He is a Harvard Man. How different from the statement: he is a Yale Man. He is a regular fellow. He is a West Pointer. He is an old army sergeant. He is a Greenwich Villager: what don't we know about him then, and about her? He is an international banker. He is from Main Street.[10]

Despite the drawbacks of stereotypes, Lippmann argued that their use is both inevitable and in some ways helpful:

> We are told about the world before we see it. We imagine most things before we experience them. . . . Were there no practical uniformities in the environment,

there would be no economy and only error in the human habit of accepting foresight for sight. But there are uniformities sufficiently accurate, and the need of economizing attention is so inevitable, that the abandonment of all stereotypes for a whole innocent approach to experience would impoverish human life.[11]

One of the most fascinating and elaborate stereotypes ever developed was the so-called criminal type. Many fiction writers, average people, and even criminologists of the late nineteenth and early twentieth centuries believed one could tell a criminal by physical appearance alone (see Box 6.1).

BOX 6.1
Lombroso's Criminal Types

The nineteenth-century Italian doctor Cesare Lombroso popularized the idea of a "criminal type." His theory was inspired by Charles Darwin's studies of evolution, then a novel idea, and the beliefs in "higher" and "lower" races that were also popular at the time. Lombroso argued that many criminals were actually genetic throwbacks to earlier evolutionary stages. These people were uncivilized and uncivilizable—born to a life of crime.[1]

Lombroso remains famous, or infamous, for his generalizations about born criminals' physical characteristic. He argued that many criminals had physical features reminiscent of those found in apes and other animals:

Thus was explained the origin of the enormous jaws, strong canines . . . and strongly developed orbital arches [brow line] which he had so frequently remarked in criminals, for these peculiarities are common to carnivores and savages who tear and devour raw flesh. Thus also it was easy to understand why the span of the arms in criminals so often exceeds the height, for this is a characteristic of apes. . . . The other anomalies exhibited by criminals—the scanty beard as opposed to the general hairiness of the body, prehensile foot, diminished number of lines in the palm of the hand, cheek pouches, enormous development of middle incisors and frequent absence of the lateral ones, flattened nose and angular or sugar-loaf form of the skull, common to criminals and apes; the excessive size of the orbits [eye sockets], which, combined with the hooked nose, so often imparts to criminals the aspect of a

(continues)

(continued)

BOX 6.1
Lombroso's Criminal Types

bird of prey, the . . . supernumerary teeth (amounting in some cases to a double row as in snakes) . . . all these characteristics pointed to one conclusion[:] the . . . criminal . . . reproduces physical, psychic, and functional qualities of remote ancestors.[2]

Criminals supposedly had sharp teeth, like rats, and, Lombroso claimed, some had the vestiges of a tail. They were more likely to be left-handed than "normal" people. It is from Lombroso's work that we derive the old saying that criminals have "shifty" eyes, "difficult to describe but . . . nevertheless apparent to all observers."[3]

Lombroso even argued that one could tell which sorts of crimes a born criminal might commit by looking at his or her physical characteristics:

The lips of violators of women and murderers are fleshy, swollen, and protruding. . . . Swindlers have thin, straight lips. . . . Dark hair prevails especially in murderers, and curly or woolen hair in swindlers. . . . Those guilty of crimes against the person have short, clumsy fingers and especially short thumbs. Long fingers are common to swindlers, thieves, sexual offenders, and pickpockets.[4]

Writers of both fiction and nonfiction became fascinated with this vision of the born criminal, and echoes of Lombroso's work appear in many popular works of that era, including Sherlock Holmes stories. Even today, fictional villains often have many of the characteristics of the "born criminal."

---

[1] Leonard D. Savitz, introduction to Gina Lombroso-Ferrero, *Criminal Man According to the Classification of Cesare Lombroso* (1911; Montclair, NJ: Patterson Smith, 1972); Lombroso-Ferrero, *Criminal Man According to the Classification of Cesare Lombroso.*

[2] Lombroso-Ferrero, *Criminal Man According to the Classification of Cesare Lombroso,* 7–8.

[3] Ibid., 14.

[4] Ibid., 14, 18, 20.

Cognitive Function of Stereotypes

Stereotypes are a "cognitive consolidation" of how the world works. They are so fundamental to the way that we make sense of the world that we often do not realize we are using them at all. Just think: every time you observe, "Men would rather die than ask directions" or "Politicians are corrupt," you are making use of stereotypes. The alternative to using stereotypes is to treat each individual as a unique person, having nothing in common with anyone else. In other words, stereotypes are necessary if we are going to generalize about others. Without stereotypes, we cannot even begin to discuss culture, which reflects a group's shared characteristics and behaviors. For example, we can talk about an "American" culture, which may include "African American" culture, "Asian American" culture, and "Irish American" culture. Our generalizations about these cultures should be cautious rather than absolute, but not to generalize at all seems too austere. At the same time, as Lippmann further argues, we need to consider the "gullibility with which we employ" stereotypes.[12] We must realize that our stereotypes are merely that, and we should be willing to change these viewpoints when we find out that they are inaccurate. We should also adjust our stereotypes when we find that by using them, we are hurting others or are misusing stereotypes to our benefit.

Researchers note that today, stereotypes most often refer to "socially shared sets of beliefs about traits that are characteristic of members of a social category."[13] Social psychologist Mark Snyder elaborates: "In stereotyping, the individual: (1) categorizes other individuals, usually on the basis of highly visible characteristics such as sex or race; (2) attributes a set of characteristics to all members of that category; and (3) attributes that set of characteristics to any individual member of that category."[14] Crucially, stereotypes are *socially shared* by many people. That is, people in a society may accept a particular stereotype, both in the language they use to describe a social group and in how they treat its members. Indeed, research from Clark and Kashima demonstrates that when stereotypes are seen as widely accepted by society, people are more likely to communicate those stereotypes to others.[15] Often these stereotypes come to us from what we are told by other people or by the media, rather than through direct experience. For example, Dixon has found that people who view more network news are more likely to endorse common stereotypes, which in turn influence support for the death penalty.[16] Other research shows that depictions of racial and gender stereotypes generate quicker responses to negative terms, such as "aggressive," than positive terms, such as "sincere."[17] These effects are demonstrated in non-news content as well. One recent study demonstrated that a comedy film can also encourage the audience to naturalize racial differences instead of challenging stereotypes.[18]

A recent polarizing event provides a vivid and disturbing example of how negative stereotypes can result in a catastrophic series of events. After Darren Wilson, a Ferguson, Missouri, police officer, fatally shot Michael Brown, an unarmed, eighteen-year-old African American teenager, in August 2014, the story quickly spread on traditional and social media. On traditional media, the first circulated image of Brown showed him holding his hands in a position that some perceived as a gang sign.[19] Shortly thereafter, Twitter user CJ Lawrence created the Twitter hashtag #iftheygunnedmedown and posted two photos of himself: one that was racially stereotypical and one that was not. In the nonstereotypical picture, he is speaking at his college graduation with President Clinton behind him. In the other, he poses with a bottle of liquor. His question is: "Which photo [do] the media use if the police shot me down?"[20] The hashtag quickly became a trending topic on Twitter and demonstrated the all-too-frequent reliance on stereotypical images of African Americans in the news, which, as shown in Dixon's research, has negative effects on viewers' perceptions of African Americans. This hashtag, along with others, propelled the story into a national and international spotlight and resulted in numerous protests and riots, which some authorities blamed squarely on social media.[21] This event, along with many other examples, demonstrates the role of the media (in their many forms) as conveyor and portrayer of stereotypes—and of public opinion. (See Chapter 11 for more on public opinion and the media.)

The concept of *social identity* helps us understand stereotypes. Social identity is a "definition of the self in terms of group membership shared with other people."[22] The main thrust behind social identity is that people develop perceptions of themselves based on the groups and categories with which they identify.[23] In other words, one's identity is developed through "actual or symbolic perceived affiliation with others who share similar experiences, perceptions, and values."[24] In contrast, *personal identity* refers to individual traits that are unique, while social identity is derived from affiliation with social groups, from religious organizations to sports teams to fan fiction.[25]

Individuals "fit" themselves into various groups, often depending on the context. For example, a student from Mississippi might identify as "southern" in a conversation with students from the North, but simply as "American" when interacting with people from other countries. Most in-group identities imply out-groups: someone is southern, not northern; someone is American, not French. However, the salience of out-groups varies across people and circumstances. (Most Americans, most of the time, are not very invested in being not-French.)

Typically, the more strongly people identify with a group, the more group members agree with each other's opinions. Moreover, communication among in-group members tends to increase agreement with stereotypes, especially about the in-group, but also about out-groups.[26] Both in-group and out-group stereotypes may be positive, negative, neutral, or mixed. For example, Green-wald and Banaji note that the stereotype of cheerleaders may "simultaneously include the traits of being physically attractive (positive) and unintelligent (neg-ative)."[27] However, people do tend to hold positive stereotypes of in-groups and negative stereotypes of out-groups. For example, you may think of members of your sorority as "highly intelligent" and members of a nearby sorority as "all about the partying"—and members of that sorority may think exactly the opposite.

Daniel Katz and Kenneth Braly[28] were among the first to study the stereo-types people hold concerning specific social groups. In a 1933 study, they asked college students to select, from a long list, adjectives that they considered typical of various groups such as Jews, Irish, and Turks. Then each respondent chose the five adjectives that seemed most characteristic of each group. Katz and Brady found often high levels of agreement. For example, 79 percent of respondents characterized Jews as "shrewd"; large numbers chose "mercenary," "industri-ous," "grasping," and "intelligent." The Irish were widely characterized as "pug-nacious," "quick-tempered," "witty," "honest," and "very religious." Turks were most often characterized as "cruel." In almost every case, the stereotypes were a mix of positive, negative, and ambiguous adjectives, yet they tended to be consis-tent: no group was seen, say, as both "lazy" and "industrious."

Reading lists of stereotypes from over eighty years ago, one might imagine that our society has moved on—and certainly in some ways it has. But we are far from dispensing with stereotypes altogether, if that is even imaginable. Ask a friend, acquaintance, or parent to say whatever words or phrases come to mind when you refer to "Asians" or "veterans" or "football players" or "blacks" or "un-documented immigrants." People are unlikely to be at a loss for words, although they may be reluctant to say some of them. (Even positive stereotypes can be embarrassing.) Moreover, much research indicates that even people who ver-bally reject stereotypes often are influenced by them, perhaps unconsciously. For example, there is wide evidence that employers are influenced by racial, ethnic, gender, and class stereotypes in hiring decisions. Scholars from a variety of disci-plines have concluded that employers often conform to gender stereotypes in making decisions about hiring, even when those stereotypes are inaccurate. One study demonstrated these inaccuracies, showing that in some domains, females applying for jobs that are stereotypically associated with males had higher levels of skills than male applicants.[29] Often, people not only perceive that others possess certain stereotypical traits but also act toward individuals or groups of people as if they possess these traits. In fact, researchers have found that stereotypes can be "self-fulfilling prophecies" through a process called *behavioral confirmation*. According to D. W. Rajecki, behavioral confirmation occurs "when a holder of a stereotype behaves consistently with that attitude and elicits the expected behavior from" the individual about whom the attitude is held, whether or not the individual being stereotyped "really has a personal disposition to act in that fashion."[30] Behavioral confirmation can have wide-ranging effects in the real world. For example, whatever group stereotypes teachers may hold about their students are likely to affect how they treat them, and in turn, how those students perform.

Stereotypes are also used unconsciously as we determine whom to be friends with or whom to date. In a classic study, Mark Snyder, Elizabeth Tanke, and Ellen Berscheid[31] investigated behavioral confirmation of the social stereotype that attractive people have more socially desirable traits. The researchers placed men and women in separate rooms, explaining that they would be interacting socially with each other on the telephone and that the researchers would be "studying the acquaintance process." Before the telephone conversations, the researchers asked these men and women to write down general background information on a form, stating that the forms were to be exchanged as an aid to getting acquainted.

Each man received a woman's form with a photograph attached. The women, however, only received the form. Each man naturally assumed that the photograph was of the woman he would talk to on the telephone, but in reality it was the picture of a paid model. Moreover, half of the men were given photographs of women who had been rated (by other college-age men) as highly attractive; the other half received photos with low attractiveness ratings. Based on this information and misinformation, before the conversations even occurred, the men reported their initial impressions of the women. The supposedly more attractive women were considered "comparatively sociable, poised, humorous and socially adept" relative to the supposedly less attractive women.[32]

After ten-minute phone conversations, twelve "observer judges" listened to recordings of the conversations and rated the women on various scales. The results gave strong evidence of behavioral confirmation. For example, the observer judges—who had seen neither the women nor the misleading photographs—rated the supposedly more attractive women as manifesting "greater confidence, greater animation, greater enjoyment of the conversation, and greater liking for their partners."[33] Evidently the men had treated the women differently based on their expectations, and the women had responded to those differences.

Another, more recent study asserted that physically attractive people are expected to be more extroverted and friendly than less attractive people. This study concluded that the "beautiful is better" stereotype does indeed exist; people are more likely to want to know more physically attractive people and will work harder to get to know them.[34] This stereotype persists even in an online environment. A study found that more attractive photos garnered higher ratings of those users' profiles.[35]

Other Functions of Stereotypes

Just as theorists have reasoned about the functions of attitudes (see Chapter 5), they have considered the various functions of stereotypes. So far we have emphasized the *cognitive* function: helping people make sense of their world (although not always accurately). Tajfel[36] describes other functions, both individual and social, that can inform our understanding of public opinion.

Evaluative Function. Stereotypes can directly influence a person's value system and self-perception. Consider the Boy Scouts' "Scout Law," which states: "A Scout is trustworthy, loyal, helpful, friendly, courteous, kind," and so on. A Scout who accepts these characteristics as stereotypes probably will take pride in belonging to a group of virtuous people. He may well also try to live up to the standard, although in Scouting as elsewhere, belief that one's group is virtuous does not always lead to virtuous behavior.

Many stereotypes assert the superiority of the in-group and stigmatize out-groups. For example, in the United States immigrants often have been stereotyped as lazy drunkards who do not appreciate the importance of hard work and thrift. An individual who accepts this stereotype affirms the value of work and thrift *and* his or her superiority to immigrants. A recent study demonstrates the effects of such stereotypes, concluding that such negative stereotypes result in negative attitudes toward immigrant groups.[37]

As Lippmann summed up in 1922, "A pattern of stereotypes . . . is the guarantee of our self-respect; it is the projection upon the world of our own sense of our own value, our own position and our own rights. [Our] stereotypes . . . are the fortress of our tradition, and behind its defenses we can continue to feel ourselves safe in the position we occupy." People do not easily question their assumptions about Us versus Them.

Social Causality. According to Tajfel, social causality is the search for a shared understanding of "complex and usually distressing large-scale social events." It typically results in "scapegoating," in which out-groups are seen as the cause of the distress.[38] For example, many denizens of Oxford, England, in the seventeenth century, trying to account for a plague outbreak, blamed it on Catholic sorcery. It may seem bizarre to call that attribution "functional"; the people of Oxford would have been far better off if they had correctly traced the plague to poor sanitation and a lack of quarantine practices. But even wrong explanations can provide some satisfaction.

Baumeister and Bushman talk about *scapegoating theory*, the process by which people tend to blame their problems on certain out-groups, and this blaming subsequently leads to increased negative feelings toward that group (even when the blame is unfounded). This dynamic can obviously create tension between different groups. Baumeister and Bushman cite the example of Jews being blamed for the death of Jesus, although it was actually the Romans—who later became Christians—who killed Jesus.[39]

Public opinion about economic problems in the United States has been directed against undocumented immigrants, particularly from Mexico, for "taking" American jobs (even though many of the jobs undocumented immigrants do are not ones that Americans want to do). Politicians also rely on scapegoating discrete sections of the American population as out-groups in order to increase their chances of political success. While there may be some connection between economic difficulties and immigration, and other attacks may likewise have some partial factual basis, it is clear that social causality is at work to the extent that blame is placed on others rather than on aspects of our own system that might explain the situation.

Social Justification. Sometimes stereotypes are used to justify actions against a particular group. As an example, Tajfel describes how colonial powers constructed derogatory stereotypes of the natives in countries they occupied. As Hogg and Abrams[40] note, such stereotypes can make a group's "exploitation seem justified, natural and unproblematic" to the exploiters.

In the United States, a strong and very popular segment of the music industry at the end of the nineteenth and the beginning of the twentieth centuries took a decidedly racist turn, aimed at maintaining status differentials and segregation between whites and African Americans, with heavy use of derogatory stereotypes in lyrics and titles in such chart-topping "Coon songs" as "Stay in Your Own Backyard," "Mammy's Little Piccaninny Boy," and "All Coons Look Alike to Me." Songs like these helped reinforce existing laws and social rules that segregated African Americans, kept them from voting, and prevented them from joining unions or obtaining many kinds of jobs.

Since September 11, 2001, the world has seen a rise in terrorist attacks around the world and many of these attacks have been attributed to followers of Islam. This assumption has often been, and continues to be, caricatured in American films and television programs. Villains in these narratives are often portrayed as Muslim or brown-skinned men, who are ultimately thwarted by Americans. This stereotypical dramatization of a real-world problem provides a degree of social justification to US government attempts to contain terrorism, which has resulted in a limitation of civil liberties for Arab and Muslim men.

Social Differentiation. If group-based stereotypes can confer the evaluative benefits that we described above, then clearly group members have a common stake in setting their group apart from out-groups or society at large. Stereotypes can serve this function of social differentiation. Certainly the popularity of "Coon songs" can be understood in part as bolstering white identity (differentiation) as well as justification. The reaction to rock and roll in the 1950s is perhaps a purer example of differentiation. White teenagers flocked to performances of black music by white and black performers. Both performers and audiences danced in ways that were widely seen as sexual, vulgar, and transgressive. In response, educators and parents joined forces in denigrating African influences on popular music, calling it the "devil's music." On national television in 1956, Steve Allen appeared to ridicule—or perhaps attempted to domesticate—Elvis Presley's performance of "Hound Dog" (a song first written for and recorded by African American blues singer Big Mama Thornton) by having Elvis perform the song in a tuxedo, singing to a real hound dog. Such efforts to differentiate polite white culture from suspect influences seem instead to have fostered the "generation gap" between teenagers and their hopelessly "square" parents.

The implications of social differentiation for public opinion formation, though potentially vital, have not been researched in any consistent fashion. It is difficult at best to study social change closely over an extended period of time. Many scholars believe that the failed backlash against rock music in the 1950s, and the generational differentiation it entailed, contributed to political and social protests in the 1960s. But even if people can agree in principle about what kinds of evidence could be used to test this idea, it would be difficult to gather such evidence half a century later.

In general, the effects of stereotyping on public opinion have been under-studied by scholars, but our discussion should give you some idea of the major impact this human tendency may have on public opinion outcomes.

SOCIAL NORMS

Webster's defines a norm as "a principle of right action binding upon the members of a group and serving to guide, control and regulate proper and acceptable behavior."[41] Hogg and Abrams define norms more broadly, as "the stereotypic perceptions, beliefs, and modes of conduct associated with a group."[42] That is, norms influence how we behave and how we interpret other people's behavior. For example, take a look at how we communicate on the social network Facebook. It's perfectly normal for someone to post good news about his or her family, career, or social life. Rarely do we see people only posting bad news (and if we do, we might choose to hide that person!). This is the norm of the social network. Yet when you are having dinner with a close friend, you may disclose more "bad news" than you would in your Facebook profile. These norms of communication vary across media and even with different types of people.

Interest in social norms dates back to the late nineteenth century, when scholars began attempting to measure the force of custom and tradition on society[43] and began investigating social control mechanisms.[44] In a widely held view, social norms "arise to govern and ensure smooth and predictable social interaction and thus enable society to exist as a cohesive and stable entity. Norms suppress strife and conflict by furnishing consensus and agreement on an acceptable modus operandum for social life."[45] Yet as we will discuss, social norms can be changeable and contested.

Just as attitude research has undergone harsh criticism, skeptics argue that social norms are vaguely defined and lend themselves to "Just-So stories" rather than good measurement and prediction.[46] Frankly, social science's predictive ability is weak with or without the concept of social norms; as Yogi Berra pointed out, it's tough to make predictions, especially about the future. Nevertheless, we find the concept of social norms invaluable for thinking about public opinion processes, as well as for understanding what many researchers have to say about those processes.

Social norms can exist not only for behaviors but also for attitudes, opinions, and tendencies toward certain behaviors.[47] Current scholarship applies the idea of social norms as predictors of behaviors, particularly in the context of health communication campaigns.[48] For example, some programs on college campuses aimed at reducing binge drinking and other risky behaviors examine social norms associated with consuming alcohol.[49]

Descriptive and Injunctive Norms

Cialdini, Kallgren, and Reno distinguish two types of social norms: descriptive norms and injunctive norms.[50] *Descriptive norms* characterize what most people commonly do. *Injunctive norms* characterize what most people approve or disapprove—what ought to be done. In short, descriptive norms have an informational function, whereas injunctive norms have a sanctioning function. More recently, Cialdini concluded that ignoring the role of descriptive social norms has consequences for citizens and authorities.[51] Moreover, although most successful health campaigns are focused on descriptive norms, it may actually be that injunctive norms are more likely to predict antisocial behavior because of their punitive associations.[52] Other research confirms that descriptive norms may not exert a direct influence on behavior, but perceived benefits and perceived similarity can have moderating effects.[53]

Descriptive norms motivate people by providing evidence of effective or appropriate actions. Imagine yourself in an unfamiliar situation—perhaps trying sushi for the first time—watching the people around you for cues about what to do. Other people's behaviors and opinions offer information not only about their social expectations, but to some extent about how the wider world works: what classes are most worthwhile, whether and when to marry, what to think about various political and social issues. Leon Festinger's social comparison theory suggests that descriptive norms play a crucial role in allowing people to validate opinions that cannot readily be tested against physical reality.[54] Festinger wrote in 1950 that "where the dependence upon physical reality is low the dependence upon social reality is correspondingly high. An opinion, a belief, an attitude is 'correct,' 'valid,' and 'proper' to the extent that it is anchored in a group of people with similar beliefs, opinions and attitudes."[55] Thus, descriptive norms play an important role in opinion formation.

In contrast, injunctive norms specify what ought to be done; they are the "moral rules of the group."[56] Obviously, injunctive norms can affect our opinions. Moreover, they can affect expression of public opinion through a phenomenon known as "social desirability": by informing our judgments of whether it is inappropriate or risky to reveal some aspect of our opinions.[57] We have all found ourselves "biting our tongues" not to say something that would be true but unhelpful, and this behavior carries through to survey research.[58] A clever 1991 study found that over half of white respondents felt anger toward "black leaders asking for affirmative action," but many of them would not have said so if asked directly. [59] For them, the injunctive norm against racism affects what they say, quite apart from what they think (although it may affect that, too). Descriptive and injunctive norms do have an effect on each other. One study found that when a negative descriptive norm for healthy eating was made salient, those exposed to a positive injunctive norm reported less intention to engage in healthy behaviors.[60]

Generating Norms

Some social norms, in Hogg and Abrams's words, "are so pervasive and so saturate society that they are 'taken for granted' and are invisible,"[61] except perhaps on rare occasions when they are challenged. Most Americans take the norm against public nudity for granted. Other norms, however, develop and change frequently, such as norms about appropriate skirt lengths for women. Skirt length is hardly a "principle of right action" as in the *Webster's* definition, but a woman whose skirt violates the prevailing norm is likely to be treated as if she has done something wrong. Of course, norms can be particular to groups or cultures. Women sunbathing topless in America violates a social norm. Women sunbathing topless in Norway does not.

Some of the earliest studies of group norms explored the ways in which such norms develop. Sherif conducted the first social psychological studies of norms.[62] His classic experiments took advantage of what is called the "autokinetic phenomenon." Subjects shown a point of light in a darkened room, with no point of reference for it, will perceive the light to be moving even though it is stationary. Sherif showed such a light to groups of experimental subjects. He found that in this situation, people interacted socially to resolve the ambiguity of the light "movement." Eventually, members of the group "converged upon a consensual group decision concerning the supposed movement of the light."[63]

When social norms are in flux, people often are uncomfortable. The historian Ken Cmiel has documented how the civil rights movement, the "hippies," and others challenged prevailing norms of politeness—for example, the norm that much public space should be for whites only. Cmiel argues that these challenges led to an informalization of American culture, entailing less conformity to rigid standards of behavior and appearance and greater acceptance of diversity.[64] In 1950 it was generally considered rude for men to wear long hair. Now, it is generally considered rude to react to the length of men's hair. The authors are young enough to smile at that example, but old enough to remember our surprise when facial piercings became common and to wince—not visibly, we hope—when a young cashier says "no problem" instead of "you're welcome."

Of course, that discomfort demands nothing of us, except perhaps not to take (or give) gratuitous offense. Other changing norms entail more social negotiation. With the rise of the women's rights movement, the social norm that men should open and hold doors for women became the focus of wide-ranging private and public debate. Did door-holding evince courtesy and respect? Did it reek of sexist condescension? Was it appropriate in some circumstances and not in others? Some people complained about the triviality of the discussion: Did it really matter who holds doors for whom, when? It did, not because the stakes were high, but because so many people regularly confronted the situation.

It may seem from our discussion so far that social norms are universal within a society, albeit changeable. Clearly they are not. Indeed, often they are coterminous with various groups: one group holds one set of norms, another holds a completely different set of norms. The conflict view of norms sees society as a "heterogenous collection of different groups of different sizes which stand in power and status relations to each other."[65] In this view, norms more generally serve the function of social differentiation that Tajfel ascribed to stereotypes: they provide a basis for unity within groups and distinction between groups.

Social Norms and Public Opinion

Many scholars conclude that social norms can play an important part in opinion formation and expression. In an influential 1930s study, Theodore Newcomb found evidence that women from a conservative background who attended Bennington College were rapidly influenced by the liberal political, economic, and social norms of that college.[66] For example, he found that "conservative" juniors who were members of sororities with liberal seniors rapidly conformed to the more liberal norms. In a follow-up study in 1960–1961, Newcomb found that these changes generally had endured.[67] To be sure, one might account for these changes without invoking norms at all. (For example, one can say that the younger students were persuaded by arguments that they hadn't previously encountered.) Whatever theoretical framework one adopts, something of lasting importance happened to those students within a few years, and similar processes presumably work on other people's opinions.

Recent changes in public opinion can also demonstrate the role that social norms play. For example, in 2004 many states, including Ohio, Oregon, and Missouri, introduced constitutional amendments to define marriage as being between a man and a woman. By 2011 American public opinion had turned, so that more people expressed favorability toward same-sex marriage than opposed it.[68] This is born out by recent research, which demonstrates that new social norms, in the form of an Iowa state court decision establishing same-sex marriage, have pressured residents to modify their negative attitudes.[69] A similar shift is occurring in the debate over legalization of marijuana. These changes in social norms demonstrate a gradual, but significant, shift in public opinion that results in real policy change.

It is clear that norms fulfill a critical function for the individual: "They simplify, render predictable, and regulate social interaction. Without them social life would be unbearably complex and stressful: the individual would collapse beneath the tremendous cognitive overload involved in interaction."[70] But how can norms help us understand public opinion formation and expression? Social norms can provide a common perspective from which to view social conditions. Emile Durkheim, who viewed society as consensual, called such common perspectives "collective representations." Serge Moscovici, who focused on the conflict view of society, called them "social representations." Moscovici notes that we derive only a small fraction of our knowledge and information from direct interactions between ourselves and the world.[71] Instead, most of our knowledge is supplied to us by communication, which affects our way of thinking and creates new content via social representations. According to Moscovici, then, social representations refer to the ideas, thoughts, images, and knowledge that members of a collectivity share.[72]

Through these representations, members of a society are able to construct "social reality."[73] As a society, for example, we may choose to act on certain social problems and to not act on others. For the most part, our shared perceptions of these problems (our social representations) determine the amount of effort we put into their resolution. Thus, to the extent that our perceptions of certain issues and events are similar, we can talk about a specific social problem. These social problems become public issues that can be debated and discussed and that eventually may be slated for public action. To the extent that we all share these perceptions, our society can coordinate its efforts and set priorities. The more we share similar perceptions, the more likely we are to agree on social problems and their solutions.

While many researchers construe norms as emerging from the majority, some research, such as that conducted by Moscovici, explores minority influences on norms. In an influential early study on color perceptions in small groups, Moscovici and his colleagues[74] enlisted two confederates per group to say that blue disks were actually green. Not only were other members more likely to say that the disks were green than if no confederates were present, but they measurably adjusted their subsequent color judgments toward perceiving more disks as green. If a consistent minority can persuade others to change their definitions of "green," presumably they can influence other social norms, at least under some circumstances. Indeed, in later work Moscovici and Willem Doise[75] found that when small groups discussed controversial issues, participants often tended to move *away* from their initial average position toward a more extreme position, what Moscovici and Doise called *group polarization*. You may have seen a similar dynamic in real life. If some people argue forcefully for a controversial position, and others are more moderate or ambivalent, the "zealots" seem more likely to persuade the moderates (at least to some extent) than vice versa. Of course, it is not always obvious whether the moderates are persuaded or just shrug and go along in order to end the argument. But Moscovici and Doise found evidence of real and lasting opinion change. Recent research from Mannix and Neale shows that support from the majority leader can be critical in getting minority opinions to be accepted.[76]

Moscovici's research illuminates how norms can change within groups. Another line of work on *social categorization* theory illuminates how divergent group identities and differences in norms can reinforce each other.[77] Social categorization research has shown that the simple act of classifying others into social categories can provoke discrimination between in-group and out-group members, cohesion within a group, and ethnocentric biases favoring the in-group— even when the distinctions between groups are meaningless.[78] This is demonstrated in the ongoing conflict between Israelis and Palestinians. In a study that examined intergroup dialogue between Israeli and Palestinian youths, Pilecki and Hammack found that Palestinian narratives reflected a theme of victimization, while Israeli dialogue demonstrated justification.[79]

A classic Dr. Seuss story depicts two kinds of "Sneetches"—some with stars on their bellies, some without. The narrator muses, "Those stars weren't so big. They were really so small, you might think such a thing wouldn't matter at all." Yet the Star-Belly Sneetches scorn and ostracize the Plain-Belly Sneetches. A sly stranger persuades the Plain-Belly Sneetches to pay to have stars put on their bellies, making them indistinguishable from the "real" Star-Belly Sneetches. Then he persuades the other group to pay to have their stars removed, thus reasserting their differentiation and superiority. The cycle continues until all the Sneetches run out of money—and belatedly conclude that it is ridiculous to discriminate on the basis of belly star status.[80]

But the Sneetches are characters in a children's story. Has anybody, anywhere, ever thought, "The distinction I'm making between my group and that group is just like what the Sneetches did"? Perhaps not. However, researchers have repeatedly found that people randomly assigned to groups have a propensity to discriminate against each other. In the classic 1954 "Robbers Cave" experiment, Muzafer Sherif had two groups of boys camp in separate parts of a large campground for a week, then he organized competitions between them. Soon the groups were not only disparaging each other but also conducting raids on each other's turf.[81] Perhaps even stranger, when people are randomly assigned to groups and then play cooperation games, they tend to favor members of their own groups, even at their own expense, and even if they have had no contact with the other people. This propensity to favor in-groups is not quite the same as social discrimination against out-groups, but it seems to foster intergroup conflict. Hammond and Axelrod concluded that our predisposition toward in-groups explains to some extent how manipulating group differences can be a powerful political strategy.[82] The famous Stanford prison study (see Box 6.2) takes group categorization to an appalling conclusion, and recent research comes to much the same conclusions on even larger scales.[83]

BOX 6.2

Group Identity and Group Polarization:
The Stanford Prison Study

In the early 1970s a group of researchers at Stanford University wanted to find out how prison conditions affected the people who lived and worked in them. Many people believed that prisons were harsh places because only the worst kinds of people were locked up there. Others believed that prisons were bad because those who chose to become guards often had a sadistic streak. Both these hypotheses make some sense, but the researchers—Craig Haney, W. Curtis Banks, and Philip Zimbardo—suspected fundamental attribution error: falsely attributing outcomes to personalities instead of circumstances. They wanted to see how guards and prisoners behaved when there were *no prior differences between* the two groups.

First they prescreened a group of men for their psychological stability. Then they selected the twenty-two who were the most psychologically "normal" for the study. These men were randomly assigned to be either a prisoner or a guard in a simulation that was to last two weeks. All subjects were told that "prisoners" would be guaranteed "a minimally adequate diet, clothing, housing and medical care"[1] for the duration of the study.

(continues)

(continued)   BOX 6.2
Group Identity and Group Polarization:
The Stanford Prison Study

The day before the "prisoners" arrived, the "guards" were issued uniforms and met with the experimenters to create rules for the prison. Upon arrival, the randomly assigned "prisoners" were "deloused" and assigned uniforms with prisoner numbers, then confined in the basement of a Stanford campus building until the experiment ended. The "guards" worked eight-hour shifts and spent the other sixteen hours each day doing what they normally did. The prisoners and guards were not given instructions on how to behave, except that guards were instructed not to use violence against prisoners.

As the researchers had hypothesized, the participants quickly adopted group norms and identities that encouraged intergroup polarization—and, as it happened, inhumane treatment on the part of the "guards." Routine bodily functions like eating and using the bathroom became privileges for the "prisoners," to be earned with good behavior. The "guards" developed a group norm of never questioning another guard's treatment of a "prisoner," no matter how harsh. "Not to be tough and arrogant was taken as a sign of weakness by the other guards." The "prisoners" began to lose self-esteem and respect for each other; they developed a norm of passivity as a means to cope with the arbitrary authority of the "guards."

The researchers had not anticipated the human cost of their experimental success. Within a few days, five of the prisoners manifested signs of "extreme emotional depression, crying, rage, or acute anxiety"; over time, they were sent home. The researchers decided to end the experiment after just six days. They reported that "most of the guards seemed to be distressed by the decision to stop the experiment. It appeared to us that the guards had become sufficiently involved in their roles so that they now enjoyed the extreme control and power they exercised and were reluctant to give it up."[2]

On the other hand, the "prisoners" were delighted to be set free. One remarked, "I learned that people can easily forget that others are human."[3]

SOURCE: Craig Haney, W. Curtis Banks, and Philip G. Zimbardo, "Interpersonal Dynamics in a Simulated Prison," in M. Patricia Golden, ed., *The Research Experience* (Itasca, IL: F. E. Peacock Publishers, 1976), 157–177.

[1]Haney, Banks, and Zimbardo, "Interpersonal Dynamics in a Simulated Prison," 159.
[2]Ibid., 164.
[3]Ibid., 173, 170.

Another example of social categorization can be found in the issue of abortion. Many people self-identify as either "pro-life" or "pro-choice." We rarely encounter, on either side of the issue, the sentiment that people on the other side have good intentions or are "a lot like us." On the contrary, people on each side seem confident not only that they are right on the issue, but that they have better morals in general than the people on the other side. We are not qualified to adjudicate people's morals, but we are skeptical about these attributions of general moral superiority. In many ways, most "pro-life" and "pro-choice" people behave similarly; neither group, taken as a whole, lives up (or down) to the other side's stereotypical expectations.

This intergroup polarization may deepen when groups interact. For example, imagine loggers and environmentalists arguing about policy in an "old growth" forest. Suppose that initially, some of the environmentalists support limited logging, believing that the forest can support it and that loggers' jobs should be protected. For their part, some of the loggers support restrictions on logging in order to preserve the forest for the long haul. Surely these two sides can find common ground? Maybe they can. But you might not be surprised to see the discussion deteriorate, with participants getting angrier at each other until ultimately the two sides only agree that "*those people* just can't be reasoned with!" People who were relatively conciliatory on the issue may come to believe that a harder line—favoring an absolute ban on logging or an end to all restrictions— actually makes more sense. Certainly this may be more comfortable than trying to stake out an awkward position between one's friends and one's adversaries.

Vincent Price[84] suggests that news stories cue their recipients to think about issues in terms of their particular group's (or groups') perspective. If, as we have discussed, people are likely to perceive group opinion as more polarized (extreme) than it is, they may report relatively polarized opinions themselves. Price interprets his data as indicating that media reports that emphasize group conflicts may thus influence public opinion. In this way, groups may affect public opinion even without any personal interaction.

Conforming to Norms

Group conformity (and the enforcement of group norms) is of interest to public opinion scholars, who examine how and why people conform to group pressure when forming and expressing their opinions. Conformity is the mechanism by which norms affect public opinion. Thus, understanding group conformity can be critical to understanding the relationship of norms to the public opinion process.

Solomon Asch conducted some of the first studies that attempted to look at the pressure groups can exert on individuals to conform. In these studies, groups of seven to nine people sitting in a semicircle were shown lines of clearly varying lengths and were asked which lines were the longest and which were the shortest. Only the last person to respond in the group was a true "naive" subject. All of the other members of this group were confederates (people who were "planted" in the group by the experimenter). When it was their turn to speak out loud, the confederates would give a unanimous incorrect judgment.[85] Obviously, Asch was interested in how the subjects would respond to group pressure, since in reality there was only one clearly correct answer—that the lines varied significantly in size (see Figure 6.1). However, it is interesting to note that the subjects accepted the incorrect group position about one-third of the time.

The fact that some people conform more than others has led to a great deal of research on establishing whether there may be a "conformist syndrome" or a "conformist personality."[86] However, Stanley Milgram showed in his experiments that "average" people conform to authority when they are placed in situations in which that authority seems relevant.[87] A recent study found that women who were labeled by their peers as beautiful were more likely to conform to social norms. They were also more likely to put their own interests before those of others. Segal-Caspi and colleagues concluded that, despite the "what is beautiful is good" stereotype, beautiful women are more likely to conform and be concerned with self-promotion.[88]

Actually, people may conform publicly without changing their attitudes. Eagly and Chaiken suggest that when influence is of an injunctive nature (when it is socially desirable to conform), social pressures may produce public agreement with other group members but provide little or no private acceptance.[89]

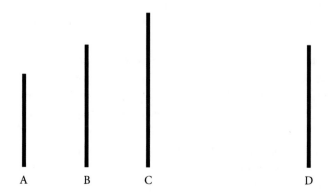

A   B   C   D

FIGURE 6.1. **The Asch Lines.** Which line is longer?

For example, imagine that you and some friends are watching TV and a show you particularly enjoy comes on. One of your friends calls the show stupid, and another person quickly agrees. Another chimes in, then asks you what you think. Faced with feeling different, many people in this kind of situation will verbally conform to the group norm—not liking the program—while not actually changing their attitude toward the program at all.

Paul Nail has suggested a useful typology of various forms of conformity.[90] *Conversion* is when people are persuaded to accept group norms, conforming both privately and publicly. *Compliance* is when they conform publicly but do not alter their attitudes. *Anticompliance* is the somewhat unusual case in which people alter their attitudes but do not publicly conform. You may have friends who appear prone to anticompliance, arguing a point after they presumably must realize that it is wrong. And *independence* is when people do not conform to a norm either publicly or privately. Note that in this typology, "private" refers to someone's internal beliefs and opinions, and "public" refers to interactions with other people, even if those interactions are more private than public.

Michael Hogg and John Turner argue that the distinction between public and private compliance can be construed in terms of two forms of social influence: normative influence and informational influence.[91] According to Morton Deutsch and Harold Gerard,[92] *normative influence* results from the individual's need for social approval and acceptance. It produces public compliance, not conversion. People can be subject to normative influence when they perceive that the group (or an individual) has the power to reward or punish them. Often these rewards and punishments are intangible, such as praise or criticism. Normative influence generally depends on a perception of surveillance: individuals are unlikely to comply unless they believe they might get "caught." Moreover, normative influence may be powerful if the reference group is very important to the individual.[93] For example, people are more likely to conform to the norms within a tight circle of friends than among strangers: what the people we care about think of our behavior matters more to us than what strangers think.

Unlike normative influence, *informational influence* results from the individual's need to be correct.[94] It thus leads to conversion, that is, private as well as public conformity. According to Hogg and Abrams, the power of informational influence "resides in the perceived expertise or expert power (i.e., possession of knowledge that others repeatedly need to draw upon), or the informational power (possession of a specific piece of information that is needed) of others. The precondition for informational influence is subjective uncertainty or lack of confidence in the validity of one's beliefs, or opinions."[95]

So where does all this leave us? Clearly stereotypes and norms, foundations for a lot of our attitudes and behaviors, can have a profound impact on public opinion formation and change (or lack of change). Public opinion scholars recognize that these are important concepts for understanding how people are motivated to change, to act on, and to express their opinions, whether by participating in elections through their vote or with demonstrations, riots, and protests. For example, while there was initial enthusiasm and support for "Occupy Wall Street," the American public largely rejected the movement when it became widely agreed that the group had no cohesive message, and protesters were painted as unorganized and incompetent.

Public opinion scholars have been using conformity research as a basis for some of their theoretical work on public opinion formation. For example, Elisabeth Noelle-Neumann used conformity studies for much of her research on the spiral of silence (see Chapter 7). Her "fear of isolation" concept is based in part on the experimental work of Asch[96] and Milgram.[97] Noelle-Neumann states that people often fear isolation because of their need to be associated with others; they have a strong need to conform in order to be accepted. More recently, Andrew Hayes and others have suggested that certain personality characteristics make people more or less likely to censor their opinions.[98] The development of this scale clarified some inconsistent findings in the spiral of silence literature, and it continues to be applied in numerous contexts in public opinion research.[99]

SOCIOLOGICAL ACCOUNTS OF OPINION: TRACES OF IN-GROUP CONFORMITY?

You might wonder whether the discussion so far has anything to do with large-scale public opinion surveys, through which we attempt to investigate and understand public opinion. Consider Table 6.1, which looks at selected differences in public opinion across various demographic groups. Demographic "groups" do not neatly correspond to social groups with shared norms. Nevertheless, there are differences across groups, and it is very plausible that these differences are partly explained by mutual influence, shared norms.

Influential research into such group differences was conducted by sociologists at Columbia University in the 1940s.[100] Paul Lazarsfeld and his Columbia colleagues found that people of low economic status, Catholics, city dwellers, and young people were more likely than others to vote Democratic and to take "liberal" as opposed to "conservative" positions on economic policy issues. These findings are still generally true well over half a century later, despite some change over time. But why do these differences exist?

TABLE 6.1. **Differences in Support for Marijuana Legalization across Demographic Groups**

	% Saying Marijuana Should be Legalized (March 2010)	% Saying Marijuana Should be Legalized (March 2013)	Change between 2010 and 2013
Men	45	57	+12
Women	38	48	+10
Non-Hispanic White	42	52	+10
Non-Hispanic Black	41	56	+15
Hispanic	35	51	+16
18–29 years old	58	64	+ 6
30–49 years old	42	55	+13
50–64 years old	40	53	+13
65+ years old	22	33	+11
College Grad+	39	52	+13
Some College	45	59	+14
High School or Less	41	47	+ 6
Republican	24	37	+13
Conservative Republican	20	29	+ 9
Moderate/Liberal Republican	36	53	+17
Democrat	48	59	+11
Conservative/ Moderate Democrat	44	52	+ 8
Liberal Democrat	57	73	+16
Independent	49	60	+11

SOURCE: Adapted from Pew Research Center, U.S. Politics and Policy, "Majority Now Supports Legalizing Marijuana," April 4, 2013, http://www.people-press.org /2013/04/04/majority-now-supports-legalizing-marijuana/#marijuana-partisan.

Some of these differences might be attributed to economic self-interest; it is no great wonder, perhaps, that relatively poor people are more likely to favor liberal economic policies that might benefit them directly. Various religious traditions may inculcate particular social values. But the Columbia sociologists argued that the differences had much to do with people's personal interactions with family and friends, coworkers, fellow churchgoers, and so on. These interactions, later described by other sociologists in terms of social "networks," provide mechanisms for people to directly influence or reinforce each other's opinions. People may rely on particular family members or friends or others in their network for information. Lazarsfeld and his colleagues characterized some people as "opinion leaders." Opinion leaders paid regular attention to issues and politics and had well-formed opinions or partisan views that affected their reactions to events. Through interactions and discussion with these opinion leaders, *especially in the same social environment*, other people tended to adopt their opinions. Lazarsfeld's research explored social influences by asking many people, in a limited geographic area, detailed questions about their conversations with other people. This tradition has been carried on, for example in the research of Robert Huckfeldt and John Sprague.[101]

The sociological approach to understanding public opinion has wide appeal. News reports and public discussions of issues very often cite subgroup reactions. For example, reporting on the same-sex marriage debate has often emphasized the large differences in opinion related to age, party identification, and religious beliefs and practices. It is easy to believe that these differences relate to shared values within subgroups, reinforced by people's interactions with others in those subgroups—although these subgroups are far from insular ("white evangelical Protestants" do not interact only with each other, nor do "Democrats" or "18-to-29-year-olds"). A sociological approach is useful in understanding large, persistent differences associated with demographic and social characteristics. By itself, it is less useful in explaining the *dynamics* of public opinion—for example, why Americans in practically every measurable subgroup have become more supportive of same-sex marriage in recent years. Presumably a sociological account would emphasize the role of opinion leaders in swaying other people's opinions, but that leaves us to wonder why the opinion leaders changed their minds: Who (or what) led the leaders?

CONCLUSION

Much social science research pays lip service to social and institutional influences but actually relies exclusively on individualistic explanations. This propensity applies even to the study of collective behavior—whether organized expressions of opinion such as strikes and sit-ins, or disorganized expressions of opinion such as riots, fads, and episodes of "mass hysteria." Although these phenomena are clearly social in nature, much of the research on collective behavior has focused on psychological characteristics of the participants; few studies have provided a larger-picture sociological explanation of public opinion.[102] A social psychologist might say that the research agenda seems to embrace the fundamental attribution error: attributing to personalities what is better explained by circumstances.

There are many more articles that attempt to understand the individual and individual opinion expression than there are articles on understanding national or even global shifts in public opinion. Scholars in political science, communication, and sociology are moving more toward understanding this process from a broader perspective. In fact the use of "big data" is becoming an increasingly important part of understanding the process in both academics and industry.[103] Yet many in the academic community are concerned about the implications and ethics of such large-scale studies.[104]

It is obviously becoming increasingly critical to examine the public opinion process from broader sociological perspectives. Many more issues are affecting entire towns, cities, countries—and even the world—than ever before. Global warming, hydraulic fracking, Ebola, terrorism, and so forth are all issues that affect humanity as a whole. Understanding the movement of a "public's" opinions about these issues will become critical in the years to come.

NOTES

1. Richard E. Petty and John T. Cacioppo, *Attitudes and Persuasion: Classic and Contemporary Approaches* (Dubuque, IA: William C. Brown, 1981), 163.

2. Alice H. Eagly and Shelly Chaiken, *The Psychology of Attitudes* (Orlando, FL: Harcourt Brace Jovanovich, 1993), 351.

3. Ibid.

4. Stephen A. Rains, "The Anonymity Effect: The Influence of Anonymity on Perceptions of Sources and Information on Health Websites," *Journal of Applied Communication Research* 35, no. 2 (2007): 197–214.

5. Denise M. Polk, "Communication and Family Caregiving for Alzheimer's Dementia: Linking Attributions and Problematic Integration," *Health Communication* 18, no. 3 (2005): 257–273.

6. Donald P. Haider-Markel and Mark R. Joslyn, "Beliefs about the Origins of Homosexuality and Support for Gay Rights—An Empirical Test of Attribution Theory," *Public Opinion Quarterly* 72, no. 2 (2008): 291–310. See also Andrew L. Whitehead,

"Politics, Religion, Attribution Theory, and Attitudes Toward Same-Sex Unions," *Social Science Quarterly* 95, no. 3 (2014): 701–718.

7. Walter Lippmann, *Public Opinion* (New York: Harcourt, Brace, 1922).

8. Michael A. Hogg and Dominic Abrams, *Social Identifications: A Social Psychology of Intergroup Relations and Group Processes* (New York: Routledge, 1988).

9. Lippmann, *Public Opinion*, ch. 6, quoting William James, *Principles of Psychology* (New York: Holt, Rinehart and Winston, 1890), I:488.

10. Ibid., 59.

11. Ibid., 59–60

12. Ibid., 60.

13. Anthony G. Greenwald and Mahzarin R. Banaji, "Implicit Social Cognition: Attitudes, Self-Esteem, and Stereotypes," *Psychological Review* 102 (1995): 14.

14. Mark Snyder, "On the Self-Perpetuating Nature of Social Stereotypes," in D. Hamilton, ed., *Cognitive Processes in Stereotyping and Intergroup Behavior* (Hillsdale, NJ: Erlbaum, 1981), 183–212, quoted in Greenwald and Banaji, "Implicit Social Cognition," 15.

15. Anna E. Clark and Yoshihisa Kashima, "Stereotypes Help People Connect with Others in the Community: A Situated Functional Analysis of the Stereotype Consistency Bias in Communication," *Journal of Personality and Social Psychology* 93, no. 6 (2007): 1028–1039.

16. Travis L. Dixon, "Psychological Reactions to Crime News Portrayals of Black Criminals: Understanding the Moderating Roles of Prior News Viewing and Stereotype Endorsement," *Communication Monographs* 73, no. 2 (2006): 162–187; Travis L. Dixon, "Network News and Racial Beliefs: Exploring the Connection Between National Television News Exposure and Stereotypical Perceptions of African Americans," *Journal of Communication* 58, no. 2 (2008): 321–337.

17. Sonja M. Brown Givens and Jennifer L. Monahan, "Priming Mammies, Jezebels, and Other Controlling Images: An Examination of the Influence of Mediated Stereotypes on Perceptions of an African American Woman," *Media Psychology* 7 (2005): 87–106.

18. Ji Hoon Park, Nadine G. Gabbadon, and Ariel R. Chernin, "Naturalizing Racial Differences through Comedy: Asian, Black, and White Views on Racial Stereotypes in *Rush Hour 2*," *Journal of Communication* 56 (2006): 157–177.

19. Layla A. Jones, "#Iftheygunnedmedown: How the Media Killed Michael Brown," philly.com, April 21, 2014, http://www.philly.com/philly/blogs/lifestyle/Iftheygunnedmedown-How-media-the-killed-Michael-Brown.html.

20. Ibid.

21. Tanzina Vega, "Shooting Spurs Hashtag Effort on Stereotypes," *New York Times* online, August 12, 2014, http://www.nytimes.com/2014/08/13/us/if-they-gunned-me-down-protest-on-twitter.html.

22. S. Alexander Haslam, Penelope J. Oakes, Katherine J. Reynolds, and John C. Turner, "Social Identity Salience and the Emergence of Stereotype Consensus," *Personality and Social Psychology Bulletin* 25, no. 7 (1999): 809–818.

23. Michael A. Hogg and Scott A. Reid, "Social Identity, Self-categorization, and the Communication of Group Norms," *Communication Theory* 16 (2006): 7–30.

24. Michael D. Slater, "Reinforcing Spirals: The Mutual Influence of Media Selectivity and Media Effects and Their Impact on Individual Behavior and Social Identity," *Communication Theory* 17, no. 3 (2007): 281–303.

25. Ibid.

26. "Social Identity Salience and the Emergence of Stereotype Consensus," 811.

27. Greenwald and Banaji, "Implicit Social Cognition," 14.

28. Daniel Katz and Kenneth W. Braly, "Social Stereotypes of One Hundred College Students," *Journal of Abnormal and Social Psychology* 28 (1933): 280–290.

29. Eric Luis Uhlmann and Raphael Silberzahn, "Conformity under Uncertainty: Reliance on Gender Stereotypes in Online Hiring Decisions," *Behavioral and Brain Sciences* 37 (2014): 103–104. See also Elizabeth H. Gorman, "Gender Stereotypes, Same-Gender Preferences, and Organizational Variation in the Hiring of Women: Evidence from Law Firms," *American Sociological Review* 70, no. 4 (2005): 702–728.

30. D. W. Rajecki, *Attitudes*, 2nd ed. (Sunderland, MA: Sinauer, 1990), 2:282.

31. Mark Snyder, Elizabeth D. Tanke, and Ellen Berscheid, "Social Perception and Interpersonal Behavior: On the Self-Fulfilling Nature of Social Stereotypes," *Journal of Personality and Social Psychology* 35 (1977): 656–666.

32. Ibid., 661.

33. Ibid., 662.

34. Genevieve L. Lorenzo, Jeremy C. Blesanz, and Lauren J. Human, "What Is Beautiful Is Good and More Accurately Understood: Physical Attractiveness and Accuracy in First Impressions of Personality," *Psychological Science* 21, no. 12 (2010): 1777–1782. See also Edward P. Lemay Jr., Margaret S. Clark, and Aaron Greenberg, "What Is Beautiful Is Good Because What Is Beautiful Is Desired: Physical Attractiveness Stereotyping as Projection of Interpersonal Goals," *Personality and Social Psychology Bulletin* 36, no. 3 (2010): 339–353.

35. Rebecca J. Brand, Abigail Bonatsos, Rebecca D'Orazio, and Hilary DeShong, "What Is Beautiful Is Good, Even Online: Correlations between Photo Attractiveness and Text Attractiveness in Men's Online Dating Profiles," *Computers in Human Behavior* 28 (2012): 166–170.

36. Henri Tajfel, *Human Groups and Social Categories: Studies in Social Psychology* (Cambridge, UK: Cambridge University Press, 1981).

37. Christine Reyna, Ovidiu Dobria, and Geoffrey Wetherell, "The Complexity and Ambivalence of Immigration Attitudes: Ambivalent Stereotypes Predict Conflicting Attitudes Toward Immigration Policies," *Cultural Diversity and Ethnic Minority Psychology* 19, no. 3 (2013): 342–356. See also Lingyu Lu and Sean Nicholson-Crotty, "Reassessing the Impact of Hispanic Stereotypes on White Americans' Immigration Preferences," *Social Science Quarterly* 91, no. 5 (2010).

38. Henri Tajfel, *Human Groups and Social Categories: Studies in Social Psychology* (Cambridge, UK: Cambridge University Press, 1981).

39. Roy F. Baumeister and Brad J. Bushman, *Social Psychology and Human Nature, Brief Version*, 3rd ed. (Belmont, CA: Wadsworth, 2014).

40. Hogg and Abrams, *Social Identifications*, 77.

41. *Webster's New Collegiate Dictionary* (Springfield, MA: G. and C. Merriam Company, 1981), 776.

42. Hogg and Abrams, *Social Identifications*, 159.

43. Walter Bagehot, *Physics and Politics* (1869; New York: Knopf, 1946); William G. Sumner, *Folkways* (Boston: Ginn, 1906).

44. Edward A. Ross, *Social Control: A Survey of the Foundations of Order* (New York: Macmillan, 1901).

45. Hogg and Abrams, *Social Identifications*, 159.

46. Dennis L. Krebs and Dale T. Miller, "Altruism and Aggression," in Gardner Lindzey and Elliott Aronson, eds., *Handbook of Social Psychology* (New York: Random House, 1985), 2:1-71. See also Margaret M. Marini, "Age and Sequencing Norms in the Transition to Adulthood," *Social Forces* 63 (1984): 229-244.

47. Carroll J. Glynn and Michael E. Huge, "Opinions as Norms: Applying a Return Potential Model to the Study of Communication Behaviors," *Communication Research* 34, no. 5 (2007): 548-568.

48. P. Niel Christensen, Hank Rothgerber, Wendy Wood, and David C. Matz, "Social Norms and Identity Relevance: A Motivational Approach to Normative Behavior," *Personality and Social Psychology Bulletin* 30 (2004): 1295-1309. See also Rajiv N. Rimal, Maria K. Lapinski, Rachel J. Cook, and Kevin Real, "Moving toward a Theory of Normative Influences: How Perceived Benefits and Similarity Moderate the Impact of Descriptive Norms on Behaviors," *Journal of Health Communication* 10 (2005): 433-450.

49. Brian Borsari and Kate B. Carey, "Descriptive and Injunctive Norms in College Drinking: A Meta-Analytic Integration," *Journal of the Study of Alcohol* 64, no. 3 (2003): 331-341.

50. Robert B. Cialdini, Carl A. Kallgren, and Raymond R. Reno, "A Focus Theory of Normative Conduct: A Theoretical Refinement and Reevaluation of the Role of Norms in Human Behavior," in Mark P. Zanna, ed., *Advances in Experimental Social Psychology* (San Diego, CA: Academic Press, 1991), 201-234.

51. Robert B. Cialdini, "Descriptive Social Norms as Underappreciated Sources of Social Control," *Psychometrika* 72, no. 2 (2007): 263-268.

52. Glynn and Huge, "Opinions as Norms."

53. Rajiv N. Rimal, Maria K. Lapinski, Rachel J. Cook, and Kevin Real, "Moving Toward a Theory of Normative Influences: How Perceived Benefits and Similarity Moderate the Impact of Descriptive Norms on Behaviors," *Journal of Health Communication* 10 (2005); 433-450.

54. Leon Festinger, "A Theory of Social Comparison Processes," *Human Relations* 7 (1954): 117-140.

55. Leon Festinger, "Informal Social Communication," *Psychological Review* 57 (1950): 272–273.

56. Cialdini, Kallgren, and Reno, "Focus Theory of Normative Conduct," 203.

57. Glynn, "Public Opinion as a Normative Opinion Process."

58. Glynn and Huge, "Opinions as Norms."

59. James Kuklinski et al., "Racial Prejudice and Attitudes Toward Affirmative Action," *American Journal of Political Science* 41 (1997): 402–419.

60. Mina Staunton, Winnifred R. Louis, Joanne R. Smith, Deborah J. Terry, and Rachel I. McDonald, "How Negative Descriptive Norms for Healthy Eating Undermine the Effects of Positive Injunctive Norms," *Journal of Applied Social Psychology* 44, no. 4 (2014): 319–330.

61. Hogg and Abrams, *Social Identifications*, 159.

62. Muzafer Sherif, "A Study of Some Social Factors in Perception," *Archives of Psychology* 27 (1935): 1–60; Muzafer Sherif, *The Psychology of Social Norms* (New York: Harper and Brothers, 1936).

63. Sherif, "Study of Some Social Factors in Perception"; Vincent Price and Hayg Oshagan, "Social-Psychological Perspectives on Public Opinion," in Theodore L. Glaser and Charles T. Salmon, eds., *Public Opinion and the Communication of Consent* (New York: Guilford Publications, 1989), 177–216; Muzafer Sherif, B. Jack White, and O. J. Harvey, "Status in Experimentally Produced Groups," *American Journal of Sociology* 60 (1955): 370–379.

64. Kenneth Cmiel, "The Politics of Incivility," in David Farber, ed., *The Sixties: From Memory to History* (Chapel Hill: University of North Carolina Press, 1994), 263–290.

65. Hogg and Abrams, *Social Identifications*, 159.

66. Theodore M. Newcomb, *Personality and Social Change: Attitude Formation in a Student Community* (New York: Holt, Rinehart and Winston, 1943).

67. Theodore M. Newcomb et al., *Persistence and Change: Bennington College and Its Students After Twenty-five Years* (New York: Wiley, 1967).

68. Pew Research Center, "Data Trend: Gay Marriage," http://www.pewresearch .org/data-trend/domestic-issues/attitudes-on-gay-marriage/.

69. Rebecca J. Kreitzer, Allison J. Hamilton, and Caroline J. Tolbert, "Does Policy Adoption Change Opinions on Minority Rights? The Effects of Legalizing Same-sex Marriage," *Political Research Quarterly* 67, no. 4 (2014): 795–808.

70. Hogg and Abrams, *Social Identifications*, 159.

71. Serge Moscovici, "On Some Aspects of Social Representations" (paper presented at the symposium "Representations" of the American Psychological Association, Anaheim, CA, 1983).

72. Serge Moscovici, *La psychanalyse, son image et son publique* (Paris: Presses Universitaires de France, 1961); Serge Moscovici, "The Coming Era of Representations," in Jean-Paul Codol and Jacques-Philippe Leyens, eds., *Cognitive Analysis of Social Behavior* (The Hague: Martinus Nijhoff, 1982), 115–119.

73. Glynn, "Public Opinion as a Normative Opinion Process."

74. S. Moscovici, E. Lage, and M. Naffrechoux, "Influence of a Consistent Minority on the Responses of a Majority in a Color Perception Task," *Sociometry* 32 (1969): 365–380.

75. Serge Moscovici and Willem Doise, *Conflict and Consensus: A General Theory of Collective Decisions* (Thousand Oaks, CA: Sage Publications, 1994).

76. Elizabeth Mannix and Margaret A. Neale, "What Differences Make a Difference? The Promise and Reality of Diverse Teams in Organizations," *Psychological Science in the Public Interest* 6, no. 2 (2005): 31–55.

77. See, for instance, Vincent Price and Hayg Oshagan, "Social-Psychological Perspectives on Public Opinion," in Theodore L. Glasser and Charles T. Salmon, eds., *Public Opinion and the Communication of Consent* (New York: Guilford Publications, 1989), 177–216; Henri Tajfel, "The Social Psychology of Intergroup Relations," *Annual Review of Psychology* 33 (1982): 1–39; John C. Turner and Penelope J. Oakes, "Self-Categorization Theory and Social Influence," in Paul B. Paulus, ed., *Psychology of Group Influence* (Hillsdale, NJ: Lawrence Erlbaum, 1989), 233–278.

78. John C. Turner, "Towards a Cognitive Redefinition of the Social Group," in Henri Tajfel, ed., *Social Identity and Intergroup Relations* (Cambridge, UK: Cambridge University Press, 1982), 15–40; John C. Turner, "Some Comments on . . . 'the Measurement of Social Orientations in the Minimal Group Paradigm,'" *European Journal of Social Psychology* 13 (1983): 351–367.

79. Andrew Pilecki and Phillip L. Hammack, "'Victims' versus 'Righteous Victims': The Rhetorical Construction of Social Categories in Historical Dialogue Among Israeli and Palestinian Youth," *Political Psychology* 35, no. 6 (2014): 813–830.

80. Dr. Seuss, *The Sneetches and Other Stories* (New York: Random House, 1961).

81. Bernard E. Whitley and Mary E. Kite, *The Psychology of Prejudice and Discrimination* (Belmont, CA: Wadsworth, 2010).

82. Ross A. Hammond and Robert Axelrod, "The Evolution of Ethnocentrism," *Journal of Conflict Resolution* 50, no. 6 (2006): 926–936.

83. Gudrun Ostby, "Polarization, Horizontal Inequalities, and Violent Civil Conflict," *Journal of Peace Research* 45, no. 2 (2008): 143–162.

84. Vincent Price, "Social Identification and Public Opinion: Effects of Communicating Group Conflict," *Public Opinion Quarterly* 53 (1989): 197–224.

85. Solomon E. Asch, *Social Psychology* (Englewood Cliffs, NJ: Prentice-Hall, 1952).

86. Hogg and Abrams, *Social Identifications.*

87. Stanley Milgram, "Nationality and Conformity," *Scientific American* 205, no. 6 (1961): 45–51.

88. Lihi Segal-Caspi, Sonia Roccas, and Lilach Sagiv, "Don't Judge a Book by Its Cover, Revisited: Perceived and Reported Traits and Values of Attractive Women," *Psychological Science* 23, no. 10 (2012): 1112–1116.

89. Eagly and Chaiken, *Psychology of Attitudes.*

90. Paul R. Nail, "Toward an Integration of Some Models and Theories of Social Response," *Psychological Bulletin* 83 (1986): 603–627.

91. Michael A. Hogg and John C. Turner, "Social Identity and Conformity: A Theory of Referent Information Influence," in Willem Doise and Serge Moscovici, eds., *Current Issues in European Social Psychology* (Cambridge, UK: Cambridge University Press, 1987), 139–182.

92. Morton Deutsch and Harold B. Gerard, "A Study of Normative and Information Social Influence upon Individual Judgment," *Journal of Abnormal and Social Psychology* 51 (1955): 629–636.

93. Hogg and Turner, "Social Identity and Conformity"; Harold H. Kelley, "Two Functions of Reference Groups," in Guy E. Swanson, Theodore M. Newcomb, and Eugene L. Hartley, eds., *Readings in Social Psychology* (New York: Holt, 1952), 410–414.

94. Deutsch and Gerard, "Study of Normative and Information Social Influence upon Individual Judgment"; Kelley, "Two Functions of Reference Groups."

95. Hogg and Abrams, *Social Identifications*, 167. See also M. A. Hogg, D. Abrams, S. Otten, and S. Hinkle, "The Social Identity Perspective—Intergroup Relations, Self-conception, and Small Groups," *Small Group Research* 35 (2003): 246–276.

96. Solomon E. Asch, "Effects of Group Pressure upon the Modification and Distortion of Judgments," in H. Guetzkow, ed., *Groups, Leadership, and Men* (Pittsburgh: Carnegie Press, 1951), 177–190.

97. Stanley Milgram, "Nationality and Conformity," *Scientific American* 205, no. 6 (1961): 45–51.

98. A. F. Hayes, C. J. Glynn, and J. Shanahan, "Willingness to Self-censor: A Construct and Measurement Tool for Public Opinion Research," *International Journal of Public Opinion Research* 17 (2005): 299–323; A. F. Hayes, C. J. Glynn, and J. Shanahan, "Validating the Willingness to Self-censor Scale: Individual Differences in the Effect of the Climate of Opinion on Willingness to Express an Opinion," *International Journal of Public Opinion Research* 17 (2005): 443–445.

99. J. Matthes, A. F. Hayes, H. Rojas, F. Shen, S. J. Min, and I. B. Dylko, "Exemplifying a Dispositional Approach to Cross-cultural Spiral of Silence Research: Fear of Social Isolation and the Inclination to Self-censor," *International Journal of Public Opinion Research* 24 (2012): 287–305.

100. Paul F. Lazarsfeld, Bernard Berelson, and Hazel Gaudet, *The People's Choice: How the Voter Makes Up His Mind in a Presidential Campaign* (New York: Columbia University Press, 1968 [1944]); Bernard R. Berelson, Paul F. Lazarsfeld, and William N. McPhee, *Voting: A Study of Opinion Formation in a Presidential Campaign* (Chicago: University of Chicago Press, 1954); Elihu Katz and Paul Lazarsfeld, *Personal Influence: The Part Played by People in the Flow of Mass Communications* (Glencoe, IL: The Free Press, 1955).

101. Robert Huckfeldt and John Sprague, *Citizens, Politics, and Social Communication: Information and Influence in an Election Campaign* (New York: Cambridge University Press, 1995). For more on network analysis and theory in sociology, see Mark S. Granovetter, "The Strength of Weak Ties," *American Journal of Sociology* 78 (1973):

1360–1380; Duncan J. Watts, *Six Degrees: The Science of a Connected Age* (New York: W. W. Norton & Company, 2003).

102. Jeff Manza and Clem Brooks, "How Sociology Lost Public Opinion: A Genealogy of a Missing Concept in the Study of the Political," *Sociological Theory* 30, no. 2 (2012): 89–113.

103. See, e.g., the controversial Facebook-sponsored experiment on social contagion: Adam D. I. Kramer, Jamie E. Guillory, and Jeffrey T. Hancock, "Experimental Evidence of Massive-scale Emotional Contagion through Social Networks," *Proceedings of the National Academy of Sciences of the United States of America* 111, no. 24 (2014): 8788–8790.

104. Danah Boyd, "What Does the Facebook Experiment Teach Us? Growing Anxiety About Data Manipulation," medium.com, July 1, 2014, https://medium.com /message/what-does-the-facebook-experiment-teach-us-c858c08e287f.

7

Perception and Opinion Formation

You have probably heard the saying, "perception is reality." In much of our lives, what we perceive is the only reality that matters. If you perceive a homeless man on the street corner to be dangerous, you will behave accordingly, perhaps crossing the street to stay at a safe distance from him. Your perception, not the homeless man's actual intentions, determines your behavior. Our perceptions are subjective, even when we might think we are simply observing objective physical reality. (Recall, from Chapter 6, the experiment in which participants apparently altered their standards for the colors green and blue.) As research psychologist Drew Westen notes, people essentially "twirl the cognitive kaleidoscope until they get the conclusions they want."[1] We do not simply take in facts through our eyes and ears; we make inferences and derive meanings, and those inferences affect what we "see."

We make judgments about other people all the time, and we base these judgments on our perceptions. Think of the many times you rely on your perceptions. If a recent acquaintance walks past you without saying hello, you may perceive the action as coming from either rudeness or preoccupation. A fellow student who expounds loudly and extensively in class may be seen as either obnoxious or extremely intelligent. You may perceive that people are angry or sad, that they are dishonest or sincere. Naturally, such perceptions are likely to affect your actions. We all continually try to interpret other people's motives so we can explain and predict their behaviors. In many ways, these perceptions provide the foundation for a public's opinion. And these perceptions can be very important. In trials, perceptions of the accused as well as the victim can influence jury members and have important implications for the outcome. When you apply for a job, the employer's perception of you can provide you with a job opportunity or keep you in the ranks of the unemployed.

Our perceptions help us understand the world around us. We try to predict what others will do or say and rationalize their motives to provide explanations for their behaviors. We constantly perceive our world, and we rationalize what is going on in that world based on our perceptions.

As Walter Lippmann describes, there is a world outside, and there are the pictures in our heads. He argues:

> Whatever we believe to be a true picture, we treat as if it were the environment itself. . . . For the real environment is altogether too big, too complex, and too fleeting for direct acquaintance. . . . The analyst of public opinion must begin then, by recognizing the triangular relationship between the scene of action, the human picture of that scene and the human response to that picture working itself out upon the scene of action.[2]

This chapter concentrates on perceptions of other people's opinions and how they influence the public opinion process. Psychologists tend to construe "perception" as a process: the processing of information received through the five senses. We use the term in a way closer to its usual conversational meaning: a "perception" is a summary attitude based (perhaps not very accurately) on our past and present sensory information. We now turn our attention to this fascinating world of perception—a world that is both internal and external to ourselves, one that not only influences what we think or say but how we act. In essence, the perceptual world is the world of public opinion.

THE LIMITS OF PERCEPTION

Human beings face physical and cognitive limitations that constrain our perceptions, including our perceptions of other people's actions and motives. Some of these are obvious. As George McCall and J. L. Simmons note, the "physical characteristics of our sense organs impose limitations on both the breadth and the acuity of our perceptions."[3] We can only see so far, and we cannot clearly see small objects at a distance. In addition, our perceptions are limited by our physical perspective: if we are looking straight ahead, we cannot see behind us. If we look to our left, we cannot see to our right.

But as McCall and Simmons argue, our cognitive limitations matter even more. Our perceptions are subject to our selective attention and inattention. For example, people tend to pay attention to social objects (people and events) that are most relevant to their lives and to the obviously unfamiliar. Attending to these things, we may be unable to "see" other people and events, as surely as if we turned our heads away from them.

Our perceptions of others are always incomplete and are generally less than accurate.[4] As Jerome Bruner comments, we tend to "'recode' into simpler form the diversity of events that we encounter" and so "not only is information lost, but also misinformation is added."[5] People actually tend to fill in events that "should" have happened, given their overall perceptions. Magicians often rely on these processes to convince audiences that they have seen the impossible. Most of the time, the processes are ubiquitous yet almost unnoticeable.

Suppose we are talking with a friend while attending a soccer game. We will have to narrow our focus so that we can alternate our attention, in order to carry on the conversation but also keep track of the main occurrences during the game. We will then alter the information we receive from the game in order to simplify this perceptual challenge. For example, we will monitor crowd noise to get an idea of what is happening on the field. We may begin to clap whenever the people around us clap, with only the vaguest sense of what they are clapping about. If they seem really excited, we may turn our full attention to the field, where (say) a player is sprinting toward the goal, and semiconsciously attempt to reconstruct the last few seconds of play that led to this scoring chance. Bruner adds that people often turn to "technological aids" to manage their attention processes.[6] Indeed, we will probably "keep an eye" (or some fraction of an eye) on the scoreboard to judge how close the game is, how much time is left, and whether we should pay closer attention. We may even think that we have "multitasked" almost flawlessly, focusing on the conversation and also taking in the game— although a few well-chosen questions could reveal just how selective our attention was. People are always multitasking, far from flawlessly. Our perceptual limitations—and our mechanisms for coping with it—can restrict, confine, and help define public opinion.

PERCEPTION AND OPINION: SOCIALIZATION AND SOCIAL COMPARISON

Crucially, yet often subtly, people's opinions, as well as their behaviors, are shaped by comparisons with others, including perceptions of others' opinions. Even the influence of group norms (discussed at length in Chapter 6) largely depends on how people perceive those norms.

Socialization

One way our opinions and behaviors are shaped is through socialization: the lifelong process by which people learn norms, beliefs, and behaviors from the people around us. In childhood, parents and close adults play a large role in socialization. There are as many forms of socialization as there are kinds of beliefs and behaviors. In this book we are especially (but not exclusively) interested in political socialization: how people develop particular ideological orientations and policy preferences. Political socialization is enormously difficult to study because it is very hard to track individuals over time, from their earliest political experiences (e.g., shaking a congressperson's hand at age eight) to their adult voting choices. Moreover, researchers cannot readily distinguish between the social influence of trusted adults and the independent impact of political events themselves.

One of the authors of this book recalls a specific example of the impact of political socialization on his life in 1973, when he heard his first political joke. His father said, "Behind every Watergate there is a Milhous." "Milhous" was President Richard Nixon's middle name, so the pun meant that Nixon was responsible for the Watergate scandal (he resigned the following year). In one sense, the coauthor's family and other people around the country were reacting to the emerging revelations about Nixon's involvement. In another sense, the actual events were somewhat irrelevant. Everything the coauthor learned about Watergate he learned from his family. His perceptions and opinions depended in large part on theirs.

Several scholars have tried to document the political socialization process.[7] For example, political scientist Paul Abramson has studied how people's party identification, feelings of political efficacy, and trust in government change during their lives. Some observers have supposed that people tend to become more conservative, and therefore to move toward the Republican Party, as they age. Abramson concluded that on the contrary, people tend to keep their party affiliations even as they grow older, find partners, and advance in their careers. Similarly, in recent research Yair Ghitza and Andrew Gelman conclude that people's propensity to vote for Democratic or Republican presidential candidates is most strongly influenced by events that occurred when they were between ages fourteen and twenty-four; events that happened at age forty or older make far less difference. (Ghitza and Gelman use presidential approval ratings to measure events, so their model focuses on when people were socialized, not with whom they were socialized.)[8]

Interestingly, Abramson found that young adults feel more efficacious (able to influence the course of government) than do older adults. Perhaps parents and teachers try to express more efficacy to their children than they actually feel, or perhaps youths tend to be more optimistic. However, later research finds that young adults in recent years tend to have less efficacy and trust in government than young people did in the 1970s and 1980s.[9] This result could mean that young people are gradually learning cynicism from their parents. It could also mean that Americans of all ages are becoming more skeptical about government, for whatever reasons. As we said before, political socialization is difficult to study.

Social Comparison

Leon Festinger's discussion[10] of how social comparison informs opinions is so important for our purposes that we summarize his major points in Box 7.1. Festinger argues that when we cannot readily test our opinions against physical reality, we resort to comparing ourselves, our opinions, and our beliefs with the opinions and beliefs of others around us. How we make these social comparisons depends on various factors, some of which are mentioned in Box 7.1. Festinger argues that social communication results from this desire to test our opinions, and further, that people strive for consensus: agreement on what opinion is correct or valid. Of course in some cases, people comfortably accept some disagreement, but they prefer to have the widest possible range of shared social facts. People generally react to disagreement either by changing their opinions to achieve the desired consensus or by changing their relationships—ceasing to use those people or groups who disagreed as a basis of comparison. In social comparison theory, social influence does not depend on the existence of a social norm. Rather, we influence each other (and norms tend to emerge) as we look to others for comparative social appraisals, even when there is no real social comparison information.[11]

Kruglanski and Mayseless[12] present a more complex view of motives for social comparison. They identify three distinct motives: fear of holding an invalid (inaccurate) opinion; need for cognitive structure, or the "desire to possess some knowledge . . . , any knowledge as opposed to confusion or ambiguity"; and the wish to maintain beliefs that are pleasing, even if not entirely accurate. Kruglanski and Mayseless find that people seek out particular others for comparison based on their goal. For example, people who seek an accurate opinion on a controversial issue (perhaps the economic effects of tax cuts) may actively seek out dissimilar people most likely to hold opposing views. However, people who want

BOX 7.1

Festinger's Social Comparison Theory

Here are some of the hypotheses and corollaries from Leon Festinger's original statement of social comparison theory that have proved especially useful (we have paraphrased for clarity):

- **Hypothesis 1:** People have a drive to evaluate their opinions and their abilities.

- **Hypothesis 2:** To the extent that objective, nonsocial means are not available, people evaluate their opinions and abilities by comparing them with those of others.

- **Hypothesis 3:** The more different another person is in opinion or ability, the less likely people are to compare themselves to him or her.

- **Hypothesis 6 and corollary:** The cessation of comparison with others (because they differ too much) will be accompanied by hostility or derogation in the case of opinions, generally not in the case of abilities. (People tend to "write off" people with whom they sharply disagree, not so much people who are more or less talented.)

- **Corollary 7a:** The stronger the attraction to a comparison group, the stronger will be the pressure toward uniformity concerning abilities and opinions within that group.

- **Corollary 7b:** The greater the relevance of the opinion or ability to the comparison group, the stronger will be the pressure toward uniformity concerning that opinion or ability.

- **Hypothesis 9:** Where there is a range of opinion or ability in a group, people close to the mode (most common position) of the group will have (1) stronger tendencies to change the positions of others, (2) relatively weaker tendencies to narrow the range of comparison, and (3) much weaker tendencies to change their own position, compared to those who are distant from the mode.

This last hypothesis has been modified by other researchers, such as Elisabeth Noelle-Neumann.[1] Some studies have found that to maintain a

(continues)

(continued)   BOX 7.1
                    Festinger's Social Comparison Theory

distinctive group identity, groups sometimes adopt an opinion that is
more extreme than that of the mode of the group. This more extreme
opinion helps the group differentiate itself from other groups.[2] However,
many of Festinger's hypotheses have been confirmed in multiple studies
that show the importance of social comparison in opinion formation.[3]

SOURCE: Leon A. Festinger, "A Theory of Social Comparison Processes," Human
Relations 7 (1954): 117–140.

---

[1]Elisabeth Noelle-Neumann, The Spiral of Silence. Public Opinion—Our Social Skin
(Chicago: University of Chicago Press, 1984).

[2]Serge Moscovici, La psychanalyse, son image et son publique (Paris: Presses Universitaires de France, 1961); Serge Moscovici, "The Coming Era of Representations," in Cognitive Analysis of Social Behavior, ed. Jean-Paul Codol and
Jacques-Philippe Leyens (The Hague: Martinus Nijhoff, 1982), 115–119.

[3]A summary of the hypotheses and recent support for them is found in K. Corcoran,
J. Crusius, and T. Mussweiler, "Social Comparison: Motives, Standards, and Mechanisms," in D. Chadee, ed., Theories in Social Psychology (Oxford, UK: Wiley-Blackwell, 2011), 119–139.

to hold a pleasing belief will probably seek out similar people who can be expected to tell them what they want to hear. People who seek cognitive structure
with regard to an issue also are likely to seek out similar people to tell them what
to think. If you think that accuracy should matter most, two of these three motives may seem rather shallow to you. Like it or not, probably everybody holds
each of these motives toward some issues, sometimes.

PERCEPTION AND PUBLIC OPINION FORMATION

Since Festinger, several theoretical frameworks have treated the role of perception in public opinion formation. These perspectives share basic assumptions:
that individuals care what others think about public issues; form perceptions of
what others think; and to an extent, modify their own opinions or behaviors, or
both, on the basis of these perceptions.[13] Together, these perspectives construe
our everyday lives as rich tapestries of "interwoven roles, groupings and social

norms to which the individual continually adapts, obtains information and provides information for others."[14]

This section examines seven public opinion perspectives: (1) looking-glass perception, (2) pluralistic ignorance, (3) disowning projection, (4) conservative/liberal/ideological biases, (5) false consensus effect, (6) impersonal impact and unrealistic optimism, and (7) the third-person effect. (Self-censorship, a burgeoning area of research, is explored in more detail later in this chapter, as part of the spiral of science discussion.) These perspectives examine different parts of the process and, in fact, define public opinion in different ways. Some perspectives appear to present public opinion as the majority opinion; others present it as generated within individuals.

Because public opinion research spans several academic disciplines, including sociology, social psychology, political science, and communication, some of these perspectives have emerged from parallel investigations in different fields. Where different terms have very similar meanings, we have discussed them together or have used the most commonly employed label. We urge you, in your own research, not to limit your literature explorations to one field. At first glance it may seem as if the discussion below is simply a potpourri of terms, definitions. and descriptions. In fact the various approaches taken toward understanding public opinion can be seen as building blocks in a young field as we attempt to understand the complexities of perceptions and opinions. Much rich understanding can come from incorporating the ideas of scholars working in multiple disciplines.

The typology developed by Glynn, Ostman, and McDonald,[15] shown in Figure 7.1, summarizes the differences among several of these approaches. One corner of this typology deals with people to whom Glynn and associates refer as "hard core." These are people who hold minority views and are aware of the fact that most people disagree with them. Because this chapter is primarily concerned with how others' opinions affect our own, we do not consider "hardcore" people here.

Looking-Glass Perception

Looking-glass perception can be simply defined as "the belief that others think the same as oneself."[16] Research has found that in many situations and for many public or social issues, most people believe that most other people have opinions similar to their own. Often this perception is correct; on uncontroversial issues, most people may guess—rightly—that theirs is the majority opinion. Indeed, in

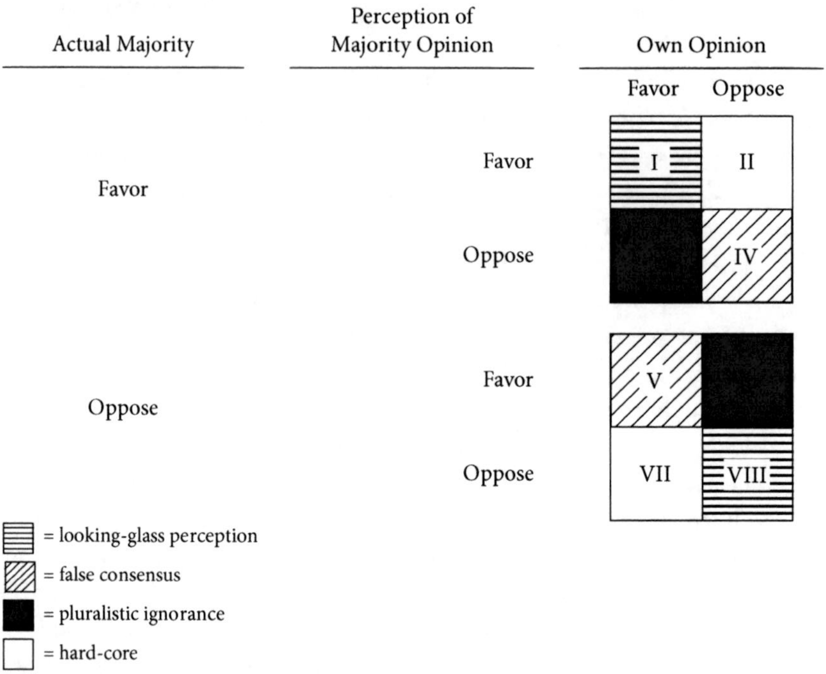

Actual Majority	Perception of Majority Opinion	Own Opinion	
		Favor	Oppose

FIGURE 7.1. **The Distribtion of Public Opinion on an Issue.**
SOURCE: Adapted from Carroll J. Glynn et al., "Opinion, Perception, and Social Reality," in Theodore L. Glasser and Charles T. Salmon, eds., *Public Opinion and the Communication of Consent* (New York: Guilford Press, 1995).

the typology, the term applies to these correct inferences. However, on divisive issues, some people in the minority may wrongly perceive that most people agree with them. In this case, looking-glass perception becomes "false consensus," which we discuss further below.[17]

The term "looking-glass perception" does implicitly suggest a particular source of this belief: people examine their own opinions and project them on other people. As Ruben Orive[18] argues, when individuals cannot conveniently compare their opinions with actual others, they may engage in "social projection" to create a "self-generated" consensus. That is, people (unconsciously) assume that other people agree with their opinion and use that putative agreement as another reason to hold the opinion. Of course, social projection is only one way that people might decide that others agree with them.

A modern-day example of the looking-glass perception is the ever-present "selfie" on social media. The photos we take of ourselves and then share online and use as our profile pictures enable us to develop a sense of self based on the perceptions of those with whom we interact.[19] Did your last selfie get a lot of likes? How did that impact your perception of self?

Pluralistic Ignorance

According to Glynn, Ostman, and McDonald, pluralistic ignorance is among the most extensively researched concepts in the perceptual influence literature.[20] In their framework, *pluralistic ignorance* occurs when people who hold the majority position on an issue incorrectly perceive it to be the minority position (see Figure 7.1). Several scholars use the term pluralistic ignorance to describe all misperceptions of others' opinions.[21] Richard Schanck originally labeled this phenomenon "misperceived consensus" or "misperceived sharing."[22] For example, suppose you believe that abortion is wrong yet perceive that your friends think abortion is appropriate in most situations. If, in fact, most of your friends actually think abortion is wrong in most situations, this is a case of pluralistic ignorance. Thus, pluralistic ignorance entails people underestimating the proportion of others who think, feel, or act as they themselves do.

Other definitions of pluralistic ignorance refer to either underestimating *or* overestimating other people's agreement with one's opinions.[23] (Glynn, Ostman, and McDonald would typically call the latter case "false consensus.") For example, Hubert O'Gorman and Stephen Garry describe pluralistic ignorance as the "false ideas held by individuals regarding the groups, social categories and collectivities to which they belong."[24] O'Gorman and Grady assert that "even members of small and relatively cohesive groups frequently misjudge the values and attitudes of other members," but that pluralistic ignorance is more common in larger, more impersonal settings. They add that in times of "accelerated social change it tends to become extensive."[25] (O'Gorman and Grady do not elaborate, but presumably in times of change, it is difficult to tell how many other people have or haven't changed their opinions.)

Often, pluralistic ignorance is tested by asking someone's opinion on a particular issue and then asking the same individual his or her perception of majority opinion. For example, in their 1970 study, O'Gorman and Garry[26] asked white respondents around the country whether they favored "desegregation, strict racial segregation, or something in between." Then they asked, "How about white people in this area? How many of them would you say are in favor of strict segregation of the races—all of them, most of them, about half, less than half, or none of them?" They also asked a similar question about "desegregation." As shown in Table 7.1, most white respondents, even in the South, said they did not personally support segregation. However, white respondents tended to markedly overestimate support for segregation. Pluralistic ignorance appeared in every demographic group O'Gorman and Garry examined, although some variables such as education were associated with both people's opinions and their perceptions of other people's opinions.

TABLE 7.1. **White Support for Racial Segregation and Whites' Perception of White Support for Racial Segregation in Area, by Region and Education**

	Favors Segregation	Perceives at Least Half Support[1]	Perceives Majority Support[2]
North[3]			
Grammar school[4]	23%	65%	32%
High school	12%	52%	28%
College	4%	36%	16%
All respondents[5]	12%	50%	25%
South[6]			
Grammar school	49%	84%	54%
High school	27%	76%	48%
College	18%	70%	36%
All respondents	30%	77%	47%

SOURCE: Adapted from Hubert O'Gorman and Stephen L. Garry, "Pluralistic Ignorance—A Replication and Extension," *Public Opinion Quarterly* 40 (1976): 452, 454, Tables 1 and 2.

NOTES:

[1] Responded that "half," "most," or "all" whites in the area favored racial segregation.

[2] Responded that "most" or "all" whites in the area favored racial segregation.

[3] Lived in any state not considered the South (see n. 6).

[4] Less than a high school diploma.

[5] Excludes respondents who did not answer at least one of the two questions reported here.

[6] Alabama, Arkansas, D.C., Florida, Georgia, Kentucky, Louisiana, Maryland, Mississippi, North Carolina, Oklahoma, South Carolina, Tennessee, Texas, Virginia, and West Virginia.

A recent study by Leviston and colleagues published in *Nature Climate Change* demonstrated a strong false consensus effect for people's estimates of others' beliefs in climate change. The authors conducted two surveys twelve months apart in Australia with over 5,000 participants, who were asked their own opinion about the nature of climate change and then asked to estimate the general population's opinion. The results demonstrate that people overestimate the number of people who reject climate change in the general public. The authors also conclude that people with high false consensus are *less* likely to change their opinions.[27]

Another recent study of pluralistic ignorance at work examined college students' perceptions of "hooking up." Both women and men rated their peers as being more comfortable with hooking up than they were themselves. Men expressed more comfort with hooking up than women, but both overestimated the other gender's level of comfort with these behaviors.[28]

Glynn and associates note that research in pluralistic ignorance generally has provided little or no explanation for it. "Pluralistic ignorance merely describes the coincidence of an issue with inaccurate perceptions."[29] Dale Miller and Cathy McFarland suggest that fear of embarrassment is a key motivation behind some cases of pluralistic ignorance.[30] If you believe your opinion is socially unacceptable, you may state the opposite opinion, and other people may do exactly the same, not realizing that all of your opinion expressions are equally insincere. You may remember the folk story "The Emperor's New Clothes," in which the emperor supposedly is wearing a spectacular suit of clothes invisible to stupid people. In fact, he is naked, but nobody wants to say so for fear of being thought stupid—until a young child calls out the truth, that he is wearing nothing at all. Miller and McFarland produce experimental evidence for a similar dynamic, in which people conform to what they believe is majority opinion, while wrongly believing that other people are much less conformist than themselves. A similar account may help to explain O'Gorman and Garry's findings. Some whites may have privately turned against racial segregation while being reluctant to say so; they may sometimes even have expressed support. But this is only one possibility. Another is that supporters of segregation were more vocal than opponents, creating the illusion that they were more numerous. And yet another possibility is our next topic: disowning projection.

Disowning Projection

Disowning projection is the pot calling the kettle black, when the kettle is shinier than the pot. More formally, as Norman Cameron defined it in 1947, *disowning projection* occurs when an individual "tends to attribute selfish motives, evil intent and stupid attitudes to others and to disclaim them for oneself, even though objectively the reverse of this may seem true to an impartial observer."[31] As Cameron describes:

> A child accused by a playmate of some act, attitude, motive or characteristic, which his peers condemn or ridicule, commonly denies it and immediately ascribes it to his accuser—"I am not! You are!"—or shifts the accusation at once to a scapegoat whom everyone dislikes. . . . The average adult still uses direct denial and counteraccusation when he is surprised into it, and when he is frightened or angry. When a person is normally on guard and neither angry nor frightened, his denials, counteraccusations and scapegoating are carried out by indirect techniques—by implication, by stressing opposite trends, by distracting others, etc.[32]

Thus, disowning projection is common, although how common depends on the person and the circumstances. You may know a classmate who habitually complains about how competitive other students are, when he or she is the most competitive student of all. Cameron's discussion focuses on pathological cases: people suffering from schizophrenia and paranoia often exhibit disowning projection, "reacting to their own behavior as if it were the behavior of others."

O'Gorman and Garry's evidence of pluralistic ignorance on segregation might be partly explained by disowning projection, or at least by social desirability bias. By 1970 many whites had seen violent attempts to defend segregation and had decided that it was wrong—or at least socially unacceptable—to side with the defenders. Yet many whites remained deeply uncomfortable with black people. Some may have dealt with this dissonance by saying, in effect, "Of course *I* don't support segregation, but those *other* people. . . ." Such people may actually have exaggerated other whites' support for segregation (true disowning projection), or they may have accurately reported widespread support for segregation while refusing to admit to it themselves.[33] In either of these related accounts, some people's expressions of opposition to segregation reflect social desirability bias—a desire to give the socially acceptable answer—rather than true opinion. At first glance, it may seem nonsensical to suggest that "social desirability" explains why many white respondents cast other whites as *more* supportive of segregation than they themselves were. But this sort of moralizing is not uncommon. The classmate who hypocritically condemns other students' competitiveness is appealing to a widely shared value that people *should not* be so competitive, even if they often are.

This explanation is almost the opposite of the pluralistic ignorance account given above, which posited that many white people were *less* supportive of segregation than they seemed to be. Which account is correct? We suspect that both accounts have some validity for various people, but we cannot go back to 1970 to test them. Even if we could, we would be hard pressed to learn what people were saying about segregation in ordinary conversation or to sort out their ambivalent opinions and attitudes based on their answers to survey questions.

A series of studies[34] conducted in Detroit, Michigan, between 1956 and 1971 provides further evidence about white racial attitudes at the time. The researchers, James Fields and Howard Schuman, presented various scenarios such as the following:

> One day a six-year-old asks her mother if she can bring another girl home to play. The mother knows that the other girl is a Negro, and that her own daughter has only played with white children before. What should the mother do? Here are three possible responses:
>
> A. She should tell her daughter that she must never play with Negroes;
>
> B. The daughter should be told that she may play with Negro children in school, but not at home; or
>
> C. The Negro child should be permitted to come to the home.[35]

(Today, the word "Negro" is no longer an appropriate term to use to describe African Americans, but even as late as 1971, it was still considered a respectful term for referring to blacks.) The researchers went on to ask whether "most people in the Detroit area" and "most people in this neighborhood" would agree, and if not, what answer they would give. In the 1969 study, the vast majority of respondents (76 percent) answered that the child should be permitted to come to the home. However, only 33 percent believed this to be the majority opinion in the Detroit area, and only 38 percent believed it to be the majority opinion in their own neighborhoods.

Fields and Schuman argue that this contradiction probably does not reflect disowning projection or social desirability bias. They reach this conclusion in part by analyzing a separate measure of people's behaviors. Respondents in the 1969 survey who said they favored open housing—that is, prohibiting discrimination against would-be homebuyers and renters on the basis of race—were subsequently asked to sign a petition stating this position. One might expect that people who gave lip service to open housing but refused to sign the petition would be more likely to attribute pro-segregation views to others than people who did sign the petition. But Fields and Schuman found otherwise: the two groups' estimates of other people's opinions were indistinguishable. While some people may have misstated their own views about segregation, the evidence for pluralistic ignorance in Detroit is probably best explained by real misperception.

More recent research on racial attitudes concludes that when blacks and whites are asked about the relevance of race in everyday issues, each group expects to agree more with its own race than with the other. Yet the groups reported remarkably similar scores. Perceptions matter.[36]

Ideological Biases

Fields and Schuman describe their findings on segregation—that people exaggerate the racial conservatism of others—as an example of conservative bias. They and others have pointed to other instances of apparent conservative bias or liberal bias. For example, Fields and Schuman note that in 1956, 79 percent of respondents said that a child should be allowed to refuse to recite the Pledge of Allegiance in school, but only 65 percent perceived this as the majority opinion. People who said that a child should *not* be allowed to refuse to recite the pledge were far more likely to think that theirs was the majority opinion than the people actually in the majority.[37] Fields and Schuman describe this result as another example of conservative bias. Glynn[38] notes that the meanings of "conservative" and "liberal" can change over time, and suggests using the broader term *ideological bias* to describe apparent misperceptions of majority opinion that have some ideological content.

In a study of neighbor perceptions of others' opinions on local, state, and national issues, Glynn[39] found evidence of ideological biases in both directions. In Glynn's study, individuals in thirty-one neighborhoods in a midwestern city were asked their own opinions, and their perceptions of other people's opinions, on eight issues: two each from the national level, the state level, the city level, and the neighborhood level. People were asked separately what they thought people in the city, and in their neighborhood, thought about each issue (except for the neighborhood issues, for which they were only asked about people in the neighborhood). Glynn summarizes the results:

> [O]n every issue without exception, respondents viewed individuals living in
> the city as having more "liberal" opinions than their own, regardless of whether
> it was a national, state or local issue. On the other hand, with only one

exception, respondents viewed their neighbors as having more "conservative" opinions on issues than their own . . . [providing] considerable evidence for . . . the existence of a "conservative bias" at least at the local level. . . . [The findings indicate] that respondents can, and do, have differing perceptions about different groups of people.[40]

Some of these differences were large. For example, 39 percent of respondents thought their neighbors were more supportive of increasing military spending (here considered a conservative opinion), while only 21 percent thought they were less supportive. Conversely, 35 percent thought others in the city were *less* supportive of increasing military spending, while only 24 percent thought they were more supportive. The largest biases appeared in the neighborhood questions. Fully 61 percent thought their neighbors were less supportive of (more "conservative" about) building a home for the mentally retarded, while only 5 percent thought the neighbors were more supportive.

Glynn's findings are remarkable because the people she interviewed were residents of both the neighborhoods and the city. They believed opinion in their city was more liberal than their own and that opinion in their neighborhood was more conservative than their own, even though they themselves were the elements composing the "public" they were speculating about.

A more recent example of ideological biases at work concerns beliefs about public officials, like the president of the United States. A 2014 study found that one in five Americans still believed the incorrect assumption that President Barack Obama was a Muslim, even after he had been in the White House for years. Although race and religious affiliation influenced this belief, so did ideology.[41]

There is also a lot of discussion of ideological bias in the media. Do a search online for "media bias," and you are sure to come across a plethora of cases and examples deriding media (fairly or not) for favoring one side over the other. Research demonstrates that more liberal Americans deem FOX News to be biased, and conservatives view CNN and the *New York Times* as biased.[42] And these perceptions can have real, behavioral effects. Rojas (2010) concluded that perceptions of media bias can lead to "corrective" political participation; those who perceive bias will often seek to rectify the unfair portrayal by engaging in political activity.[43]

False Consensus Effect

False consensus is the tendency for individuals "to see their own behavioral choices and judgments as relatively common and appropriate to existing circumstances while viewing alternative responses as uncommon, deviant and inappropriate."[44] Richard Schanck[45] originally labeled this phenomenon "misperceived consensus" or "misperceived sharing." False consensus can occur on a variety of issues. One study examining the death penalty, gun regulation, and teaching morality in schools found that those who strongly favored the policies estimated public support to be higher. Moreover, if respondents reported engaging in disagreement with others about the issues, the association between the individual opinion and false consensus declines.[46]

False consensus also means that people who engage in a given behavior, or who hold a given opinion, believe it to be shared by a larger proportion of people in the group than those with an alternative behavior or a differing opinion.[47] Lee Ross, David Greene, and Pamela House, in a 1977 study of college students, found false consensus on a variety of beliefs, preferences, and traits.[48] For example, students who preferred brown bread to white estimated, on average, that about 52 percent of students agreed with them; students who preferred white bread estimated that only about 37 percent of students preferred brown bread. On some issues, there was practically no difference: both students who considered themselves "politically left of center" and those who didn't estimated, on average, that just under 60 percent of students were left of center. The largest difference appeared on a question about whether there would be a woman on the Supreme Court within a decade. Students who thought that there would estimated that 63 percent of students agreed with them; students who thought that there wouldn't estimated that only 35 percent of students thought there would be. Thus, students on each side thought that nearly two out of three students agreed with their views. (As it happened, Sandra Day O'Connor joined the court in 1981.)

Other studies have found even more extreme examples of false consensus. For example, a 2013 study on youth delinquency shows a strong false consensus effect. Young people who report engaging in and supporting delinquent activities are more likely to exaggerate how much delinquent behavior their friends engage in. This perception has potential behavioral effects, as it may encourage more delinquent behavior. Indeed, the study showed that over time, overestimating friends' delinquency led to more delinquent behavior and friends.[49]

Why does false consensus occur? Lee Ross suggests two sets of reasons. On the one hand, false consensus can reflect a perceptual distortion that emerges from selective exposure to and recall of other people's opinions. If we disproportionately spend time with people who agree with us (or who politely downplay their disagreements), it's no wonder we tend to exaggerate the extent to which other people do agree. On the other hand, false consensus can arise from motivated bias: the desire to feel or to appear normal, appropriate, and rational.[50]

False consensus can have a major impact on public opinion formation and on public debate. In the case of the abortion debate, public discourse was radically altered by a case of false consensus (see Box 7.2).

BOX 7.2

A Case of False Consensus:
Origins of the Pro-Life Movement

The origins of the pro-life movement provide a remarkable example of the effects of false consensus. Prior to the Supreme Court's 1973 decision in *Roe v. Wade*, which protected a woman's right to an abortion in the first six months of pregnancy, many activists were working to make abortions easier to obtain legally, but there was almost no grassroots movement opposed to abortion. Kristin Luker argues that most people who opposed abortion believed that theirs was the majority view:

> Perhaps the most important reason why pro-life activists were not well prepared to resist abortion reform was that they simply couldn't believe such a movement would get very far. They tacitly assumed that the unsavory connotation of abortion rested on a deep belief in the sacredness of embryonic life, and they found it hard to understand how such a belief could be changed so quickly. They counted on public opinion to be outraged and were stunned when most of the public was either unaware or unconcerned.

Luker's qualitative interviews with pro-life activists show that this case of false consensus stemmed in part from their selective exposure to the social world. Most pro-lifers had never had abortions themselves, nor did they know anyone who had experienced an abortion (or who admitted to it). Thus, they believed that it was an uncommon event. These people also misperceived the "unsavory connotation of abortion":

> In particular, they interpreted the relative invisibility of abortion prior to the 1960s as proof that their opinion was the common one. And in a way, their assumption was plausible. If people didn't talk about abortion very much (or talked about it only in hushed tones in back rooms), wasn't that because

(continues)

(continued)

BOX 7.2
A Case of False Consensus:
Origins of the Pro-Life Movement

most people believed it was the taking of an innocent life, hence morally re-
pugnant? What these early pro-life activists did not understand was that for
many people abortion was "unspeakable" not because it represented the
death of a child but because it represented "getting caught" in the consequences of sexuality. Sex, not abortion, was what people didn't talk about.

Because of this false consensus effect, many abortion opponents were
shocked not only by the *Roe v. Wade* decision itself, but also that so few
people shared their horror about it. They had difficulty formulating
persuasive arguments to support their opinions:

Their belief that everyone accepted a common definition of the meaning and
moral nature of abortion left these pro-life people with few arguments to use
against the abortion reformers. They tried to appeal to what they thought
was the commonly shared value, but when it turned out to be not so common after all, they were literally at a loss for words.

As you can see, false consensus can have both psychological and
social consequences. In this case, the shape of public debate was altered
by people's perceptions of majority opinion.

SOURCE: Kristin Luker, *Abortion and the Politics of Motherhood* (Berkeley: University of California Press, 1984), quoted passages from pp. 128–131.

Unrealistic Optimism and Impersonal Impact

A very different, but important, perceptual influence on public opinion is called
unrealistic optimism. The basic idea is as simple as it sounds: people tend to over-
state the probability that good things will happen to them and to understate the
probability that bad things will happen to them.[51] As Neil Weinstein says, people
"expect others to be victims of misfortune, not themselves."[52] Similarly, they think
that good things are more likely to happen to them than to others. Researchers
have found that this phenomenon occurs across a wide range of topic areas, from
perceptions of being murdered to perceptions of winning the lottery.[53]

James Shepperd and colleagues note that the bias toward favorable outcomes occurs for many negative events, including diseases, natural disasters, unwanted pregnancies, and even the end of a romantic relationship.[54] These scholars further distinguish between two types of unrealistic optimism: unrealistic absolute optimism and unrealistic comparative optimism. Simply put, the former occurs when a person's estimate of his or her personal risk is too low relative to some specific standard. The latter, on the other hand, occurs when a person incorrectly judges how his or her risk compares with that of other people.

The related concept of *impersonal impact* holds that mass media information influences people's perceptions of risk to others, but not (or more weakly) their perceptions of risks to themselves.[55] For example, Tyler and Cook found that people who had seen a television newsmagazine story about fraud in home health care services were more likely afterward to view the problem as serious—but were no less confident in their own ability to secure good home health care for themselves or their relatives.[56] Impersonal impact has been considered a separate area of research, but it dovetails with unrealistic optimism: impersonal impact suggests that people will tend to perceive social risks as other people's problems.

Weinstein conducted a study that looked at college students' perceptions of future life events and the extent to which students expressed unrealistic optimism about these life events.[57] As shown in Table 7.2, unrealistic comparative optimism was widespread among these students. When you read the table, note that a positive value in the first column indicates that the students tended to believe chances were greater than average that a good thing would happen to them; a negative value indicates that students believed the chances were less than average that a bad thing would happen to them. The numbers in the second column indicate the ratio of optimistic to pessimistic responses.

Students in the study thought they were, on average, 50 percent more likely than other students at their college to like their first job after graduation, 44 percent more likely to own a home, and 35 percent more likely to travel to Europe. They also thought they were 58 percent less likely than others to have a drinking problem, 56 percent less likely to attempt suicide, and 49 percent less likely to be divorced a few years after marriage. (The optimism was not universal; for example, people were not relatively optimistic about being the same weight in ten years or about not being burglarized.) Individually, some of these optimistic judgments may have been reasonable, but it isn't reasonable for so many students to have above-average prospects *compared to each other.* Although researchers have raised questions about Weinstein's measures,[58] many studies with various measurement strategies have found broadly similar results.[59]

TABLE 7.2. **Unrealistic Optimism about Future Life Events**

	Measures of Optimism	
Abbreviated Event Description	Mean Comparative Judgment of Own Chances vs. Others' Chances (%)[a, b]	Number of Optimistic Responses Divided by Number of Pessimistic Responses[b, c]
POSITIVE EVENTS		
Liking your postgraduation job	50.2[f]	5.93[f]
Owning your own home	44.3[f]	6.22[f]
Traveling to Europe	35.3[f]	2.25[f]
Starting salary > $15,000	21.2[e]	1.56[d]
Graduating in top third of class	14.2	1.02
Your work being recognized with an award	12.6[d]	1.72[d]
Not spending a night in the hospital for 5 years	8.5	1.23
Having a gifted child	6.2[d]	2.26[e]
In 10 years, earning > $40,000 a year	-0.7	0.64[d]
Marrying someone wealthy	-9.1	0.36[d]
NEGATIVE EVENTS		
Having a drinking problem	-58.3[f]	7.23[f]
Getting divorced a few years after getting married	-48.7	9.50[f]
Being fired from a job	-31.6[f]	7.56[f]
Dropping out of college	-30.8[f]	3.49[f]

(continues)

(continued)

TABLE 7.2. **Unrealistic Optimism about Future Life Events**

	Measures of Optimism	
Abbreviated Event Description	Mean Comparative Judgment of Own Chances vs. Others' Chances (%)[a, b]	Number of Optimistic Responses Divided by Number of Pessimistic Responses[b, c]
NEGATIVE EVENTS		
Having a heart attack	-23.3[f]	3.18[f]
Not finding a job for 6 months	-14.4[f]	2.36[f]
Buying a car that turns out to be a lemon	-10.0[d]	2.12[e]
Tripping and breaking a bone	-8.3[d]	1.66[d]
Being sued by someone	-7.9	2.38[f]
Being a victim of mugging	-5.8	3.17[f]

NOTES:

[a] In making a comparative judgment, students estimated the difference in percent between the chances that an event would happen to them and the average chances for other students at their college of the same sex. $N = 123$ to 130, depending on rating form and missing data. Student's t was used to test whether the mean is significantly different from zero.

[b] For positive events, the response that one's own chances are greater than average is considered optimistic, and the response that one's own chances are less than average is considered pessimistic. For negative events, the definitions of optimistic and pessimistic responses are reversed.

[c] Significance levels refer to a chi-square test of the hypothesis that frequencies of optimistic and pessimistic responses are equal.

[d] $p < .05$.

[e] $p < .01$.

[f] $p < .001$.

SOURCE: Adapted from Neil D. Weinstein, "Unrealistic Optimism About Future Life Events," *Journal of Personality and Social Psychology* 39 (1980): 806–820.

How might unrealistic optimism affect public opinion? That depends on how it interacts with other aspects of people's thinking. For example, if people's policy preferences tend to coincide with their perceived self-interest, then unrealistic optimism could bias them toward weaker "safety net" programs than they otherwise would support. However, if people tend to take a society-wide view of policy impacts, then unrealistic optimism may not bias their policy preferences, although it may influence their private choices. (For example, people may tend to underinvest in insurance for themselves, but may still be supportive of government health care for the unfortunate even if they dismiss the prospect of being so unfortunate themselves.)

The concept of impersonal impact ultimately suggests that people assume media are powerful in influencing others, which can influence cognitions and behavior. A study by Hoffman concluded that political discussions in the media influenced citizens' perceptions of which presidential candidate would win their state in an election.[60] Mutz noted that the mechanism driving impersonal influence is likely to be different for "citizens with differing levels of information,"[61] which is borne out by Hoffman's study. Hoffman found that citizens who read more content in their local papers and talked more about the Democratic candidate were more likely to be influenced in their perception that the candidate would win.

Third-Person Effect

The third-person effect describes the fact that when individuals are exposed to a persuasive message, such as an advertisement on television, they often perceive greater effects on others (i.e., the "third person") than on themselves. The term was established by sociologist W. Phillips Davison in 1983.[62] Using his own personal experiences with journalists, he examined the phenomenon in which some journalists seemed to be convinced that editorials had an effect on others' attitudes, but not on people like them. Or, you might think to yourself, that ad for sugary soda might influence other people to buy it, but definitely not me!

The third-person effect is similar to the idea of unrealistic optimism, only instead of referring to the chances of good or bad events, the concern is about the perceived effects of the mass media. Davison's ideas have generated a good deal of research. For example, Jeremy Cohen, Diana Mutz, Vincent Price, and Albert Gunther studied the third-person effect by asking people to read defamatory newspaper articles. They found that readers who were exposed to these newspaper articles estimated that others would be significantly more affected by the messages than they themselves had been.[63]

The third-person effect has two components: perceptual and behavioral. The *perceptual* component is just that: the perception that others are more influenced by content. The *behavioral* component proposes that biased third-person effects will result in behavioral action. The most commonly studied behavioral outcomes are support for censorship and willingness to speak out.

Why do people engage in third-person effects? One analysis suggested that "people project negative effects onto others in order to avoid the discomfort caused by admitting that such content affects themselves."[64] There are other motivations for this perception. Hoffman and Glynn also note that in addition to unrealistic optimism, whereby people are motivated to believe that unfortunate events are more likely to happen to others than to themselves, individuals are also motivated to protect their self-concept from threatening messages and maintain general control over their environment.

In addition to the third-person effect, some research has found a "reverse first-person effect," wherein people perceive a greater effect on themselves than on others, as long as the content is positive and desirable. So if a person were watching a media message encouraging healthy eating habits, he or she might be more likely to say he or she is affected by the content than are others.[65]

In the age of microtargeted messaging, when an online search can result in tailored ads displayed for different users, the third-person effect might take on a different role. Even in the "old days" of mass-targeted messages, we saw that ads can influence us even when we don't think they do. But now, the likelihood of being impacted by highly targeted ads should arguably be much higher.

PUBLIC OPINION AS A SOCIAL PROCESS

The theories we have considered so far in this chapter operate at the individual level, although they involve people's opinions about social groups. Such theories are useful, but they have limited capacity to describe or explain some of the ways in which public opinion changes The theories we turn to next describe public opinion more as a *social* process: how groups, or even the entire public, behave and change collectively. There are a number of public process models; we briefly discuss several in this section.

Foote and Hart's (1953) Developmental Model

Following Herbert Blumer's lead, Foote and Hart[66] construe a public as created and defined by its members' discussion of some issue. (Thus, many publics exist simultaneously, and they change size and shape as the discussion evolves.) First comes the problem phase, in which some people—a nascent public—come to agree that a problem exists. Next comes the proposal phase, in which members of the public consider various ways to deal with the problem. Then come the policy and program phases, by the end of which a course of action is decided on, typically with broad public support. The final phase is the appraisal stage, in which the public periodically reevaluates the policy.

This model is idealized; issues and publics do not have to develop in this linear manner, or at all. (And it may be hopelessly unclear who belongs to a particular public.) It may be most useful for the questions it prompts us to ask about "public opinion" on an issue, such as: Who is thinking about it? Who is talking about it, and to whom? How specific are those conversations, and what kinds of information (accurate or inaccurate) do they incorporate? How many people are saying "Do something," and how many know what they want to have done? The common idea of an *issue public* has roots in Foote and Hart's model.

Davison's (1958) Communication and Opinion Leadership Model

W. Phillips Davison's model[67] is grounded in individual behaviors, but it ultimately portrays broader social dynamics. Davison starts from a famous discussion of public opinion by the German poet Christoph Wieland in 1798. Wieland wrote that he understood "public opinion" to mean

> an opinion that gradually takes root among a whole people, especially among those who have the most influence when they work together as a group. In this way it wins the upper hand to such an extent that one meets it everywhere.... It is an opinion that without being noticed takes possession of most heads, and even in situations where it does not dare to express itself out loud it can be recognized by a louder and louder muffled murmur. It then only requires some small opening that will allow it air, and it will break out with force. Then it can change whole nations in a brief time and give whole parts of the world a new configuration.[68]

In this view, then, a public is defined by the opinion it shares, an opinion that may not often be openly expressed but nonetheless can have momentous consequences.

Somewhat like Foote and Hart, Davison emphasizes the role of issues in public opinion formation. For Davison, the formation process begins with issue presentation, in which people communicate ideas—potential issues—to each other. When an issue is passed to a third and fourth and fifth person, it begins to take root. Most potential issues disappear from attention before this "human chain" grows to an appreciable length, but the few that remain form the basis for public opinion. A contemporary analogy might be how a YouTube video can either "go viral" or remain obscure, depending on how many people share it.

Davison emphasizes the role of groups in determining how opinions are communicated. Opinions initially spread within a primary group—a group of people who converse together on an issue. Most opinions never progress beyond a primary group, but some find "leadership transcending the original primary group."[69] The most influential opinion leaders have the means to publicize their views, as well as the skill to simplify and generalize their ideas so that they will appeal to the largest possible audience. If many in that audience accept the new idea, a widely held public opinion may develop. Face-to-face discussion proceeds in other primary groups, and these new discussions lead to more public communication about the issue.

Davison's model also integrates people's perceptions of others' opinions. As public discussion of an issue increases, individuals begin to form expectations about what others' opinions are likely to be. As we have seen, those expectations may rely on particular conversations, on social projection, on assumptions about other people's thought processes, and so on. Individuals decide what to say about their opinions—whether to speak, remain silent, or even express the opposite of their private views—considering the opinions of salient others. Davison argues, "A process is set up in which expectations produce behavioral adjustments, and these in turn reinforce expectations. When this has happened, public opinion has been formed."[70]

Price and Roberts's Communication and Reciprocal Relationships Model

Price and Roberts's 1987 model of public opinion processing[71] shares many basic elements with Davison's approach. Price and Roberts describe public opinion as a "process of social organization through communicating." In their model, (1) a public is not organized in any fixed fashion until forced to communicate in resolving issues; and (2) public opinion is decidedly not the distribution of opinions within a public, but is instead a complex function of processes in which disparate ideas are expressed, adjusted, and compromised en route to collective determination of a course of action.

According to Price and Roberts, the public opinion process may be conceptualized as communication between political actors who are pursuing public recognition and support for views and members of the interested public who are trying to understand the issue and decide whom to support. Price and Roberts observe that many people "deciding their stand on a public issue are not so much deciding their own opinion (or where they stand on the matter) but instead deciding on their social loyalties (in other words, with whom they stand)."[72] They call public opinion a social process, and more specifically, they emphasize the important role of communication, suggesting that the relationship between cognitions and behavior is a "continuing dialectic," in which individuals incorporate new information with preexisting opinions.[73] The public, then, is formed by the issue, not the other way around. A public is composed of various groups, some of them interpersonal, others broadly social, "attempting through discursive means to resolve a common issue."[74] The process of forming and changing public opinion is a complex one that involves political actors, media, and an interested public, and all these elements attempt to ascertain and influence opinions on social issues. Thus, the public opinion process is a process of social accommodation.

Hoffman and her colleagues built on this model by identifying sources of influence: (1) predispositions and interests (i.e., intrapersonal filters); (2) the media, which disseminate public opinion and issue specific information (i.e., media filters); and (3) interpersonal political discussion, which gives an issue momentum and strengthens opinion, as well as supplying additional relevant information (i.e., social filters).[75] They concluded that interpersonal factors largely accounted for how public opinion was formed around a community issue.

Noelle-Neumann's Social System Process Model: The Spiral of Silence

Whereas Davison's model considers both how opinions spread and how contrary opinions may go unspoken, Elizabeth Noelle-Neumann's *spiral of silence theory*[76] focuses squarely on the latter. Noelle-Neumann, a German political scientist and pollster, posits that our relationships with others are so important to us that we will willingly change or repress our opinions in order to be accepted by others. She states that to the individual, "not isolating himself is more important than his own judgment."[77]

Perhaps surprisingly, spiral of silence theory began with a voting behavior puzzle. In 1965 Noelle-Neumann polled and studied the West German federal elections, in which the ruling Christian Democratic Union coalition was challenged by the Social Democrats.[78] She found that for many months before the election, the polls showed the parties essentially tied, yet they also showed a steady shift toward believing that the Christian Democrats would remain in power. Then, just before the election, about 3–4 percent of voters suddenly switched their support to the Christian Democrats, who won by a decent margin. During the 1972 election, Noelle-Neumann noticed a similar pattern: a late shift to support the expected winners. Surprised, Noelle-Neumann decided to investigate, and her research on the spiral of silence began.

Spiral of silence theory posits that one's perception of the distribution of public opinion affects one's willingness or unwillingness to express opinions.[79] Individuals who notice that their personal opinions are spreading will voice these opinions self-confidently in public; those who notice their opinions are "losing ground" will be inclined to adopt a more reserved attitude and remain silent. These perceptions of reality become reality as people's opinions are swayed by the increasingly one-sided content of public discourse. The result is a spiral of silence, as the expression of dissenting opinion becomes smaller and fainter.[80]

The theory is complex, and it is not possible to present the details here. However, it is important to note that four key elements enter into the theory: (1) one's own opinion on an issue; (2) one's perception of the predominant public opinion; (3) one's assessment of the likely future course of public opinion; and (4) one's willingness to support one's opinion with action, verbal statements, or other signs of commitment.[81] One's own opinion, and one's perception of predominant opinion, both are assumed to influence one's judgment of the future course of opinion. One's willingness to speak out then depends on the interaction among these variables—basically, on whether one expects to end up in the majority or the minority.

Noelle-Neumann's full conception of the public opinion process contains several important aspects, including (1) societal functions of public opinion, (2) moral and behavioral components of public opinion, (3) the importance of perception in the public opinion process, and (4) the importance of communication in opinion outcomes. The spiral of silence theory attempts to describe impacts on public opinion that go far beyond interpersonal interaction.

Since Noelle-Neuman's initial research, more public opinion research has been conducted on the spiral of silence than on almost any other single public opinion approach, thesis, or question.[82] An updated meta-analysis concluded with essentially the same findings: perceived opinion climate continues to have an effect on opinion expression.[83] Yet several of the most recent studies in this review demonstrated small, sometimes not significant, effects when other key variables were included. More recent research suggests that opinion expression is affected by the climate of opinion only when opinions are of low or moderate certainty, but it doesn't matter for those with high certainty about their opinions.[84] Another study concluded that communication apprehension (anxiety about communicating), along with fear of isolation, can also impact opinion expression.[85] Carroll Glynn and Jack McLeod[86] argue that the spiral of silence theory is important because it describes how, through social interaction, people influence each other's willingness to express opinions.

Other scholars have identified a personality characteristic that might explain opinion expression better than fear of isolation: self-censorship. "Willingness to Self-Censor" was developed by Glynn and colleagues to address conflicting results in the spiral of silence literature.[87] The eight-item validated scale draws from research in social psychology, specifically on conformity, which suggests there is a lot of variability in individuals' willingness to offer an opposing opinion in a confronting opinion climate. It is also rooted in research on individuation, which suggests that a person's willingness to engage in behaviors that make him or her be distinctive from others in a group could impact opinion expression.

Noelle-Neumann also ascribes importance to the mass media's impact on the formation and presentation of the public's opinions. According to Noelle-Neumann, the media play a crucial role in that their messages are "ubiquitous" (everywhere) and "consonant" (they repeat the same messages over and over).[88] Essentially, the media continually bombard us with information that frames our social reality—and regardless of the reporter or the medium, the messages tend to be the same. According to Noelle-Neumann, we learn most of our societal norms, customs, and so forth from the media. That is, media messages continually reinforce accounts of what we should believe about any numbers of issues.

It is clear that the spiral of silence is an important theory that the student of public opinion should understand. Although many researchers have found problems with the theory,[89] it is widely regarded as a major contribution to public opinion theory and research. If anything, the most simple of its premises attest to its importance: we are social, others are important to us, we want others to like us, and we want to fit in. These factors clearly influence public opinion formation. Of all the approaches discussed in this chapter, Noelle-Neumann's spiral of silence theory may be the most broadly applicable.

CONCLUSION AND IMPLICATIONS FOR THE FUTURE

These theories are exciting yet incomplete. What is fascinating for the student of public opinion is that we know that psychological, social, and political factors can change or motivate public opinion outcomes, but we are not sure what these factors are or exactly when these outcomes will occur.

We know that the media are important in the formation of public opinion, but we do not know enough about how people are influenced by these powerful transmitters of information. Politicians know there are ways to manipulate the public through the media, yet public opinion scholars do not know enough about the public opinion process to be able to determine how and when this manipulation will occur. The public is arguably more vulnerable and more susceptible because of this lack of research in this important area.

Perception has been defined throughout this chapter as a summary attitude based on all of our past and present sensory information. Perceptions are limited because they are selective. Perceptions also play a comparative role; we compare our perceptions to those of others. Socialization, the influence of what others important to us think, and social comparison, the comparison of one's opinion to others to test its validity, have become important theories used to explain how individuals apply their perceptions to the larger social context.

Public opinion is clearly more than responses to public opinion polls. It is a verbal expression of culture, of social interactions, of psychological processes. Students of public opinion should understand the approaches described in this chapter, but should also make sure they have a solid grasp of theories developed in other fields, especially sociology, social psychology, and psychology. It is important that we understand how public opinion works so that we can go beyond mere speculation or description. The field is exciting, and there continues to be much to learn. Public opinion scholars of the future can help us understand this important and fundamental social process that is vital to our very survival.

NOTES

1. Drew Westen, Pavel S. Blagov, Keith Harenski, Clint Kilts, and Stephan Hamann, "Neural Bases of Motivated Reasoning: An fMRI Study of Emotional Constraints on Partisan Political Judgment in the 2004 U.S. Presidential Election," *Journal of Cognitive Neuroscience* 18, no. 11 (2006): 1947–1958.

2. Walter Lippmann, *Public Opinion* (New York: Harcourt, Brace, 1922), 4, 11.

3. George J. McCall and J. L. Simmons, *Identities and Interactions: An Examination of Human Associations in Everyday Life,* 2nd ed. (New York: Free Press, 1978), 104.

4. Ibid.

5. Jerome S. Bruner, "Social Psychology and Perception," in Eleanor E. Maccoby, Theodore M. Newcomb, and Eugene L. Hartley, eds., *Readings in Social Psychology* (New York: Holt, Rinehart and Winston, 1958), 86.

6. Ibid.

7. Paul R. Abramson, *Political Attitudes in America: Formation and Change* (San Francisco: W. H. Freeman and Co., 1983); M. Kent Jennings and Richard G. Niemi, *Generations and Politics: A Panel Study of Young Adults and Their Parents* (Princeton, NJ: Princeton University Press, 1981); Roberta L. Sangster and Robert W. Reynolds, "A Test of Inglehart's Socialization Hypothesis for the Acquisition of Materialist/Postmaterialist Values: The Influence of Childhood Poverty on Adult Values," *Political Psychology* 17 (1996): 253–269.

8. Yair Ghitza and Andrew Gelman, "The Great Society, Reagan's Revolution, and Generations of Presidential Voting" (working paper, July 7, 2014).

9. Erica Weintraub Austin, "Apathy, Voter," in Lynda Lee Kaid and Christina Holtz-Bacha, eds., *Encyclopedia of Political Communication* (Thousand Oaks, CA: Sage Publications, 2007), 37.

10. Leon Festinger, "A Theory of Social Comparison Processes," *Human Relations* 7 (1954): 117–140.

11. Hyun Soon Park and Charles T. Salmon, "A Test of the Third-person Effect in Public Relations: Application of Social Comparison Theory," *Journalism & Mass Communication Quarterly* 82 (2005): 25–43.

12. Arie W. Kruglanski and Ofra Mayseless, "Motivational Effects in the Social Comparison of Opinions," *Journal of Personality and Social Psychology* 5, no. 53 (1987): 834–842.

13. See, e.g., Albert C. Gunther and Stella Chih-Yun Chia, "Predicting Pluralistic Ignorance: The Hostile Media Perception and Its Consequences," *Journalism and Mass Communication Quarterly* 78, no. 4 (2001): 688–701; Diana C. Mutz, *Impersonal Influence: How Perceptions of Mass Collectives Affect Political Attitudes* (Cambridge, UK: Cambridge University Press, 1998); Jordon M. Robbins and Joachim I. Krueger, "Social Projection to In groups and Out groups: A Review and Meta-Analysis," *Personality and Social Psychology Review* 9 (2005): 32–47; Jounghwa Choi, Myengja Yang, and Jeongheon J. C. Chang, "Elaboration of the Hostile Media Phenomenon: The Roles of Involvement, Media Skepticism, Congruency of Perceived Media Influence, and Perceived Opinion Climate," *Communication Research* 36 (2009): 54–75; Lindsay H. Hoffman and Carroll J. Glynn, "Media and Perceptions of Reality," in Wolfgang Donsbach, ed., *The International Encyclopedia of Communication*, (Malden, MA: Blackwell, 2008), VII:2945–2959; Tien-Tsung Lee, "The Liberal Media Myth Revisited: An Examination of Factors Influencing Perceptions of Media Bias," *Journal of Broadcasting & Electronic Media* 49 (2005): 43–64; Tien-Tsung Lee, "Why They Don't Trust the Media: An Examination of Factors Predicting Trust," *American Behavioral Scientist* 54 (2010): 8–21; Jonathan S. Morris, "Slanted Objectivity? Perceived Media Bias, Cable News Exposure, and Political Attitudes," *Social Science Quarterly* 88, no. 3 (2007): 707–728.

14. Glynn, Ostman, and McDonald, "Opinions, Perceptions and Social Reality"; Carroll J. Glynn, "Public Opinion as a Normative Opinion Process," in Brant R. Burleson, ed., *Communication Yearbook 20* (Thousand Oaks, CA: Sage Publications, 1996), 157–183.

15. Glynn, Ostman, and McDonald, "Opinions, Perceptions and Social Reality."

16. James M. Fields and Howard Schuman, "Public Beliefs About the Beliefs of the Public," *Public Opinion Quarterly* 40 (1976): 445.

17. Lauren J. Human and Jeremy C. Biesanz, "Through the Looking Glass Clearly: Accuracy and Assumed Similarity in Well-adjusted Individuals' First Impressions," *Journal of Personality and Social Psychology* 100, no. 2 (2011): 349–364; Slavko Splichal, "The Public in the Private, Privately about the Public: Opinion Polls in the Political Process," *Javnost-The Public* 16 (2009): S81; Serena Chen, Helen C. Boucher, and Molly P. Tapias, "The Relational Self Revealed: Integrative Conceptualization and Implications for Interpersonal Life," *Psychological Bulletin* 132, no. 2 (2006): 151–179.

18. Ruben Orive, "Social Projection and Social Comparison of Opinions," *Journal of Personality and Social Psychology* 54, no. 6 (1988): 953–964.

19. Christine Erickson, "The Social Psychology of the Selfie," mashable.com, February 15, 2013, http://mashable.com/2013/02/15/social-media-and-the-selfie/.

20. Classic influential discussions include Frank H. Allport, *Social Psychology* (Cambridge, MA: Riverside Press, 1924); Richard Louis Schanck, "A Study of a Community and Its Groups and Institutions Conceived of as Behaviors of Individuals," *Psychological Monographs* 43, no. 2 (1932): entire issue; Hubert O'Gorman and Stephen L. Garry, "Pluralistic Ignorance—A Replication and Extension," *Public Opinion Quarterly* 40 (1976): 449–458; Dale T. Miller and Cathy McFarland, "Pluralistic Ignorance: When Similarity Is Interpreted as Dissimilarity," *Journal of Personality and Social Psychology* 53, no. 2 (1987): 298–305; and D. Garth Taylor, "Pluralistic Ignorance and the Spiral of Silence: A Formal Analysis," *Public Opinion Quarterly* 46 (1982): 311–355.

21. William P. Eveland Jr., "The Impact of News and Entertainment Media on Perceptions of Social Reality." in James Price Dillard and Michael Pfau, eds., *The Persuasion Handbook: Developments in Theory and Practice* (Thousand Oaks, CA: Sage, 2002), 691–727; Fields and Schuman, "Public Beliefs about Beliefs of the Public;" Hoffman and Glynn, "Media and Perceptions of Reality."

22. Schanck, "A Study of a Community and Its Groups and Institutions."

23. Patricia Moy, "Pluralistic Ignorance and Nonattitudes," in Wolfgang Donsbach and Michael W. Traugott, eds., *SAGE Handbook of Public Opinion Research* (Thousand Oaks, CA: SAGE Publications, 2007), ch.15.

24. O'Gorman and Garry, "Pluralistic Ignorance," 450.

25. Ibid.

26. Ibid.

27. Z. Leviston, I. Walker, and S. Morwinski, "Your Opinion on Climate Change Might Not Be as Common as You Think," *Nature Climate Change* 3 (2013): 334–337.

28. Tracy A. Lambert, Arnold S. Kahn, and Kevin J. Apple, "Pluralistic Ignorance and Hooking Up," *Journal of Sex Research* 40, no. 2 (2003): 129–133.

29. Glynn, Ostman, and McDonald, "Opinions, Perceptions and Social Reality," 262.

30. Miller and McFarland, "Pluralistic Ignorance."

31. Norman Cameron, *The Psychology of Behavior Disorders: A Biosocial Interpretation* (Boston: Houghton Mifflin, 1947), 168.

32. Ibid.

33. Fields and Schuman discuss both these possibilities in "Public Beliefs about the Beliefs of the Public," 434.

34. Fields and Schuman, "Public Beliefs about the Beliefs of the Public."

35. Ibid., 430.

36. Diana E. Betz, Laura R. Ramsey, and Denise Sekaquaptewa, "Perceiving Race Relevance in Everyday Events: Target Race Matters, Perceiver Race Does Not," *Group Processes & Intergroup Relations* 16, no. 6 (2013): 699–716.

37. Fields and Schuman, "Public Beliefs about the Beliefs of the Public," 432. (The 65 percent figure is calculated from numbers reported in the text.)

38. Carroll J. Glynn, "Perceptions of Others' Opinions as a Component of Public Opinion," *Social Science Research* 18 (1989): 64.

39. Ibid.

40. Ibid., 63.

41. Michael A. Cacciatore, Sara K. Yeo, Dietram A. Scheufele, Michael A. Xenos, Doo-Hun Choi, Dominique Brossard, Amy B. Becker, and Elizabeth A. Corley, "Misperceptions in Polarized Politics: The Role of Knowledge, Religiosity, and Media," *PS—Political Science & Politics* 47, no. 3 (2014): 654–661.

42. Carroll J. Glynn and Michael E. Huge, "How Pervasive Are Perceptions of Bias? Exploring Judgments of Media Bias in Financial News," *International Journal of Public Opinion Research* 26, no. 4 (2014): 543–553; Lee, "The Liberal Media Myth Revisited" and Lee, "Why They Don't Trust the Media."

43. Hernando Rojas, "'Corrective Actions' in the Public Sphere: How Perceptions of Media and Media Effects Shape Political Behaviors," *International Journal of Public Opinion Research* 22, no. 3 (2010): 343–363.

44. Lee Ross, David Greene, and Pamela House, "The 'False Consensus Effect': An Egocentric Bias in Social Perception and Attribution Processes," *Journal of Experimental Social Psychology* 13 (1977): 280.

45. Schanck, "A Study of a Community and Its Groups and Institutions."

46. Magdalena Wojcieszak and Vincent Price, "What Underlies the False Consensus Effect? How Personal Opinion and Disagreement Affect Perception of Public Opinion," *International Journal of Public Opinion Research* 21 (2009): 25–46.

47. Brian Mullen et al., "The False Consensus Effect: A Meta-Analysis of 115 Hypothesis Tests," *Journal of Experimental Social Psychology* 21 (1985): 262–283.

48. Ross, Greene, and House, "The 'False Consensus Effect.'"

49. Jacob T. N. Young and Frank M. Weerman, "Delinquency as a Consequence of Misperception: Overestimation of Friends' Delinquent Behavior and Mechanisms of Social Influence," *Social Problems* 60, no. 3 (2013): 334–356.

50. Lee Ross, "The Intuitive Psychologist and His Shortcomings: Distortions in the Attribution Process," in Leonard Berkowitz, ed., *Advances in Experimental Social Psychology* (New York: Academic Press, 1977), 150–195.

51. Roger A. Drake, "Lateral Asymmetry of Personal Optimism," *Journal of Research in Personality* 18, no. 4 (1984): 497–507.

52. Neil D. Weinstein, "Unrealistic Optimism About Future Life Events," *Journal of Personality and Social Psychology* 39, no. 5 (1980): 806.

53. Hugh M. Culbertson and Guido H. Stempel, "Media Malaise: Explaining Personal Optimism and Societal Pessimism About Health Care," *Journal of Communication* 35 (1985): 180–190.

54. James A. Shepperd, William M. P. Klein, Erika A. Waters, and Neil D. Weinstein, "Taking Stock of Unrealistic Optimism," *Perspectives on Psychological Science* 8, no. 4 (2013): 395–411.

55. Patricia Moy, "Social Perception: Impersonal Impact," in Donsbach, ed., *International Encyclopedia of Communication*.

56. Tom R. Tyler and Fay L. Cook, "The Mass Media and Judgments of Risk: Distinguishing Impact on Personal and Societal Level Judgments," *Journal of Personality and Social Psychology* 47 (1984): 693–708.

57. Weinstein, "Unrealistic Optimism About Future Life Events."

58. Adam J. L. Harris and Ulrike Hahn, "Unrealistic Optimism About Future Life Events: A Cautionary Note," *Psychological Review* 118 (2011): 135–154.

59. See, e.g., the references cited in Neil D. Weinstein and William M. Klein, "Unrealistic Optimism: Present and Future," *Journal of Social and Clinical Psychology* 15 (1996): 1–8, and in Harris and Hahn, "Unrealistic Optimism."

60. Lindsay H. Hoffman, "When the World Outside Gets Inside Your Head: The Effects of Media Context on Perceptions of Public Opinion," *Communication Research* 40, no. 4 (2013): 463–485.

61. Mutz, *Impersonal Influence*, 216.

62. W. Phillips Davison, "The Third-Person Effect in Communication," *Public Opinion Quarterly* 47 (1983): 1–15.

63. Jeremy Cohen et al., "Perceived Impact of Defamation: An Experiment on Third-Person Effects," *Public Opinion Quarterly* 52 (1988): 161–173.

64. Hoffman and Glynn, "Media and Perceptions of Reality."

65. Anita G. Day, "Out of the Living Room and into the Voting Booth: An Analysis of Corporate Public Affairs Advertising under the Third-person Effect," *American Behavioral Scientist* 52, no. 2 (2008): 243–260.

66. Nelson N. Foote and Clyde W. Hart, "Public Opinion and Collective Behavior," in Muzafer Sherif and M. O. Wilson, eds., *Group Relations at the Crossroads* (New York: Harper and Row, 1953), 301–332; Vincent Price, *Public Opinion* (Newbury Park, CA: SAGE Publications, 1992), 29–30.

67. W. Phillips Davison, "The Public Opinion Process," *Public Opinion Quarterly* 21 (1957): 103–118.

68. Christoph Martin Wieland, *Gespräch unter vier Augen* (1798), 103.

69. Davison, "The Public Opinion Process," 106.

70. Ibid.

71. Vincent Price and Donald F. Roberts, "Public Opinion Processing," in C. R. Berger and S. H. Chaffee, eds., *Handbook of Communication Science* (Beverly Hills, CA: Sage Publications, 1987), 781–816.

72. Ibid., 800.

73. Ibid., 789.

74. Ibid., 803.

75. Lindsay H. Hoffman, Carroll J. Glynn, Michael E. Huge, Tiffany Thomson, and Rebecca Border Seitman, "The Role of Communication in Public Opinion Processes: Understanding the Impacts of Individual, Media, and Social Filters," *International Journal of Public Opinion Research* 19, no. 3 (2007): 1–26.

76. Elisabeth Noelle-Neumann, "Return to the Concept of a Powerful Mass Media," *Studies of Broadcasting* 9 (March 1973): 67–112; Elisabeth Noelle-Neumann, *The Spiral of Silence: Public Opinion—Our Social Skin* (Chicago: University of Chicago Press, 1984).

77. Elisabeth Noelle-Neumann, "Turbulences in the Climate of Opinion: Methodological Applications of the Spiral of Silence Theory," *Public Opinion Quarterly* 41 (1977): 143–158.

78. The Christian Democratic Union was allied with the much smaller Christian Social Union. For simplicity, we use "Christian Democrats" as shorthand for the two parties together.

79. Carroll J. Glynn, "The Communication of Public Opinion," *Journalism Quarterly* 64 (1987): 688–697.

80. Noelle-Neumann, *The Spiral of Silence.*

81. Taylor, "Pluralistic Ignorance and the Spiral of Silence."

82. Carroll J. Glynn, Andrew F. Hayes, and James Shanahan, "Spiral of Silence: A Meta-Analysis," *Public Opinion Quarterly* 61, no. 3 (1997): 452–463.

83. Carroll J. Glynn and Michael E. Huge, "Speaking in Spirals: An Updated Meta-analysis of the Spiral of Silence," in Wolfgang Donsbach, Charles T. Salmon, and Yariv Tsfati, eds., *The Spiral of Silence: New Perspectives on Communication and Public Opinion* (New York: Routledge, 2014).

84. Jörg Matthes, Kimberly Rios Morrison, and Christian Schemer, "A Spiral of Silence for Some: Attitude Certainty and the Expression of Political Minority Opinions," *Communication Research* 37, no. 6 (2010): 774–800, doi: 10.1177/0093650210362685.

85. K. Neuwirth, E., Frederick, and C. Mayo, "The Spiral of Silence and Fear of Isolation," *Journal of Communication* 57, no. 3 (2007): 450–468.

86. Carroll J. Glynn and Jack M. McLeod, "Implications of the Spiral of Silence Theory for Communication and Public Opinion Research," in Keith R. Sanders, Lynda Lee

Kaid, and Dan D. Nimmo, eds. *Political Communication Yearbook* (Carbondale: Southern Illinois University Press, 1985), 43–68.

87. Carroll J. Glynn, Andrew F. Hayes, and James Shanahan, "Perceived Support for One's Opinions and Willingness to Speak Out: A Meta-analysis of Survey Studies on the "Spiral of Silence," *Public Opinion Quarterly* 61 (1997): 452–461.

88. Noelle-Neumann, *The Spiral of Silence*; Noelle-Neumann, "Return to the Concept of a Powerful Mass Media"; Andrew F. Hayes, Carroll J. Glynn, and James Shanahan, "Willingness to Self-censor: A Construct and Measurement Tool for Public Opinion Research," *International Journal of Public Opinion Research* 17 (2005): 299–323; Andrew F. Hayes, Carroll J. Glynn, and James Shanahan, "Validating the Willingness to Self-censor Scale: Individual Differences in the Effect of the Climate of Opinion on Willingness to Express an Opinion," *International Journal of Public Opinion Research* 17 (2005): 443–445.

89. Glynn, "Perceptions of Others' Opinions as a Component of Public Opinion"; Dominic L. Lasorsa, "Real and Perceived Effects of 'Amerika,'" *Journalism Quarterly* 66 (1989): 373–378; Charles T. Salmon and Chi-Yung Moh, "The Spiral of Silence: Linking Individual and Society Through Communication," in J. David Kennamer, ed., *Public Opinion, the Press, and Public Policy* (Westport, CT: Praeger, 1994), 145–161; Glynn, Hayes, and Shanahan, "The Spiral of Silence: A Meta-Analysis"; Glynn and McLeod, "Implications of the Spiral of Silence Theory"; Carroll J. Glynn and Jack M. McLeod, "Public Opinion du Jour: An Examination of the Spiral of Silence," *Public Opinion Quarterly* 48, no. 4 (1984): 731–740; Charles T. Salmon and F. Gerald Kline, "The Spiral of Silence Ten Years Later," in Sanders, Kaid, and Nimmo, eds., *Political Communication Yearbook*, 3–30; Charles T. Salmon and Hayg Oshagan, "Community Size, Perceptions of Majority Opinion and Opinion Expression," *Public Relations Research Annual* 2 (1990): 157–171; Wolfgang Donsbach and Robert L. Stevenson, "Challenges, Problems and Empirical Evidence of the Theory of the Spiral of Silence" (paper presented at the International Communication Association Conference, San Francisco, 1984); Frank L. Rusciano, *Isolation and Paradox: Defining "the Public" in Modern Political Analysis* (New York: Greenwood Press, 1989).

8

Economic Approaches

The last three chapters have described various psychological and sociological perspectives and influences on public opinion. This chapter[1] introduces an approach from another social science: economics. Economics may seem basically irrelevant to the study of social and political attitudes and opinions. After all, people usually construe economics as the study of the "money economy": how goods are produced and consumed, bought and sold, and so forth. However, the basic concepts of microeconomics—the assumptions about how individuals make decisions about, say, what to buy or how many hours to work—can readily be extended to choices that have little or nothing to do with money. Economic theories can be used to explain (or, skeptics might say, at least to characterize) how people decide what policies, political parties, and candidates to support, and how much time and effort to invest in various forms of political activity. The economist Gary Becker wrote in 1976, "I have come to the position that the economic approach is a comprehensive one that is applicable to all human behavior."[2] Although Becker did not claim that economists by themselves could explain all aspects of human behavior, his statement captures the sweeping ambition of much work in the economic tradition.

This chapter considers economic accounts of political opinions and behavior. Economic reasoning can be extended to social attitudes and behavior,[3] but the political applications have been more thoroughly considered and debated.[4]

INDUCTION AND DEDUCTION

As we have seen, psychological theories can be varied and complex, as they seek to explain a wide variety of behavior with reference to multifarious mental and social processes. In contrast, basic economic approaches build on simple assumptions about human decisionmaking.

Often these contrasting assumptions are rooted in distinct approaches to research. Many social science researchers generally seek answers *inductively*: starting with observed human behavior and formulating and testing possible explanations for regularities and patterns in that behavior. The alternative is to reason *deductively*: to begin with a few principles or *assumptions* about human behavior and from these to derive testable predictions about that behavior. We think both approaches are valid, and even essential. Inductive public opinion research tends to be messy, as various researchers posit competing concepts (often of mental or social processes that cannot be directly observed), and it is unclear whether and how these concepts should be combined. Deductive research can be simpler in the sense of using fewer concepts, but researchers still debate how much the chosen concepts really explain. Similar trade-offs exist in all scientific inquiry; ultimately, theory and evidence need to come together.

Advocates of an economic or what is known as a *rational choice* perspective, in particular, have argued forcefully that deductive theorizing is crucial to seeking and understanding important tendencies and regularities in public opinion and political behavior. While sociological and psychological theorizing have also attempted to be deductive, economic or rational choice approaches have done so more explicitly—and exclusively.

ECONOMIC EXPLANATIONS AND RATIONAL CHOICE PERSPECTIVES

While psychology attempts to explain both simple and complex forms of behavior, including the expression of attitudes, the range of the psychological explanations for the complexities of behavior may seem daunting. Indeed, they are. Chapters 5–7 provide a view of public opinion and behavior that has enormous complexity; using all these concepts may seem like fitting together a jigsaw puzzle with too many pieces to keep track of. But in examining political attitudes and behavior, to what extent do we really have to keep track of all the pieces? That is, to what extent do we have to emphasize and fully track the unstructured complexity of psychological processes and also (the somewhat simpler) sociological influences? The answer, from the standpoint of economic approaches, is "not so much." Economic approaches or rational choice models seek *parsimony*, or simplicity: to explain a wide range of behaviors—not only of ordinary citizens, but of political leaders, candidates, and parties—using just a few postulates.

Self-interest, Rationality, and the Ends of Political Behavior

The rational choice perspective we consider here fundamentally assumes that agents (individuals, political parties, and other decisionmakers) pursue whatever they value most. More specifically, it assumes that they maximize expected *utility*, where utility is an abstract measure of value. Rational agents may have different "utility functions"; that is, they may value different things to varying extents. For example, some people may work more hours than others because they place relatively greater value on money (and/or other work outcomes) vis-à-vis leisure time. These values are not necessarily "selfish"; people may spend their money in all sorts of generous ways. However, as we will see, particular rational choice models usually assume that utility functions are simple and reflect a rather narrow conception of self-interest.

We said that, in a rational choice perspective, actors seek to maximize their *expected* utility. Most human decisionmaking involves uncertainty: we cannot be sure of the consequences of our choices. The quality of our decisions depends in part on how much information we have about possible consequences, as well as our capacity to reason about that information. As you might expect, *rational* choice accounts typically assume that people reason accurately to advance their interests (utility) based on the information they have. On that assumption, what looks like a bad decision typically is either a calculated risk that turned out poorly or a decision based on incomplete information.

A rational choice approach does not insist that *all* behavior is rational. Anthony Downs, in his influential *An Economic Theory of Democracy* (1957), says that his model "ignores all forms of irrationality and subconscious behavior even though they play a vital role in real-world politics."[5] It might seem odd to exclude "vital" behaviors from a model, but that can be justified in at least three ways. First, rational choice modelers often argue that their models capture the most important elements of political behavior. These models may perform especially well in systems that impose the largest costs for irrational behavior. For example, if elected officials are likely to be punished for irrational behavior by losing their seats, then a good rational choice model may splendidly predict their behavior. Second, rational choice models might capture the *predictable* elements of political behavior better than alternative models. Irrational behaviors, however important they may sometimes be, may be essentially unpredictable. Third, even if some irrational behaviors can be predicted by other theories, it may be fruitful to see how much we can explain by assuming rational behavior.

Modeling Ends as Economic Self-interest

The premise that agents pursue what they value most does little good unless we know what they value. We have already noted that people probably value various things to various extents—but in order to generalize about their likely behavior, we will need a relatively simple model of their utility functions. Many rational choice models assume that all utility functions are identical: that everyone wants the same things to the same degree. Slightly more complicated models assume that there are a few kinds of rational agents—say, candidates and voters—and that each kind has its distinctive utility function. Beyond that, any variation among agents is generally treated as random noise, unpredictable and unimportant to the model. Of course this treatment is too simple, but the rationale is to explain as much as possible, as simply as possible. This is the idea of *parsimony* mentioned previously, which can be as persuasive and relevant in social science research as it is in the physical sciences.[6]

Moreover, many rational choice models assume that people (or other agents) pursue narrow economic self-interest. As the nineteenth-century economist and philosopher John Stuart Mill said of political economy, the models treat each person as "a being who inevitably does that by which he may obtain the greatest amount of necessaries, conveniences, and luxuries, with the smallest quantity of labour and physical self-denial with which they can be obtained."[7] In the simplest models, agents maximize profit or wealth. In more complicated models, they face trade-offs among competing goods—such as material possessions and leisure—but often these trade-offs can be expressed in monetary terms. Thus, in some models, a person works additional hours until the amount he or she would pay (or forgo) *not* to work an additional hour equals what he or she would be paid to work that hour. As a comprehensive theory of human nature, this assumption of narrow economic self-interest may seem simplistic or worse. It may nonetheless be highly useful for describing and predicting some aspects of human behavior. Bear in mind, too, that nothing in the logic of rational choice requires self-interest to be measured in terms of money.

To bring these words down to earth, consider a simple economic rational choice model of opinion applied to a means-tested social welfare program such as food stamps (which has been renamed SNAP, the Supplemental Nutrition Assistance Program). In our model, each person makes a straightforward cost-benefit calculation—straightforward in concept, at least. By assumption, the *cost* of the program to the person is that person's expected share of the taxes that must be collected to pay for it. The *benefit* of the program is the person's expected income from food stamps, which depends in part on how likely he or she is to use them. (Granted, in real life a person will not know just how likely that is.) Even without being able to fill in all the numbers, we can infer that high-income people will generally be less likely to support food stamps than low-income people, for two reasons: their costs probably are larger (they are in a higher income tax bracket), and their benefits are smaller (they are less likely to use food stamps). Sure enough, US polling data consistently show that high-income respondents are less supportive of food stamps and other social welfare programs to improve the standard of living for the poor. The same self-interested economic motivations explain why there is also less support among members of high income groups than lower income groups for spending overall in other areas, including health care, education, "improving the conditions of blacks," environmental protection, "solving the problems of big cities," dealing with drug addiction, and fighting crime. There is also less support for government action to reduce income differences between the rich and the poor, and less agreement that "differences in income in America are too large."[8]

It may strike you, however, that this model is not very satisfactory. For one thing, we cannot actually say what numbers *any* respondent would place in that cost-benefit calculation. In fact, it is difficult to imagine anyone doing the calculation, much less everyone doing it. How likely are you to use food stamps during your life? You probably have never thought about it, and you may not know where to begin—and that is just one piece of the equation. Moreover, if people did do this calculation, would they be as supportive of food stamps as they are? Even people in high income brackets who seem particularly unlikely ever to need food stamps often oppose reducing food stamp spending. Why? One possibility is that their utility calculation diverges from dollars alone, because the benefit of (say) $100 in food stamps when times are bad substantially outweighs the utility cost of $100 in taxes paid when times are good. That reasoning makes some sense. But another explanation also makes some sense: most people derive some utility—personal satisfaction—from knowing that needy families receive food stamps, quite apart from any expectation of ever receiving food stamps themselves. That satisfaction can be construed as a kind of self-interest, but it isn't the narrow self-interest that informs basic rational choice models. A researcher might extend the model to incorporate one or both of these explanations (or perhaps others) or might prefer the simpler version. After all, even the simple version makes an interesting and correct *comparative* prediction.

As the previous example suggests, behaviors that are irrational in one model may be rational in another model. In particular, rational choice models can be expanded to incorporate psychological and sociological mechanisms such as the ones we have discussed. Consider a woman whose stock portfolio is likely to fare better under one candidate than under another. At first glance, she has a strong incentive to vocally support the candidate who will enrich her. However, suppose she knows that a close friend vehemently opposes that candidate. Arguably, if the psychic cost of offending one's friend exceeds the benefit of speaking out, then it is rational to suppress one's opinion.[9] So a rational choice model can account for self-censorship by incorporating a wider range of costs and benefits. However, most rational choice modelers are reluctant to incorporate theories from psychology and sociology. One reason is that narrower economic models may capture the most important aspects of other theories. Downs suggests that while various sociological "primary groups" may have diverging predispositions, "we may provisionally regard the peculiarities of each such group as counterbalanced by opposite peculiarities of other primary groups."[10] In effect, these variations amount to random noise. Whatever differences remain among groups are likely to reflect larger economic or political interests. For example, union members can be expected to support social insurance programs not because of a shared primary group membership, but because of a shared economic interest. Indeed, researchers have found that union members, as well as farmers, tend to support policies that advance their economic interests. Similarly, as you might expect—and as a rational choice theorist almost certainly would—smokers and drinkers of alcohol tend to oppose increased taxes on their respective habits, whereas other people tend to support them.[11]

However, many researchers are more struck by the limits of explanations based on self-interest.[12] Some group differences do not seem to comport with self-interest. Men are typically more supportive of capital punishment than women; this difference seems to have more to do with values than economic or personal stakes. Some differences even seem contrary to self-interest. Consider the military draft. Young adults of draft age seem to have the most to lose, but they were not the most opposed to the draft. Nor were they most likely to oppose US entry into the wars in Korea and Vietnam, fought primarily by conscripts. Other examples from a range of studies include issues such as affirmative action, unemployment, health insurance, public education, economic issues, and policies concerning women. Studies of opinion toward school busing to achieve desegregation do not find large differences between parents of children who might be bused and other responses; people's other attitudes, especially on race, are far stronger predictors. However, self-interest *can* explain why politically active opponents of busing are disproportionately likely to be parents of children who would be affected. Similarly, it can explain why people who will be most affected by a proposed new tax are far more likely to organize to oppose it than people who are unaffected. What may matter here is how self-interest leads people to pay particular attention to specific issues and the extent to which that attention occurs because an issue is important to them *personally*, so that self-interest weighs in only on selected issues.[13]

One might suppose that self-interest would do fairly well in predicting voting behavior. In 2012 Republican presidential candidate Mitt Romney told a gathering of supporters that at least 47 percent of voters would prefer Democratic incumbent Barack Obama because they "are dependent upon government" and pay no federal income taxes. Romney, apparently, was positing a very high level of *pocketbook voting* based on material self-interest. Similarly, many Obama supporters perceived Romney's support as concentrated among voters who stood to gain the most from Romney's tax cut proposals. In 2012 as in other elections, such expectations were exaggerated. According to national exit polls, among voters with annual household incomes under $30,000, Obama got 63 percent of the vote; among those with incomes over $100,000, 44 percent voted for Obama. This difference is substantial, but it still leaves huge numbers of voters voting against their supposed material interests. Similarly, studies have shown that in choosing a presidential candidate, voters seem to weigh changes in their own financial circumstances less heavily than their *perceptions* of how the national economy is doing. This phenomenon is an example of *sociotropic* voting, based on perceptions of society's overall interests rather than personal interest in isolation. Moreover, these perceptions may not fully reflect actual national—or even personal—economic conditions and circumstances. They may depend on exposure to news media coverage and attitudes toward the partisan political leaders involved in debating and producing economic policies and outcomes.[14] For example, Democrats tend to be more cheerful than Republicans about the national economy when a Democrat is president.

Thus, a narrow economic approach that emphasizes material self-interest as a goal is less useful than one might expect in explaining public opinion and political behavior. As one set of researchers conclude: "To summarize, self-interest ordinarily does not have much effect on the mass public's political attitudes. There are occasional exceptions as when there are quite substantial and clear stakes which individuals perceive as very important to them personally (especially regarding personal tax burdens), including ambiguous and dangerous threats. But even these conditions only infrequently produce systematic and strong self-interest effects, and then, ones that are quite narrowly specific to the interest in question. The general public thinks about most political issues, most of the time, in a disinterested frame of mind."[15] "Disinterested" may be a misleading word if it suggests that people strive for objectivity. Their opinions may be very subjective indeed. But they generally do not seem to be based on financial calculations or even on more complicated reckonings of self-interest in isolation from the interests and values of other people.

This apparent dismissal of self-interest has been sharply criticized. Jason Weeden and Robert Kurzban assert that many researchers have dismissed the importance of self-interest because they have defined it too narrowly.[16] Weeden and Kurzban propose that people's "fundamental, everyday motives" include "satisfying immediate physiological needs . . . , defending themselves and those they value, establishing social ties, gaining and maintaining social status and esteem, attracting and retaining mates, and parenting."[17] If these are (reasonably) seen as elements of self-interest, then many attitudes and behaviors that don't promise direct financial advantage may nonetheless be self-interested. For example, people's differing views on social issues such as abortion and homosexuality may reflect the different social contexts in which they seek status and esteem. Weeden and Kurzban add that many social scientists have attributed attitudes to broad dispositions that may well be rooted in self-interest. For example, some people's opposition to affirmative action for blacks might be attributed to broad "symbolic racism," but the people who espouse "symbolic racism" may generally be those whose interests are most threatened by affirmative action provisions.

Critics of Weeden and Kurzban believe that their understanding of self-interest is too broad to be useful. The fundamental motives mentioned above sometimes point in opposite directions; if self-interest can "explain" both sides of opposing opinions or behaviors, then it seems not to explain much at all. However, a larger problem may be that the concept of "self-interest" is so value-laden that social scientists find it difficult to agree on what it means or should mean. If researchers set aside the question of whether various motivations are "self-interested" or not—as we generally did throughout Chapters 5 through 7—it may be possible to reach wider agreement about which motivations matter most in what circumstances. Bear in mind that the economic approach fundamentally assumes that people maximize their expected utility, not necessarily their income, wealth, or any particular definition of self-interest.

Rational Choice: Rationality of Means

So far we have focused on decisions about modeling people's utility functions, or their ends: what they value most. Suppose that the work is done, that we understand people's interests and motivations at least reasonably well. Then, perhaps, it is a straightforward task to predict their opinions and behaviors without paying much attention to psychological and sociological complications. Differently put, even if we are uneasy characterizing people's ends as rational, we can still adopt the assumption that people are rational in their *means*.

In this more general form, rational choice theory assumes that individuals have goals, and "it is taken as fundamental that individuals have beliefs and preferences." Given this, "a rational individual is one who combines his or her beliefs about the external environment and preferences about things in that environment in a consistent manner."[18] Individuals are assumed to be persistent and directed in their efforts to achieve their goals. It does not matter whether they are self-interested, are collectively or altruistically oriented, or have a mix of these motives. What matters is *how* people pursue those goals. Rational choice theory asks: Given particular desired ends, what political choices and behavior can be expected in rational pursuit of such ends?

More formally, we expect people to act consistently with *instrumental* rationality, by minimizing their costs and maximizing their benefits—that is, by using "the least possible input of scarce resources per unit of valued output."[19] In choosing among various objects—including opinions and behaviors—"a choice is rational if the object chosen is at least as good as any other available object according to the chooser's preferences. Put differently but equivalently, an object is a rational choice if no other available object is better according to the chooser's preferences."[20] Rational choice theory typically assumes that people pursue their goals through planning and forward-looking behavior, taking into account and *anticipating* the opinions and behavior of other individuals or political actors involved. Rational choice approaches specialize in exploring these interactions using *formal mathematical models* and *game theory* or game theoretic models of behavior.[21] For example, rational choice theorists have created elaborate models of how legislators bargain and maneuver to promote their policy agendas.

You might wonder, however, how much a rational choice approach could say about public opinion. If the essence of rational choice is that people choose in accordance with their goals, that means that people choose their opinions or express preferences based on the goals they want to pursue—or that they want the government or some other actor to pursue. This may or may not sound like an insight, and we may need to go beyond the expression of opinions. Indeed, rational choice theory may be more useful in explaining people's political behavior than their opinions per se. Nevertheless, it offers a striking perspective on how people form their opinions, rooted in the same constraints that face other political actors in various settings: the costs of information; the costs of participating in politics; and also the uncertainty that voters and other political actors face, especially in their communications and interactions with each other.[22]

First let's consider a relatively simple model of the strategic interaction between voters and the political parties (and candidates) who compete for their votes. This is a *spatial model*: it assumes that policy positions can be depicted as positions in a policy space—in this case, a one-dimensional "spectrum" from low to high.[23] For simplicity and specificity, this model posits a single quantifiable issue: How much money should the federal government spend, compared to what it is spending now? Figure 8.1(a) shows the preferred positions of each of eleven voters, from number 1, who prefers a 12 percent reduction in spending, to number 11, who prefers a 7 percent increase. It also shows the preferences of two competing political parties, A (which ideally prefers a 10 percent decrease) and B (which ideally prefers a 5 percent increase). The model assumes that each voter's utility function is *single-peaked* and symmetrical; basically, the closer the policy outcome is to the voter's preferred position, the happier the voter will be. (This assumption seems reasonable, but it may not always hold true. For example, in real life, a voter might think that the United States should spend either much more or much less on military interventions around the world: "either win or get out."[24]) The model also assumes that voters have *complete information*—that is, all the information they need in order to know their own utility functions as well as the parties' positions—and that there are no costs to political participation. Under the latter assumption, we expect everyone to vote. In fact, we expect each voter to vote for the party whose position is closest to his or her own, thus seeking to maximize utility by bringing about the best possible outcome. Thus, in order to predict a voter's vote choice, we only need to know his or her ideal point and the positions of the parties.

What do the competing parties do? Whatever its ideal policy preferences, each party prefers to win most of the votes. After all, the power of elected officials hinges on being elected. We assume that the parties, like the voters, have complete information about everybody's positions. The vertical dotted line is halfway between the two party's positions. In this scenario, party A is the loser. Seven of the voters are closer to party B's position than to party A's. In order to win them back, A will have to move toward the middle. In Figure 8.1(b), party A has promised a 4 percent reduction in spending—not as dramatic as it would prefer, but enough to persuade/win two voters (numbers 5 and 6) and the election. Only of course, party B will not sit back and wait to lose. It will move toward the middle itself, trying to win a majority of the votes.

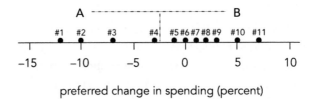

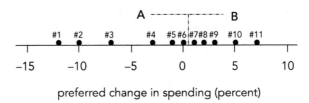

FIGURE 8.1. **Spatial Model of Preferences for Government Spending.**

You can probably see where this game is headed. (By assumption, the parties saw it all along, so they wouldn't actually make all these intermediate moves.) The parties have to compete for the voter in the middle (number 6), known as the *median voter*. Under the assumptions of the model, the parties have no viable alternative except to move to the median voter's position; any other position would mean certain defeat. What will voters do then? They cannot distinguish the parties based on their issue positions, because their issue positions are identical. So they will need some other decision rule. One possibility is called *retrospective voting*: voters can base their votes on how well the incumbent party (the one currently in power) has performed, quite apart from its policy positions. If it has performed well enough, voters will vote to reelect it; otherwise, they will vote for the other party.[25] Another possibility, which can be compared with past performance but can be a separate evaluation and standard of judgment for individuals, is *prospective* voting: that is, projecting how the parties will perform going forward and voting for the party expected to perform better.[26]

It has been said that "all models are false, but some models are useful." What is useful about the model we just considered? You may reasonably object to the assumption that all voters vote based on a single issue—especially one based on budget totals. However, this assumption may be somewhat useful as a crude approximation: many people identify themselves and candidates along a single *ideological* dimension from "liberal" to "conservative," and they may vote accordingly. Perhaps a bigger problem, though less present in the polarized politics of the United States today than in past years,[27] is that political parties and candidates may not generally have distinguishable positions. A more complicated model could account for this fact in one or more ways. Perhaps the most important complication, in national politics, is the primary election campaigns in which the party nominees often are chosen. In presidential primaries, Democratic candidates tend to take relatively liberal positions and Republican candidates, relatively conservative positions—vying for the votes of party loyalists. Then the nominees "race to the center," downplaying their more controversial views and often portraying their opponents as "extreme." However, the nominees cannot abandon their earlier positions altogether without being (correctly) accused of inconsistency. Also, the candidates often fear that if they stray too far from their party supporters' preferences, some voters simply will not vote. This possibility is assumed away here, since participation is costless, so voters should always vote for the party they would rather have in power—that is, the party closer to them. But in present-day ideologically charged partisan politics, voters with intense opinions (on either side, or in the middle) may prefer not to vote if they perceive that no party speaks for their views.[28] While our simple model does not capture these and other complications, it focuses our attention on a crucial fact that casual political observers often overlook: parties and candidates vying for a bare majority of the votes face strong incentives not to stray too far from the median voter.

But now we must consider another complication with broad implications for public opinion. So far we have assumed that voters have complete information and that political participation has zero cost. In the real world, voting takes time, effort, and sometimes money (to get to the polling place). Gathering information on the candidates and issues is likely to take even more time and effort; gathering "complete" information is inconceivable. What are the countervailing benefits? In Anthony Downs's basic theory of voting, the primary benefit of voting depends on how much policy difference the voter perceives between the two candidates—and the probability that the voter will cast the deciding vote. After all, if someone's vote cannot possibly affect the outcome, there is no real advantage in casting it, no matter how strongly one prefers one candidate over the other. In fact, Downs's simplest model implies that nobody should vote in any but the smallest elections, because the costs of voting are sure to exceed the benefits.

Obviously something is wrong here. Voting confers some intangible benefits, such as the feeling of having done one's civic duty, and these evidently suffice to inspire many people to vote. Nevertheless, voting rates are far lower than many people say they should be. In the 2012 presidential election, an estimated 58.6 percent of potentially eligible adults voted.[29] In many local elections, less than 10 percent of potentially eligible adults vote. A rational choice model provides a way of thinking about why turnout is disappointingly low. It also suggests ways to increase turnout by affecting the perceived costs and benefits of voting. For example, studies indicate that people are more likely to vote in elections that they perceive as close; their vote is, at least subjectively, more likely to matter, so the benefit is greater. They also are more likely to vote if they are not required to register before election day, if they have more choices about when to vote (e.g., early and absentee voting prior to election day), and if wait times at polling places are short. All these circumstances, among others, reduce the cost of voting.[30]

Granted that many people vote despite the minimal direct benefit, the question remains: If it hardly matters *whom* you vote for, how much effort should you spend deciding? Probably not much at all, unless the effort appeals to you on other grounds. This reasoning leads Downs to his prediction of *rational ignorance:* we should expect people to have little political information beyond whatever comes to them without effort, perhaps in casual conversations or in television commercials. This information presumably allows people to express some policy preferences and to draw some distinctions between the candidates, but it is far from the perfect knowledge that would compel candidates to cater to the preferences of the median voter. In fact, it might be more important to cater to whoever will pay for the television commercials! So, in a world in which most voters are rationally ignorant, the behavior of candidates becomes more difficult to predict; ideally, other actors (such as campaign contributors) should be incorporated into the model. But even if voters do not know very much, they still may know enough to withhold their votes from candidates who take positions far from their own views. (We say more about how voters may assess candidates in Chapter 9.)

You might object that the concept of rational ignorance expects too little of citizens in a democratic society. Shouldn't we all pay some attention to politics, cast informed votes, and participate in other ways? Many people would agree that we should. But here we all confront a *collective action problem:* our individual incentives don't correspond with our shared interests. Suppose we all agree that we would all be better off if *at least* (say) two-thirds of us spent (say) thirty minutes or more per week learning about politics—the more of us, the better. Will this agreement in itself lead most of us to spend that time? Probably not.

The problem, from a rational choice standpoint, is that for any one of us to spend that time makes almost no difference to the entire electorate. Each of us has an incentive to be a *free rider*: to rely on other people to contribute to the benefits of an informed electorate, while we do something else we prefer (unless we already prefer to follow politics). This is not necessarily a matter of being selfish; bear in mind that our personal decision to follow politics, in itself, does very little good. Similarly, most people would rather give $100 to a local charity than send it to, say, the Defense Department; no matter how strongly we favor national defense, our $100 will not help it very much. In fact, providing for national defense is a classic example of a *public good*—basically, something that everyone can benefit from—that tends to be underprovided unless people are somehow forced to cooperate.[31] In the case of national defense, that generally means imposing taxes. Despite all complaints, most people accept that some taxes are necessary. But it is not obvious how to require that everyone be well-informed.

Whatever one thinks of rational ignorance from an ethical standpoint, it fares well as a prediction. For example, in a March 2011 Pew survey, only 38 percent of respondents knew (or correctly guessed) that the Republican Party controlled the House and not the Senate. It seems difficult for citizens to hold incumbents accountable if they don't know which party holds power where. In the following chapters we say more about the limits of public knowledge and its implications. As we have already hinted, the fact that voters have far from perfect information opens room for *persuasion*. Candidates (and other political actors) can now try to convince voters to change their issue positions; they can misrepresent their own issue positions; and they can promote candidacies on grounds that—good or bad—have nothing to do with issue positions. (Think of ads that show candidates' smiling families or that lambaste the supposed character flaws of other candidates.) They can try to lead—or manipulate—public opinion, in addition to responding to it.[32]

To elaborate on misrepresentation, when candidates take positions that are far from the median voter's, they have incentives not to state those positions, or to obscure them. To the extent that they succeed, voters are more likely to ignore those issues or to misperceive candidates as relatively moderate on them. Of course, opposing candidates face similar incentives not only to expose such misrepresentations, but to portray their opponents' centrist (near the median voter) views as extreme. If voters could easily establish the truth, then candidates would have no incentive to misrepresent their and their opponents' issue positions. In real life, they often have wide leeway. For various reasons, media reports often do not evaluate whether candidates' claims are factual, or tend to speak euphemistically. Even concerted journalistic efforts to fact-check candidates' claims seem to have had limited effects (see Chapter 11). Whether lulled by a lack of information about controversial policy positions or buffeted by competing claims, some voters end up perceiving candidates as indistinguishable on the issues even when they are not. The expected outcome, paradoxically, is similar to the expected outcome under the assumption of complete information: these voters will vote based on their perception of the incumbent's performance (retrospective voting) or other shortcuts.

RATIONAL CHOICE AND PSYCHOLOGY

For some advocates, rational choice research is the most intellectually rigorous approach to understanding public opinion and political behavior. For some critics, rational choice offers big promises but relatively small payoffs: rational choice models can reach diametrically opposed predictions, and (in critics' view) many of the most famous predictions of these models by no means depend on rationality assumptions. In practice, rational choice research has fruitfully coexisted with other approaches; rational choice models sometimes borrow from psychological and sociological theory, and psychological and sociological research sometimes draws on rational choice concepts. What you do with rational choice reasoning is likely to depend on the questions that interest you most.

We have heard advocates of rational choice approaches ask, "What is the alternative to assuming rationality: assuming *irrationality*? What good does that do?" Indeed, assuming "irrationality" alone doesn't lend itself to predicting or explaining human behavior. However, psychologists have posited important challenges to rational choice assumptions, involving psychological processes that would be difficult to deduce from rational first principles and that influence people in predictable and systematic ways.

For example, research in *behavioral economics* has identified behavioral patterns that defy simple rational choice explanations; they require psychological explanations.[33] Rational choice theory entails that given the choice between two options with specific consequences, a rational actor should always choose the same option, because the utility calculation should be identical. This principle is called *invariance*. In particular, how a choice is described or *framed* should not matter. A pessimist may see a glass as half empty when an optimist sees it as half full, but a rational actor understands that half empty means half full. Consider the following survey experiment, in which respondents were asked to choose between two medical treatments: surgery and radiation therapy.[34] One group of respondents was given the following choice (called the survival frame):

Surgery: Of 100 people having surgery 90 live through the post-operative period, 68 are alive at the end of the first year and 34 are alive at the end of five years.

Radiation Therapy: Of 100 people having radiation therapy all live through the treatment, 77 are alive at the end of one year and 22 are alive at the end of five years.

The other respondents were given the following choice (the mortality frame):

Surgery: Of 100 people having surgery 10 die during the surgery or the post-operative period, 32 die by the end of the first year and 66 die by the end of five years.

Radiation Therapy: Of 100 people having radiation therapy none die during treatment, 23 die by the end of one year and 78 die by the end of five years.

Substantively, these two sets of options are identical: "90 live" means "10 die," and so forth. However, in the survival frame, only 18 percent of respondents chose radiation. In the mortality frame, support more than doubled, with 44 percent preferring radiation. These percentages imply that over a quarter of respondents would make a different decision depending on how the choice was worded or how they thought about it. Apparently, for many people the difference between "10 die" and "none die" is larger than the difference between "90 live" and "all live"—although it is the same difference. Remarkably, the researchers found that this *framing effect* was as large for physicians and for statistically knowledgeable business students as for a group of clinic patients.

Framing can dramatically affect how people judge *risk*—the possibility that some bad outcome will occur. Consider the survey experiment in which participants were told to imagine that the United States is preparing for the outbreak of an unusual Asian disease, which is expected to kill 600 people, and that two alternate programs to combat the disease have been proposed. Again, one group was given a survival frame, and the other was given a mortality frame. Here is the survival frame:

If Program A is adopted, 200 people will be saved.

If Program B is adopted, there is a 1/3 probability that 600 people will be saved, and a 2/3 probability that no people will be saved.

Note that the mathematical "expected value" of Program B is that 200 people will be saved. (If this scenario were repeated many times, on average we would expect 1/3 × 600 = 200 to survive.) So Program B has the same expected value as Program A, but involves an element of risk. Which program would you favor? In the study, 72 percent of respondents favored Program A. This preference is *risk averse*: most respondents preferred the certainty of saving 200 people to the chance of saving all or none of the 600. Now consider the mortality frame:

> If Program C is adopted 400 people will die.
> If Program D is adopted there is a 1/3 probability that nobody will die, and 2/3 probability that 600 people will die.

Which of these programs would you choose? You may be influenced by the fact that these are the *same programs* as A and B, only stated in negative instead of positive terms. But the respondents in this group had never heard about A and B, only about C and D—and they took a very different view. Fully 80 percent chose program D. This choice is *risk seeking*: the expected value of both programs is 400 deaths, but most people preferred to take a chance that "nobody will die." For rational choice theory, the difference between the two groups is inexplicable; the choices are identical. We must turn to psychology for an explanation.

You might wonder whether these odd results really need to be explained. One might object that survey experiments are like "word problems" in math class: some people give strange answers, but that tells us almost nothing about how they behave in the real world. However, many lines of evidence indicate that people violate rational choice expectations as brazenly in daily life as in these experiments. For example, people are sensitive to *anchoring effects*. Most people are *loss-averse*; basically, they dislike losses more than they like gains. What people construe as a loss or a gain depends on their reference point—and it turns out that people sometimes re-anchor their reference points in ways that make no rational sense. For example, gambling casinos often offer "free chips." People who pay $500 for a casino package that includes $50 of free chips, then spend all the chips, tend to feel that they broke even gambling, as if those chips really were free. Paying $450 for an otherwise identical package without the free chips, then buying $50 worth of chips and spending them all, feels like a loss, because the reference point is different—even though, either way, the person has spent $500.

From the standpoint of ascertaining individuals' opinions and preferred choices and hence measuring the public opinion regarding some issue or topic, how an issue or choice is framed can make a big difference. Psychological explanations have to be brought into play to understand such decisions, which should lend themselves to economically rational choices. This not only has relevance to understanding why individuals might voice support for one policy choice over another, but it also provides insight into how to get the public to make rational choices. To this end choices need to be framed so that the public can readily see how to make the correct cost-benefit calculation that leads to the utility maximizing choice. To the same end, understanding human psychology and behavior apart from rational calculations can also lead to the construction of policy choices themselves that can directly produce rational choices.

Consider situations in which individuals have to make choices that directly affect them and that involve calculations and initiative, even if the calculations are not complicated. One way to encourage a rational choice is to legally require it. Every state except New Hampshire requires automobile drivers to wear seat belts, largely because seat belts greatly reduce injury and fatality rates in accidents. Lawmakers assume that this safety benefit to drivers exceeds the cost (in comfort and convenience) of wearing seat belts. Seat belt laws help drivers behave rationally by providing an additional incentive to buckle up. In other cases it is helpful to provide a "default choice," which is itself the more rational, utility-maximizing choice.[35] Having a default choice takes advantage of what, for lack of a better term, can be called "inertial" or the "status quo bias" in human behavior; in some cases it is just delay or "procrastination" in making choices. That is, people have difficulty making decisions that lead to changes, which means they may miss an opportunity to make change for the better. To address this problem and encourage rational choice, if the default choice—the choice that is made without an individual having to make any choice—is itself the rational choice for most individuals, then status quo bias will lead to better decisions.

One good—and important—example of this is the policy question of how to encourage individuals to benefit from employer-sponsored contributory retirement plans. In these plans, employers match contributions that the employees themselves make. If employees do not make contributions, then they are missing out on "free money"; they are leaving money on the table, so to speak. If in order to participate the employees have to actively decide and sign up to make these contributions, then inertia can—and in fact does—lead to individuals not contributing and receiving employer contributions that can grow substantially through interest and/or investments made as part of the retirement plans. How can this problem be dealt with so that more individuals make the rational choice to contribute? The answer is simple: make the default choice an automatic employee contribution of a specific percentage of income, a percentage small enough that employees can afford it. In this case the active choice that the employee would be asked to make is whether he or she prefers to opt out of the contributory plan, in contrast to having to opt into it. In the case of having to opt out, the likely result of inertia is that more employees will benefit from the plan's employer contributions and subsequent growth. When done on a large scale, this setup of employer or individual pensions might improve national retirement savings. One early study found that the opt-in approach produced participation of 20 percent after three months, increasing to 65 percent after three years. In contrast, automatic enrollment led immediately to a full 90 percent participation rate, increasing even more to 98 percent (nearly full participation) after three years. Thus, with automatic enrollment, employees participated sooner and in very large numbers—a good application of behavioral economics to encourage rational choices.[36]

CONCLUSION

Sorting out social science theories is not easy. The good news is that there is no lack of theories, and the bad news is the same: often we confront multiple explanations of people's opinions and behavior. Economic theorizing has tried to cut through the complexity of individual-level psychology and social relations to focus on enduring regularities, and often to illuminate the strategic interactions of different kinds of "players" (such as voters and candidates) rather than consider one in isolation from the other. All this is good, but it is far from perfect. In our view, no one approach provides a complete explanation for opinion holding and political behavior. It is important to consider and apply sociological, psychological, and economic approaches to explain the broadest range of attitudes and behavior. As we now turn our attention to specific topics in public opinion, we draw on all these fields.

NOTES

1. We thank Charles Cameron for his past comments in drafting this chapter.

2. Gary S. Becker, *The Economic Approach to Human Behavior* (Chicago: University of Chicago Press), 8.

3. A classic treatment is Becker's *The Economic Approach to Human Behavior*. For popular audiences, Steven Levitt and Stephen J. Dubner's *Freakonomics* (New York: William Morrow, 2005) applies economic theory to a wide variety of human behaviors.

4. Still a fine introduction to the debate is Donald P. Green and Ian Shapiro, *Pathologies of Rational Choice Theory: A Critique of Applications in Political Science* (New Haven, CT: Yale University Press, 1994), and the ensuing discussion in "Critical Review," special issue, *Rational Choice Theory and Politics* 9 (Winter-Spring 1995).

5. Anthony Downs, *An Economic Theory of Democracy* (New York: Harper & Row, 1957), 34.

6. For example, see Elliott Sober, "The Principle of Parsimony," *The British Journal for the Philosophy of Science* 32 (1981): 145–156; Daniel Nolan, "Quantitative Parsimony," *The British Journal for the Philosophy of Science* 48 (1997): 329–343.

7. John Stuart Mill, *Essay on Some Unsettled Questions of Political Economy*, 2nd ed. (London: Longmans, Green, Reader, and Dyer, 1874), essay V, par. 46.

8. See Leslie McCall and Jeff Manza, "Class Differences in Social and Political Attitudes in the United States," in Robert Y. Shapiro and Lawrence R. Jacobs, eds., *The Oxford Handbook of American Public Opinion and the Media* (Oxford: Oxford University Press, 2011), 552–570; and Hart Research Associates to Jim Weill, Food Research and Action Center, "Recent Survey Results Related to Public Support for the Food Stamp Program," August 12, 2013.

9. Downs gives a similar example, involving a married couple, in *An Economic Theory of Democracy*, 7.

10. Ibid., 8.

11. See Benjamin I. Page and Robert Y. Shapiro, *The Rational Public: Fifty Years of Trends in Americans' Policy Preferences* (Chicago: University of Chicago Press, 1992), 285–286.

12. See, e.g., the various contributions to Jane J. Mansbridge, ed., *Beyond Self-interest* (Chicago: University of Chicago Press, 1990).

13. See Page and Shapiro, *Rational Public*, 285–286, 304–305; David O. Sears and Carolyn L. Funk, "Self-interest in Americans' Political Opinions," in Mansbridge, ed., *Beyond Self-interest*, 147–170; Charles S. Taber, "Political Cognition and Public Opinion," in Shapiro and Jacobs, eds., *Oxford Handbook of American Public Opinion and the Media*, 368–383, esp. 377; and Cynthia J. Thomsen, Eugene Borgida, and Howard Levine, "The Causes and Consequences of Personal Involvement," in Richard E. Petty and Jon A. Krosnick, eds., *Attitude Strength: Antecedents and Consequences* (Hillsdale, NJ: Lawrence Erlbaum, 1995), 191–214.

14. For a summary, see Sears and Funk, "Self-interest in Americans' Political Opinions," 156–157; see also Taber, "Political Cognition and Public Opinion"; and Jason Barabas, "'Public Opinion, the Media and Economic Well-Being," in Shapiro and Jacobs, eds., *Oxford Handbook of American Public Opinion and the Media*, 589–604.

15. Sears and Funk, "Self-interest in Americans' Political Opinions," 170.

16. Jason Weeden and Robert Kurzban, *The Hidden Agenda of the Political Mind: How Self-Interest Shapes Our Opinions and Why We Won't Admit It* (Princeton, NJ: Princeton University Press, 2014).

17. Ibid., 35. Weeden and Kurzban attribute this understanding to research psychologist Douglas Kenrick. See Douglas T. Kenrick, *Sex, Murder, and the Meaning of Life: A Psychologist Investigates How Evolution, Cognition, and Complexity Are Revolutionizing Our View of Human Nature* (New York: Basic Books, 2011), and Douglas T.

Kenrick and Vladas Griskevicius, *The Rational Animal: How Evolution Made Us Smarter Than We Think* (New York: Basic Books, 2013).

18. Kenneth A. Shepsle and Mark S. Bonchek, *Analyzing Politics: Rationality, Behavior, and Institutions* (New York: W.W. Norton, 1997), 17.

19. Downs, *An Economic Theory of Democracy*, 5.

20. Shepsle and Bonchek, *Analyzing Politics*, 25.

21. For an exploration of how game theory can be used to explain individuals' behavior from the standpoint of *behavioral economics*, see Colin F. Camerer, *Behavioral Game Theory: Experiments in Strategic Interaction* (New York and Princeton, NJ: Russell Sage Foundation and Princeton University Press, 2003).

22. The discussion that follows draws heavily on and offers further interpretation of Part I and Part II of Downs, *An Economic Theory of Democracy*; and Benjamin I. Page, *Choices and Echoes in Presidential Elections: Rational Man and Electoral Democracy* (Chicago: University of Chicago Press, 1978).

23. The ideas presented here were originally put forth by economists Harold Hotelling, Arthur Smithies, Duncan Black, and Anthony Downs. See Downs, *An Economic Theory of Democracy*, 114–119; and, for example, Melvin J. Hinich and Michael C. Munger, *Analytic Politic* (New York: Cambridge University Press, 1997), 24–27. However, the example is ours.

24. The assumption of symmetry is not crucial to all the model results, but it allows us to say simply that, given a choice between two policy positions, voters will prefer the one closer to their own ideal position. Like single-peakedness, this assumption may not hold in real life. For example, there may be voters whose ideal position is no change in spending, but who would rather see (say) a 5 percent decrease in spending than a 2 percent increase even though the latter is closer to their ideal.

25. See Morris P. Fiorina, *Retrospective Voting in American National Elections* (New Haven, CT: Yale University Press, 1981). Evidence on retrospective voting is discussed in Warren E. Miller and J. Merrill Shanks, *The New American Voter* (Cambridge, MA: Harvard University Press, 1996).

26. On retrospective versus prospective voting, see Michael B. MacKuen, Robert S. Erikson, and James A. Stimson, "Peasants or Bankers? The American Electorate and the U.S. Economy," *American Political Science Review* 86 (September 1992): 597–611; and Michael S. Lewis-Beck, William G. Jacoby, Helmut Norpoth, and Herbert F. Weisberg, *The American Voter Revisited* (Ann Arbor: University of Michigan Press, 2008), 378–381.

27. See Joseph Bafumi and Robert Y. Shapiro, "A New Partisan Voter," *Journal of Politics* 71 (January 2009): 1–24.

28. See ibid.

29. United States Election Project, "2012 November General Election Turnout Rates," http://www.electproject.org/2012g (accessed May 12, 2015).

30. On the usefulness of rational choice theorizing in restrictive contexts like these, see Morris P. Fiorina, "Rational Choice, Empirical Contributions, and the Scientific

Enterprise," in *Critical Review, Rational Choice Theory and Politics* 9 (Winter-Spring 1995): 85–94. See also Melanie Springer, *How the States Shaped the Nation: American Electoral Institutions and Voter Turnout 1920-2000* (Chicago: University of Chicago Press, 2014); Jan E. Leighly and Jonathan Nagler, *Who Votes Now? Demographics, Issues, Inequality, and Turnout in the United States* (Princeton, NJ: Princeton University Press, 2013).

31. A classic discussion of public goods and free riding is Mancur Olson, *The Logic of Collective Action* (Cambridge, MA: Harvard University Press, 1965).

32. See Lawrence R. Jacobs and Robert Y. Shapiro, *Politicians Don't Pander: Political Manipulation and the Loss of Democratic Responsiveness* (Chicago: University of Chicago Press, 2000).

33. The discussion that follows is based on Amos Tversky and Daniel Kahneman, "Rational Choice and the Framing of Decisions," in Robin M. Hogarth and Melvin W. Reder, eds., *Rational Choice: The Contrast Between Economics and Psychology* (Chicago: University of Chicago Press, 1987), 67–94.

34. B. J. McNeil, S. G. Pauker, H. C. Sox Jr., and A. Tversky, "On the Elicitation of Preferences for Alternative Therapies," *New England Journal of Medicine* 306 (1982): 1259–1262.

35. This discussion is taken from Richard H. Thaler and Cass R. Sunstein, *Nudge: Improving Decisions About Health, Wealth, and Happiness* (New Haven, CT: Yale University Press, 2008).

36. Ibid., 108–109.

9
CHAPTER

Content and Conflict in Public Opinion

In Chapter 1, one reason we gave for studying public opinion was that it "constrains (or should constrain) political leaders"—that it should influence policy. Now that we have examined some of the processes that influence people's opinions and attitudes, it is time to return to that claim. Some observers argue that policy should have little if anything to do with public opinion. General William Sherman, writing to his wife during the Civil War, declared, "Vox populi, vox humbug."[1] Like many other leaders and political writers, Sherman vigorously denied the public's *democratic competence*.

How (or whether) we think about democratic competence may depend on our normative beliefs about what role the public should play in policy formation. As we noted in Chapter 4, some theories of representative democracy assume that people need only enough wisdom to vote for responsible political leaders. Other theories hold that, at least in some circumstances, public opinion should substantially dictate government policy. Presumably these theories demand more of the public, as well as government. However, regardless of your normative views about what the public's role should be, if you think that public opinion at least sometimes *does* influence policy, then you will have questions about how people form and express their opinions.

In this chapter we consider some of the basic content of US public opinion: the elements that might be expected to influence policy. We pay special attention to major disagreements among the public: the contested terrain that provides the context for political and social debates. (We focus on the United States partly because that is the democratic country that we and most of our readers know best, and partly because the topic seems complex enough without trying to draw comparisons among many countries.)

THE PUBLIC'S LEVEL OF POLITICAL KNOWLEDGE

Many political observers believe or suspect that most Americans simply know very little about politics in general—far too little for their thinking about political issues to be other than profoundly misguided. Figure 9.1 examines trends in public knowledge by looking at the answers to a basic question: Which political party controls the most seats in the US House of Representatives? The percentage of correct answers sometimes changes in reaction to political events. For example, it plummeted from 71 percent in 1980 to 32 percent in 1982, after the election of Republican president Ronald Reagan—although Democrats remained in control of the House. Overall, knowledge of this question does not seem to be increasing, despite significant growth in Americans' formal education over the last 50 years. Americans remain widely underinformed about politics.

However, the evidence may not be as discouraging as it appears at first glance. Arguably, survey questions like these amount to surprise trivia quizzes removed from any political context. In practice, it is more important for people to recognize or find relevant names and facts when they need them, such as when they are voting or when an issue is prominent in the news. If people showed little ability to learn about an issue as it became more salient, that would indeed be discouraging.

We do find evidence that the public can learn—and also that it can "unlearn." For example, Scott Althaus has shown that respondents are more likely to know which party controls each branch of Congress and to recognize the names of political leaders in presidential election years than in other election years— which implies that at least some Americans go through cycles of learning and forgetting.[2] But the level of knowledge is never very high. In the 2012 American National Election Study, about 62 percent of respondents correctly said that the Republican Party controlled the House of Representatives before the election, and about 55 percent correctly said that the Democratic Party controlled the Senate; 43 percent got both questions right. Arguably these particular questions are uncommonly important, because the division of power between the two parties sets the stage for many political disputes. How can voters assess political parties' performance if they don't know who controls what?

Perhaps you can think of some possible answers. Below we consider arguments about how people can use simple decision rules to at least vote somewhat reasonably based on very little information. Nevertheless, even the most optimistic analysts concede that people's general indifference to the details of politics limits their ability to participate usefully in the political process. As we noted in Chapter 8, this indifference can be construed as *rational ignorance*: for most

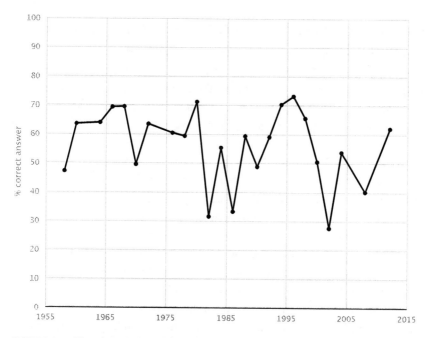

FIGURE 9.1. **Trends in Public Knowledge: Party Control of US House of Representatives.**
NOTE: Percentage of respondents who correctly named the political party that had the most seats in the US House of Representatives (prior to the election).
SOURCE: *American National Election Studies*, 1958–2012, available at http://election studies.org.

people, tending to family, work, and personal life has greater and more immediate payoffs than studying political issues. Yet the collective implications are alarming: if almost everyone ignores politics, how can the public possibly form sensible policy preferences, much less make sure the government follows these preferences?

Part of the answer, some believe, is that the public performs better as a whole—collectively—than most citizens do individually. One reason is that citizens adopt a tacit division of labor. Not only do some know more about politics than others, but different issues engage different people. A multiplicity of "issue publics" exists, each consisting of people who follow a particular issue. Moreover, issue publics can grow; more people can learn about an issue as it becomes (or remains) prominent. It may be, then, that these more informed citizens have a decisive influence on their particular issues, because they are disproportionately likely to lobby for their opinions and to influence other people's opinions.

How Do People Vote? The Early Columbia and Michigan Models

As we have seen, representative democracy rests on the ability of citizens collectively to choose—to elect—officials who will generally pursue the public interest, as opposed to their own interests. Given the centrality of elections, how citizens decide whom to vote for, or whether to vote at all, is crucial. Beyond its inherent importance, how people think about voting may influence how they think about other issues.

Between 1940 and the mid-1960s researchers at Columbia University and the University of Michigan developed voting models that have had enduring influence. The Columbia model focused on *sociological* processes: how people's social environments and relationships influenced their votes. The Michigan model placed more emphasis on *psychological* variables: how people thought about the parties, candidates, and issues, and how these factors influenced their votes. The models had more in common than these descriptions suggest, but the differences were substantial, and they inspired very different research strategies.

The Columbia model emphasized the influence of social groups and relationships on voting decisions. Paul Lazarsfeld and his colleagues conducted a groundbreaking study of Erie County, Ohio, during the 1940 presidential campaign, in which Democratic president Franklin D. Roosevelt ran for reelection against Republican candidate Wendell Willkie.[3] Remarkably, as part of the study, they interviewed almost 600 respondents *seven* times, from May through November, in order to trace changing opinions. (Most surveys interview respondents only once or, at most, twice.) They learned, first, that very few people—about 12 percent—altered their voting intentions from one candidate to the other at any time during the campaign, and about one-third of them changed back by election day. Thus, the campaign did not win many converts, although it apparently did get many people to "pay attention" and eventually to vote. Many more voters moved from "don't know" to a candidate (28 percent) or from a candidate to "don't know" and then back to the same candidate (11 percent). Thus, a small majority of voters did change preferences at some point in the campaign.[4]

The direction of these changes was fairly predictable, at least in retrospect. People usually ended up voting as most people of their social class, religion, and place of residence (urban or rural) did. Upper-class rural Protestants were very likely to vote Republican, and lower-class urban Catholics to vote Democratic. The Columbia scholars attributed these patterns to how people's closest relationships—with family and friends, coworkers, fellow churchgoers, and so on—affected their political views. The intensive interview format allowed the scholars to trace, to some extent, how these influences actually worked. Some people tended to be "opinion leaders": highly interested in politics, usually with a distinctly partisan outlook that colored their reactions to events. And through discussing politics with opinion leaders in the same social setting—for example, Aunt Mary at family gatherings—other people tended to adopt the same partisan line. Of course some social settings were more diverse than others, and some people received mixed or opposing signals, or "cross-pressures," that might lead them to delay voting decisions or to skip voting entirely. But in the end most people turned in the direction of most of their social cohort.

To illustrate the power of social influences, the Columbia scholars combined their three key social variables (class, religion, and urban/rural residence) into a seven-point index of political predisposition (IPP). The IPP was a very strong predictor of people's votes, as shown in Figure 9.2. Lazarsfeld and his associates summed up their findings this way: "A person thinks, politically, as he is, socially. Social characteristics determine political preferences."[5] A rational choice theorist (Chapter 8) might retort that on the contrary, simple self-interest can explain the IPP's predictive success; for example, Roosevelt's New Deal policies tended to benefit the working poor and unemployed, city dwellers, and Catholic constituencies, arguably at others' expense. But even if self-interest can broadly explain the overall results, it says nothing about the social processes that influenced uncertain voters. The Columbia scholars argued that uncertain voters "turn to their social environment for guidance, and that environment tends to support the party that is 'right' for them also."[6]

A crucial limitation of the IPP is that it does not explain how the political preferences of social groups vary over time or in different places. Think about creating such an index now. Very likely your thoughts turn to race; for example, as we discuss below, self-identified African American voters are presently far more likely to vote Democratic than self-identified white voters. But in 1940 that was far less true. The Columbia model's focus on social processes seems as applicable now as it was then—although social media have emerged as a new means of influence—but by treating the "social environment" as a given, it leaves many questions unexplored. Another limitation is that researchers cannot directly observe the social processes of persuasion. Through intensive interviewing, researchers can establish that people tend to vote for the same candidates that other people in their social networks do, but it is much harder to establish that they are persuading each other, not just coming to the same conclusions.

In some respects, the Michigan school took a more comprehensive approach; its first book, *The American Voter*, was over 500 pages long.[7] Like the Columbia school, the Michigan school combined a powerful predictive model with a

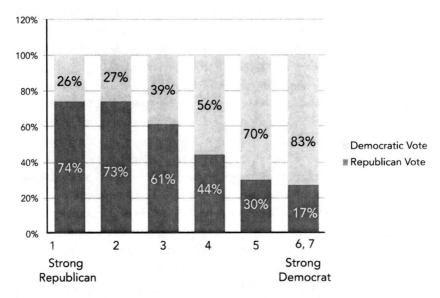

FIGURE 9.2. **Index of Political Predisposition and Political Vote, 1940.**
SOURCE: Adapted from Paul Felix Lazarsfeld, *The People's Choice* (New York: Columbia Unviersity Press, 1968).

broader causal theory, but the Michigan theory, the *funnel of causality*, could be construed to explain all kinds of changes. The National Election Studies conducted by Michigan's Survey Research Center (now in collaboration with Stanford University), dating back to 1948, have given the Michigan approach extensive influence. We consider the predictive model first.

The Michigan model emphasized three variables that influenced voting, the most important being party identification. Often called "party ID" for short, *party identification* is the attitude of considering oneself a Republican, Democrat, or whatever—having a party attachment—as opposed to being an official party member or even voting for the party's candidates. Since 1952 the National Election Studies (NES) have measured party identification by asking, "Generally speaking, do you usually think of yourself as a Republican, a Democrat, an Independent, or what?" Follow-up questions pin down Republicans and Democrats as "strong" or "weak" and classify independents as leaning toward one party, the other, or neither. Self-identified Democrats and Republicans, as we would expect, tend to vote for candidates of their favored party. For some voters, party ID functions as a *heuristic*—a cognitive shortcut—for deciding how to vote: just vote for the candidate of your party. People's party identification is relatively

stable over time. For example, many participants in the 2000 NES were reinter-
viewed in 2004; over 80 percent reported the same basic party identification (Republican, Democratic, independent, or other), and fewer than 2 percent switched
between the two major parties. Thus party ID is far from frozen in place, but it is
more consistent than responses on many other questions. Similarly, the five
presidential elections between 1960 and 1976 included two landslides with 23-
point popular vote margins in opposite directions, as well as three very close
contests, but the balance of Democrats and Republicans on party ID questions
was far more stable.[8]

Party identification predicts individuals' votes better than social characteristics do, but it cannot predict or explain differences between elections, such as the
opposite landslides mentioned above (in 1964 and 1972), or even differences
among contests in the same election. To overcome this weakness, the Michigan
model also considers people's issue opinions and their images of the candidates.
Of course, party identification tends to influence both these areas. As we would
expect from the discussion of consistency theories in Chapter 5, strong partisans
tend to perceive that they agree with the candidate of their party on the issues,
even if they don't. Partisans also tend to like their own party's candidates, accept
positive messages about these candidates, and reject negative ones—and, conversely, to think the worst of candidates of other parties.[9] Still, issues and candidates do matter in themselves, even for strong partisans, and especially for
independents or weaker partisans. In 1980, 35 percent of "weak Democrats"
voted for the Republican challenger, Ronald Reagan, whereas only 5 percent of
"weak Republicans" voted for the Democratic incumbent, Jimmy Carter; independents favored Reagan by more than two to one.[10] Here, broad unhappiness
with Carter probably accounted for his weak performance.

A model based on party ID, issues, and candidates can easily be applied to any
presidential election. It can make better predictions about voting across more
places and times than the IPP; unsurprisingly, people's candidate evaluations say
more about their likely vote choice than do sociological variables such as religion.
(Figure 9.3 shows some results from a party-candidate-issue model for the 2012
presidential election. These results are not really predictions—they were produced
after NES respondents reported their vote choices in the postelection survey—but
they illustrate how these and similar variables could be used to predict voting
choices.) However, it may strike you that the model explains little beyond the obvious. People tend to vote for people they like, who hold positions they like, from the
party they like—and party matters most. These facts are important, and maybe
even reassuring ("issues" do seem to matter), but they do not seem to explain political *change* any better than the Columbia model does.

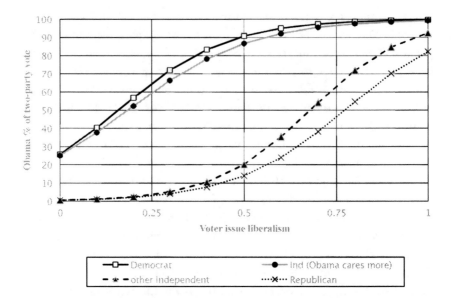

FIGURE 9.3. **Party, Candidates, and Issues in the 2012 Presidential Election.**
The graph depicts how the 2012 presidential election was affected by voters' party
identification, candidate evaluation, and issue positions. Most Democrats voted for
Democratic incumbent president Barack Obama; most Republicans voted for the
Republican nominee, Mitt Romney. However, many of the least issue-liberal
Democrats—and the most issue-liberal Republicans—voted for the other party's
candidates. (These voters are relatively unusual.) Among independents, those who gave
Obama a higher rating for "really car[ing] about people like you [the respondent]" were
almost as likely to vote for him as were Democrats, and far more likely than other
independents; issue positions were also important. *Note:* Using 2012 NES data, five issue
positions—support for government spending and services, whether the government
should guarantee jobs and standards of living, whether the government should provide
health insurance, how much the government should do to help blacks, and in what cases
abortion should be legal—are combined to form a 0-1 scale of issue liberalism (the
average score is 0.48). The results in the graph are smoothed by estimating separate
logistic regressions for each of the four categories. (Note that votes for minor-party
candidates are excluded.) Many other measures of candidate evaluation could be used,
but the caring question was an especially strong predictor in 2012.

To give their analysis explanatory power, the Michigan scholars proposed
their complex *funnel of causality*, which incorporated a wide range of variables
(see Figure 9.4). The funnel began, at the wide end, with the social sources of
political cleavages, such as the conflict between North and South. These sources
were often rooted in events that occurred before the respondents were born and

did not directly influence people's political beliefs. Yet they profoundly influenced the basic values and group loyalties that people formed in childhood and generally held all their lives. These early-formed attitudes in turn influenced people's party ID; party ID influenced people's views of the issues and the candidates—the factors nearest the "tip of the funnel," where people actually decided how to vote. Major events, election-year economic and social conditions, media coverage, campaign activities, and the opinions of friends (among other things) could also affect people's partisanship and views of the candidates and issues. Just about everything fit into the model—although, in practice, it was almost impossible to juggle all the pieces at once. Few, if any, scholars ever tried to "test" the funnel theory as a whole. Instead, many studies investigated how party ID, issue opinions, and candidate ratings influenced each other and voting decisions. Scholars recognized that how party ID changed over time might matter even more. But it would take many years of data collection to learn much about that.

Arguably, the Columbia and Michigan schools did not really disagree on much. What really set the Columbia school apart was its interest in how social

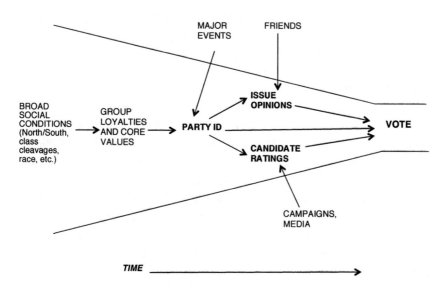

FIGURE 9.4. The "Funnel of Causality."

SOURCE: Adapted from Russell J. Dalton, *Citizen Politics in Western Democracies* (Chatham, NJ: Chatham House Publishers, 1988).

relationships—with family, friends, coworkers, and other acquaintances—influenced people's attitudes. As we noted in Chapter 6, Lazarsfeld and his colleagues explored social influences by asking many people, in a limited geographic area, detailed questions about their conversations with other people. (This tradition has informed the research of Robert Huckfeldt and John Sprague and the work of Betsy Sinclair.)[11] The Michigan scholars preferred to conduct national surveys that gathered valuable data about how people all around the country thought about politics but revealed less about the social processes that influenced people's thinking.

What does all this voter research imply for democratic competence? There is no simple answer. At first glance the Columbia model seems to offer the bleaker view: people apparently cast their votes by following the people around them. However, as Walter Lippmann noted, of course people tend to rely on the judgments of people around them: "Complete independence in the universe is simply unthinkable."[12] Moreover, people in similar settings often have the same interests at stake in an election, so voting alike—however they manage to do it—may evince good sense, not blind followership. The Michigan model allowed for great individuality. Its voters could form their party identifications, opinion stances, and candidate evaluations through highly sophisticated processes. But these voters could just as well be mindlessly parroting their parents' party affiliations, their friends' opinions, and their newspapers' candidate endorsements. Although no one claimed that "the American voter" was mindless, the evidence on political knowledge suggested that most voters might not be thinking very hard.

Rational Ignorance, Ideological Innocence, and Nonattitudes

For people to vote wisely, perhaps they do not need much "quiz-show knowledge" about facts like those in Figure 9.1, but surely they should know something more than their party ID. Political *ideology*—liberalism, conservatism, and so forth—could plausibly be the thread connecting many people's issue stands, party ID, candidate evaluations, and votes. The most common model of US ideology is a simple "spectrum," with liberals on the left and conservatives on the right. Liberals tend to support (among other things) government spending on social problems, gun control laws, and abortion rights; conservatives tend to oppose these. Conservatives tend to be more supportive of military spending, capital punishment, other policies seen as tough on crime, and prayer in the schools than are liberals. There is no logical reason that these issue positions must go together; indeed, many people stake out what they regard as more philosophically consistent positions that straddle "Left" and "Right."[13] Nevertheless, if a politician is described as, say, "ultraliberal" or "right-wing," any politically knowledgeable observer can make good guesses about the politician's views on many issues. Like party identification, ideology is one simplifying heuristic that can help people make consistent judgments based on limited information. Journalists routinely characterize politicians in terms of this liberal-conservative continuum. Do most Americans also make use of this ideological approach?

In *The American Voter*, the Michigan scholars concluded that very few Americans used ideology to judge political parties and candidates. Respondents in the 1956 National Election Study were asked to list things that they liked and disliked about the parties and presidential candidates. The researchers used these "open-ended" responses to assign people to *levels of conceptualization*, or what we might call levels of political sophistication (see Table 9.1).[14] According to the analysts, ideology mattered to only 11.5 percent of the respondents. Of those, only 2.5 percent were "ideologues" who used abstract concepts such as liberalism to evaluate the parties and candidates; the other 9 percent, dubbed "near ideologues," used abstract concepts, but in vague or inaccurate ways. The largest group, 42 percent, focused on tangible group benefits (e.g., "the Democrats are for the common man"). Of the rest, 24 percent relied on the "nature of the times." For example, they credited or blamed President Dwight Eisenhower, who was seeking reelection, for the state of the national economy. The remaining 22.5 percent of the population offered no issue content at all. Critics pointed out that judging Eisenhower on his economic performance or attentiveness to group interests might be at least as sensible as trying to judge his (notoriously vague) ideology. Still, the failure of the vast majority even to mention ideological principles raised doubts about their grasp of political issues, at least in the terms that political leaders and journalists grasp these issues.

Philip Converse, building on his collaboration in *The American Voter*, argued that "ideological innocence" was widespread among the American public, and even more disturbing, that most people had hardly any real opinions on many political issues. Converse's 1964 article "The Nature of Belief Systems in Mass Publics" introduced the concept of *ideological constraint*, or the degree of consistency among a person's beliefs. The "ultraliberal" and "right-wing" politicians we described earlier evince high constraint: their beliefs across a wide range of issues are highly predictable. Converse argued that mass public opinion (i.e., most people's thinking) showed very little constraint: many people seem unaware of what issues "go together." Mass belief systems tended to be disorganized and tended not to depend on "abstract, 'ideological' principles." People more often built their political beliefs—such as they were—around charismatic leaders, family life, and other concrete objects.

TABLE 9.1. **Levels of Conceptualization, 1956**

Category	Examples	Proportion of Sample
A. Ideology	"I think [the Democrats] are . . . a more liberal party, and I think of the Republicans as being more conservative and interested in big business."	11.5%
B. Group benefits	"I've just always before been a Democrat. . . . I just don't believe [the Republicans] are for the common people."	42.0 %
C. Nature of the times	"[My husband's] stocks are up. They go up when the Republicans are in."	24.0%
D. No issue content	"I'm a Democrat. *(Is there anything you like about the Democratic Party?)* I don't know." "Parties are all about the same to me. . . . I really don't care which man is best or otherwise."	22.5%

SOURCE: Adapted from A. Campbell, P. Converse, W. E. Miller, and D. E. Stokes, *The American Voter*, unabridged ed. (New York: John Wiley, 1960).

To illustrate this disregard for ideology, Converse closely analyzed in-depth interviews in which respondents were asked, "What do the terms liberal and conservative mean to you?" Fully 37 percent of the respondents could not name any difference between "liberal" and "conservative"; beyond that, only about one-half gave answers that Converse judged even roughly correct. Only 17 percent demonstrated a "broad understanding" of the terms, by what Converse considered quite generous criteria.

People who struggle to define the terms "liberal" and "conservative" may nonetheless have some understanding of what these terms mean for political leaders. In the 2012 NES, about three-quarters of respondents were able to place the major presidential candidates (Barack Obama and Mitt Romney) on a seven-point ideology scale and to identify Obama as more liberal than Romney, as almost all expert observers would. Past performance has been weaker, but still better than Converse might expect; in 1988, 54 percent of respondents rated the Republican candidate, George H. W. Bush, as more conservative than the Democratic candidate, Michael Dukakis. We noted earlier that many citizens may not spontaneously remember the names of political leaders or other political facts but can easily be reminded of them. Likewise, it appears that many citizens do not spontaneously use the "liberal" and "conservative" categories often used by political elites, but nonetheless they can at least partly understand political debates that use these terms.

However, when it came to people's own stated issue positions, Converse found that familiar ideological categories failed to explain their positions. Converse presented two strong lines of evidence that they were not grounded in highly constrained belief systems of any kind. First, he compared the opinions of an "elite" group of congressional candidates and a mass public sample from the 1958 NES survey. Converse found many pairs of issues for which candidates' views on one issue powerfully predicted their views on the other—apparent evidence of ideological constraint among this elite sample. For the NES respondents, the relationships between issues were generally much weaker, suggesting that most people's issue opinions were not well anchored in broader belief systems of any kind.

Worse, Converse found evidence that many of these opinions weren't well anchored at all. Many people appeared to be making them up as they went along. Converse examined an NES "panel study" in which a group of potential voters were asked the same questions (among many others) in 1956, 1958, and 1960. On each issue, so many people's responses changed from one survey to the next that many respondents seemed to be answering at random. Especially discouraging was the pattern of change over time. For instance, on one question about job guarantees, about 40 percent of respondents changed their basic response (support, opposition, or "not sure") from 1956 to 1958. Suppose that most of these people had really changed their political opinions during this time. Even more people would change their views from 1958 to 1960, and perhaps some people would return to their 1956 position. Overall, we should find that from 1956 to 1960, considerably more than 40 percent of respondents changed their position on job guarantees. But in fact only about 42 percent did. Many, even most, of the people who changed *answers* over time might not really have changed their minds.

Converse suggested a simple explanation: a small number of people—around 20 percent—answered the question identically each time, while the vast majority answered pretty much *at random*. This "black-and-white" model of the opinion-ated and the clueless did not fit the data perfectly (although for some questions it came very close) and could not be literally true. Nevertheless, Converse was con-vinced that many, indeed most, respondents were answering the questions es-sentially at random. They could not consult their considered opinions on, for example, whether "the government should leave things like electric power and housing for private businessmen to handle," because they had never formed any opinions. As Converse summed up his argument: people's policy attitudes were in fact largely *nonattitudes*.[15]

The proposition of "nonattitudes" posed a challenge not only to democratic competence, but also to public opinion analysis itself. If people had no real opin-ions, why attempt to study them? And how could government be accountable to public opinion if it did not exist? Today many, if not most, analysts find Con-verse's emphasis on nonattitudes overdrawn. They see more stability and coher-ence of various sorts in public responses across issues and over time. Nonetheless, any account of people's political opinions must reckon with Converse's closely argued skepticism.

Collective Deliberation: The Rational Public?

Benjamin Page and Robert Y. Shapiro offer a forceful response to Converse's dismissal of nonattitudes. They strongly affirm that citizens can and should steer policy—and, implicitly, that surveys are useful to identify public preferences. In Page and Shapiro's view, "the American public, as a collective body, does seem to have a coherent set of policy preferences that fit with people's basic values and that respond to changing realities and changing information. Lacking a supply of philosopher kings or a reliable means of identifying them, it is not easy to find a better source of guidance on what a government should do than the prefer-ences of its citizenry."[16]

Page and Shapiro draw on the aggregate opinion of many people, expressed in many surveys over time, as opposed to individual responses. They find, first of all, that aggregate public opinion is generally stable. That is, if a question about policy preferences is asked repeatedly over several years, overall opinion is un-likely to bounce around sharply and unpredictably. This typical stability in ag-gregate public opinion comes as a surprise to many observers, who expect to find that public opinion is volatile—continually changing for no good reason. One might think that if individuals mostly respond at random to survey questions, then overall opinion should change randomly also. Indeed it might, but only very slightly. (For example, suppose that *everyone* answers a particular question by flipping a coin. Individual responses will be completely random and unpredictable, but the overall split will always be about 50–50, give or take a few percentage points.) So by itself, the finding that overall opinion is usually stable doesn't tell us much about its rationality. Indeed, if overall opinion were perfectly stable, that would imply that people were oblivious to new events and information that might be expected to change their minds.

Yet Page and Shapiro's trend data show that public opinion does sometimes "move." They argue that these moves seem to happen for identifiable, and usually sensible, reasons. For example, during the Cold War, when people expressed greater or lesser fear of the Soviet Union, they were apparently responding to new information about Soviet power and intentions. (Sometimes the new information may have been wrong, but that was not the public's fault.) Moreover, Page and Shapiro observe that various demographic groups usually respond similarly—as "parallel publics"—to changing circumstances. This parallel movement suggests that members of these various groups are interpreting new information in the same way (on average), using common standards of judgment. Much of this new information is transmitted by the mass media; some comes from personal experience of a changing society. Page and Shapiro argue that survey trends reveal a *rational public* that responds to new information in reasonable ways.[17]

Figures 9.5 through 9.7 illustrate the rational public at work. Figure 9.5,[18] which addresses the question of women working outside the home, shows the largest opinion change that Page and Shapiro found—about a 70-percentage-point increase in public support for allowing a married woman to work if she has a husband to support her. It may be difficult nowadays to imagine this as a burning policy issue, but during the Great Depression in the 1930s, Illinois and Massachusetts considered passing laws that would ban most married women from working.[19] Judging from the polls, such laws would have been fairly popular. The enormous change in opinion from 1936 to 1998—after which year researchers stopped asking questions about this issue—can readily be explained by changes in the lives and roles of women. While people's views on these questions may not be entirely taken into consideration, some aspect of prevailing beliefs obviously has changed fundamentally and dramatically. (Later we consider changes in people's attitudes toward frequently stigmatized groups, including communists and homosexuals.)

Figure 9.6 traces an issue often found on the public agenda: crime and criminal punishment.[20] It shows three general trends, each explicable and reasonable. First, we see a decline in support for capital punishment in the 1950s and early 1960s, associated with concerns that some capital defendants would not get fair

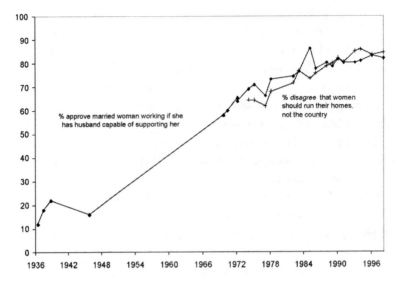

FIGURE 9.5. **Women Working Outside the Home, 1936–1998.**
SOURCE: Based on Gallup and NORC-General Social Survey polls from 1937 to 1998.

trials. At this time, people generally felt safe on dark city streets and in their homes. Beginning in the 1960s, violent crime rates (and corresponding news reports) increased sharply. In response, public support for capital punishment rose, as did support for less lenient treatment of criminals by the courts. As violent crime rates began to decline sharply after 1992, public support for these punitive policies also declined. By 2012 the violent crime rate had declined to a level last seen around 1970, and public attitudes had changed accordingly.

While the opinion *trends* on criminal justice issues seem reasonable, the percentages themselves should not be taken at face value: Here, as elsewhere, the wording of questions can greatly influence the results. For example, Figure 9.6 shows that when Americans are asked whether they "favor or oppose the death penalty for persons convicted of murder," in recent years about two-thirds have expressed support. However, other surveys find that when Americans are asked whether they prefer the death penalty or "life in prison with no chance of parole," they are almost evenly divided between the two options.[21] Arguably, this discrepancy shows that public opinion results are indeed volatile: people "should" be able to think of life imprisonment without parole as an alternative to the death penalty whether or not it is mentioned in the survey question.

Figure 9.7 illustrates the movement of "parallel publics" in a period of great political change. The figure shows parallel opinion changes by region in support

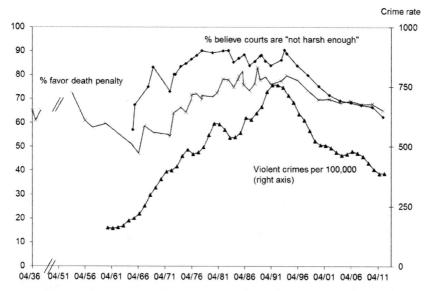

FIGURE 9.6. **Attitudes toward Capital Punishment and Courts' Treatment of Criminals, 1936–2012.** SOURCE: Data from various Gallup, NORC-General Social Survey, *Los Angeles Times*, CNN, and *USA Today* polls between 1936 and 2012.

for increased defense spending. (Note that the South is generally most support-ive.) The low level of support in 1973 can be seen as a national reaction to the costly, unsuccessful, and intensely controversial US involvement in the Vietnam War. The "spike" in 1980 occurred after the Iran hostage crisis and the Soviet invasion of Afghanistan. This was a time of widespread and plausible concern about the country's military capability, concern fed by political rhetoric that ex-pressed hostility toward the Soviet Union and criticism of the Carter administra-tion. The subsequent reversal of opinion was a response to three factors: a decline in anti-Soviet rhetoric; an actual increase in defense spending (which had al-ready begun under President Carter); and the advent of the 1981–1982 reces-sion, in which the public gave lower priority to defense spending. Support for higher defense spending hit its lowest level in 1993, after the breakup of the So-viet Union and during another recession. Support then trended gently upward, with a smaller spike after the attacks that occurred on September 11, 2001. Thus, this figure shows people around the country responding similarly to circumstances.

Changes in opinion like those shown in Figures 9.5 through 9.7 suggest that public opinion is meaningful and sensible: people are exposed to new

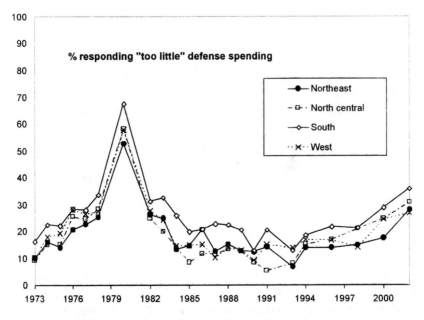

FIGURE 9.7. **Defense Spending, 1973–2002: Opinion by Region.**
SOURCE: Based on NORC-General Social Survey polls from 1973 to 2002.

information, pay attention to this information, and change their opinions (survey responses) as a result. As the defense spending example shows, these changes are often similar across smaller subgroups, suggesting that however polarized the public may seem in its reactions to events, people tend to move in the same direction. Similarly, James Stimson and his colleagues have found evidence for a "public mood"—sometimes more liberal, sometimes more conservative—that appears both to influence and to respond to policy changes.[22]

If most people know very little about political issues, how do their aggregate or collective responses manage to make sense? Page and Shapiro argue that people participate (to varying degrees) in a process of *collective deliberation*. Policy-making elites and expert analysts often provide much of the substance of this collective debate. However, they do not supply the results. In the end, the public makes "a multitude of individual decisions about who and what is right."[23] For better or worse, sometimes a prevailing public decision emerges that goes sharply against most "expert" opinion. Page and Shapiro concede that collective deliberation is no democratic panacea, particularly if political elites can manipulate the information that people receive.[24] Nevertheless, they conclude that the public's collective policy preferences are intelligible and important. In other words, analysts can tell coherent stories about "what Americans really think" about the issues—climate change, economic inequality, health reform, immigration—because Americans really do think about the issues, or at least (in the aggregate) they answer polls as if they do.

Still, the rational public is not all that rational. One issue is that some people receive new information much faster than others do. For example, in the first few years after the Soviet Union broke up in 1991, the most politically informed respondents became far less supportive of defense spending than they had been, whereas there was little change among the 60 percent of the public with the least information about politics.[25] One might say that apparently most Americans hadn't noticed that the Cold War was over. How large a problem this sluggishness is may depend on how policymakers interpret public opinion. If policymakers tend to follow majority opinion, informed or not, then they may repeatedly react far too late to changing circumstances. If policymakers are more attentive to trends, or to informed opinions, then it may not matter how slowly most people change their opinions. (We say much more about policy impacts later.)

Another issue is that the differences between subgroups can be startlingly large, even when they change substantially in parallel. The Pew Research Center asked repeatedly between 2006 and 2013: "From what you've read and heard, is there solid evidence that the average temperature on earth has been getting warmer over the past few decades, or not?" Overall, the share of respondents who said yes fell from 77 percent in 2006 and 2007 to 57 percent in 2009—perhaps in reaction to the economic hardship of that year—rebounding to 69 percent by 2013. In that year, 87 percent of Democrats—but only 44 percent of Republicans—answered yes.[26] Partisans did move in parallel, but they were nowhere near each other. That wide disagreement may be more important than the parallel movement.

A third issue may have occurred to you as you read the previous example: sometimes the information that apparently influences people's survey opinions has no logical relevance to the survey questions they are answering. One might expect the 20-point drop in belief in rising global temperatures, circa 2009, if there had been new evidence that temperatures were not increasing, but there was no such evidence. (Every year from 2000 through 2014 has been warmer than the average year in the 1990s.)[27] As the US unemployment rate increased from around 5 percent in early 2008 to 10 percent by October 2009, one might expect to find that people were less willing to pay for programs to combat global warming. But temperatures are a matter of fact, not of policy preference or even scientific theory. Why would so many people change their minds about facts that had not changed? Perhaps some had forgotten the facts amid the economic concerns. Probably many interpreted the factual question as if it were really a policy question. Arguably, some were choosing the facts to fit the circumstances.

So we see again that survey responses cannot always be taken at face value, even when their wording seems unambiguous. This problem applies even to policy issues that receive heavy attention. For example, in the mid-1990s political controversy swirled around a proposed constitutional amendment that would have required the federal government to balance its budget. Many surveys showed strong support for such an amendment. For instance, a CBS News survey at the end of January 1997 asked, "Would you favor or oppose a balanced budget amendment to the Constitution that would require the federal government to balance its budget by the year 2002?" Fully 76 percent said they favored such an amendment.[28] But another survey just two weeks earlier had evoked a very different result. The earlier survey asked, "Do you think requiring the federal government to balance the budget is the kind of issue you would like to change the Constitution for, or isn't balancing the budget that kind of issue?" Only 39 percent said that it was.[29] Apparently, in responding to the "favor or oppose" question, people tended to focus on the desirability of a balanced budget; in responding to the "that kind of issue" question, they focused on the seriousness of changing the Constitution. So, what did Americans really think about a balanced budget amendment? Evidently they had mixed feelings, but beyond that, it is difficult to say.

"Gut Rationality," Heuristics, and Political Judgments

Whereas Page and Shapiro focused on collective rationality, other researchers have explored mechanisms by which individuals achieve some degree of rationality—not just rational ignorance, but reasoned thought and action—despite the incentives to limit their effort. One influential work, Samuel Popkin's *The Reasoning Voter*, helped to draw attention to people's use of heuristics to attain what Popkin calls *gut rationality* in presidential voting. Popkin's basic approach draws upon insights of the Columbia school and cognitive psychology, as well as Anthony Downs's account of "information shortcuts":

> People learn about specific government programs as a by-product of ordinary activities. . . . They obtain economic information from their activities as consumers, from their workplace, and from their friends. They also obtain all sorts of information from the media. Thus they do not need to know which party controls Congress, or the names of their senators, in order to know something about the state of the economy or proposed cuts in Social Security or the controversies over abortion.[30]

Similarly, voters use "campaign competence as a proxy for competence in elected office—as an indication of the political skills needed to handle the issues and problems confronting the government." And voters "use evaluations of personal character as a substitute for information about past demonstrations of political character."[31] If certain candidates have made a mess of their campaigns or their personal lives, maybe they should not be trusted to direct the national government. Because it is difficult to pin down candidates on the issues, and because presidents often cannot enact their policy preferences anyway, basing votes on "personalities instead of issues" makes more sense than policy experts may want to admit. In fact, some research indicates that even well-informed people often give more weight to personalities than to issues.[32] Thus voters use heuristics in gathering and analyzing information, so that they can make good—or at least better than random—voting decisions without much hard work.

Researchers have found that people employ heuristics in making all kinds of political judgments, such as taking positions on policy issues.[33] Different people use different heuristics, depending on their political sophistication and their cognitive styles. Some heuristics are group based and follow the logic of attitudinal consistency ("balance theory"), as we discussed in Chapter 5. A person may "reason" as follows: "African Americans like affirmative action, and I like (dislike) African Americans, so I like (dislike) affirmative action." "Republicans favor lower taxes on capital gains, and I am a Democrat, so I oppose them." Similar heuristics can be based on individuals: "Ralph Nader endorsed this referendum, and I respect Nader, so I will vote for it."[34] Other heuristics engage simple values; for example, Paul Sniderman and his colleagues argue that people evaluate some social policies by asking whether the likely beneficiaries are deserving (a "desert heuristic").[35] For some people, although (as we have seen) not very many, ideological beliefs such as liberalism or conservatism serve as powerful heuristics. Heuristics, by definition, do not require very much thought, but they may be very reasonable, in that they sometimes enable people to reason and act effectively with minimal knowledge and effort.

One especially powerful heuristic for voting decisions, which we discussed in Chapter 8, is *retrospective voting*, or voting on the basis of incumbent performance (rather than issue positions or other criteria). In Chapter 4 we quoted Lippmann's view that the essence of democratic governance is "to support the Ins when things are going well; to support the Outs when they seem to be going badly." Many studies indicate that voters do weigh incumbent performance, as well as economic conditions, very heavily in determining their presidential votes.[36] Of course, people's perceptions of performance—and even economic conditions—can be heavily influenced by their predispositions. In the 2012 National Election Study, 57 percent of self-identified strong Democrats said that the national economy had gotten better in the last year, and 13 percent said that it had gotten worse. Meanwhile, 66 percent of strong Republicans said that it had gotten worse, and just 6 percent that it had gotten better. Nevertheless, researchers have consistently found that incumbent presidents, and successors from the incumbent party, do better in good economic times.[37]

However, retrospective voting is at best a blunt instrument. One pitfall is that the retrospection may not go very far. Larry Bartels has found that voters seem to consider only the previous year's economic conditions when casting their votes for president.[38] Thus, voters effectively ignore much of the record and may credit or blame incumbents for short-run conditions beyond their control. Bartels finds that this shortsightedness may have altered the outcomes of several elections. Moreover, Christopher Achen and Bartels adduce evidence that people's votes are influenced not just by economic conditions that are largely beyond presidents' control, but by events that they could not possibly control, including droughts, floods, and even shark attacks![39] Achen and Bartels substantially qualify this finding: incumbents are punished for natural events when their response is plausibly (even if unreasonably) criticized as inadequate, not when almost everyone agrees that they bear no responsibility for the disaster. Nevertheless, in their account, retrospective voting begins to look indiscriminate or even superstitious.

Heuristics are better than nothing, but clearly they do not resolve all the problems of limited political information. Delli Carpini and Keeter found that among the least politically knowledgeable respondents—unlike the most knowledgeable—issue positions poorly predict their presidential votes, and ideology is hardly a predictor at all.[40] This result implies, of course, that uninformed voters do not use issues and ideology to decide their votes. But it also implies something more disturbing: that despite whatever heuristics these voters use, they are more likely than informed voters to vote contrary to their stated preferences. Unfortunately, not all such heuristic failures "wash out" at the aggregate level. Larry Bartels, studying presidential elections from 1972 through 1992, estimates that incumbent presidents on average won about 5 percent more of the vote—and Democratic candidates about 2 percent more—than they would have if all voters were fully informed.[41] In an experimental study, Anthony Fowler and Michele Margolis found that providing political information led low-information participants to shift their preferences toward the Democratic Party.[42] In individual elections (and perhaps especially in congressional elections), voters' lack of information could lead to even more dramatic distortions. Scott Althaus[43] finds that lack of information also affects people's positions on policy issues themselves. So, as Delia Baldassarri comments, heuristics "should not be invested with virtues that they do not possess,"[44] such as an uncanny capacity to distill high-quality decisions from low-quality information.

Zaller's Theory of the Survey Response

Given the skepticism we have expressed about survey responses, we want to present one more model that helps to bridge the apparent gap between Converse's "nonattitudes" and the "rational public." John Zaller, in *The Nature and Origins of Mass Opinion*,[45] agrees with Converse that people do not have predetermined "true" attitudes on most survey questions. Yet Zaller argues that people do have predispositions—values, interests, and ideological views—that have important implications for the issues treated in political surveys. Zaller's model is consistent with most of Page and Shapiro's analysis, yet he does not believe that public opinion should be as influential in policymaking as Page and Shapiro would like.

Zaller argues that people make up responses to survey questions spontaneously, based on whatever relevant consideration first comes to mind. (A consideration is simply "any reason that might induce [someone] to decide a political issue one way or the other.")[46] However, for considerations to "come to mind," they have to be in the mind first. Zaller proposes a three-step *receive-accept-sample (RAS) model* that pivots on political awareness:

1. People who pay closer attention to politics—who are more politically aware and knowledgeable—are more likely to *receive* new political messages that can serve as considerations.[47] When President Barack Obama argued in 2009 that a new national health care program was needed to protect the uninsured, some people noticed his arguments, and others never did. But political messages come from many sources—ranging from news to popular culture—and often do not explicitly refer to politicians or even to policy issues.

2. Politically aware respondents are also more likely to *accept* messages that suit their predispositions—and to reject messages that do not. For example, knowledgeable liberals were more likely to "buy" President Obama's argument about the uninsured than either unknowledgeable liberals or knowledgeable conservatives. Conversely, knowledgeable conservatives were more likely to accept the argument that Obama's proposal would impose onerous restrictions. However, many people accepted some considerations on both sides. Bear in

mind that not all considerations are arguments (or depend on ideology). For example, a person might simply have figured, "Obama supports this plan, and I like/hate him, so that's a reason to support/oppose it."

3. When asked a survey question, people *sample* from among whatever considerations they have received, both pro and con, that are "accessible" and seem relevant to the question. A consideration's accessibility partly depends on how recently it has been called to mind. It also depends on political knowledge: for example, respondents can't base their opinions of the Affordable Care Act on their opinions of Obama unless they know—or unless the survey question mentions—that Obama supported the act. For a yes-or-no question, it is almost as if people throw the accessible considerations into a hat, then pull one out at random to decide how to answer. (For more complicated questions, people "average" the accessible considerations.)

Although the RAS model cannot literally be true—people do not collect considerations like marbles—it is a relatively simple framework for understanding many aspects of survey responses. For example, it provides a way to think about the effects of question wording. Imagine a survey question in 2009 that asks respondents, "Do you support the health care proposal now before Congress?" Now reword the question: "Do you support Barack Obama's health care proposal, now before Congress?" Now change "Barack Obama's" to "President Obama's." In policy terms, these questions are identical, but they would not evoke identical considerations. Naming Obama increases the accessibility of people's attitudes toward Obama himself; referring to him as president increases the accessibility of their attitudes toward the presidency. Moreover, by altering the wording and order of *earlier* questions in the survey, researchers can profoundly influence what people are thinking about when they answer a question on health care reform. These effects challenge simplistic accounts of "what Americans really think," and they can lead to deeper understanding of *how* Americans really think when they respond to surveys.

Zaller's RAS model has plausible and subtle implications for how people respond to new information (political messages). Most important for Page and Shapiro's argument is that we can predict that the public as a whole *will* respond to new messages, although some people will either ignore or reject them. For example, if most major sources of political information agree that the United States needs a military buildup, public opinion will probably move in that direction, as it did in 1980—in what Zaller calls a "mainstream effect." However, if Democratic and Republican leaders sharply disagree about an issue, politically aware Democrats and Republicans will tend to move in opposite directions—a "polarization effect"—for two reasons: they are more likely to *receive* messages from like-minded leaders than from other leaders, and they are more likely to *accept* those messages. Perhaps surprisingly, the model predicts that in some cases people who are moderately politically aware will be more influenced by new information than will people who are either less or more politically aware: they are attentive enough to *receive* the new information, but not so attentive that they refuse to *accept* the new information because of their predispositions.

Zaller's perspective on democratic competence is less positive than Page and Shapiro's. He writes that many citizens, who have relatively low political awareness, "are blown about by whatever current of information manages to develop the greatest intensity," while "most of the rest respond mechanically on the basis of partisan cues," tending to rely on elites that share their predispositions.[48] Zaller therefore asks baldly, "If, as I have implied, only specialists are competent to conduct political debate, why bring the public into it at all?" Why not just leave government to the experts? Zaller answers: because "government, in the absence of checks, invariably goes astray and becomes overbearing or worse. . . . It is the collective ability of citizens in a democracy to pressure leaders in useful directions and, when necessary, to remove the leaders, more than the collective wisdom of the people, that seems to me critical."[49] For Zaller, like Lippmann, the public's crucial role is to choose between the Ins and the Outs—in effect adjudicating the various debates among political leaders, although not as neutral observers.

AMERICAN PUBLIC OPINION: CONSENSUS AND CONTESTATION

Robert Benchley famously observed that there are two kinds of people in the world: those who constantly divide people into two kinds, and those who don't.[50] Some observers of the American public emphasize partisan, ideological, and demographic divides; others cite areas of widespread agreement and moderation. As Morris Fiorina has written,[51] some perceive the United States as a "50–50 nation" more or less evenly divided between liberals and conservatives; others—including Fiorina—see it as a "so-so nation" in which most people are not far from the middle. A well-rounded understanding of American beliefs and values should give careful consideration to both these approaches.

Democracy and Its Core Values

Americans consistently express considerable pride in their political system. Typically, in a 2011 survey 77 percent of respondents agreed that "whatever its faults, the United States still has the best system of government in the world"—down from 89 percent in a 2000 survey, but a large majority nonetheless.[52] (Yet as we will see, Americans express less satisfaction in how their political system actually functions.) In particular, most Americans express strong support for *democracy*. In Wave 6 of the World Values Survey (WVS), conducted between 2010 and 2014, respondents were asked, "How important is it for you to live in a country that is governed democratically?" On a scale from 1 for "not at all important" to 10 for "absolutely important," 74 percent of US respondents who answered the question rated democratic governance 8 or higher This is far from the warmest embrace of democracy, ranking twenty-sixth among the 59 countries in which the WVS was fielded, far behind Sweden (89 percent). Still, it evinces strong majority support.

If most Americans support the US political system in part because it is democratic, what do they understand by "democratic"? The World Values Survey asks whether each of nine factors is an "essential characteristic of democracy," again on a 1 through 10 scale. For Americans, two responses stand out: free elections and equal rights for women. About three-quarters of respondents rated each of these 8 or higher on the scale. These were also the most popular factors among respondents from other countries, chosen by about two-thirds of them. The third most essential characteristic among both Americans and other respondents was "civil rights [to] protect people from state oppression," chosen by 57 percent of Americans and 56 percent of other respondents. However, Americans differ sharply from non-Americans on some other items. "People receive state aid for unemployment" was chosen by slightly over half of non-American respondents, but only about a quarter of Americans. "Governments tax the rich and subsidize the poor" and "The state makes people's incomes equal" similarly were chosen far less frequently by Americans than by non-Americans.

Bearing in mind the pitfalls of overinterpreting survey results, these responses dovetail with some common generalizations about widely held American values. Most Americans value certain forms of *liberty* and *equality*. Many believe that in the United States at its best, people are free from governmental tyranny, free to speak their minds, practice their religions, and pursue happiness and prosperity in any way that does not impose on others. The Bill of Rights, which comprises the first ten amendments to the US Constitution, protects freedom of speech, religion, and the press; freedom from arbitrary punishment; and other crucial aspects of liberty.

Americans generally also believe that the United States is (or should be) committed to political and social equality. The Declaration of Independence affirms the "self-evident" proposition that "all men are created equal." For many, that principle means that each person is entitled to a vote and to some say in political decisions, and that no one should be subservient because of differences in social class or condition. This support for equality extends, in part, to the economic realm. Most Americans support public schools as a way of providing equal opportunity to succeed through education. Most even support assistance to the poor, although they tend not to support "welfare" as such.[53] However, they are substantially less supportive of intervention to equalize economic *outcomes* than are people in many other countries.

To some Americans, it is obvious that the United States stands for liberty and equality, perhaps more so than any other country. Yet the substantive content of those ideals has been contested throughout the country's history. For example, not only did slavery persist until after the Civil War, but in the South most blacks were effectively denied voting rights and equal access to public facilities until the 1960s. While Americans generally support the abstraction of "equal rights," they often disagree sharply on how it should be applied. As Jennifer Hochschild points out, many Americans even argue with themselves. In her interviews, "when respondents used a political perspective to consider the possibility of redistributing wealth, they often endorsed it. . . . But when the same respondents used an economic perspective to think about redistributing wealth, they usually opposed it." When asked to reconcile these views, "most respondents simply stammered apologetically and changed the subject."[54] We return to some of these conflicts below.

Americans typically do *not* identify public participation in decisionmaking as a key democratic ideal. According to John Hibbing and Elizabeth Theiss-Morse, most Americans are not interested in politics, dislike political debate and compromise, and do not want to spend more time following political issues. "As a result, people most definitely do *not* want to take over political decision making from elected officials. . . . Americans do not even want to be placed in a position where they feel obligated to provide input to those who *are* making political decisions."[55] What Americans would like best, Hibbing and Theiss-Morse argue, is rule by experts who are selflessly devoted to the common good—or, as they put it, "empathetic, non-self-interested decision makers (ENSIDs)."[56] From the standpoint of rational ignorance, it is easy to understand why Americans do not want to participate more extensively in politics. If Americans believed that their political leaders were ENSIDs, they might participate in and think about politics even less.

Partisan Disagreements: 50–50 or So-So?

How is it that some observers see Americans as polarized on major issues, while others see most Americans as moderate? One way to start thinking about the conundrum is to examine responses to some National Election Study questions that ask people to place themselves on seven-point opinion scales. One of these questions is worded as follows:

> Some people feel the government in Washington should see to it that every person has a job and a good standard of living. Suppose these people are at one end of a scale, at point 1. Others think the government should just let each person get ahead on their own. Suppose these people are at the other end, at point 7. And, of course, some other people have opinions somewhere in between, at points 2, 3, 4, 5, or 6. Where would you place YOURSELF on this scale, or haven't you thought much about this?

In the 2012 NES, among the people who placed themselves on this scale, the largest share—about 23 percent—put themselves in the middle, at point 4. (If we count the people who said they "hadn't thought much about this" as also in the middle, the proportion increases to 29 percent.) On this question, more people are on the conservative side of the scale, points 5 through 7 (43 percent), than on the liberal side (28 percent), another example of Americans' limited support for economic equality. But over half the respondents are within one point of the midpoint.[57]

Now let us expand the analysis to five such questions about government policy. (In brief, the questions are about government spending, government services, health insurance, aid to black Americans, and environmental protection at the risk of jobs.[58]) When people's answers to these questions are correlated, those who take a liberal ("big government") position on one question tend to do likewise on the others, and the result is similar for those with conservative ("small government") positions. For four of the five questions, the midpoint is the most common response—and the *average* response of most respondents is, again, within one point of the midpoint, between 3 and 5. The distribution of average scores looks somewhat like a bell curve: some people are more conservative than others, but Americans don't look especially "divided" on political lines, just as they don't appear to be "divided" between tall people and short people. Of course, we cannot be sure how people interpret these particular questions and scales. However, Fiorina's analysis of widely varied policy questions suggests that the same broad pattern obtains: there are real differences in opinion among people and across issues, but there is no great division between two camps.

However, as critics have pointed out—and Fiorina concedes—the data show a different kind of polarization: the policy opinions of self-identified Democrats and Republicans are farther apart than they used to be. Back in the 1972 NES, the average Democrat and the average Republican were less than a point apart on the guaranteed job question (3.92 for Democrats, 4.78 for Republicans). By 2012 the gap had roughly doubled: 3.54 for Democrats, 5.24 for Republicans. The Pew Research Center, analyzing a ten-item scale of political values in its own surveys between 1994 and 2014, similarly found a sharp increase in partisan disagreement. In 1994 the opinions of Democrats and Republicans largely overlapped; the median Democrat was only slightly to the left of the median Republican. By 2014, 94 percent of Democrats were to the left of the median Republican, and the gap between the median Democrat and the median Republican had more than tripled. Pew summarized these and other findings: "Republicans and Democrats are more divided along ideological lines—and partisan antipathy is deeper and more extensive—than at any point in the last two decades."[59]

You might wonder whether this change is a side effect of a move away from identification with either party. Perhaps relatively moderate voters were more likely to call themselves independent in 2012 than forty years earlier. That idea does not pan out: about 63 percent of respondents identified as Democrats or Republicans in 2012, almost exactly the same as in 1972. Party identification did shift repeatedly over this period, but not necessarily away from the parties. (The proportion of independents did sharply increase between 1952 and the early 1970s—a shift heralded in such works as *The Changing American Voter*[60]—but then that particular change slowed or even stopped.)

As Fiorina and his colleagues have noted, two other broad explanations for the growing partisan division merit consideration. One is true polarization: Democrats have moved to the left, while Republicans have moved to the right, leaving fewer people in the middle. The other is what Fiorina and colleagues call *sorting*: people who once identified, or might have identified, as conservative Democrats or liberal Republicans are now more likely to identify with the party closer to their policy positions. Fiorina argues that sorting is a better explanation than polarization.[61] His argument is particularly plausible in the southern states, which mostly elected conservative Democrats to Congress for most of the twentieth century, but by the 2014 election were dominated by conservative Republicans.[62]

Yet other observers, including Pew, argue that true polarization is an important part of the story. Pew reports that in 1994 only 10 percent of respondents expressed consistently liberal or consistently conservative positions in its ten-question index; by 2014, the proportion had more than doubled, to 21 percent.[63] Granted, 21 percent is still far from a majority. Pew acknowledges that most Americans have more moderate opinions, both about policy and about the importance of compromise. However, Pew adds, "the most ideologically oriented and politically rancorous Americans make their voices heard through greater participation in every stage of the political process" than their more moderate counterparts.[64] On that point, Pew and Fiorina agree: unsurprisingly, less moderate Americans tend to be more politically active. Even a rather small increase in polarization may therefore lead to greater polarization in various political arenas. Moreover, partisan sorting may actually encourage polarization, if partisan settings increasingly become "echo chambers" in which the least moderate voices ring loudest. Sorting may also reduce political leaders' propensity or ability to seek policy compromises, as they find ever less basis for actual agreement with leaders from other parties. We consider these possibilities further in Chapter 10.

Political and Social Tolerance

Political theorists have often argued that *political tolerance* for dissenting views, manifested in civil liberties including freedom of speech and of the press, is a core democratic principle. Freedom to dissent is a crucial (albeit incomplete) protection against tyranny, whether of an autocratic minority or of a heedless majority. A political order that silences some or many of its citizens is unlikely to serve their legitimate interests. However, in the United States, as elsewhere, the scope of political tolerance has always been contested; civil liberties have never been absolute.

Distinct from political tolerance is the more ambiguous concept of *social tolerance*. Social tolerance is the degree to which deviant behavior (contrary to prevailing social norms) is not met by active intervention to oppose, suppress, eliminate, or discourage it.[65] Such intervention could take many forms, from a policy that bans some behaviors in particular places, to individual decisions to criticize (or just glare at) someone who is perceived as violating a norm. Obviously some manifestations of social intolerance are more forceful than others. Under this definition, social intolerance (like political intolerance) is directed against behaviors, rather than people or social groups per se—but in practice, this distinction does not always amount to much. We can fairly say, for example, that racial segregation represents social intolerance directed against an entire group. Social tolerance is even more intensely contested than political tolerance, because people disagree about which behaviors should be banned or discouraged and which ones should be tolerated or even welcomed as expressions of diversity.

For many social scientists in the 1950s, the depredations of the Nazi Party in Germany highlighted the importance, and the fragility, of political and social tolerance. Although Adolf Hitler never won a free election,[66] he gained great popularity, largely due to the effectiveness of Josef Goebbels's propaganda efforts and the suppression of dissenting voices. The Nazi regime's plans, which included military conquest and the extermination of German Jews, proceeded with little evident opposition from the German public. Reflecting on these events, political observers and social scientists wondered whether some flaw in German *political culture* was to blame for the demise of democracy and the advent of a ruthless dictatorship—and many worried about the long-term prospects in other countries, including the United States.

One team of researchers, led by German émigré Theodor Adorno, related the collapse of democracy in Germany to a generalized *authoritarian personality*.[67] The authoritarian mind-set, according to Adorno and his colleagues, was marked by rigid adherence to conventional values, excessive submissiveness to authority, and a propensity to condemn and even punish deviants. Writing in 1950, the researchers saw these traits as ominously widespread among Americans. The concept of authoritarianism has provoked much debate over the years, but never did the debate seem more urgent than in the shadow of World War II. If authoritarian values were widely held, could democracy survive?

For many observers, the rise of "McCarthyism" underscored the threat to democracy. The Cold War was well under way, and the Soviet detonation of an atomic bomb in August 1949, as well as the Communist victory in China that October, deepened American fears of communism abroad—and of spies and sympathizers at home. In February 1950 Senator Joseph McCarthy claimed to have evidence that eighty-one people in the State Department were Communists. Over the next four years, McCarthy launched several congressional investigations into suspected Communists in federal jobs. McCarthy also opened a campaign against what he considered anti-American books in American libraries and an investigation into "Communist thinkers" in colleges and universities. Although many of McCarthy's charges were completely unsubstantiated, he had considerable public support—as well as strong public opposition. McCarthy's critics argued that he had created a climate of suspicion in which merely associ-ating with accused Communists, or even denying the truth of particular accusa-tions, could expose patriotic Americans to charges of treachery. For McCarthy's detractors, "McCarthyism" became, in Richard Rovere's words, "a synonym for the hatefulness of baseless defamation, or mudslinging"; McCarthy himself said in 1952 that "McCarthyism is Americanism with its sleeves rolled."[68]

In the midst of this controversy, in mid-1954, Samuel Stouffer led the re-search that resulted in his book *Communism, Conformity, and Civil Liberties*. In Stouffer's words, the study examined Americans' reactions to two dangers: "One, from the Communist conspiracy outside and inside the country. Two, from those who in thwarting the conspiracy would sacrifice some of the very liberties which the enemy would destroy."[69] The study interviewed almost 5,000 ordinary Americans, plus 1,500 selected local community leaders in medium-sized cities. Respondents were asked a variety of questions, including open-ended questions about threats facing America; questions about Communists in America; and questions about possible restrictions on "nonconformists" such as Communists, Socialists, and atheists.

The results painted a complex and troubling picture of American views on political tolerance. Community leaders were generally more tolerant—more in-clined to express support for civil liberties—than the public at large. For exam-ple, 64 percent of community leaders said that a speech "against churches and religion" should be allowed, compared with only 39 percent of other respon-dents in the same cities. On other questions, solid majorities of both groups sup-ported civil liberties. Respondents were asked whether an accused Communist "who swears under oath he has never been a Communist" should be fired from a high school teaching job. Only 16 percent of community leaders, and 22 percent of the national sample, said that he should be fired.[70] But admitted Communists received much less tolerance. For example, fully 89 percent of community lead-ers, and 91 percent of the national sample, said that an admitted Communist should be fired from a high school teaching job. Most thought that books by ad-mitted Communists should be removed from public libraries.[71]

How was the government supposed to find out who were Communists? Some 62 percent of community leaders, and 64 percent of the national sample, thought "the government should have the right to listen in on people's private telephone conversations, in order to get evidence against Communists," al-though the question did not ask whether any limits should be placed on that power. Somewhat larger majorities said it was a "good idea . . . for people to re-port to the F.B.I. any neighbors or acquaintances who they suspect of being Communists."[72] This idea becomes unnerving when one considers some of the reasons that various respondents gave for suspecting that someone they knew might be a Communist: "He was always talking about world peace." "He brought a lot of foreign-looking people into his home." "During the war I used to say Russia was our enemy and he got mad at me." "My husband's brother drinks and acts common-like. Sometimes I kind of think he is a Communist."[73] Stouffer emphasized that such responses were uncommon, but he also quoted community leaders who felt that they could not speak their minds for fear of having their loyalty questioned.

Stouffer emphasized that community leaders were generally (although not always) more tolerant. Stouffer also found that younger people, people with more education, and city dwellers were more tolerant of political nonconformists than their older, less educated, and rural counterparts. Stouffer argued that growing access to higher education, increased geographic mobility and the influx into cities, and modern media were among the forces that helped spread the idea that people who are different, with different value systems, "can be good people, too."

Some observers took a darker view of what they saw as a widespread willingness to abridge basic rights. Granted, if American Communists had forsworn loyalty to the United States and were potential spies and saboteurs, then one might reasonably support some abridgment of their rights, although that judgment was open to debate. Abridgment of the rights of *accused* Communists was harder to stomach. To the extent that community leaders supported civil liberties, or at least did not act to turn repressive sentiments into policy, they could be seen as bulwarks of democratic values against a profoundly undemocratic public. It seemed that the fate of democracy might depend on ordinary citizens not taking too strong an interest in what the government actually did. One group of scholars asked, "How could mass democracy work if all the people were deeply involved in politics? . . . Extreme interest goes with extreme partisanship and might culminate in rigid fanaticism that could destroy democratic processes if generalized throughout the country."[74]

James Gibson later presented evidence that the actual course of anticommunism depended more on elites than on the public.[75] Using Stouffer's data, Gibson showed that the states with the least tolerant *elites* (community leaders) tended to have the most repressive policies, while the tolerance or intolerance of the mass public seemed to make no difference. Gibson conceded that "elites tend to be relatively more tolerant than the masses." Yet he insisted, "it is difficult to imagine that the repression of the 1950s was inspired by demands for repressive public policy from a mobilized mass public," especially because (as Stouffer also had pointed out) very few among the public identified the Communist threat as a major issue.[76] Mass intolerance may have *permitted* anticommunist repression, but it did not drive it.

Recall that Stouffer had expected political tolerance—and indeed, the general belief that "people are different from me . . . and they can be good people, too"— to increase over time. Since 1972 the General Social Survey (GSS) has repeated many of the questions on Stouffer's tolerance scale, enabling us to track trends over time. For the most part, Stouffer's expectation has held true. Willingness to "tolerate" anti-religionists, Communists, militarists (who "advocate[e] doing away with elections and letting the military run the country"), and homosexuals as speakers, college teachers, and authors in a local library has increased dramatically since 1976 (the first year all these categories were asked about). The increases in tolerance range from 13 to 35 percentage points, with homosexuals registering the greatest increases. (Figure 9.8 shows trends for college teachers. The trend for "somebody who is against all churches and religion" not shown, is almost indistinguishable from that for Communists.) In the 2014 GSS, solid majorities "tolerate" each of these groups in each of these contexts, although support is weakest for allowing militarists and Communists to teach in college (61 percent and 57 percent, respectively). Of the groups that the GSS asks about, only "racists" have evoked little increase in tolerance since 1976. In 2014 about 48 percent of respondents said that racists should be allowed to teach in college—just six points above the 1976 level. A 60 percent majority did say in 2014 that racists should be allowed to speak in the community, but this figure was actually three points lower than in 1976. A slightly larger majority, 63 percent, said that racists' books should not be removed from libraries, a small increase since 1976.

Why are trends in tolerance toward racists different than trends in tolerance toward Communists, homosexuals, or anti-religionists? Certainly prevailing views about homosexuals and anti-religionists have warmed considerably over this time period. Some scholars have questioned whether the upward trends in Figure 9.8 should be considered increases in "tolerance." As Sullivan and colleagues put it, political tolerance "implies a willingness to permit the expression of those ideas or interests that one opposes" and thus "presumes opposition or disagreement."[77] Arguably some of the apparent growth in tolerance is better understood as a decline in opposition or disagreement. By the same token, since (as we discuss below) support for racist beliefs has declined since 1976, the fact that "tolerance" for racists has not actually *decreased* may imply an increase in actual tolerance for these now unpopular views.

To some extent, these trends can be interpreted as supporting the idea of a rational democratic public: specifically, a public that balances the value of free

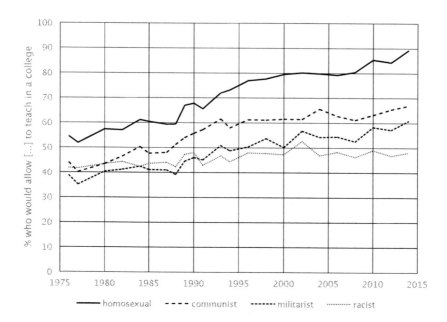

FIGURE 9.8   **Civil Liberties of College Teachers, 1976–2014.**

QUESTION (NORC-General Social Survey):

"There are always some people whose ideas are considered bad or dangerous by other people. ["Racist"] " . . . consider a person who believes that Blacks are genetically inferior. . . . Should such a person be allowed to teach in a college or university, or not?" ["Communist"] "Now I would like to ask you some questions about a man who admits he is a Communist....Suppose he is teaching in college. Should he be fired, or not?" ["Militarist"] "Consider a person who advocates doing away with elections and letting the military run the country. . . . Should such a person be allowed [etc.]?" ["Homosexual"] "And what about a man who admits he is a homosexual? . . . . Should such a person be allowed [etc.]?"

SOURCE: *Survey dates: 3/1976–3/2014.*

speech against specific threats posed by various groups. Why were Americans in 1976 almost as willing to allow a racist to speak as a Communist, while in 2014 they were substantially more willing to allow a Communist to speak than a racist? Especially since the collapse of the Soviet Union in 1990, it has become increasingly difficult to imagine that a Communist speaker could pose a serious threat. On the other hand, it is easy for many to imagine that a racist speaker could at least incite a riot. Since the attacks of September 11, 2001, Americans have debated how to treat accused or suspected terrorists, as well as how far to accept routine government surveillance. Issues of political tolerance and civil liberties may shift, but they show no signs of disappearing.

Changes in attitudes toward homosexuality bear special mention. In the 1950s, many Americans perceived homosexuality as a threat to the American way of life, as insidious in its own way as the Communist threat. Indeed, Joseph McCarthy and his allies targeted suspected homosexuals (the most common polite term at the time) as well as suspected Communists. Homosexuals were said to be subject to blackmail, despite the lack of evidence that any American civil servant had been blackmailed based on his or her sexual orientation. Untold thousands of gay men and lesbians were forced out of government service.[78] Homosexuals were also widely portrayed as agents of moral perversion and decay. This sense of threat gradually subsided, but moral disapproval of homosexual behavior remained. The GSS documents that between 1973 and 1991, even as tolerance toward homosexuals increased, large majorities said that "sexual relations between two adults of the same sex" were "always wrong." In 1991, 77 percent gave this response, tied for the greatest disapproval in GSS history.

Then began a dramatic shift in opinions. By 2002 only 56 percent of GSS respondents said that same-sex sexual relations were always wrong, while 32 percent said they were "not wrong at all" (up from 15 percent in 1991). The trend toward greater acceptance seems to have faltered over the next few years, then resumed after 2006. By 2014 just 40 percent of respondents said that same-sex relations were always wrong, and 49 percent said that they were not wrong at all. Meanwhile, similar large changes unfolded in support for civil rights for lesbians and gay men, including the right to marry someone of the same sex. In Gallup polls, support for marriage equality increased from just 27 percent in 1996 to 55 percent by 2014.[79]

UNDERSTANDING AMERICAN ATTITUDES ABOUT RACE

Discussions of racial attitudes often seem sharply polarized—often along racial lines. In a study published in 2011, online samples of self-identified black and white Americans[80] were asked to indicate, on a 1 to 10 scale from "not at all" to "very much": "How much do you think blacks [whites] were/are the victims of discrimination in each of the following decades?" from the 1950s through the 2000s. White and black respondents agreed that in the 1950s discrimination against blacks was intense—on average, over 9 on the scale. Black respondents said on average that by the 2000s, anti-black discrimination had declined to about 6.0 on the scale. White respondents, on the other hand, said that anti-black discrimination had declined to about 3.6 on the scale, more than a point lower than discrimination against whites.[81] Such differences go far beyond assessments of discrimination. Countless questions from past and present surveys evince large disagreements along racial lines about widely varied social and political issues. Donald Kinder and Lynn Sanders commented in 1996 that the "racial divide" is a "divide without peer."[82] The literature on racial attitudes is vast,[83] and we will not attempt to survey it; we simply sketch some major themes and challenges for American democracy.

What do we mean by "race," anyway? Race is a social construct rather than a biological concept. For example, some groups that used to be distinct—and stigmatized—ethnic minorities within the United States, such as the Irish, now tend to blend in with the "white" majority. In the last century the terms "Negro," "colored," "African American," and "black"—among others—all have been respectable labels (some of which have since fallen out of favor) for people who self-identify, or are identified by others, as appearing to be of African ancestry or, perhaps, as having dark skin. From our perspective as public opinion observers, racial and ethnic differences are precisely as real and important as people think they are. However, though racial categories are not objective or immutable, it would be naïve to conclude that they are inconsequential; they are part of how people understand social reality.

Some basic facts about race and ethnicity in America condition our discussion. In the 1970 census, blacks made up about 11 percent of the US population, and people of Hispanic origin constituted less than 5 percent. By the 2010 census, the Hispanic or Latino respondents outnumbered non-Hispanic black respondents, 16.3 percent to 12.2 percent. Setting aside several complications,[84] you can see that the Hispanic population has grown rapidly. The Asian American population has also grown rapidly, although not as much in absolute terms: from 0.8 percent of the population in 1970 to 4.8 percent in 2010. Meanwhile, over much of the twentieth century, African Americans were moving out of southern rural areas into southern and northern cities. All these changes (among many others) have altered Americans' experience of racial and ethnic difference. They have also altered the shape of survey research; as racial and ethnic minorities grow larger, it becomes easier to conduct national surveys of these groups. Here we focus primarily on certain aspects of white-black relations. We pay more attention to white attitudes, partly because more is known about them (because they dominate typical national samples by sheer numbers), and partly because majority beliefs have special political importance.

Unquestionably, whites' attitudes toward African Americans have warmed over time. One measure of this change is attitudes toward racial intermarriage, which we can trace for more than half a century. In 1958 Gallup asked, "Do you approve or disapprove of marriage between white and colored people?" Just 4 percent of all respondents said they approved; another 3 percent were unsure. By 2011, when Gallup asked about "marriage between blacks and whites," 86 percent of respondents—including 83 percent of whites—said they approved. That change is huge, although there are still tens of millions of American whites who do *not* approve of racial intermarriage. Meanwhile, in the 2012 General Social Survey, 21 percent of whites said they would be somewhat or very opposed to "having a close relative marry a black person," down from 65 percent in 1990, albeit far from a small number.[85]

Opinions about direct discrimination have also shifted. When the GSS began in 1972, 37 percent of white respondents supported laws to ban racial intermarriage. By 2002 (the last time this question was asked), only about 11 percent did.[86] Similarly, in 1972, 39 percent of white respondents agreed that whites "have a right to keep [African Americans] out of their neighborhoods"; in 1996 (the last time asked), only 12 percent agreed.[87] However, even in 2012, 29 percent of white GSS respondents thought, for whatever reasons, that homeowners should be allowed not to sell their homes to blacks—down sharply from 64 percent in 1973, but little changed from 1996.[88]

In interpreting these and other survey data, one always has to wonder how accurately people are reporting their racial (and other) attitudes. In Chapters 6 and 7 we considered the possibility of "social desirability" bias: people reporting what they think is acceptable or appropriate to say, rather than how they really think or feel. Moreover, individuals' racial attitudes may be complex and apparently contradictory; some of them may be inaccessible even to the individuals themselves. Various studies using the Implicit Association Test have found that even whites who report (and apparently believe) that they harbor no prejudices against blacks often manifest negative "implicit" associations that affect their response times on simple tasks,[89] although the implications are disputed.[90] More generally, Pearson, Dovidio, and Gaertner argue that in the United States social categorization along racial lines is "largely automatic," and spontaneously activates more positive feelings and beliefs about in-group members than out-group members. Among whites, it activates "stereotypes of whites as intelligent, successful, and educated, and of blacks as aggressive, impulsive, and lazy."[91] Many experimental studies evince substantial proportions of whites, consciously or not, applying different standards to blacks than whites—for example, discriminating against qualified African American job candidates.[92] Such findings do not necessarily reflect upon whites' subjective intentions: group-based stereotypes and other social-psychological shortcuts seem to be deeply rooted in human psychology. But we should not assume that unintended discrimination matters less than willful bias.

For whatever combination of reasons, whites and blacks radically disagree in their explanations of racial gaps in economic and social conditions. Following are a few examples of those gaps. As of 2009, the median white household[93] income was about $52,000, almost 60 percent higher than the median black household income (under $33,000). This gap was modestly narrower than the 74 percent gap reported in 1980.[94] The wealth gap—based on the household net worth, including the value of real estate, stocks and bonds, and all other assets minus debts—was far wider. In the 2013 Survey of Consumer Finances, the median white household wealth was almost $142,000, against just $11,000 for black households. This 13:1 gap was substantially wider than the gap in 1983 (roughly 8:1).[95] How should we account for these and many other differences?

In the 2012 National Election Study, respondents were asked their opinions about four statements about blacks. A summary of (non-Hispanic) white and black responses appears in Table 9.2.

These four questions, plus two others, were designed by Kinder and Sanders as a *racial resentment* scale. Racial resentment, in their account, describes the joint contentions "that blacks do not try hard enough to overcome the difficulties they face and they take what they have not earned."[96] But these statements do not directly measure resentment against blacks. More cautiously, we can interpret the scale as measuring a spectrum of causal attribution. At one end, black economic outcomes primarily depend on blacks' individual choices (agreement with the first and last statements). At the other, they largely depend on circumstances beyond blacks' control (agreement with the second and third statements). As you can see, both whites and blacks often offer mixed responses to these statements, but whites are substantially more likely to score high on racial resentment—to say that blacks should try harder, with no "special favors." These statements are ambiguous and open to interpretation, but it seems hard to believe that the legacy of slavery and discrimination *doesn't* make it difficult for blacks to improve their circumstances, or that blacks can obliterate the 13:1 wealth gap if they just try harder. Those positions might be construed as prejudiced, rhetorical, or wishful—the American Dream posits that anyone can succeed through hard work[97]—but not as factual.

These differences in opinion carry over to policy, and sometimes even widen. In the 2012 NES, only 33 percent of (non-Hispanic) whites, as opposed to 70 percent of blacks, said that "government in Washington [should] see to it

TABLE 9.2. **A Summary of Responses from (Non-Hispanic) Whites and Blacks to Race-related Statements**

QUESTIONS	Non-Hispanic Whites		Non-Hispanic Blacks	
	Agree (%)	Disagree (%)	Agree (%)	Disagree (%)
"Irish, Italians, Jewish and many other minorities overcame prejudice and worked their way up. Blacks should do the same with no special favors."	70	14	41	38
"Generations of slavery and discrimination have created conditions that make it difficult for blacks to work their way out of the lower class."	31	57	64	18
"Over the past few years, blacks have gotten less than they deserve."	12	65	54	19
"It's really a matter of some people not trying hard enough; if blacks would only try harder they could be just as well off as whites."	52	23	32	45

SOURCE: 2012 American National Election Study, available at http://electionstudies.org.

that black people get fair treatment in jobs"; most of the rest said that "this is not the federal government's business." Only 11 percent of whites said they favored "preferential hiring and promotion of blacks" (67 percent said they were strongly against it), while 60 percent of blacks favored it.[98] This is not to say that differences in racial resentment or attribution entirely explain racial disagreements on these or other issues. For example, even most whites who strongly *disagree* that blacks should work their way up without "special favors" also oppose racial hiring preferences. Part of the difference can be attributed to the obvious divergence of *group interests*. Presumably most white respondents perceive hiring preferences for blacks as preferences against whites; perhaps we should be surprised that whites *ever* support such preferences. More subtly, people's life experiences influence their perceptions of social causality and social justice, and in the United States, these experiences often depend substantially on race. For example, blacks are more likely to know stories of (black) friends and relatives who feel they have been hurt by white racial discrimination; whites are more likely to know stories of (white) friends and relatives who feel they have been hurt by affirmative action. These differing experiences are likely to influence policy beliefs in ways not fully captured by the racial resentment questions.

Barack Obama's successful presidential campaign in 2008 triggered wide-ranging commentaries and speculation about changing racial attitudes; some observers suggested that the United States was rapidly becoming "post-racial." By any standard, Obama's election marked a watershed in US racial politics. In 1958 Gallup asked for the first time whether people would vote for a "generally well-qualified" black for president; only 37 percent of *all* respondents said they would. By 2012, 96 percent said they would.[99] To be sure, "well-qualified" is open to interpretation; how fairly did white voters assess Obama's qualifications? It is difficult to say; we cannot know what voters would have thought of a white candidate with identical qualifications and characteristics. One study that uses Google search data to measure "racial animus" suggests that such animus cost Obama "about four percentage points of the national popular vote in both 2008 and 2012."[100] On the other hand, Obama's share of the white vote, according to exit polls, was not much different from the shares of previous Democratic candidates. For that matter, his share of the black vote was higher, but not much higher.[101]

It can be argued that racial attitudes primarily affected the 2008 election not through people's reactions to Obama, but through their preexisting attitudes toward the political parties. Many whites, especially in the South, shifted from the Democratic to the Republican Party in the years after President Lyndon Baines Johnson signed major civil rights acts and undertook various social welfare initiatives known as the "War on Poverty." (Whites who score high on racial resentment are more likely to oppose social welfare programs, apparently because they perceive it as disproportionately benefiting blacks.) For their part, black voters have overwhelmingly favored Democratic presidential candidates from at least 1964 on.

In any case, Obama's presidency has been consequential for American politics. Michael Tesler and David Sears have documented an increased *racialization*: across a wide range of issues and questions—party identification, health care reform, economic conditions—racial attitudes matter more than in the recent past. Racialization is not new; Kinder and Sanders demonstrated in the mid-1990s that racial resentment appeared to influence people's opinions on many issues even when other more obvious influences were taken into account. They further found that its apparent effects on voting varied across elections, probably depending on the content of the campaigns.[102] Probably, then, we should not be surprised that racialization has intensified during Obama's presidency.

One odd manifestation of widespread alienation from Obama is the prevalent belief that he was born in another country—making him constitutionally ineligible to serve as president—despite having a birth certificate from the state of Hawaii. Remarkably, in the 2012 NES, 25 percent of respondents said that Obama was "probably" or "definitely" born in another country. Surely many of these people did not realize that they were declaring Obama an illegitimate president; over one-eighth of them said they had voted for him in 2012. While some observers perceive animus toward Obama as distinctively evincing racial and ethnocentric attitudes, others underscore that partisans often strongly dislike presidents from the other party, whatever reasons they might offer. In 2012 about 15 percent of NES respondents rated Obama 0 on a 0 to 100 "feeling thermometer," barely more than the 13 percent who rated Republican incumbent George W. Bush 0 in 2004. On the subject of Obama's presidency, like so many other topics, one should not expect agreement on the role of racial attitudes.

The "Gender Gap"

The "gender gap" between men's and women's voting choices, although much smaller than the racial gaps we just considered, is a notable feature of contemporary American politics. In the 2012 presidential election, according to exit polls, Democratic president Barack Obama beat Republican challenger Mitt Romney by eleven points among women, but Romney won by seven points among men. This gap was unusually wide—although the gap in 2000 between George W. Bush and Al Gore was even wider[103]—but according to National Election Studies, it has existed in presidential elections since at least 1980. Many people assume that the gap has to do with attitudes toward abortion, but the truth is more complicated.

Abortion is widely considered one of the most controversial issues in American politics. One reason is that the public—depending on the exact wording of the question—is evenly divided. In a 2014 Gallup poll, 47 percent of respondents said they were "more pro-choice"; 46 percent said they were "more pro-life."[104] But this result is misleading if it conjures the image of two opposed camps with nobody in the middle. In the 2012 GSS, respondents were asked if "it should be possible for a pregnant woman to obtain a legal abortion" under various circumstances. Forty-three percent of respondents said it should be possible if "the woman wants it for any reason"; 87 percent said it should be possible if "the woman's own health is seriously endangered by the pregnancy." At the same time, other questions show strong majority support for certain restrictions on abortion rights, especially after the first trimester (three months) of pregnancy. Characteristically, in a 2013 Gallup poll, 20 percent of respondents said abortions should be "illegal in all circumstances," 26 percent that they should be "legal under any circumstances," and a slight 52 percent majority that they should be "legal only under certain circumstances." As we have seen on many other issues, many Americans are somewhere in the middle—in fact, more than the Gallup question indicates.[105]

Interestingly, there is very little "gender gap" on the abortion issue itself. In General Social Surveys between 2008 and 2012, 43 percent of men and 42 percent of women said that abortion should be legal if the woman wants it for any reason. Indeed, combining all the GSS data on this question back to 1977, men on average were slightly more supportive of abortion rights. (Abortion could explain the gender gap, if women who favor abortion rights give more weight to the issue in deciding their votes than other people do, but this explanation does not fit the evidence.) Abortion has been an important part of political campaigns not so much because it separates men from women, but because it separates the parties. Supporters of abortion rights strongly support the Democratic Party, and opponents of abortion rights more often support the Republican Party.[106] As with other issues, strong partisans of the two parties tend to have less moderate positions; candidates must balance those often intense preferences against the greater moderation of the electorate at large. In 2012 the Republican candidate for the US Senate in Missouri, Todd Akin, explaining why he opposed an exception to allow abortion in cases of rape, commented in part that "if it's a legitimate rape, the female body has ways to try to shut that whole thing down."[107] The ensuing furor is widely believed to have cost Akin the election, but there is little evidence that it cost him more dearly among women than men.

What, then, explains the gender gap in voting? The answer is not entirely clear; after all, the gap is not an immutable fact in itself, but emerges from millions of individual voting decisions that elude complete understanding. As with abortion, so with other issues pertaining to women's rights and roles: the differences between men and women tend to be small. However, women on average tend to support greater social welfare spending than men do and are less supportive of military spending and wars—issues that often seem to influence people's votes (and possibly influence women's more than men's). Various studies have attempted to measure the effects of such differences on vote choice and to move beyond generalizing about men or women to consider particular groups thereof.[108] Although the gender gap is large enough to interest political observers (and candidates), it is much smaller than the racial divide we considered earlier.

Considered Opinions and Deliberative Research

As you have noticed, a shadow hangs over most discussions of public opinion as it relates to policy. Most Americans, judging from the results of various surveys and experiments, do not have fixed opinions on most policy issues. As we will underscore in Chapter 10, there is evidence that policymakers do respond to public opinion, but it simply is not possible for them to slavishly obey opinions that do not exist. It *is* often possible for them to claim public support for their policy positions, even on opposite sides of the same issue. We do not mean to imply that survey responses are infinitely malleable; they aren't. It would be difficult to argue from survey results that most Americans oppose Social Security, believe the government should own all large businesses, or favor invading Canada. But on hugely consequential issues such as the 2010 health care reform ("Obamacare"), confusion reigns.

Some observers have proposed and experimented with *deliberative research* as a way to give citizens an intelligible voice in public policy debates. The term is ours, not necessarily the researchers', although it has increasingly caught on.[109] Deliberation most broadly means "thinking," and deliberative research attempts to probe beneath people's off-the-top-of-the-head survey responses to evoke and record their *considered opinions* on policy issues.[110] Not all research on deliberation is designed to give the public a clearer voice; for example, James Kuklinski and his colleagues have investigated the effects of deliberation on political tolerance judgments, and these experiments were not intended to affect policy debates.[111] Much of the impetus for policy-relevant deliberative research has come from people outside academia.

Deliberative research often, but not always, falls into one of two paradigms: survey-based research that hinges on the individual (such as Kuklinski et al.'s research[112]); or group-based research that emphasizes a search for shared understanding and, if possible, consensus. The very word "deliberation" fosters this duality. Sometimes deliberation refers to the individual act of carefully considering the consequences of a decision before one decides. At other times, it means a group activity of attempting to come to a decision together through mutual persuasion, such as when a jury deliberates about a defendant's guilt. (Indeed, one prominent form of deliberative research is called a Citizens Jury.)[113]

These two broad models of deliberative research have complementary strengths and weaknesses. In the survey model, unlike the group-based model, the large number of participants and the scripting of the interviews make the results fairly reliable. (Reliability is quite distinct from validity. *Reliability* means that the survey would be expected to yield similar results each time, unless people's actual beliefs or "considerations" change. Whether deliberative surveys offer a *valid* and useful measure of "considered opinions" on policy issues is open to debate.) But the limits of a telephone survey assure that people will not have much time to think through difficult issues, and by design, they have no opportunity to discuss their differences face to face. A group-based model can offer abundant time and opportunity for mutual persuasion as well as individual thought. However, because a group discussion is influenced by many factors that are difficult to control or even to measure—such as the role of the moderator, the influence of de facto group leaders, and even the body language of the expert witnesses—the results are less reliable. In other words, we cannot tell whether five different groups would come to five radically different conclusions.

James Fishkin's Deliberative Polling' attempts to combine some of the strengths of individual- and group-based approaches. The first large-scale deliberative poll, the 1996 National Issues Convention, brought more than 400 randomly selected citizens together in Austin, Texas, for a weekend of intense engagement with a variety of domestic and foreign issues. They received carefully prepared briefing books, heard talks by policy analysts, and engaged in extended discussions with each other. Surveys conducted before and after the event measured changes in participants' opinions on various policy issues. Thus, the project combined face-to-face deliberation with basic properties of survey research. Since then, deliberative polls have been conducted in over a dozen countries. In 1993 Fishkin described his purpose as follows:

> An ordinary poll models what the electorate thinks, given how little it knows. A deliberative opinion poll models what the electorate would think, if, hypothetically, it could be immersed in intensive deliberative processes. The point of a deliberative opinion poll is prescriptive, not predictive. It has a *recommending force*, telling us what the entire mass public would think about some policy issues or some candidates if it could be given an opportunity for extensive reflection and access to information.[114]

Fishkin has not explicitly defined "recommending force," but he implies that the results of a well-done, deliberative poll should, and to some extent will, be valued by other citizens and by policymakers as an expression of—so to speak—what people would think about an issue if they thought about it.[115]

Of course there is no assurance that policymakers will pay attention to the opinions of deliberative poll participants no matter how carefully considered those opinions are. Even policymakers who think that, ideally, they should follow the dictates of deliberative public opinion, will be reluctant to do so if it puts them at political risk. Increasing the influence of deliberative polling and similar methods therefore entails concerted efforts to make their results better known and respected. The National Issues Convention employed an elaborate media strategy, including extensive public television coverage and outreach to reporters and columnists. Other projects have incorporated direct involvement of politicians and elected officials, who then have some stake in the results. Bruce Ackerman and Fishkin have suggested setting aside a national Deliberation Day in October, on which citizens would be systematically recruited (and paid) to deliberate on topics related to the upcoming elections.[116] This proposal seems very unlikely to be adopted: eliciting and reporting considered public opinion is not widely regarded as a high priority. But considering this and other proposals to foster democratic deliberation among citizens conceivably could promote interest in actually doing so. If we want informed public participation in policy debates, why not work at it?

CONCLUSION

We end this chapter with a conundrum. In terms of their basic values, Americans seem reasonably democratic: generally favorable to civil liberties (although, for better or worse, far from being doctrinaire civil libertarians); generally inclined to seek and to support some sort of common good; more often similar than sharply divided in basic policy priorities. However, Americans are not well equipped for much of the work of democracy, if that work goes beyond merely "supporting the Ins [or the Outs]." Many do not know much about political issues; their votes are often not closely related to their expressed positions on issues, and those positions are often changeable and inconsistent, almost to the vanishing point. Indeed, as mentioned earlier, many Americans explicitly shy away from political debate and disagreement, which makes it hard to judge whether they do or could have meaningful positions on the most difficult decisions facing the country.[117] Nevertheless, we argue in the next chapter that public opinion palpably does have an ongoing influence on government policy—an influence that we believe generally is for the better.

NOTES

1. Hugh Rawson and Margaret Miner, eds., *The Oxford Dictionary of American Quotations* (New York: Oxford University Press, 2005), 508.

2. Scott L. Althaus, *Collective Preferences in Democratic Politics: Opinion Surveys and the Will of the People* (New York: Cambridge University Press, 2003), 208.

3. Paul F. Lazarsfeld, Bernard R. Berelson, and Hazel Gaudet, *The People's Choice* (New York: Duell, Sloan, and Pierce, 1944).

4. Ibid., 65–66.

5. Ibid., 27.

6. Bernard R. Berelson, Paul F. Lazarsfeld, and William N. McPhee, *Voting: A Study of Opinion Formation in a Presidential Campaign* (Chicago: University of Chicago Press, 1954), 293. This book describes a 1948 study in Elmira, New York.

7. Angus Campbell, Philip E. Converse, Warren E. Miller, and Donald E. Stokes, *The American Voter*, unabridged ed. (New York: Wiley, 1960; Chicago: University of Chicago Press, 1976).

8. Using the NES's "Party ID collapsed (1)" measure (VCF0303), the proportion of self-identified Democrats ranged from 52 to 55 percent except in 1964, when it spiked to 61 percent; the proportion of self-identified Republicans ranged from 30 to 36 percent. For further information, refer to the NES Web site, http://www.electionstudies.org, or the SDA data archive hosted by the University of California, Berkeley, at http://sda.berkeley.edu/sdaweb/analysis/?dataset=nes2004c.

9. A rich account of how partisanship influences people's political thinking and voting is Donald P. Green, Bradley Palmquist, and Eric Schickler, *Partisan Hearts and Minds: Political Parties and the Social Identity of Voters* (New Haven, CT: Yale University Press, 2002).

10. These figures—which exclude votes for independent candidate John Anderson—come from the 1980 National Election Study. Here we combine all self-described independents, including those who said that they leaned toward one party or the other.

11. Robert Huckfeldt and John Sprague, *Citizens, Politics, and Social Communication: Information and Influence in a Presidential Campaign* (New York: Cambridge University Press, 1995); Betsy Sinclair, *The Social Citizen: Peer Networks and Political Behavior* (Chicago: University of Chicago, 2012).

12. Walter Lippmann, *Public Opinion* (New York: Harcourt, Brace, 1922; New York: Free Press, 1965), 143.

13. For instance, the US Catholic bishops oppose both abortion rights and capital punishment, in what is sometimes called a "consistent pro-life" or "seamless web of life" ethic. Interestingly, people who favor abortion rights while opposing capital

punishment (liberals) or vice versa (conservatives) often criticize their counterparts' inconsistency but see no inconsistency in their own views. In fact, philosophically consistent arguments can be made for any of these positions.

14. This chapter touches on several measures of political sophistication, but in limited detail. A good overview can be found in Robert C. Luskin, "Measuring Political Sophistication," *American Journal of Political Science* 31 (1987): 856–899.

15. See Philip E. Converse, "Attitudes and Non-attitudes: Continuation of a Dialogue," in Edward R. Tufte, ed., *The Quantitative Analysis of Social Problems* (Boston: Addison-Wesley, 1970), 168–169. This paper was originally presented in 1963.

16. Benjamin I. Page and Robert Y. Shapiro, "The Rational Public and Democracy," in George E. Marcus and Russell L. Hanson, eds., *Reconsidering the Democratic Public* (University Park: Penn State University Press, 1993), 61.

17. Benjamin I. Page and Robert Y. Shapiro, *The Rational Public: Fifty Years of Trends in Americans' Policy Preferences* (Chicago: University of Chicago Press, 1992). We emphasize here, as we will again, that "information" is not necessarily factual.

18. See Page and Shapiro, *Rational Public*, 90–97, for further discussion.

19. See the 1939 Gallup surveys cited in Page and Shapiro, *Rational Public*, 100.

20. See Page and Shapiro, *Rational Public*, 100–104 and 378–379, for further discussion.

21. This wording was used in three Quinnipiac University Polls between December 2004 and April 2013; in the 2013 survey, 48 percent said they preferred the death penalty, 43 percent said they preferred a life sentence, and 9 percent said they were unsure or did not answer. (The survey results and trends are available at http://www.quin nipiac.edu/news-and-events/quinnipiac-university-poll/national/release-detail?Re leaseID=1891, accessed December 2014.) Other surveys have produced similar results.

22. James A. Stimson, *Public Opinion in America: Moods, Cycles, and Swings* (Boulder, CO: Westview Press, 1991); Robert S. Erikson, Michael B. Mackuen, and James A. Stimson, *The Macro Polity* (New York: Cambridge University Press, 2002).

23. Page and Shapiro, *Rational Public*, 365.

24. In their own words, "Government responsiveness to the public would constitute a hollow victory, for example, if public opinion were itself manipulated by elites or interest groups in such a way that policy followed the mistaken wishes of a deceived public." Page and Shapiro, "Educating and Manipulating the Public," in Michael Margolis and Gary A. Mauser, eds., *Manipulating Public Opinion: Essays on Public Opinion as a Dependent Variable* (Pacific Grove, CA: Brooks/Cole, 1989), 294.

25. Larry M. Bartels, "The American Public's Defense Spending Preferences in the Post-Cold War Era," *Public Opinion Quarterly* 58, no. 4 (Winter 1994): 479–508.

26. Pew Research Center, "More Say There Is Solid Evidence of Global Warming," October 15, 2012, 1, http://www.people-press.org/files/legacy-pdf/10–15–12%20 Global%20Warming%20Release.pdf; Pew Research Center, "Keystone XL Pipeline Draws Broad Support," April 2, 2013, 3, http://www.people-press.org/files/legacy -pdf/4–2–13%20Keystone%20Pipeline%20and%20Global%20Warming%20 Release.pdf.

27. Global temperature averages can be retrieved from the National Climatic Data Center, http://www.ncdc.noaa.gov/cag/time-series/global.

28. CBS News, field dates 1/30/97–2/1/97 (Roper Center accession number 0272753); 76 percent responded "favor," 17 percent "oppose."

29. CBS News and *New York Times*, field dates 1/14/97–1/17/97 (Roper Center accession number 0271190); 39 percent responded "the kind of issue," 49 percent "not the kind of issue."

30. Samuel Popkin, *The Reasoning Voter* (Chicago: University of Chicago Press, 1991), 213.

31. Ibid.

32. David P. Glass, "Evaluating Presidential Candidates: Who Focuses on Their Personal Attributes?," *Public Opinion Quarterly* 49 (1985): 517–534.

33. A useful overview of the political heuristics literature through the early 1990s is Jeffery J. Mondak, "Cognitive Heuristics, Heuristic Processing, and Efficiency in Political Decision Making," *Research in Micropolitics* 4 (1993): 117–142. More recent and critical appraisals include Richard R. Lau and David P. Redlawsk, "Advantages and Disadvantages of Cognitive Heuristics in Political Decision Making," *American Journal of Political Science* 45 (2001): 951–971, and Delia Baldassarri, *The Simple Art of Voting: The Cognitive Shortcuts of Italian Voters* (New York: Oxford University Press, 2013), chs. 2–3.

34. See Arthur Lupia, "Short Cuts Versus Encyclopedias: Information and Voting Behavior in California Insurance Reform Elections," *American Political Science Review* 8 (Spring 1994): 63–76.

35. Paul M. Sniderman, Richard A. Brody, and Philip E. Tetlock, *Reasoning and Choice: Explorations in Political Psychology* (New York: Cambridge University Press, 1991).

36. Morris P. Fiorina, *Retrospective Voting in American National Elections* (New Haven, CT: Yale University Press, 1981), is the seminal work. On economic conditions in particular, see, e.g., Michael S. Lewis-Beck, *Economics and Elections: The Major Western Democracies* (Ann Arbor: University of Michigan Press, 1988), and Gregory Markus, "The Impact of Personal and National Economic Conditions on the Presidential Vote: A Pooled Cross-Sectional Analysis," *American Journal of Political Science* 32 (1988): 137–154. Michael B. Mackuen, Robert Erikson, and James Stimson have argued that future economic prospects matter more than "retrospective" evaluations, in "Peasants or Bankers? The American Electorate and the U.S. Economy," *American Political Science Review* 86 (1992): 597–611.

37. For example, economist Ray C. Fair finds that the rate of growth in gross domestic product, the number of quarters of high growth, and the inflation rate all are strong predictors of presidential vote shares. See, e.g., Ray C. Fair, "Presidential and Congressional Vote-Share Equations," *American Journal of Political Science* 53 (2009): 55–72.

38. Larry M. Bartels, *Unequal Democracy: The Political Economy of the New Gilded Age* (Princeton, NJ: Russell Sage Foundation and Princeton University Press, 2008), ch. 4.

39. Christopher H. Achen and Larry M. Bartels, "Blind Retrospection: Electoral Responses to Drought, Flu, and Shark Attacks" (working paper, January 27, 2004, http://qssi.psu.edu/files/AchenBartels_Sharks.pdf). See also Christopher H. Achen and Larry M. Bartels, "Blind Retrospection: Why Shark Attacks Are Bad for Democracy" (working paper 5-2013, Center for the Study of Democratic Institutions, March 22, 2012, http://www.vanderbilt.edu/csdi/research/CSDI_WP_05-2013.pdf).

40. Michael X. Delli Carpini and Scott Keeter, *What Americans Know About Politics and Why It Matters* (New Haven, CT: Yale University Press, 1996), 256–257.

41. Larry M. Bartels, "Uninformed Votes: Information Effects in Presidential Elections," *American Journal of Political Science* 40 (1996): 194–230. Here Bartels uses only demographic characteristics, not political attitudes, to predict vote choice. Although this choice is limiting, it spares him from the objection that information may also affect people's political views, as argued by Althaus, below.

42. Anthony Fowler and Michele Margolis, "The Political Consequences of Uninformed Voters," *Electoral Studies* 34 (2014): 100–110.

43. Scott L. Althaus, "Information Effects in Collective Preferences," *American Political Science Review* 92 (September 1998): 545–558; Scott L. Althaus, *Collective Preferences in Democratic Politics: Opinion Surveys and the Will of the People* (New York: Cambridge University Press, 2003).

44. Baldassarri, *Simple Art of Voting*, 76.

45. John R. Zaller, *The Nature and Origins of Mass Opinion* (New York: Cambridge University Press, 1992); John Zaller and Stanley Feldman, "A Simple Theory of the Survey Response: Answering Questions Versus Revealing Preferences," *American Journal of Political Science* 36 (1992): 579–616.

46. Zaller, *Nature and Origins*, 40.

47. What we call "political messages," Zaller usually calls "information," but he emphasizes that he does *not* mean neutral facts. Notice, however, that there is no neat distinction between "political" and "nonpolitical" messages.

48. Zaller, *Nature and Origins*, 311; see also 328.

49. Ibid., 331, 332.

50. Benchley's comment appears in a mock review of the 1920 New York City telephone book: Robert C. Benchley, *Of All Things* (New York: Henry Holt, 1921), 187.

51. Morris P. Fiorina with Samuel J. Abrams and Jeremy C. Pope, *Culture War? The Myth of a Polarized America*, 3rd ed. (New York: Pearson, 2010).

52. Jon Cohen and Dan Balz, "Poll: Spreading Gloom about Government; Most Dissatisfied with Political System," *Washington Post*, August 10, 2011, http://www.washingtonpost.com/politics/poll-spreading-gloom-about-government-most-dissatisfied-with-political-system/2011/08/10/gIQAXsUB7I_story.html; ABC News/*Washington Post* survey, field dates December 14–15, 2000 (Roper Center accession number 0375554).

53. An excellent, albeit dated, introduction to this complex issue is Martin Gilens, *Why Americans Hate Welfare: Race, Media, and the Politics of Antipoverty Policy* (Chicago: University of Chicago Press, 2000). For a classic discussion of whether and how

Americans extend equality to the economic realm, see also Jennifer L. Hochschild, *What's Fair? American Beliefs about Distributive Justice* (Cambridge, MA: Harvard University Press, 1981).

54. Jennifer L. Hochschild, "Disjunction and Ambivalence in Citizens' Political Outlooks," in George E. Marcus and Russell L. Hanson, eds., *Reconsidering the Democratic Public* (University Park: Penn State University Press, 1993), 192–193; Hochschild, *What's Fair?*

55. John R. Hibbing and Elizabeth Theiss-Morse, *Stealth Democracy: Americans' Beliefs About How Government Should Work* (New York: Cambridge University Press, 2002), 130–131.

56. Ibid., 161.

57. In the 2012 NES dataset, this variable is named GUARPR_SELF. The results here were obtained using the SDA 4.0 interface hosted by the University of California at Berkeley, http://sda.berkeley.edu/sdaweb/analysis/?dataset=nes2012.

58. The variable names are SPSRVPR_SELF, INSPRE_SELF, AIDBLACK_SELF, and ENVJOB_SELF. The spending and services variable was reverse-coded so that the most liberal position would be at point 1 on the scale, instead of point 7 as in the original wording.

59. Pew Research Center, "Political Polarization in the American Public," June 2014, 6, http://www.people-press.org/files/2014/06/6-12-2014-Political-Polarization-Release.pdf.

60. Norman H. Nie, Sidney Verba, and John R. Petrocik, *The Changing American Voter* (Cambridge, MA: Harvard University Press, 1976).

61. Fiorina, *Culture War?*; Morris P. Fiorina and Samuel Abrams, "Americans Aren't Polarized, Just Better Sorted," *Monkey Cage* (blog), *Washington Post*, January 21, 2014, http://www.washingtonpost.com/blogs/monkey-cage/wp/2014/01/21/americans-arent-polarized-just-better-sorted/.

62. Another kind of "sorting" is geographical: Bill Bishop argues that Americans are more ideologically segregated than they used to be, as they have tended to move nearer to like-minded people. Bill Bishop, *The Big Sort: Why the Clustering of Like-Minded America Is Tearing Us Apart* (New York: Houghton Mifflin, 2008).

63. Pew Research Center, "Political Polarization," 6.

64. Ibid., 8.

65. Thomas J. Durant Jr. and Cecilia Chan, "Social Tolerance for Crime and Deviance: An Exploratory Analysis," *Deviant Behavior* 1 (1980): 261–262.

66. Hitler was appointed chancellor in January 1933, having lost two presidential elections in 1932, but the Nazis were the largest party in the parliament (Reichstag), with about one-third of the seats.

67. T. W. Adorno, Else Frenkel-Brunswik, Daniel J. Levinson, and R. Nevitt Sanford, *The Authoritarian Personality* (New York: Harper & Brothers, 1950).

68. Richard H. Rovere, *Senator Joe McCarthy* (New York: Harper & Row, 1959; 1973), 7–8.

69. Samuel A. Stouffer, *Communism, Conformity, and Civil Liberties: A Cross-section of the Nation Speaks Its Mind* (Garden City, NY: Doubleday, 1955), p. 13.

70. Ibid., 38.

71. Ibid., 40–43.

72. Ibid., 44–45.

73. Ibid., 176–178.

74. Berelson, Lazarsfeld, and McPhee, *Voting*, 314.

75. James L. Gibson, "Political Intolerance and Political Repression During the McCarthy Red Scare," *American Political Science Review* 82, no. 2 (June 1988): 511–529.

76. Ibid., 518–519.

77. John L. Sullivan, James Piereson, and George E. Marcus, "An Alternative Conceptualization of Political Tolerance: Illusory Increases 1950s–1970s," *American Political Science Review* 73, no. 3 (September 1979): 784.

78. David K. Johnson, *The Lavender Scare: The Cold War Persecution of Gays and Lesbians in the Federal Government* (Chicago: University of Chicago Press, 2004).

79. Justin McCarthy, "Same-Sex Marriage Support Reaches New High at 55%," http://www.gallup.com/poll/169640/sex-marriage-support-reaches-new-high.aspx. Before 2006, the question was worded, "Do you think marriages between homosexuals should or should not be recognized by the law as valid, with the same rights as traditional marriages?" Starting in 2006, "same-sex couples" replaced "homosexuals."

80. In using the descriptors whites and blacks here, we follow the lead of the researchers, who used those terms throughout their study.

81. Michael I. Norton and Samuel R. Sommers, "Whites See Racism as a Zero-Sum Game That They Are Now Losing," *Perspectives on Psychological Science* 6 (2011): 215–218. In the 2000s, white respondents on average rated discrimination against whites at 4.7 on the scale; blacks rated it at 1.8, less than a point from the bottom of the scale.

82. Donald R. Kinder and Lynn M. Sanders, *Divided by Color: Racial Politics and Democratic Ideals* (Chicago: University of Chicago Press, 1996), 27.

83. In the US context, some important surveys are Howard Schuman and Charlotte Steeh, *Racial Attitudes in America: Trends and Interpretations*, rev. ed. (Cambridge, MA: Harvard University Press, 1998); Lawrence D. Bobo, "Racial Attitudes and Relations at the Close of the Twentieth Century," in Neil J. Smelser, William Julius Wilson, and Faith Mitchell, eds., *America Becoming: Racial Trends and Their Consequences* (Washington, DC: National Academies Press, 2001), 1:264–301; Michael Tesler and David O. Sears, *Obama's Race: The 2008 Election and the Dream of a Post-Racial America* (Chicago: University of Chicago Press, 2010); and Michael C. Dawson, *Not in Our Lifetimes: The Future of Black Politics* (Chicago: University of Chicago Press, 2011), esp. chs. 1–3.

84. In 2010, about 2.9 percent of respondents identified themselves as belonging to two or more races; about 0.4 percent identified themselves as Hispanic (or Latino) and black.

85. "What about having a close relative marry a black person? Would you be very in favor of it happening, somewhat in favor, neither in favor nor opposed to it happening, somewhat opposed, or very opposed to it happening?" (variable name MARBLK).

86. "Do you think there should be laws against marriages between [Negroes/Blacks /African-Americans] and whites?" (variable name RACMAR; the wording has varied over the years).

87. "White people have a right to keep [Negroes/Blacks/African-Americans] out of their neighborhoods if they want to, and [Negroes/Blacks/African-Americans] should respect that right" (variable name RACSEG).

88. "Suppose there is a community-wide vote on the general housing issue. There are two possible laws to vote on: (A.) One law says that a homeowner can decide for himself whom to sell his house to, even if he prefers not to sell to [Negroes/Blacks /African-Americans]. (B.) The second law says that a homeowner cannot refuse to sell to someone because of their race or color. Which law would you vote for?" (variable name RACOPEN).

89. A book-length discussion is Mahzarin R. Banaji and Anthony G. Greenwald, *Blindspot: Hidden Biases of Good People* (New York: Delacorte/Random House, 2013).

90. Hart Blanton and James Jaccard, "Unconscious Racism: A Concept in Pursuit of a Measure," *Annual Review of Sociology* 34 (2008): 277–297.

91. Adam R. Pearson, John F. Dovidio, and Samuel L. Gaertner, "The Nature of Contemporary Prejudice: Insights from Aversive Racism," *Social and Personality Psychology Compass* 3 (2009): 316.

92. On employment, for example, see Devah Pager, Bruce Western, and Art Bonikowski, "Discrimination in a Low-Wage Labor Market: A Field Experiment," *American Sociological Review* 74 (2009): 777–799, which evinces discrimination against both black and Latino applicants.

93. In government reports, households often are categorized by the self-reported race of the head of household.

94. US Census Bureau, *Statistical Abstract of the United States, 2012* (Washington, DC: Department of Commerce, Bureau of the Census, 2011), Table 691, http://www .census.gov/prod/2011pubs/12statab/income.pdf.

95. Rakesh Kochhar and Richard Fry, "Wealth Inequality Has Widened along Racial, Ethnic Lines Since End of Great Recession," *FactTank* (blog), Pew Research Center, December 12, 2014, http://www.pewresearch.org/fact-tank/2014/12/12/racial-wealth -gaps-great-recession/.

96. Kinder and Sanders, *Divided by Color*, 106.

97. See the thorough discussion in Jennifer L. Hochschild, *Facing Up to the American Dream: Race, Class, and the Soul of the Nation* (Princeton, NJ: Princeton University Press, 1996).

98. 2012 American National Election Study, www.electionstudies.org, variable names FAIRJOB_OPIN and AAPOST_HIRE_X.

99. The 1958 wording was this: "If your party nominated a generally well-qualified man for president and he happened to be a Negro, would you vote for him?" In 2012 "man" had changed to "person," "Negro" to "black," and "him" to "that person." Gallup News Service, June [2012] Wave 1, Final Topline, available at http://www.gallup .com/file/poll/155282/Willingness_Vote_Other_Key_Groups%20.pdf.

100. Seth Stephens-Davidowitz, "The Cost of Racial Animus on a Black Presidential Candidate: Using Google Search Data to Find What Surveys Miss" (working paper, March 24, 2013, available at http://sethsd.com/).

101. Democratic nominee Al Gore is estimated to have received 42 percent of the white vote in 2000; in 2004, John Kerry received 41 percent; in 2008, Obama received 43 percent; and in 2012, he received 39 percent. (Obama won both elections largely because the nonwhite share of the electorate was larger than in previous elections.) The corresponding estimated shares of the black vote were Gore, 90 percent; Kerry, 88 percent; Obama 2008, 95 percent; Obama 2012, 93 percent.

102. Kinder and Sanders, *Divided by Color*. On differences across elections, see 251–258.

103. According to the 2000 Voter News Service exit polls, Gore beat Bush by 12 points among women, while Bush beat Gore by 10 points among men. Kristin Kanthak and Barbara Norrander, "The Enduring Gender Gap," in Herbert F. Weisberg and Clyde Wilcox, eds., *Models of Voting in Presidential Elections: The 2000 U.S. Election* (Palo Alto, CA: Stanford University Press, 2003), 141.

104. Lydia Saad, "U.S. Still Split on Abortion: 47% Pro-Choice, 46% Pro-Life," http://www.gallup.com/poll/170249/split-abortion-pro-choice-pro-life.aspx.

105. Comparing the Gallup and GSS results, it seems that many people who say that abortion should always be illegal nonetheless would make an exception if the woman's health is at risk. Contrariwise, in a 2012 Gallup survey, only 14 percent of respondents said that abortion should generally be legal in the last three months of pregnancy. Both Gallup survey results are reported in Lydia Saad, "Majority of Americans Still Support Roe v. Wade Decision," http://www.gallup.com/poll/160058/majority-americans -support-roe-wade-decision.aspx.

106. In the 2008–2012 GSS, people who favored legal abortion for any reason were 21 points more likely to identify as Democrats than as Republicans (39 percent to 18 percent); people who opposed legal abortion when the woman's health was endangered were more likely to be Republican (34 percent) than Democratic (21 percent).

107. John Eligon and Michael Schwirtz, "Senate Candidate Provokes Ire with 'Legitimate Rape' Comment," *New York Times*, August 19, 2012.

108. Some reference points in the literature are Carole Kennedy Chaney, R. Michael Alvarez, and Jonathan Nagler, "Explaining the Gender Gap in U.S. Presidential Elections, 1980–1992," *Political Research Quarterly* 51 (1998): 311–339; Kanthak and Norrander, "The Enduring Gender Gap"; and Lois Duke Whitaker, ed., *Voting the Gender Gap* (Urbana: University of Illinois Press, 2008).

109. See, for example, Simon Beste, "Contemporary Trends of Deliberative Research: Synthesizing a New Study Agenda," *Journal of Public Deliberation* 9, no. 2 (2013), http://www.publicdeliberation.net/jpd/vol9/iss2/art1/, although Beste does not strictly limit the term to the empirical research we consider here.

110. Robert C. Luskin, James S. Fishkin, and Roger Jowell, "Considered Opinions: Deliberative Polling in Britain," *British Journal of Public Opinion* 32 (2002): 455–487.

111. One such study is James H. Kuklinski, Ellen Riggle, Victor Ottati, Norbert Schwarz, and Robert S. Wyer Jr., "The Cognitive and Affective Bases of Political Tolerance Judgments," *American Journal of Political Science* 35 (1991): 1–27.

112. The most extensive example is the series of Americans Talk Issues surveys conducted from 1988 to 1998. See Alan F. Kay, *Locating Consensus for Democracy: A Ten-Year U.S. Experiment* (Washington, DC: Americans Talk Issues Foundation, 1998).

113. Citizens Juries were originally designed by Ned Crosby in the early 1970s and have been conducted under the auspices of the Jefferson Center for New Democratic Processes for over 20 years; similar programs have been conducted in many other countries. See Ned Crosby and John C. Hottinger, "The Citizens Jury Process," in *The Book of the States 2011* (Lexington, KY: Council of State Governments, 2011), 321–325, http://knowledgecenter.csg.org/kc/system/files/Crosby2011.pdf (accessed January 7, 2015); James S. Fishkin, *When the People Speak: Deliberative Democracy and Public Consultation* (New York: Oxford University Press, 2009), 55–57.

114. James S. Fishkin, *Democracy and Deliberation: New Directions for Democratic Reform* (New Haven, CT: Yale University Press, 1993), 81. See also James S. Fishkin, *The Voice of the People: Public Opinion and Democracy* (New Haven, CT: Yale University Press, 1997); Fishkin, *When the People Speak*, esp. ch. 5.

115. See, e.g., *When the People Speak*, 134, 151, 156.

116. Bruce Ackerman and James Fishkin, *Deliberation Day* (New Haven, CT: Yale University Press, 2004).

117. Nina Eliasoph, *Avoiding Politics: How Americans Produce Apathy in Everyday Life* (New York: Cambridge University Press, 1998); Hibbing and Theiss-Morse, *Stealth Democracy*.

10

Public Opinion and Policymaking

COAUTHORED WITH LAWRENCE R. JACOBS

Unless mass views have some place in the shaping of policy, all the talk about democracy is nonsense.

—V. O. KEY JR.,
PUBLIC OPINION AND AMERICAN DEMOCRACY[1]

Princeton Study: U.S. No Longer An Actual Democracy

—TALKING POINTS MEMO HEADLINE, APRIL 2014[2]

In the quote above, V. O. Key Jr. firmly emphasizes what we observed in the first chapter: when we talk about democracy, we must talk about public opinion. In Chapter 4 we considered normative issues: Just what role should public opinion play in a democracy? Here we focus on a broad empirical question: How much influence does public opinion have on policymaking? If it has none or almost none, then we might conclude, in Key's words, "that democratic government only amounts to a hoax, a ritual whose performance serves only to delude the people and thereby to convert them into willing subjects of the powers that be."[3] But in fact we will present evidence—confounding some cynics' expectations— that shows that public opinion substantially affects what government does. At the same time, the evidence in some ways is ambiguous; in other ways (as in the case of the "Princeton Study"), it depicts the role of public opinion in policy as far from most observers' ideals.

CONSTRAINT, IMPULSION, OR IRRELEVANCE?

In considering how public opinion influences policy, it is useful to distinguish among three broad possibilities: (1) public opinion may merely constrain policy; (2) it may impel, or exert strong pressure to alter, policy; or (3) it may be ignored in policymaking. To exemplify the distinction between constraining policy and impelling change, consider US foreign and military policy during the 1930s. Many historians have argued that public isolationist sentiment prevented President Franklin D. Roosevelt from moving decisively to oppose the territorial ambitions of Nazi Germany, in particular to help England defend itself (although this judgment is debatable).[4] Walter Lippmann generalized in the 1950s that in the democratic nations, "in matters of war and peace . . . , the prevailing mass opinion will [usually] impose what amounts to a veto upon changing the course on which the government is now proceeding." Lippmann added that this status quo bias operated in both directions, "compell[ing] the governments . . . to be too late with too little, or too long with too much, too pacifist in peace and too bellicose in war."[5] Lippmann was describing constraint: public opinion setting limits on what policies are possible, rather than impelling policy to change in some direction.

In other cases, changes in public opinion at least appear to impel changes in policy. Military intervention by the United States in Vietnam in 1964–1965 initially had strong public support, but—as we will show later—after the public turned against the war, the government started to withdraw troops. The historically important Civil Rights Act of 1964 and Voting Rights Act of 1965 passed after public opinion became increasingly supportive of protecting black civil rights. Even the Supreme Court's 1973 decision that constitutionally protected abortion rights (*Roe v. Wade*) followed a ten-year period of growing public support for legal abortion—although the federal courts are designed to be relatively insulated against the pressures of public opinion.[6] In any particular case, observers may disagree about whether change in public opinion impelled policy change or merely changed the constraints upon policy. It seems to us that at some point a change in constraints amounts to impelling (if not quite compelling) policy change—but readers must make their own judgments.

Conversely, sometimes policymakers appear to ignore what public opinion (as revealed by opinion polls) ostensibly wants. For example, in every General

Social Survey from 1973 on, large majorities, ranging from 59 to 79 percent, have said that the United States spends "too much" on "foreign aid." Yet foreign aid programs continue unabated. Part of the reason is that Americans grossly exaggerate foreign aid spending. In a 2013 Kaiser Family Foundation survey, respondents estimated that on average 28 percent of the US budget goes to foreign aid, and 61 percent of respondents said that the United States was spending too much. Interviewers then asked, "What if you heard that about 1 percent of the federal budget is spent on foreign aid?" (which was close to the true figure). Respondents were almost evenly divided among saying that proportion was too much, too little, or "about the right amount."[7] We do not argue that policymakers ignore public opinion on foreign aid because it is misinformed; on the contrary, we think that misinformed opinion can still be influential. Indeed, public opinion on foreign aid may function as a constraint, albeit a weak one—any politician might think twice before advocating for a large increase. However, foreign aid has not been a very *salient* issue: it receives relatively little attention in the media, and the political parties have not extensively debated it. Perhaps if foreign aid were more salient, public opinion about it would be better informed, and policymakers might not ignore it—or perhaps not.

In some cases, policymakers essentially ignore reasonably clear public opinion on highly salient issues. One interesting example is the effort to remove President Bill Clinton from office in 1998–1999 for actions related to the Monica Lewinsky sex scandal. Many public opinion polls showed that Americans generally thought Congress should censure Clinton and no more. But the House Republican leadership undertook to impeach Clinton, and the House voted for two articles of impeachment, almost entirely along party lines. If two-thirds of the Senate had voted to convict Clinton of either article, he would have been removed from office, but neither article received more than fifty votes. Republican leaders may have hoped that public opinion would turn against Clinton as the controversy continued, much as it had turned against Richard Nixon during the Watergate scandal. For their part, Democrats may have hoped that voters would punish Republicans for going forward with impeachment. Neither of these outcomes was apparent, although Democrats did gain five seats in the 1998 House elections, an unusually good midterm result for the president's party.[8] Clearly the public's wishes are not always followed. This apparent lack of responsiveness, however, may not mean that a decision is, in the end, "undemocratic." We will say more on that topic later.

A different typology of policy responsiveness deserves mention. Jeff Manza and Fay Lomax Cook argued in 2002 that much of the literature had been divided between positing "large effects" and "small effects" of public opinion on policy. Manza and Cook themselves suggest that the best model is "contingent effects": simply put, public opinion matters more in some circumstances than in others, and the better task is to understand those circumstances.[9] We hesitate to categorize researchers into "large effects" and "small effects" camps, all the more because we generally agree with Manza and Cook that researchers should strive to move beyond that dichotomy. That said, some researchers do portray a much greater degree of policy responsiveness than others. Bear this in mind as you assess the evidence and arguments presented here.

TESTING POLICY RESPONSIVENESS

In Chapter 4 we considered some theories about the effects of public opinion on policy outcomes. We might expect large effects, inasmuch as elected officials depend on people's votes to remain in office, or we might expect rather small effects, inasmuch as many interest groups seem to have far greater opportunity than ordinary citizens to promote their views. But what is the reality? How do we systematically compare public opinion and government policies to assess their relationship? It took political scientists some time to focus on this question. Some of the earliest empirical studies of policy responsiveness focused on representation in Congress. These studies of constituency representation, as we will see later, examined the votes cast by legislators on proposed laws; they did not directly compare public opinion with actual policy outcomes.

One way to tackle the problem would be to compare majority public opinion with subsequent government policy. If it takes simple majorities in the House and the Senate to pass a law, perhaps a simple majority of public opinion can also be decisive (although this assumption can easily be criticized).[10] The simplest question to ask is this: How often does majority opinion get what it wants from government? First we could look for instances of majority opinion, say, poll questions that ask about specific government policies, in which an outright majority of respondents took a clear position for or against a policy change. In each case, we could then see whether policy subsequently (within some period of time) changed or remained the same, and whether or not it ended up agreeing with majority opinion.

Conceptually, this approach to measuring policy responsiveness is simple. Practically, it has posed many challenges. Modern opinion polling began in the United States in 1935, but the polls generally were not designed with such a study in mind; the policy questions available to researchers often were vague or covered a narrow, ad hoc subset of policy debates. It took more than thirty years for enough public opinion data to become available. Finally a handful of researchers—most notably Donald Devine, Robert Weissberg, and Alan Monroe[11]—developed appropriate strategies for using these data to examine government responsiveness to public opinion.

Monroe's study, the largest of these initial studies, examined "congruence" between majority opinion and policy in much the way we just described. For example, if in response to a survey question, 51 percent or more of survey respondents opposed the United States establishing diplomatic relations with Cuba, and the government had not established such relations up to four years later, this would be a case in which government policy was consistent or "congruent" with public opinion. In this case, too, we would have majority support for existing policy, or the status quo, in Monroe's terms. If majority opinion had favored the establishment of diplomatic relations, and the government had subsequently complied, this would be a case of congruence with a "change" in policy. Table 10.1 summarizes Monroe's results. Overall, across 222 cases of nonspending issues, Monroe found that policy outcomes were congruent with public opinion in 64 percent of cases— far more than the 50 percent that one would expect to occur by chance.

Monroe, however, warned that his evidence did not establish that public opinion actually influenced policy. Take the Cuban relations example: policymakers might well oppose establishing diplomatic relations regardless of public opinion on the issue. Also, pollsters' decisions about what questions to ask (and how to ask them) affect the apparent rate of congruence. As an extreme example, if a poll asked, "Do you think the United States should launch a nuclear attack on England? . . . on France? . . . on Germany?" and so on, it could quickly establish congruence between public opinion and policy on dozens of "policy issues" that are, in most people's minds, not issues at all. Furthermore, other researchers using similar methods found weaker evidence of responsiveness, particularly in other countries.[12] Additional studies using different research methods and other data were clearly needed to confirm or challenge Monroe's findings.

Benjamin Page and Robert Y. Shapiro undertook one such different approach.[13] One part of their study used a method similar to Monroe's and found a comparable level of "majoritarian" opinion–policy congruence. But they were much more interested in finding out how often changes in public opinion were followed by changes in policy. In this analysis, they ignored whether support for a policy constituted a majority; they examined only the direction of opinion change and the direction of policy change, if any. For example, they found that support for increasing government health care spending increased (by more than the survey sampling error) from 1980 to 1982. Because this spending (adjusted for inflation) in fact increased from 1980 to 1983, this case evinced

TABLE 10.1. **Public Preference and Policy Outcome for All Nonspending Cases**

| | Public Preference | |
Policy Outcome	Status Quo	Change
Status Quo	56 (76%)	61 (41%)
Change	18 (24%)	87 (59%)
Total	74 (100%)	148 (100%)

SOURCE: Adapted from A. D. Monroe, "Consistency Between Public Preference and National Policy Decisions," *American Politics Quarterly* 7 (1979): 9.

"covariational congruence" between policy change and opinion change. Had spending decreased from 1980 to 1983, the case would have been classified as an instance of noncongruence.

In their analysis of 231 instances of changes in policy preferences and changes of policy, Page and Shapiro found that policies one year later had moved in the same direction as opinion 66 percent of the time. These results are shown in Table 10.2. Note that this percentage depended on their excluding 120 cases of "no change in policy." At least some of those cases might be construed as examples of noncongruence. However, the authors reported that in many of these cases, policy was already maximally congruent with opinion. In others, congruent policy changes occurred more than one year after public opinion changed. In still others, the increased level of support for policy change still amounted to a minority, so inaction could not reasonably be construed as a failure of democratic responsiveness.

Table 10.3 shows evidence that policy responds to the degree of change in public opinion; larger opinion changes made corresponding policy changes more likely. When opinion changed by only 6 or 7 percentage points, congruent policy change was barely more common (53 percent of cases) than one would expect by chance. When opinion changed by 20 percentage points or more, policy change was congruent in 86 percent of cases. Similarly, Monroe had found congruent policy changes more likely when there was larger majority support.[14] Page and Shapiro (as well as Monroe) also show that congruence was more likely for the most salient issues, those receiving the most attention in media reporting. All these results were consistent with theories about when democratic responsiveness should be highest.

TABLE 10.2. **Congruence Between Opinion and Policy, 1935–1979**

	Total Cases		Cases with Policy Change	
	%	N	%	N
Congruent change in opinion and policy	43	(153)	66	(153)
Noncongruent change in policy	22	(78)	34	(78)
No change in policy	33	(120)		
Uncertain	2	(6)		
Total	100	(357)	100	(231)

NOTE: Each case is an instance in which public policy preferences changed significantly, according to repeated administration of identical survey items.
SOURCE: Benjamin I. Page and Robert Y. Shapiro, 1983, table 1, p. 178.

TABLE 10.3. **Frequency of Congruence for Opinion Changes of Different Sizes**

Size of Opinion Change in Percentage Points	Congruent		Noncongruent		Total	
	%	N	%	N	%	N
6–7	53	(25)	47	(22)	21	(47)
8–9	64	(32)	36	(18)	22	(50)
10–14	62	(40)	38	(25)	29	(65)
15–19	69	(22)	31	(10)	14	(32)
20–29	86	(18)	14	(3)	9	(21)
30+	100	(10)	0	(0)	4	(10)
Total	65	(147)	35	(78)	100	(225)

SOURCE: Benjamin I. Page and Robert Y. Shapiro, 1983, table 3, p. 180.

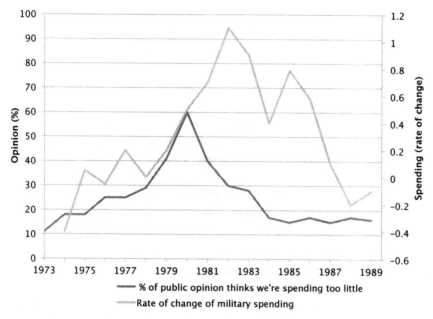

FIGURE 10.1. **The Opinion-Policy Relationship in Defense Spending.**
SOURCE: Adapted from Robert Y. Shapiro and Benjamin I. Page, "Foreign Policy and
Public Opinion," in David A. Deese, ed. *The New Politics od American Foreign Policy*
(New York: St. Martin's Press, 1994)

Time series studies of trends on particular issues have provided further evidence of democratic responsiveness. One of the most dramatic examples is depicted in Figure 10.1, which shows the relationship between public opinion and policy on defense spending from 1973 to 1989. On its face, this graph suggests that the public helped give defense spending a big boost in the early 1980s, then reversed the process. Although the graph does not prove that policy responded to public opinion, it certainly looks that way.[15] Unfortunately, good time series data on individual policy issues often are not available. (Later we consider time series analysis bearing on the effect of public opinion across a wide range of policy issues.)

Another approach to examining democratic responsiveness is to look at *cross-sectional* data, which compare various places—such as states or countries—at some point in time. Suppose that both opinions and policy outcomes can be measured on continuums: for example, from less spending to more spending, or from conservative to liberal. Then we might expect that (say) the more liberal public opinion is in a state, the more liberal its policies will be, evincing democratic responsiveness. Or, on the contrary, we might expect that there is *no* systematic relationship between public opinion and policy outcomes.

Warren Miller and Donald Stokes's pathbreaking 1963 study, "Constituency Representation in Congress,"[16] tackled a closely related question: the cross-sectional relationship between public opinion in over one hundred congressional districts (in which the 1958 National Election Study had been conducted) and how House members from those districts voted on various issues. Miller and Stokes found a relatively strong relationship between public opinion and member votes on civil rights issues, and a weaker relationship on social welfare issues. However, on issues of "foreign involvement," such as foreign economic aid and sending troops abroad, they found "no discernible agreement between legislator and district whatever"—that is, no relationship between public opinion and member votes.[17] (Various analysts have speculated about why foreign policy votes might be relatively impervious to constituent opinion.) Even so, Miller and Stokes's results suggested substantial policy responsiveness, and subsequent analyses indicated that Miller and Stokes may even have understated the case.[18]

Figure 10.2 illustrates cross-sectional analysis of actual policy outcomes across fifteen countries: specifically, the relationship between public support for reducing inequality and public social expenditures as a share of gross domestic product (all economic spending).[19] These countries are by no means representative of the world; all are among the most economically developed democracies. In fact, if one includes less wealthy and less democratic countries in the analysis, the apparent strong relationship between public opinion and social spending largely disappears.[20] That said, the United States is most often compared with countries such as these, and among them, it has the lowest level of public support for reducing income inequality (by this measure), as well as one of the lowest levels of social spending. By this metric—although, as we will see, not by all metrics—US social spending appears to correspond with public preferences.

Figure 10.3 shows Matthew Wetstein's findings for the issue of abortion at the US state level in 1988. Under the Supreme Court decision in *Roe v. Wade* (1973) and subsequent rulings, states cannot ban abortion, but they can impose various restrictions. Wetstein uses the number of restrictions as a measure of policy outcomes. As one might expect, states with higher levels of public support for abortion rights, those on the right side of the graph, on average have fewer abortion restrictions, as indicated by the downward-sloping best fit line. The relationship here is no more than modest; it might appear stronger if better state-level public opinion data were available. But it is also quite possible that states are limited in their responsiveness, issue by issue, to public opinion; citizens may typically pay (even) less attention to state policy debates than to national policy debates.

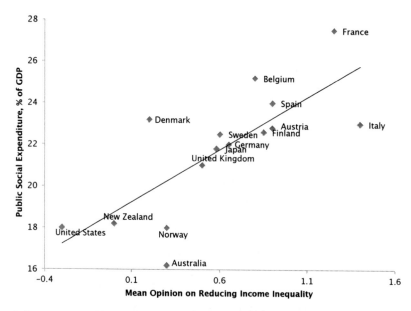

FIGURE 10.2. **Public Opinion and Social Spending in 15 Countries.**
SOURCE: International Social Survey Programme, 2009 Social Inequality IV Wave, Question 6B, OECD Social Expenditure Database (SOCX), 2011 data.

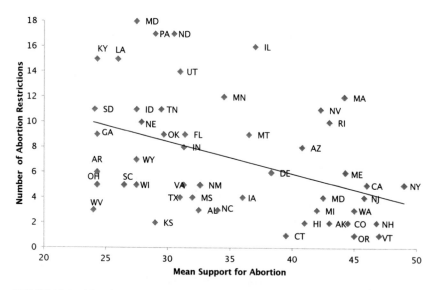

FIGURE 10.3. **Abortion Restrictions and Support for Abortion in the States, 1988.**
SOURCE: Adapted from M. E. Wetstein, *Abortion Rates in the United States: The Influence of Opinion and Policy* (Albany: State University of New York Press, 1996).

On the other hand, few issues in this millennium have attracted more attention in the United States than the debate over same-sex marriage rights. On this issue, public opinion has shifted rapidly. In May 2009 only 40 percent of respondents in a Gallup Poll said that "marriages between same-sex couples should . . . be recognized by the law as valid, with the same rights as traditional marriages"—up from 27 percent in 1996, but far from a majority. At that time, same-sex marriage was legal in five states. By May 2014, 55 percent of respondents said that same-sex marriages should be valid.[21] (Other polls showed similar trends.) Over the same period, same-sex marriage was legalized in another eleven states plus the District of Columbia.[22] By early January 2015, it had been legalized in another nineteen states, bringing the total to thirty-five. In most of these states federal judges, rather than state legislators or citizens, acted to make same-sex marriage legal. Even so, most observers agree that changing public opinion at least facilitated these judicial actions. Meanwhile, a 2009 study examined state-level public opinion and policy on eight issues relating to (in the study's terms) gay rights, including same-sex marriage, hate crime laws, and employment and housing nondiscrimination laws. It found that average public support for these rights was a strong predictor of the number of rights protected in each state (see Figure 10.4).[23] In some respects, these laws may be especially amenable to democratic responsiveness because few people have a material interest in opposing them.

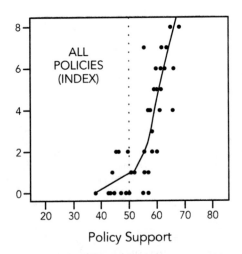

FIGURE 10.4. **Public Opinion and Gay Rights Policies in the States.**
SOURCE: Adapted from Jeffrey R. Lax and Justin H. Phillips, "Gay Rights in the States: Public Opinion and Policy Responsiveness," *American Political Science Review* 103 (2009):367-386, Figure 1.

Responsiveness to Public Mood or General Ideology

Having considered some studies that combine closely related policies, we can weigh an even broader approach: measuring a more general sense of public sentiment, to which policymakers might respond across a wide range of issues. Perhaps policymakers often consider and respond to the general predispositions or "mood" of the public, rather than to its opinions on specific issues. To be sure, issue-specific responsiveness is very plausible for the most salient issues, for which policymakers are likely to receive some clear indications of public opinion. But for many other issues, policymakers may not learn much—or worry much—about narrow opinions. For low-salience issues, even if public opinion data are available, they may not be very relevant. If survey respondents are largely improvising opinions based on their general beliefs and feelings—or even if political leaders wrongly think that they are—then public ideology or mood may tell leaders all they need to know about public opinion on most issues. (A 2015 poll found 80 percent support for "mandatory labels on foods containing DNA"—which would mean almost all foods—but failure to honor that supermajority opinion probably tells us little about democratic responsiveness.[24]) A general sense of direction may suffice; for example, do people presently want to spend more or less money addressing social problems? James Druckman and Lawrence Jacobs found evidence that Richard Nixon's White House tended to rely on such general questions for less important issues.[25]

Studies of the effect of the "public mood" on both state and national policy tend to support V. O. Key's observation:

> parallelism between action and opinion tends not to be precise in matters of detail; it prevails rather with respect to broad purpose. And in the correlation of purpose and action time lags may occur between the crystallization of a sense of mass purpose and its fulfillment in public action. Yet in the long run majority purpose and public action tend to be brought into harmony.[26]

Figure 10.5 shows a strong correlation between states' prevailing opinions and policy liberalism.[27] State-level opinion was measured by combining responses to a question about self-identified liberalism (survey respondents were asked whether they consider themselves "liberal," "conservative," or "moderate") from many years of the CBS News/*New York Times* polls. (Thus, this analysis does not attempt to track changes in mood over time.) The overall responses for individual states were compared with various policies and a combined policy measure, as shown in the figure. Although such an analysis cannot really prove

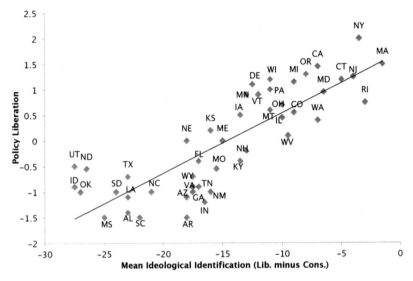

FIGURE 10.5. **Public Opinion and State Policy.**
SOURCE: Adapted from Robert S. Erikson, Gerald C. Wright, and John P. McIver, *Statehouse Democracy: Public Opinion and Policy in the American States* (New York: Cambridge University Press, 1993), p. 79.

that public opinion causes policy outcomes, it suggests a substantial degree of democratic responsiveness.

Although the *Statehouse Democracy* results are impressive, more important for national politics and policymaking is James Stimson, Michael MacKuen, and Robert Erikson's study of *dynamic representation* at the national level.[28] This research used a measure of public mood developed earlier by Stimson that combined numerous issue-specific opinion trends over time, which indeed tended to move in parallel (although not entirely so).[29] The dynamic representation research found that policymaking by various national institutions often, but not always, tends to follow trends in public mood, as we would expect in a theory of democratic responsiveness. Figure 10.6 depicts the general trend that when the public mood becomes more liberal, more liberal laws tend to pass, and other policies also tend to liberalize. Different institutions have different political dynamics—policymaking by the House of Representatives most closely follows trends in public opinion—but even the Supreme Court tends to move in the same direction as the public. The general trend includes increasing opinion and policy liberalism into the 1960s, followed by declining liberalism

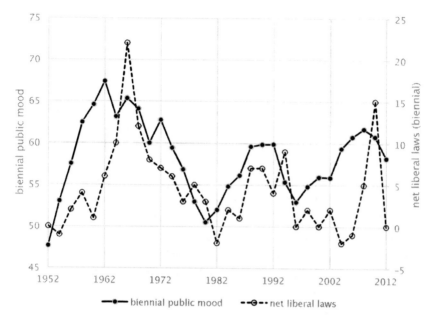

FIGURE 10.6. **Public Mood and Net Liberal Laws, 1951–2012.**
NOTE: Variables are measured over two-year periods 1951–52 through 2011–12. Public mood is measured on a 0–100 scale, where higher scores are more liberal (50 is the neutral midpoint). "Net liberal laws" is the net number of important liberal laws (liberal laws minus conservative laws). For details, see Stimson, MacKuen, and Erikson, *The Macro Polity.*
SOURCE: Adapted from Robert S. Erikson, "Income Inequality and Policy Responsiveness," forthcoming in *Annual Review of Political Science.*

into the early 1980s, and then some shorter and more ambiguous trends (increasing opinion liberalism between 1996 and 2008 was eventually met with an increase in policy liberalism in 2006). Of course, opinions on various issues do not always move in the same direction. For example, support for same-sex marriage—which certainly can be construed as a liberal position—has generally tended to increase since at least the 1990s, while the overall public mood has moved in both directions over that time. Theory would lead us to expect that public opinion trends on salient issues will trump general public mood trends when the two are at odds, as the rapid spread of same-sex marriage rights suggests.

Looking Further at Linkages: Parties, Polling, and In-Depth Case Studies

So far we have seen striking relationships between public opinion and policy outcomes. But this evidence for democratic responsiveness is largely circumstantial, since it does not directly trace the processes by which public opinion (presumably) influences policy. Indeed, in social science terms, most of these analyses have focused *only* on opinion and policy variables. We have generally disregarded intervening variables that could connect opinion to policy, as well as other variables that could influence both public opinion and policy, possibly explaining the apparent relationship between them. Also, many of these analyses have been cross-sectional, so we cannot observe whether opinion change preceded policy change. This gap leaves the direction of any causal effect in doubt. Perhaps policy tends to drive opinion, as the public ratifies or just goes along with government-enacted policies. (Several studies show that support for wars tends to increase once the wars start.[30]) To prove that opinion affects policy requires more direct evidence.

One way to address this need is to examine the role of political parties. Although political parties are not part of the US constitutional design, they emerged quickly as a means of structuring political contestation. Political leaders with similar policy goals would present themselves to voters as a team. In the United States, generally there are two major political parties at any time. An important reason is that the president and members of Congress are elected in separate winner-take-all elections; a political party that wins 20 percent of the vote could end up with no seats at all, unless some of its candidates actually win the most votes in their districts. (The same is true in most state and local elections.) As we saw in Chapter 8, candidates from the two major parties have incentives to move toward the political center, competing for the "median voter." But they also have countervailing incentives to appeal to the people who choose them—voters in primary elections, party convention delegates, and/or other party leaders—as well as to the interests that fund and otherwise support their campaigns. So political party institutions may play a crucial role in translating public preferences into policymaking.

Some studies have focused on the national party conventions that select US presidential candidates. What are the policy preferences of delegates at these conventions, how do the party platforms (official policy stances) change over time, and how do these positions compare with those of the broader electorate?[31] Table 10.4 presents opinion data for the 2008 Republican and Democratic convention delegates. On most (but not all) of the issues shown there, party delegates took more polarized positions than voters who identified with their party.

TABLE 10.4. **Delegates to the 2008 Party Conventions: How They Compare on Issues**

	Republican Delegates (%)	Republican Voters (%)	Democratic Voters (%)	Democratic Delegates (%)
Condition of national economy very bad	6	18	51	63
US should have stayed out of Iraq	13	25	84	95
Troop surge in Iraq making situation better	96	67	28	36
Health care coverage for all Americans more important than holding down taxes	7	40	90	94
Allow illegal immigrants to stay in jobs and eventually apply for citizenship	22	26	50	68
Developing new sources of energy higher priority than protecting the environment	75	81	53	37
Make Bush 2001 tax cuts permanent	91	62	34	7
Abortion should be generally available to those who want it	9	20	43	70
There should be no legal recognition of a gay couple's relationship	46	57	29	5
Gun control laws should be made more strict	8	32	70	62

SOURCE: Adapted from "*New York Times*/CBS News Poll, 2008 Republican National Delegate Survey," *New York Times*, September 1, 2008, http://graphics8.nytimes.com /packages/pdf/politics/20080901-poll.pdf.

Overall, the average difference between Republican and Democratic delegates was 61 percentage points, far wider than the average 35-point gap between Republican and Democratic voters. Thus, the party delegates magnify opinion differences in the electorate.

The consequences of this polarization are not self-evident, but many observers argue that it can enhance democratic responsiveness. The two major parties contend across a wide range of issues, and when one party wins control of the presidency and/or Congress, it has incentives to deliver results on some part of its distinctive policy agenda. Indeed, in 1950 a prestigious committee of political scientists called for a "more responsible two-party system" in which the policy differences between the two parties would be starker, enabling voters to make a clear choice between two competing visions.[32] Studies of congressional roll call voting indicate that indeed, the gap between the two major parties has grown substantially since then, and by 2009 it had reached historic highs in analyses extending back to 1879.[33]

Even as political parties attempt to appeal to their own partisans, they must also appeal to the electorate at large. Party platforms and presidential candidates' promises are two of the means by which parties balance these contending incentives in their appeals to public opinion.[34] For example, when Alan Monroe studied over 300 pledges made in party platforms from 1964 through 1980, he found that most of both parties' pledges were consistent with majority opinion: 64 percent of Republican pledges and 74 percent of Democratic pledges for which data were available.[35] This result does not mean that the party platforms were indistinguishable moderate mush, although, like party votes in Congress, they were closer in that period than they have been in recent years.[36] Rather, it suggests that both parties worked to highlight the most broadly popular elements of their policy agendas. National Election Studies over the years indicate that voters generally perceive the parties and presidential candidates as somewhat left or right of center on various issues, but not very far left or right. Nevertheless, ever-increasing polarization between the parties seems likely at some point to decrease democratic responsiveness, as both parties' preferences are far from what median voters would prefer. Morris Fiorina, in *Culture War?* (discussed in Chapter 9) and more pointedly in *Disconnect,*[37] is among the observers who have argued that responsiveness has decreased in recent years, a point to which we return later in the chapter.

No one thinks that quantitative analysis of political party behavior tells the whole story about linkages between opinion and policy. We must look further. Often, additional insight comes from historical and in-depth case study research. As we saw in Chapter 3, this research can be complex and time-consuming, entailing extensive archival searches, interviews, or other methods that illumi-nate how policymakers learn about and respond to public opinion. Such case studies have in some instances provided compelling evidence for a significant effect of public opinion on policymaking in the United States. For example, Law-rence Jacobs's study of health care policy in Britain and the United States[38] re-vealed what has been called a "recoil effect": political leaders initially tracked public opinion for the purpose of manipulating it, but wound up responding to it. (See Box 10.1.)

BOX 10.1
The "Recoil Effect"

Lawrence Jacobs examined how public opinion analysis became institu-tionalized in both the British and the US governments, and how it played a surprisingly large (and surely unanticipated) role in health care reform in both countries.[1] Studying the establishment of Britain's National Health Service after World War II and the passage of Medicare in 1965 in the United States, Jacobs found that both these initiatives, along with oth-ers, were informed by public opinion institutions that were designed for other purposes. These initiatives were notably responsive to particular val-ues and attitudes of the British and American people.

In Britain, institutional attention to public opinion began with what one might call wartime propaganda concerns:

> During the war government officials created the first administrative struc-tures to track public opinion systematically. The purpose of building an in-telligence gathering capacity was to "provide . . . [an] effective link between the people of the country and the government . . . convey[ing] the thoughts, opinions, and feelings of the public . . . [so that they were] constantly in the minds of administrators." In particular, the Ministry of Information produced two distinct types of data on public opinion: a qualitative survey conducted by the ministry's Home Intelligence Division and a statistical report by its Social Survey Division. Over the course of the war, the focus of intelligence gathering shifted from assessing the effectiveness of government publicity efforts and measuring general "morale" to studying public preferences to-ward particular government policies, especially as they related to postwar reconstruction.[2]

(continues)

(continued)   BOX 10.1
                                  The "Recoil Effect"

In both Britain and the United States, the opinion apparatus initially prioritized "the capacity to conduct public relations campaigns aimed at shaping popular preferences"—bluntly, to manipulate public opinion. But executive branch officials gradually realized that they could use public opinion analysis to inform their political strategy and tactics in domestic policymaking, offsetting the advantages possessed by the legislature and other actors. Ultimately, as British public administration expert Marjorie Ogilvy-Webb put it, the public opinion apparatus's "recoil effect [was] greater than its blast."[3] Jacobs elaborates: "In striving to have an outward effect on public opinion, the creation of this apparatus had an inward effect; it educated government officials to be aware of and sensitive to public opinion. Thus, while the apparatus originated as an attempt to manipulate popular preferences through public relations campaigns, its development over time increased senior government officials' interest in tracking and responding to public popular preferences."[4] This interest has influenced health care programs in both countries.

---

[1]Lawrence R. Jacobs, "The Recoil Effect: Public Opinion and Policy Making in the United States and Britain," *Comparative Politics* 24 (1992): *199–217;* Lawrence R. Jacobs, *The Health of Nations: Public Opinion and the Making of American and British Health Policy* (Ithaca, NY: Cornell University Press, 1993).

[2]Jacobs, "The Recoil Effect," 205.

[3]Marjorie Ogilvy-Webb, *The Government Explains: A Study of the Information Services,* (London: George Allen and Unwin, 1965), 196.

[4]Jacobs, "The Recoil Effect," 200.

Case studies of foreign policy have provided important illustrations of policy responsiveness, although one might expect the executive branch to feel less pressure to follow public opinion. For example, studies have indicated that public opinion has noticeably influenced developments in US–Chinese relations, such as the admission of China to the United Nations;[39] in US policymaking toward Nicaragua after the Sandinista Revolution of 1979;[40] and in foreign policymaking generally during the Reagan and Bush years.[41] Even when presidents profess indifference to public opinion, it still can constrain their foreign policy choices. President George W. Bush declared in 2006, "I'm not going to make decisions based upon polls and focus groups," and made many other similar statements during his presidency. Yet as did previous administrations (see our discussion below), the Bush administration conducted extensive polling, largely to look for ways to promote his policy agenda when possible.[42]

Some research has focused on identifying trends in the causal relationship between public opinion and policy. This research entails examining in detail, and over time, both how policymakers get information about public opinion and how they respond to (or are otherwise affected by) it. For instance, Thomas Graham examined nuclear arms control policy from the beginning of the Cold War to the 1980s; he found that policymakers paid more attention to public opinion than political leaders would admit.[43] Bernard Cohen reported in 1973 that State Department officials saw their role as one of shaping public opinion, not responding to it. Cohen famously quoted one official: "To hell with public opinion. . . . We should lead, and not follow."[44] However, Philip Powlick concluded in 1991 that State Department officials had become more attentive and responsive to public opinion, at least as a constraint on feasible policy.[45] Some studies suggest that the administrations of Bill Clinton and George W. Bush saw a reduced role for public opinion in policymaking, but these questions will probably be disputed for some time.[46]

One telling line of evidence that US presidents both attend to and strive to influence public opinion is the extent to which they have conducted their own public opinion research. While (as we saw earlier) presidents and politicians had long used unscientific methods to learn about public opinion, and scientific polling data were discussed and used in the White House beginning with Franklin Roosevelt,[47] since the Kennedy administration the public opinion research process has been routinized. Presidents seek this information to guide their policy strategy and tactics, often with an eye to winning reelection. The institutionalization of public opinion analysis studied by Jacobs extends to the Oval Office itself, but with a twist: presidents often use their own pollsters and consultants to conduct and analyze private polls, all of this work being paid for by the political parties or other nongovernmental sources.[48] Kennedy commissioned 16 private polls during his abbreviated presidency; Johnson commissioned 130 polls as president; and Nixon commissioned more than 200 during his first term, including 153 in 1972 as he sought reelection.

Figure 10.7 graphs the payments made to presidential pollsters during the Carter, Reagan, George H. W. Bush, and Clinton administrations. These data show that Presidents Reagan and Clinton spent the most money on—and devoted the most attention to—polling and public opinion analysis, especially between elections. They also show all four presidents spending substantially

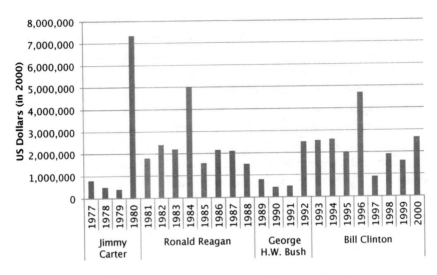

FIGURE 10.7. **Payments to White House Pollsters, 1977–2000.**
SOURCE: Adapted from S. K. Murray and P. Howard, "Variation in White House Polling Operations: Carter to Clinton," *Public Opinion Quarterly* 66 (2002); Federal Election Commission, Party Disclosure Documents, 1977–1999.

more in years when they ran for reelection. Clearly presidents can command the resources to learn a great deal about public opinion, but how much they have used this capability has varied markedly.[49] What they have done with the information has varied, too. Researchers have found examples of responsiveness to public opinion; of opinion leadership, where presidents used polls to hone their persuasive tactics; and of presidents working against public opinion rather than trying to lead it. As you might expect, presidents were often responsive on salient issues, especially those that clearly could affect their electoral prospects.[50]

When Lyndon Johnson became president in November 1963 after John Kennedy's assassination, he at first tended to respond to public opinion, seeking to build his support and win reelection. When Barry Goldwater emerged as his Republican opponent, Johnson pointedly contrasted his desire to pursue peace and disarmament with Goldwater's reported willingness to use nuclear weapons in Vietnam. (However, Johnson, like Kennedy before him, attempted to lead on the issue of foreign aid, supporting increases despite the arguably shallow public opposition we discussed earlier in the chapter.) Johnson took similarly responsive stances on many domestic issues, and he continued this approach even after it became clear he would easily defeat Goldwater. Johnson sought to maximize his public support, so he could more effectively pursue his racial and social policy agenda in his new full term as president.[51]

After the election, Johnson generally chose to lead, not follow, the public. His domestic proposals, especially the War on Poverty, had not been demanded by the public, but the public came to support this effort. Here Johnson was an effective opinion leader. Meanwhile, the Vietnam War was becoming an issue of extreme contention, and here Johnson had no intention of letting the public influence his actions. Eventually, as bad news and fatalities mounted in Vietnam, Johnson's intransigence gravely undermined his popularity. His decision not to run for reelection can be considered one last major instance of responsiveness to opinion.[52]

Richard Nixon, as we have seen, used polls even more extensively than Johnson—and the results played a surprisingly large role in his foreign policy, as well as domestic policy. (An example of the latter is that in public Nixon strongly endorsed environmental protection, although privately he was at most indifferent.) Nixon had campaigned on a vague promise that "new leadership will end the war and win the peace" in Vietnam, and he was determined not to share Johnson's fate. He closely tracked growing public hostility toward the war and gradually withdrew US troops from Vietnam, even as he tried to use air power to turn the war in the US favor.[53] Meanwhile, Nixon and his advisers detected a softening of public hostility toward Communist China in 1971, providing an opening for Nixon's efforts to improve relations with China. These efforts included a secret visit by Henry Kissinger in July 1971, US acquiescence in China's admission to the United Nations in October 1971, and Nixon's famous visit to China in February 1972. Nixon closely monitored public opinion to assure that support for rapprochement was increasing.[54] Ultimately, he raised the visibility of the issue so as to enhance his own and his party's electoral appeal. Here we see opinion leadership, and also a crucial element of democratic responsiveness: it seems unlikely that Nixon would have moved so far toward China if public opinion had vehemently objected.

CHANGES AND VARIATIONS IN RESPONSIVENESS TO PUBLIC OPINION

Given all this presidential and governmental attention to public opinion, as well as the proliferation of mass media polls, it might seem that government responsiveness should tend to increase over time. However, some evidence indicates just the opposite. When Monroe updated his findings (reported in Table 10.1) for the period from 1980 to 1993, he found a decline—to 55 percent (still significantly above the 50 percent level attributable to chance)—in overall responsiveness.[55] Comparisons across time are tenuous: this decline could represent a new and persistent trend; some aspect of the particular time period (such as the combination of Republican presidents and Democratic Congresses over most of it); or a change in polling to include more questions of lesser salience, to which elected officials may be less responsive. (Figure 10.6, based on Erikson, MacKuen, and Stimson's research, seems to depict periods of greater and lesser responsiveness.) The last possibility—a change in polling—implies that earlier research, by Monroe and other scholars, may have exaggerated policy responsiveness because of sampling bias: an overemphasis on high-salience issues, on which the public presumably has the most leverage.[56]

In their 2002 book *Politicians Don't Pander*, Lawrence Jacobs and Robert Shapiro diagnose and seek to explain a systematic decline in responsiveness.[57] Jacobs and Shapiro cite various lines of evidence that in fact policy outcomes have become less responsive to majoritarian preferences. They argue that as the political parties in Congress have become more ideologically polarized since the mid-1970s, elected officials have become more intent on promoting policy goals that may be far from those of the median voter. Of course, these officials still seek reelection, but they have strong incentives to lead, persuade, or perhaps even misdirect public opinion, rather than respond to it. (Compounding the problem, many members of Congress live in strongly partisan districts or states, where they are more likely to be defeated in a primary election than in a general election, so the reelection imperative may actually push them away from the middle toward the typically more extreme primary voters.) If officials commission their own public opinion research, it is far likelier to help them do what they want, by refining their message, than what the public would prefer. Jacobs and Shapiro's research on the Clinton administration and its Republican opposition indicates that both sides used polling primarily to promote their own agendas—opinion leadership without democratic responsiveness.

Whatever we make of the Clinton administration (or the subsequent Bush and Obama administrations), we should not expect the relationship between opinion and policy to be simple and stable. It may vary over time, and it is likely to depend on the kinds of policies at issue and the political context.[58] For example, Paul Burstein has argued that limited responsiveness to public opinion "does not mean that the public is being defeated by special interests. On many issues, the public has no meaningful opinions; organized interests, therefore, can win without the public losing."[59] It is possible, then, that the public "wins"—or at least comes closer to winning—on the issues it cares the most about.

Inequality in Democratic Responsiveness: Whose Opinion Matters?

The preceding discussion of evidence has largely danced around a major concern, which may already have struck you. In Chapter 9 we mentioned James Gibson's evidence that the course of anticommunist repression during the 1950s "Red Scare" depended more on elite opinion than on mass public opinion. If one considers *only* mass public opinion, it appears to be a decent predictor of variations in state policy. But if one considers both mass and elite opinion, elite opinion appears to be a strong predictor, and mass opinion a weak predictor, if that.[60] Gibson's study is inconclusive, due in part to limited data,[61] but it frames the possibility that policy is far more responsive to some kinds of public opinion than others—in particular, that elite opinion matters far more than most people's opinions do. For example, Larry Bartels finds that the policy preferences of relatively affluent respondents (not necessarily "elite") predict members of Congress's roll call votes more strongly than other people's preferences do, implying that members in some sense pay more attention to affluent people's preferences.[62]

Martin Gilens has marshaled perhaps the broadest evidence that, in fact, the opinions of "the few" outweigh—even swamp—those of the many.[63] (At the beginning of the chapter we referred to a "Princeton study," which is said to demonstrate that the United States is "no longer an actual democracy"—that is Gilens's work.) Gilens examined 1,779 policy survey questions asked between 1981 and 2002.[64] He found, first, a large status quo bias: "Of the 240 proposed policy changes that were favored by at least 80 percent of survey respondents, only 48 percent were adopted" within four years, and the rate was much smaller for less popular policies.[65] As Gilens notes, a status quo bias is unsurprising given all the barriers to policy change in the US system. Next, Gilens used income data to estimate support for each policy change at various income levels, especially the tenth percentile (lower income than 90 percent of the population), the median or fiftieth percentile (middle of the income distribution), and the ninetieth percentile (top 10 percent of income). For simplicity, we will call these low-income, middle-income, and high-income respondents. Gilens found that opinions at each of these income levels tended to predict policy change, but high-income opinion was the strongest predictor.[66] Moreover, Gilens found that when high-income people's opinions diverged substantially—by over 10 percentage points—from other people's opinions, only the opinions of high-income respondents appeared to affect (or at least to predict) policy outcomes. In other words, it seems that when the affluent disagree with the nonaffluent, only the opinions of the affluent matter.

Gilens emphasizes that his result does not mean that low- and middle-income Americans never get what they want. On most questions, people at various income levels largely agreed. In over 40 percent of cases, Gilens found at least a 10-point preference gap between high-income and low-income respondents; in 18 percent of cases, he found at least a 10-point gap between high-income and middle-income respondents. However, even in most of these cases, majorities of respondents at all three income levels were on the same side of the issue. Gilens found just over fifty cases (about 3 percent of his sample) in which at least 55 percent of high-income respondents were on one side and at least 55 percent of low-income respondents were on the other side.[67]

Some of these differences had little if anything to do with self-interest. For example, in a 1993 survey, about 61 percent of low-income respondents favored "formal guidelines limiting the amount of violence shown in television entertainment shows," versus about 43 percent of high-income respondents. No such guidelines were adopted. Arguably low-income respondents faced greater risk of violence, but this difference probably had more to do with formal education, which often inculcates support for free speech and civil liberties. (You might wonder whether the apparent high responsiveness to affluent people is better construed as high responsiveness to highly educated people. Gilens found that both education and income matter, but that income matters more than education does.) In two surveys in 1992, majorities of high-income respondents supported financial aid to Russia, while majorities of low-income respondents opposed it; the United States did provide aid. Here, for whatever reasons, the high-income respondents seemed more willing to set aside past animosities after the breakup of the Soviet Union.

In other cases, differences in economic interest could well explain differences in opinion. In a 1985 survey, 70 percent of high-income respondents, versus just 44 percent of low-income respondents, favored President Ronald Reagan's proposal to reduce the maximum income tax rate to 35 percent (from 50 percent); the Tax Reform Act of 1986 cut the rate even further. Affluent respondents may have been more attuned to the economic arguments for tax cuts than low-income respondents were; certainly they had more to gain in the short run.

Here are some further examples. In 1992 and 1993 high-income respondents were far more supportive of the North American Free Trade Agreement between the United States and Mexico than low-income respondents were. In 1995 they were far more supportive of a "flat tax," in which everyone would pay income tax at the same rate, no matter how high his or her income. (This proposal was not adopted.) In 1996 through 2001 they were far more supportive of proposals to move some Social Security funds into stocks and bonds, reducing guaranteed benefits while providing a possibility of higher returns. (None of these proposals was adopted.) And in 2002 they were far more supportive of providing tax cuts for businesses, which were adopted. In all these cases, some policy experts would argue that the proposals were in the best interests of the country and that high-income respondents held the more informed view. (The economist Bryan Caplan has argued at length that people tend to be systematically misinformed about economic policy.)[68] Others would argue that the proposals tended to benefit well-off Americans at others' expense. It is at least questionable whether policymakers should consider the opinions of the affluent while disregarding other people's opinions entirely, but Gilens's analysis suggests that, in general, they do.

Gilens further tests for differences in responsiveness across policy domains and for the impact of interest groups. He finds that the difference between low-income and high-income responsiveness is greatest on foreign policy issues; the difference between medium-income and high-income responsiveness is greatest on economic policy issues (like those we just considered); and the smallest differences are on social welfare issues. In fact, Gilens found that the preferences of nonaffluent Americans tended to prevail over those of affluent Americans in four social welfare areas: Social Security (as in the example above), Medicare, school vouchers, and public works spending. Gilens notes that the nonaffluent have powerful allies on these topics; for example, AARP (formerly the American Association of Retired Persons) has strongly opposed reducing Social Security guaranteed benefits. Gilens also examines the impact of forty-three powerful interest groups such as AARP, the US Chamber of Commerce, and the United Auto Workers. Overall, he finds that these interest groups apparently have considerable influence on policy outcomes, but this influence appears to be separate from the patterns we have discussed. On some issues, powerful interest groups side with the preferences of the affluent; on others, they side with the preferences of the nonaffluent. Overall, interest groups apparently neither increase nor reduce the advantage enjoyed by the affluent. This result may imply that affluent Americans exercise their influence through direct financial contributions to candidates and political parties, social influence, and various other ways[69] apart from support for traditional interest groups.

Summarizing this work, Gilens and Page suggest four alternative theories of policy outcomes, which should seem broadly familiar from Chapter 4: majoritarian electoral democracy, in which average citizens primarily dictate policy; economic-elite domination, in which economic elites have the most influence; majoritarian pluralism, in which the interests of average citizens tend to dominate indirectly through the auspices of mass interest groups; and biased pluralism, in which business-based interest groups wield the most influence. Gilens and Page conclude that "Economic-Elite Domination theories do rather well in [their] analysis," and might do even better if they had a better measure of elite preferences. (Usually the term "elite" refers to a small number of powerful "movers and shakers," not to one-tenth of the population.)[70] They also conclude that business interest groups have substantially more influence than mass interest groups, and therefore that biased pluralism fares better than majoritarian pluralism:

> It is simply not the case that a host of diverse, broadly-based interest groups take policy stands—and bring about actual policies—that reflect what the general public wants. Interest groups as a whole do not seek the same policies as average citizens do. . . . Relatively few mass-based interest groups are active, they do not (in the aggregate) represent the public very well, and they have less collective impact on policy than do business-oriented groups—whose stands tend to be negatively related to the preferences of average citizens. These business groups are far more numerous and active; they spend much more money; and they tend to get their way.[71]

It is difficult to be sure what to make of these results. Again, in most cases the preferences of affluent respondents were close to those of other respondents; it was somewhat rare for solid majorities to be on opposite sides. Benjamin Page and Lawrence Jacobs, in their 2009 book *Class War?*, demonstrate at length a wide degree of consensus for various policies to provide economic opportunity. They describe the common thread as conservative egalitarianism: conservative in its focus on opportunity rather than outcome, egalitarian in its willingness to invest in ensuring opportunity, not merely allowing it. Drawing in part on their own national survey, Page and Jacobs find strong support for investing in excellent public education as well as "government assistance to make sure that people can find jobs, get decent wages, have health-care coverage, be guaranteed adequate retirement pensions, and receive at least a minimal level of support if they cannot work. . . . Support for these government programs comes from all sectors of society: from Republicans, from self-described middle-class and upper-class people, from whites, and from those with high incomes, as well as from Democrats, working-class people, African Americans, and lower-income citizens."[72] It is possible that this support is overstated; perhaps many apparent supporters are not willing to bear the costs of such programs. However, if one concludes that policy is substantially inconsistent with widely shared public preferences, one might wonder why.

Part of the answer may turn on the preferences of a narrower economic elite. In 2011 Page, Larry Bartels, and Jason Seawright led a small pilot opinion survey targeted at the top 1 percent of wealth-holders in the metropolitan Chicago area.[73] Researchers completed eighty-three interviews with respondents whose median wealth was $7.5 million; about one-third had annual incomes of $1 million or more. (The expected "margin of error" for such a small sample is about plus or minus 11 points, far larger than in larger studies, but still small enough to draw broad conclusions if the sampling method is not very biased.)

On some issues, these wealthy respondents were not far from the public at large; for example, large majorities of both groups favored increasing federal spending on public infrastructure such as roads. Smaller but similar majorities of both groups said that "differences in income in America are too large." In other cases wealthy respondents had very different opinions. Only 17 percent agreed that the government "should redistribute wealth by heavy taxes on the rich," compared with 52 percent of the general public (still only a small majority). The wealthy were over 30 points more supportive of cutting domestic spending programs to reduce federal budget deficits—but also over 30 points more willing to pay higher taxes themselves. Whereas 87 percent of the general public agreed that "the federal government should spend whatever is necessary to ensure that all children have really good public schools they can go to," only 35 percent of the wealthy respondents agreed. Wealthy respondents also were far less supportive of national health insurance and job and income programs. These gaps are far larger than the ones studied by Gilens. If policy is disproportionately sensitive to these preferences—which seems very plausible to us—the impact could be dramatic. Unfortunately, many economic experts believe that reducing budget deficits is less important than investing in education, jobs, and other government programs. If this view prevails, even wealthy Americans' willingness to pay higher taxes to reduce deficits may not serve the national interest, as they presumably intend.

IS GOVERNMENT RESPONSIVENESS TO PUBLIC OPINION DEMOCRATIC?

Most of the evidence we have considered here indicates that the government is more than minimally responsive to public opinion—that, for whatever reasons, it often does what most people want it to do, although it is more attentive to some opinions than to others. To be sure, Monroe, Page and Shapiro, and other researchers have found many cases of nonresponsiveness—and, as Burstein has emphasized, these studies are limited by their reliance on the questions that pollsters chose to ask. That said, to the extent that policy indeed responds to public opinion, should we conclude that policymaking in the United States is largely democratic? As we noted in previous discussions, it is not only democratic governments that pay attention to public opinion. As V. O. Key Jr. stated in the very first sentence of his classic *Public Opinion and American Democracy*: "Governments must concern themselves with the opinions of their citizens, if only to provide a basis for repression of disaffection."[74] At this extreme, if opinion is coerced to support government policy, we would hardly want to say that the correspondence between them evinces "democratic responsiveness."

But short of that extreme case, which we might find in authoritarian governments, to make judgments about democracy we need to weigh both what has influenced public opinion and the quality of the opinion that has resulted: to what extent it constitutes an informed and (in language from Chapter 9) a considered judgment. We may further insist that policy outcomes should be evaluated for consistency with basic democratic norms. Many people construe that fundamental civil liberties and rights are non-negotiable requirements of democracy. To infringe upon those rights based on public opinion at a given moment might be responsive but not actually democratic. (It is tempting to argue that a democratic citizenry could never reach a considered judgment to abandon basic democratic norms, but this conclusion is not obvious; even the identity of those norms is not obvious.) To extend the argument, elected officials may act contrary to stated public opinion on the grounds that their actions are consistent with what the public would believe if it were fully informed. Remember the case of foreign aid, in which most people grossly overestimate the current level of spending. Is it undemocratic to disregard the prevailing opinion that foreign aid spending should be reduced when that opinion apparently is directly based on false information? Assuming that it isn't, how far should would-be "trustees" go in substituting their own judgments for the opinions of the voters who elected them?

As we saw in Chapter 9, the public is far from omniscient; individuals do not walk around with all the information they need to make judgments about issues that arise and to decide what government should do about them. They depend on information from others. On national issues, much of the information comes from political leaders, other elites, and organized groups with their various agendas, largely as conveyed by the mass media. The mass media themselves can have some independent impact on public opinion based on their choices of what to report about, the sources they allow to speak, and the opinions that they state or that suffuse their reporting.

The quality of this information thus is crucial. Our standards of quality should not be inappropriately high; we should never expect most citizens to function as if they were members of some blue-chip policy task force. But we can at least ask whether political and other opinion leaders, taken together, are tending to inform the attentive members of the public or solely to manipulate and deceive them. Is it easy, difficult, or practically impossible for citizens to learn the basic facts that would enable them to reason from their values to their policy preferences? If the public is essentially at the mercy of dishonest elites for its information, then following its systematically misinformed views is not what most people would consider democratic. To be sure, "basic facts" often are subject to debate, but some are less debatable than others.

Let us briefly consider some cases in which the public may have been fundamentally deceived. First consider the Tonkin Gulf incident of 1964, in which President Johnson marshaled support for an escalation of US military involvement in Vietnam by misrepresenting alleged attacks on two US ships off the coast of North Vietnam. At the time, Democrats and Republicans might have disagreed about the facts—although, in fact, hardly anyone forcefully questioned Johnson's account.[75] But now it is generally acknowledged that Johnson's portrayal of North Vietnamese aggression was willfully misleading and unfounded. Other cases, again subject to debate, include arguments that before the United States entered World War II, the Roosevelt administrations essentially goaded the Germans to attack American ships that engaged in naval reconnaissance for the British;[76] that the first Bush administration misrepresented American options prior to the start of all-out fighting in the first Gulf War against Iraq in 1990;[77] and that the second Bush administration, before the second Gulf War in 2003, misled the public about Iraqi leader Saddam Hussein's progress toward obtaining "weapons of mass destruction."[78] Although these examples can be disputed, it is no accident that they are foreign policy issues. Foreign policy issues are especially troublesome for democracy because the government often has a monopoly or near-monopoly on relevant information.[79]

Conversely, the sea change in opinion and policy on same-sex marriage can be construed as an example of relatively free and full democratic debate. Surely people on each side of the debate believe that the other side's arguments have been dishonest—and in some cases they may be right—but it seems unlikely that either side's misrepresentations have dictated the course of the debate. Apparently, many citizens have changed their minds after further thought and after hearing the stories of same-sex couples as well as many other people's views.

Many other examples of apparent democratic responsiveness likewise seem basically reasonable, whether or not one agrees with the policy outcomes.

CONCLUSION

We have covered a lot of new ground in this chapter—and we could have covered far more. Thanks to the expansion of public opinion research, there is more evidence than ever before to explore the multifaceted relationship between public opinion and policymaking. The evidence for policy responsiveness to public opinion has been extensive but often ambiguous, often difficult to evaluate on its own terms. Some researchers perceive public opinion as substantially directing many policy debates; others see it as usually only constraining policy outcomes, and perhaps not even constraining them very much. To judge the normative implications for democratic theory, we must interrogate the evidence further in complex and sometimes contentious ways. This may be yet another frustration for students of public opinion, but important questions often are.

In everyday life, we now see a more direct and dynamic role than ever before of public opinion in politics and policymaking. We see this in the reporting of opinion polls and in the continual appeals to public opinion—including all types of political advertising—that are made through the mass media by presidents, members of Congress, political parties, organized groups, and others interested and active in the political process. Some see this as a bad development that detracts from institutional consultations and deliberations among political leaders and experts, who may be best able to formulate effective policies. Others see this as bad because it gives the public itself a false sense that what government does is democratic, even as the public is then manipulated in ways that do not necessarily serve its interests. Still others see these changes as, on the whole, distinct improvements in democratic practice. Further research will help to illuminate some aspects of these debates, but we fully expect the arguments to continue.

NOTES

1. V. O. Key Jr., *Public Opinion and American Democracy* (New York: Alfred A. Knopf, 1961), 7.

2. Brendan James, "Princeton Study: U.S. No Longer An Actual Democracy," *Talking Points Memo* (blog), *LiveWire*, April 18, 2014, http://talkingpointsmemo.com/livewire/princeton-experts-say-us-no-longer-democracy.

3. Key, *Public Opinion and American Democracy*, 7; see also Benjamin Ginsberg, *The Captive Public: How Mass Opinion Promotes State Power* (New York: Basic Books, 1986). For related discussion about mass opinion and government, see Susan Herbst, *Numbered Voices: How Opinion Polling Has Shaped American Politics* (Chicago: University of Chicago Press, 1992); and James A. Morone, *The Democratic Wish: Popular Participation and the Limits of American Government* (New York: Basic Books, 1990).

4. For arguments that US public opinion was not so isolationist, see John Walko, "Isolationism: How Would We Know If We Saw It? Reopening the Case of the 1930s," *The Public Perspective* 85 (August/September 1997): 41–42; and Adam J. Berinsky et al., "Revisiting Public Opinion in the 1930s and 1940s," *PS: Political Science and Politics* 44, no. 3 (2011): 515–520.

5. Walter Lippmann, *Essays in the Public Philosophy* (Boston: Little, Brown, 1955), 19–20.

6. On some of these issues and other related research, see Paul Burstein, *Discrimination, Jobs, and Politics: The Struggle for Equal Employment Opportunity in the United States Since the New Deal* (Chicago: University of Chicago Press, 1985); Benjamin I. Page and Robert Y. Shapiro, "Effects of Public Opinion on Policy," *American Political Science Review* 77 (1983): 175–190; and Benjamin I. Page and Robert Y. Shapiro, *The Rational Public: Fifty Years of Trends in Americans' Policy Preferences* (Chicago: University of Chicago Press, 1992).

7. Kaiser Family Foundation, "2013 Survey of Americans on the U.S. Role in Global Health," 4–5, https://kaiserfamilyfoundation.files.wordpress.com/2013/11/8508 -f-2013-survey-of-americans-on-the-u-s-role-in-global-health.pdf.

8. Lawrence R. Jacobs and Robert Y. Shapiro, *Politicians Don't Pander: Political Manipulation and the Loss of Democratic Responsiveness* (Chicago: University of Chicago Press, 2000), xi–xii; on the *increase* in Clinton's job approval ratings as the Lewinsky scandal unfolded, see John R. Zaller, "Monica Lewinsky's Contribution to Political Science," *PS: Political Science and Politics* 31 (1998): 182–189.

9. Jeff Manza and Fay Lomax Cook, "A Democratic Polity? Three Views of Policy Responsiveness to Public Opinion in the United States," *American Politics Research* 30 (2002): 630–667.

10. Martin Gilens, among others, has pointed out that the 50 percent threshold is "arbitrary": "Because public preferences are only one factor affecting policy outcomes, the degree of favorability needed to tip a policy from not being adopted to being adopted may be more or less than 50 percent." Martin Gilens, *Affluence and Influence: Economic Inequality and Political Power in America* (Princeton, NJ: Princeton University Press, 2014), 67. This objection should not prevent us from examining majority opinion, but we should be cautious about interpreting the results.

11. Donald J. Devine, *The Attentive Public: Polyarchical Democracy* (Chicago: Rand McNally, 1970); Robert Weissberg, *Public Opinion and Popular Government*

(Englewood Cliffs, NJ: Prentice-Hall, 1976); Alan D. Monroe, "American Party Platforms and Public Opinion," *American Journal of Political Science* 27 (1983): 27–42.

12. Compare Devine, *Attentive Public*; Weissberg, *Public Opinion and Popular Government*; Joel E. Brooks, "Democratic Frustration in the Anglo-American Polities: A Quantification of Inconsistency Between Mass Public Opinion and Public Policy," *Western Political Science Quarterly* 38 (1985): 250–261; and "The Opinion–Policy Nexus in France: Do Institutions and Ideology Make a Difference?" *Journal of Politics* 49 (1987): 465–480.

13. Page and Shapiro, "Effects of Public Opinion on Policy"; Robert Y. Shapiro, "The Dynamics of Public Opinion and Public Policy" (PhD diss., University of Chicago, 1982).

14. See also Thomas W. Graham, "Public Opinion and U.S. Foreign Policy Decision Making," in David A. Deese, ed., *The New Politics of American Foreign Policy* (New York: St. Martin's Press, 1994), 190–215.

15. See Thomas Hartley and Bruce Russett, "Public Opinion and the Common Defense: Who Governs Military Spending in the United States?" *American Political Science Review* 86 (1992): 905–915; Christopher Wlezien, "The Public as Thermostat: Dynamics of Preferences for Spending," *American Journal of Political Science* 39 (1995): 981–1000 and "Dynamics of Representation: The Case of U.S. Spending on Defense," *British Journal of Political Science* 26 (1996): 81–103; Charles W. Ostrom Jr. and Robin F. Marra, "U.S. Defense Spending and the Soviet Estimate," *American Political Science Review* 80 (1986): 819–841; and Larry M. Bartels, "Constituency Opinion and Congressional Policy Making: The Reagan Defense Buildup," *American Political Science Review* 85 (1991): 457–474. See also Wlezien's extension to different policy areas in "Patterns of Representation: Dynamics of Public Preferences and Policy," *Journal of Politics* 66 (2004): 1–24. Note, however, that the "thermostat effect" that Wlezien describes involves subsequent reversals of public opinion at points at which the policy that initially responded to public opinion is perceived as going too far, leading (at least briefly, or longer) to a state of noncongruence. An analysis of over-responding in Congress that is related to current partisan polarization in American politics is described in Joseph Bafumi and Michael Herron, "Leapfrog Representation and Extremism: A Study of American Voters and Their Members in Congress," *American Political Science Review* 104 (August 2010): 519–542.

16. Warren E. Miller and Donald E. Stokes, "Constituency Influence in Congress," *American Political Science Review* 57 (1963): 45–56.

17. Ibid., 50.

18. Miller and Stokes's public opinion dataset relied on an average of just thirteen interviews per district; the resulting measurement error probably weakened the apparent relationship between public opinion and policy. See Robert S. Erikson, "Constituency Opinion and Congressional Behavior: A Reexamination of the Miller–Stokes Data," *American Journal of Political Science* 22 (1978): 511–535; and Benjamin I. Page,

Robert Y. Shapiro, Paul W. Gronke, and Robert M. Rosenberg, "Constituency, Party, and Representation in Congress," *Public Opinion Quarterly* 48 (1984): 741–756.

19. This figure is inspired by a similar analysis in Clem Brooks and Jeff Manza, "Social Policy Responsiveness in Developed Democracies," *American Sociological Review* 71 (2006): 474–494.

20. Larry Bartels, using different measures, finds that differences in "national economic capacity" partly account for gaps between public opinion and social spending. Bartels also concludes that "[c]itizens in every country in every year" in his study wanted additional spending in several areas. Thus, his analysis finds a lack of majoritarian congruence. Larry M. Bartels, "The Opinion-Policy Disconnect: Cross-National Spending Preferences and Democratic Representation" (paper presented at the Annual Meeting of the American Political Science Association, August 2008).

21. Gallup News Service, "Gallup Poll Social Series: Values and Beliefs. Final Topline," May 8–11, 2014, http://www.gallup.com/file/poll/169868/REV_Views_on_Same_Sex_Marriage_140521%20.pdf.

22. This count does not include Arkansas, where same-sex marriage was legal from May 9 to 16, 2014, or three other states—Oregon, Pennsylvania, and Illinois—where it was legalized by June 1.

23. Jeffrey R. Lax and Justin H. Phillips, "Gay Rights in the States: Public Opinion and Policy Responsiveness," *American Political Science Review* 103 (2009): 367–386.

24. Oklahoma State University, Department of Agricultural Economics, *FooDS: Food Demand Survey* 2, no. 9 (January 16, 2015): 4, http://agecon.okstate.edu/faculty/publications/4975.pdf.

25. James N. Druckman and Lawrence R. Jacobs, "Lumpers and Splitters: The Public Opinion Information that Politicians Collect and Use," *Public Opinion Quarterly* 70 (2006): 453–476.

26. Key, *Public Opinion and American Democracy*, 553.

27. Robert S. Erikson, Gerald C. Wright, and John P. McIver, *Statehouse Democracy: Public Opinion and Policy in the American States* (New York: Cambridge University Press, 1993).

28. James A. Stimson, Michael B. MacKuen, and Robert S. Erikson, "Dynamic Representation," *American Political Science Review* 89 (1995): 543–565; Robert S. Erikson, Michael B. MacKuen, and James A. Stimson, *The Macro Polity* (New York: Cambridge University Press, 2002); Robert S. Erikson, Michael B. MacKuen, and James A. Stimson, "The Macro Polity Updated" (paper delivered at the annual meeting of the Midwest Political Science Association, April 3–6, 2008), http://www.columbia.edu/~rse14/Erikson_MacKuen_Stimson_2008_Macro_Polity_Updated_MPSA11.pdf; Robert E. Erikson, "Income Inequality and Policy Responsiveness," *Annual Review of Political Science* (2015): forthcoming.

29. James A. Stimson, *Public Opinion in America: Moods, Cycles, and Swings* (Boulder, CO: Westview Press, 1991).

30. For example, see John Mueller, *Policy and Opinion in the Gulf War* (Chicago: University of Chicago Press, 1994).

31. A classic study of platform content is Alan D. Monroe, "American Party Platforms and Public Opinion," *American Journal of Political Science* 27 (1983): 27–42.

32. "Toward a More Responsible Two-Party System: A Report of the Committee on Political Parties, American Political Science Association," *American Political Science Review* 44 (1950): supp.

33. Keith T. Poole and Howard Rosenthal, "The Polarization of American Politics," *Journal of Politics* 46 (1984): 1061–1079; for updated data, see Poole's Web site voteview.com, especially "The Polarization of the Political Parties," http://voteview.com/political_polarization.asp.

34. See Anthony Downs, *An Economic Theory of Democracy* (New York: Harper and Row, 1957); Benjamin I. Page, *Choices and Echoes in Presidential Elections: Rational Man and Electoral Democracy* (Chicago: University of Chicago Press, 1978); Gerald M. Pomper with Susan S. Lederman, *Elections in America: Control and Influence in Democratic Politics*, 2nd ed. (New York: Dodd, Mead, 1980); Kelly D. Patterson, *Political Parties and the Maintenance of Liberal Democracy* (New York: Columbia University Press, 1996); Jeff Fishel, *Presidents and Promises: From Campaign Pledge to Presidential Performance* (Washington, DC: Congressional Quarterly Press, 1985); and John Aldrich, *Why Parties? A Second Look* (Chicago: University of Chicago Press, 2011).

35. Alan D. Monroe, "American Party Platforms and Public Opinion," *American Political Science Review* 27 (February 1983): 32, table 5.

36. Soren Jordan, Clayton McLaughlin Webb, and B. Dan Wood, "The President, Polarization and the Party Platforms, 1944–2012," *The Forum* 12 (2014): 169–189.

37. Morris P. Fiorina with Samuel J. Abrams, *Disconnect: The Breakdown of Representation in American Politics* (Norman: University of Oklahoma Press, 2011).

38. Lawrence R. Jacobs, *The Health of Nations: Public Opinion and the Making of American and British Health Policy* (Ithaca, NY: Cornell University Press, 1993).

39. Leonard A. Kusnitz, *Public Opinion and Foreign Policy: America's China Policy, 1949–1979* (Westport, CT: Greenwood Press, 1984).

40. Richard Sobel, ed., *Public Opinion in U.S. Foreign Policy: The Controversy over Contra Aid* (Lanham, MD: Rowman and Littlefield, 1993).

41. Ronald H. Hinckley, *People, Polls, and Policymakers: American Public Opinion and National Security* (New York: Lexington Books, 1992).

42. George W. Bush, "Remarks on the War on Terror and a Question-and-Answer Session in Charlotte, North Carolina," April 6, 2006, http://www.presidency.ucsb.edu/ws/index.php?pid=68481; Joshua Green, "The Other War Room," *Washington Monthly* (April 2002), http://www.washingtonmonthly.com/features/2001/0204.green.html.

43. Graham, "The Politics of Failure: Strategic Nuclear Arms Control, Public Opinion, and Domestic Politics in the United States, 1945–1985" (PhD diss., Massachusetts

Institute of Technology, 1989), and Graham, "Public Opinion and U.S. Foreign Policy Decision Making."

44. Bernard C. Cohen, *The Public's Impact on Foreign Policy* (Boston: Little, Brown, 1973), 62.

45. Philip J. Powlick, "The Attitudinal Bases of Responsiveness to Public Opinion Among American Foreign Policy Officials," *Journal of Conflict Resolution* 35 (1991): 611–641.

46. See Robert Y. Shapiro and Lawrence R. Jacobs, "Who Leads and Who Follows? U.S. Presidents, Public Opinion and Foreign Policy," in Brigitte L. Nacos, Robert Y. Shapiro, and Pierangelo Isernia, eds., *Decisionmaking in a Glass House: Mass Media, Public Opinion, and American and European Foreign Policy in the 21st Century* (Boston: Rowman and Littlefield, 2000), 223–246, and other essays in this volume; Robert Y. Shapiro and Lawrence R. Jacobs, "Public Opinion, Foreign Policy, and Democracy: How Presidents Use Public Opinion," in Jeff Manza, Fay Lomax Cook, and Benjamin I. Page, eds., *Navigating Public Opinion: Polls, Policy, and the Future of American Democracy* (New York: Oxford University Press, 2002), 184–200; Diane J. Heith, *Polling to Govern: Public Opinion and Presidential Leadership* (Stanford, CA: Stanford University Press, 2004).

47. Robert M. Eisinger, *The Evolution of Presidential Polling* (New York: Cambridge University Press, 2003). Regarding World War II, see Steven Casey, *Cautious Crusade: Franklin D. Roosevelt, American Public Opinion, and the War Against Nazi Germany* (New York: Oxford University Press, 2001).

48. Some of this history is described in Lawrence R. Jacobs and Robert Y. Shapiro, "The Rise of Presidential Polling: The Nixon White House in Historical Perspective," *Public Opinion Quarterly* 59 (1995): 163–165, and in Druckman and Jacobs, "Lumpers and Splitters." Fuller treatments are found in Eisinger, *The Evolution of Presidential Polling*, and Heith, *Polling to Govern*.

49. Shoon Kathleen Murray and Peter Howard, "Variation in White House Polling Operations: Carter to Clinton," *Public Opinion Quarterly* 66 (Winter 2002): 527–558.

50. See Lawrence R. Jacobs and Robert Y. Shapiro, "Public Decisions, Private Polls: John F. Kennedy's Presidency" (paper presented at the Annual Meeting of the Midwest Political Science Association, Chicago, 1992); "The Public Presidency, Private Polls, and Policymaking: Lyndon Johnson" (paper presented at the Annual Meeting of the American Political Science Association, Washington, DC, 1993); "Issues, Candidate Image, and Priming: The Use of Private Polls in Kennedy's 1960 Presidential Campaign," *American Political Science Review* 88 (1994): 527–540; and "Lyndon Johnson, Vietnam, and Public Opinion: Rethinking Realist Theory of Leadership," *Presidential Studies Quarterly* 29 (September 1999): 592–616; and especially the theoretical analysis in John G. Geer, *From Tea Leaves to Opinion Polls: A Theory of Democratic Leadership* (New York: Columbia University Press, 1996).

51. Jacobs and Shapiro, "The Public Presidency."

52. Ibid.; and Jacobs and Shapiro, "Lyndon Johnson, Vietnam, and Public Opinion."

53. Andrew Z. Katz, "Public Opinion and Foreign Policy: The Nixon Administration and the Pursuit of Peace with Honor in Vietnam," *Presidential Studies Quarterly* 27 (1997): 496–513.

54. See Page and Shapiro, *Rational Public*, 242–251; cf. Kusnitz, *Public Opinion and Foreign Policy*.

55. Alan D. Monroe, "Public Opinion and Public Policy 1980–1993," *Public Opinion Quarterly* 62 (1998): 6–28.

56. Benjamin I. Page, "The Semi-Sovereign Public," in Jeff Manza, Fay Lomax Cook, and Benjamin I. Page, eds., *Navigating Public Opinion* (New York: Oxford University Press, 2002), 325–344; Paul Burstein, "Why Estimates of the Impact of Public Opinion on Public Policy Are Too High: Empirical and Theoretical Implications," *Social Forces* 84 (2006): 2273–2289; Paul Burstein, *American Public Opinion, Advocacy, and Policy in Congress: What the Public Wants and What It Gets* (New York: Cambridge University Press, 2014).

57. Jacobs and Shapiro, *Politicians Don't Pander*.

58. On the importance of understanding the variations in the opinion–policy relationship and under what circumstances responsiveness occurs, see several essays in Manza, Cook, and Page, eds., *Navigating Public Opinion*; Elaine B. Sharp, *The Sometime Connection: Public Opinion and Social Policy* (Albany: State University of New York Press, 1999); Jeff Manza and Fay Lomax Cook, "A Democratic Polity? Three Views of Policy Responsiveness to Public Opinion in the United States," *American Politics Research* 30 (November 2002): 630–667; and Robert Y. Shapiro, "Public Opinion and American Democracy," *Public Opinion Quarterly* 75, no. 5 (2011): 982–1017.

59. Burstein, "Why Estimates . . . Are Too High," 2273.

60. James L. Gibson, "Political Intolerance and Political Repression During the McCarthy Red Scare," *American Political Science Review* 82, no. 2 (June 1988): 511–529.

61. David A. Freedman, "Statistical Models and Shoe Leather," *Sociological Methodology* 21 (1991): 291–313. Formally, the slope coefficient for elite opinion is statistically significant, and the coefficient for mass opinion is not, yet the difference between the coefficients is not. So, even assuming that the statistical model is correct—which Freedman challenges—it is plausible that mass opinion had at least as much influence as elite opinion did.

62. Larry Bartels, *Unequal Democracy: The Political Economy of the New Gilded Age* (New York: Russell Sage Foundation and Princeton University Press, 2008).

63. Gilens, *Affluence and Influence*; Martin Gilens and Benjamin I. Page, "Testing Theories of American Politics: Elites, Interest Groups, and Average Citizens," *Perspectives on Politics* 12 (2014): 564–581.

64. Gilens used four criteria for including a question: it had to pose a choice of supporting or opposing a policy change, it had to be specific enough to make clear whether it was adopted, it had to involve federal government policy, and it could not be conditional. Moreover, the dataset had to include income information.

65. Gilens, *Affluence and Influence*, 73.

66. Ibid., 76.

67. The data for the study are published as "Economic Inequality and Political Representation" on the Russell Sage Foundation Web site (http://www.russellsage.org/research/data/economic-inequality-and-political-representation), making it possible for us to report these and other details not cited in Gilens's book.

68. Bryan Caplan, *The Myth of the Rational Voter: Why Democracies Choose Bad Policies* (Princeton, NJ: Princeton University Press, 2007).

69. For evidence that contributions and many other forms of political activity tend to increase with higher income, see Kay Lehman Schlozman, Sidney Verba, and Henry E. Brady, *The Unheavenly Chorus: Unequal Political Voice and the Broken Promise of American Democracy* (Princeton, NJ: Princeton University Press, 2012), or earlier, Sidney Verba, Kay Lehman Schlozman, and Henry E. Brady, *Voice and Equality: Civic Volunteerism in American Politics* (Cambridge, MA: Harvard University Press, 1995).

70. Gilens and Page, "Testing Theories of American Politics," 573–574. On elite preferences, see the discussion of Page, Bartels, and Seawright below.

71. Gilens and Page, "Testing Theories of American Politics," 575.

72. Benjamin I. Page and Lawrence R. Jacobs, *Class War? What Americans Really Think about Economic Inequality* (Chicago: University of Chicago Press, 2009).

73. Benjamin I. Page, Larry M. Bartels, and Jason Seawright, "Democracy and the Policy Preferences of Wealthy Americans," *Perspectives on Politics* 11 (2013): 51–73.

74. Key, *Public Opinion and American Democracy*, 3.

75. Democratic senator Wayne Morse raised doubts about the incident, and was one of only two senators to oppose the Tonkin Gulf Resolution that expanded US intervention.

76. On these and other ostensible cases of manipulation of public opinion, see Page and Shapiro, *Rational Public*, ch. 9.

77. On political communication during the first Gulf War, see the essays in W. Lance Bennett and David L. Paletz, eds., *Taken by Storm: The Media, Public Opinion, and U.S. Foreign Policy in the Gulf War* (Chicago: University of Chicago Press, 1994); and Benjamin I. Page, *Who Deliberates? Mass Media in Modern Democracy* (Chicago: University of Chicago Press, 1996).

78. For example, see Barton Gellman and Walter Pincus, "Errors and Exaggerations: Prewar Depictions of Iraq's Nuclear Threat Outweighed the Evidence," *Washington Post National Weekly Edition*, August 18–24, 2003, 6–8; and Brigitte L. Nacos, Yaeli Bloch-Elkon, and Robert Y. Shapiro, *Selling Fear: Counterterrorism, the Media, and Public Opinion* (Chicago: University of Chicago Press, 2011).

79. See Page and Shapiro, *Rational Public*, chs. 5, 6, and 9; Shapiro and Jacobs, "Who Leads and Who Follows?"

Mass Media, Campaigning, and the Public

We have seen that public opinion is not a static, unchanging object. Rather, it is a highly dynamic, fluid process that reflects how people think, interact with one another, and deal with the bodies politic into which they have organized themselves. At the individual level, citizens continually reassess their attitudes and opinions in response to new knowledge and experience. As we saw especially in Chapters 5 through 7, these changes depend on complex psychological processes—sometimes they seem rational, sometimes irrational. At the macro, or mass, societal level, politically salient events alter political coalitions, the nature of issues, and the appropriateness of various policy options. At the level of group interaction and networking, the everyday give and take of political talk at the dinner table, at the workplace, and over the phone or the Internet reshapes what we think of one another and about politics. At each of these levels, public opinion emerges from active communication processes.

In these processes, certain actors stand out as being potentially very influential. The mass media, such as newspapers, radio stations, television networks, and Web sites, present much of the information that people incorporate into their opinions. At various times governments, corporations, other private organizations, and political candidates mount campaigns—via the mass media and by other means—to convey their messages or advance their candidacies. Understanding the effects of mass media and campaigns is thus naturally a crucial concern for public opinion scholars. With respect to the workings of American democracy, the quality of public opinion depends on the quality of communication processes at all levels. As these media and campaigns continue to evolve, scholars must keep pace. In this chapter we review some of the history of communication studies and summarize some major findings and debates about contemporary media and campaigns.

COMMUNICATION, MASS MEDIA, AND PUBLIC OPINION: EARLY DEVELOPMENT AND PERSPECTIVES

Communication serves many social functions. The sociologist Harold Lasswell defined three key functions of communication for societies, each of which also has clear ramifications for public opinion.[1] The first is *surveillance*, or monitoring events in the environment, especially those that may threaten the common good. Print and electronic news media have come to play a central role in fulfilling this function, sometimes idealized as the "watchdog" role (of which we say more below). A second function, *correlation*, is to inform us of how others are reacting to events and thinking about various topics. Lasswell compared this function to the neural processes by which the various parts of an animal act in concert, for example, to flee or to attack. Thus, correlation tends to produce social consensus—not necessarily unanimity of opinion, but at least some shared sense of where people stand. Mass media again play a crucial role in correlation, along with other opinion leaders. A third function is *transmission*, or the passing of the norms and morals of the culture to others entering the social system, especially the young. Formal education fills much of this role for society as a whole, but mass media also play an important role, as children learn from media role models (sometimes to the dismay of their parents). Other more informal communication channels also help transmit norms, initiating new members into the rituals that keep social groups together over time.

Other scholars have described functions for modern mass media besides those described by Lasswell, including entertainment[2] and economic stimulation. The modern channels of media advertising and marketing arguably are necessary to keep the US consumer-based economy operating. Many social critics also have seen mass media as promoting dysfunction. Emerging media technologies have often been blamed—convincingly or otherwise—for contemporaneous political, social, and cultural changes.

Not coincidentally, the rise of mass media coincides with the emergence of mass society theories of public opinion.[3] Western industrialized societies were viewed as moving away from clusters of closely knit communities with close personal linkages toward becoming more transient, urbanized, and impersonal. It was believed that as people moved from rural communities and farms to cities, community structures and personal relationships broke down; people became more anonymous and isolated. Theorists speculated that these new urban denizens might behave more like "masses" than publics: less socially integrated and responsible, more amenable to various forms of propaganda and demagoguery.

New mass media sources intensified the threat. Communication about politics previously had been largely an interpersonal pursuit, influenced by books and periodicals available to a relatively small, affluent audience. But new media could directly reach huge audiences—with potentially chaotic effects.

First came high-speed printing in the early and mid-1800s. Soon inexpensive daily newspapers were available to millions of urban dwellers, providing timely local and telegraph-fed national news and commentary. The technology also made a wide variety of print materials—including magazines, books, pamphlets, and catalogs—far cheaper, more available, and more appealing. Next, motion pictures became a mainstream entertainment medium in the early 1900s. Such popular films as D. W. Griffith's *Birth of a Nation* (1915) evinced the potential political and social influence of the cinema. Then came radio, which spread to over 90 percent of US households between 1920 and 1950 (and almost all of them by 1970).[4] Radio provided a diverse mix of popular and more sophisticated entertainment, commentary, and news, including live coverage of war, disasters, political speeches, and elections.

Television entered the scene on a grand scale in the 1950s and within a decade became the dominant mass medium for entertainment, as well as a widely valued source of national and international news. By the 1980s telecommunication via satellite had greatly expanded television's content capabilities to include dozens—and eventually hundreds—of cable-cast and direct satellite channels covering a much wider range of interests. The same satellite capabilities, accompanied by rapid innovation in the computer industry, allowed greatly enhanced personal interactive communications in the 1990s and the 2000s, relying on Internet capabilities and far more sophisticated telephone systems. Over these two decades, e-mail, World Wide Web sites, and social media—on computers and subsequently on mobile devices—all emerged as widely used communication channels. These new channels often bridged mass communication with interpersonal communication, blurring many distinctions between the two concepts.[5]

Each of these developments provoked some awe, and no little consternation, about its possible social impacts. Political debate was thought to be cheapened by many nineteenth-century newspapers' penchant for "yellow journalism," which included sensationalism, biased coverage, and often crude, nearly libelous attacks on public officials. (Crude political attacks were not new, but mass newspapers had an unprecedented capacity to bring these attacks to wide audiences day after day.) The movie *Birth of a Nation*, set in the post–Civil War South, romanticized the violently racist Ku Klux Klan and, for critics, epitomized the malign propaganda potential of cinema. Subsequently, observers fretted about radio's ability to provide live home access to the words of political leaders—champions and demagogues alike. Radio's propaganda value led to heated international competition on shortwave radio. This competition peaked in the 1950s, early in the Cold War, as Voice of America (and related stations such as Radio Free Europe), the British Broadcasting Corporation, and Radio Moscow vied for influence. Television seemed to combine the most disturbing elements of all these media channels in a stream made continuously available in people's homes. The Internet brought additional concerns about facilitating political radicalism and pornography and threatening individual privacy.

In sum, each new technology was seen as a threat to public opinion: it might influence many people to believe or act in ways harmful to themselves and society at large. Some of these concerns seem reasonable; others seem frankly reactionary or poorly founded, scapegoating media for wars, economic depressions, and other ills.

But how much have these new media really mattered? How greatly have they affected how public opinion is developed and shaped, for better or for worse? In truth, we will probably never really know; no one can tell how history would have unfolded without these media. Nevertheless, we can hazard some well-educated guesses and, at the least, frame the questions in ways that will help us assess the current influence of communication media. In the crudest terms, the ongoing debate offers two sharply distinct views. On the one hand, some observers perceive mass media as dominating, or unduly influencing, the publics or audiences they reach. On the other, some observers argue that these publics largely use mass media as they choose, and indeed use media in largely beneficial ways. As in other such debates, it seems unlikely that one side has the best of every argument, and we should be wary of the normative assumptions tucked into words like "unduly" or "beneficial." But this broad frame will help to organize the discussion.

Before turning to evidence about media impacts, we should say more about who determines media content. If the media are a major source of public information about the social and political world, then many people have a stake in controlling them. Who owns the media, and what are their purposes? How do various elites and political leaders go about influencing the media, and how successful are they at doing this? After answering these questions we can consider the consequences for public opinion.

WHO DECIDES WHAT THE MEDIA PRESENT?

Media play a central role in shaping our perspectives. Walter Lippmann opens his 1922 book *Public Opinion* by discussing how people rely on indirect representations of their environments: instead of the "world out-side," we react to "the pictures in our heads."[6] Media sources prodigiously supply those pictures, providing images and stories about events, issues, personalities, social situations, and other things that we will likely never encounter "live" on our own. Thus, who determines which images and stories we see, and what their intentions and biases may be, are crucial concerns for public opinion. Although it might seem natural to start with media owners and content creators (such as reporters and editors), first we will take an even broader perspective.

Much evidence points to the media's *agenda-setting* power; most major public issues attract public attention after the news media report about them.[7] The public's interest in events and issues is mostly proportional to how much news coverage those issues get. However, this relationship reflects the power of the public, as media consumers, as well as the media's own influence. Media outlets are competing for an audience; their decisions about what to cover are shaped by their perceptions of what people will read or watch and what the audience will think of it. Whether reporting on a trivial story or an important one, news organizations generally are driven by the assumption that some valuable audience will want to know about it and will "buy" the story by reading or watching it. Hence, the news agenda may be set in large part by the press's expectations of what audiences want or need. So it can be argued that the public substantially influences the news agenda, even though the media seem to direct the particular choices. Also, agenda-setting should not be overstated: sometimes the news media discover stories that are already priorities on the public agenda. Indeed, sometimes small groups of people participate in agenda-setting by speaking at local hearings, organizing demonstrations, or otherwise attracting media attention, thus generating more support for (and perhaps more opposition to) their cause.

It is also commonplace for organized interest groups—including corporations and government agencies and other elites—to try to influence the press and thereby the public agenda.[8] A cursory scan of policy news stories reveals that much of the information presented in them originates from governmental organizations, lobbying groups, corporations, and other institutions with their own agendas and influence strategies. Examples, are the Centers for Disease Control and Prevention's press releases on an outbreak of the deadly Ebola virus; an oil company's attempts to put the best possible spin on a recent spill; an environmental group's press conference on what it regards as a major threat to watershed protection; and a politician's campaign staff leaking documents that cast their opponent in an unflattering light. Although we may rely on journalists to sort out the merits of these episodes and report responsibly on the most important ones, even the most responsible news outlets are, in part, reacting to others' agendas.

Much of the US public relations industry focuses on encouraging the press to give more play to a company, person, issue, or event. Anecdotal evidence suggests that political candidates can significantly influence news coverage during campaigns and that incumbents can be highly successful at it. Research shows that presidents in particular can use the power of their office to sway the news agenda[9] and are more likely to succeed in doing so when they are more popular with the public and the press.[10] Officeholders and other individuals who are regarded by the media as public spokespersons wield influence through their increased access; journalists often seek their opinions and reactions. These leaders often can frame the context of emerging stories, leading reporters to emphasize some aspects at the expense of others.[11] For example, Robert Entman argues that during the Cold War leaders often induced the media to report on civil wars around the world in a frame of global competition between the United States and the Soviet Union. News stories might consider the prospects that a "Communist" or "Soviet-leaning" faction would gain the upper hand in some conflict, with little attention being given to important aspects of the conflict that did not fit the Cold War frame.

Often contending leaders and spokespersons promote alternative frames. Should a story on increasing Medicare costs be framed as a looming budget catastrophe, with the implication that the country must make tough choices to reduce health care expenses for the elderly? Or should it be framed as a threat to retirees' access to health care, suggesting that more funding may be needed? Even when a story presents contending perspectives on a policy issue, the initial frame—whose perspective is first presented sympathetically—may largely determine how readers or viewers perceive it. Accordingly, advocates may attempt to persuade reporters that their favored frame is most appropriate, or just that it makes the most compelling story.

As Clarice Olien, George Donohue, and Phillip Tichenor remind us, these and other influences on the news media render them far from being independent, autonomous, "objective" observers.[12] The press can be viewed as a socially controlled institution in the same sense that executive government agencies, the courts, schools, and higher education are. All respond to and are constrained by other societal forces, notably including one another and the public. Olien, Donohue, and Tichenor's studies indicate that news media often report on issue conflicts in ways that satisfy established, powerful political and social groups, perhaps at many other people's expense.

The First Amendment protections accorded the press imply that it serves something of a "watchdog" role, alerting the community at large to potential threats. Olien and her associates argue that in too many cases, the news media act more as a "guard dog," favoring more powerful and influential community interests. This does not imply that the press is an outright "lap dog" that favors the powerful no matter how poorly they behave. Rather, the news establishment is seen as having developed power relationships with other community institutions; it focuses on maintaining those relationships. Olien and her associates suggest that "guard dog" reporting emphasizes conflict between individuals within power structures rather than challenges to the power structure itself. Election campaigns are played up; threats to the political system are disregarded or trivialized. Olien and her colleagues argue, in this vein, that in 1972 "ritualistic" coverage of Richard Nixon's presidential reelection campaign against George McGovern displaced coverage of the system-threatening Watergate affair until after the election.

Edward Herman and Noam Chomsky offer an even more sharply critical view of the media.[13] They argue that dominant media voices are fundamentally biased toward powerful economic and political interests, for a variety of reasons. Some of these reasons have to do with economic incentives. Most major media outlets are owned by large corporations, whose economic interests can often be at odds with the interests of most of their readers and viewers. A relative handful of corporations controls a wide variety of media sources. For example, Comcast—best known as a cable provider—owns NBC, Telemundo, USA Network, CNBC, MSNBC, and many other cable networks, as well as Universal Pictures. Moreover, the media compete not just for an audience, but fundamentally for advertising. Broadcast television and most Internet news sources depend almost exclusively on advertising revenues; even traditional newspapers and magazines usually earn far more from advertising than from subscriptions. Thus media outlets have incentives not to alienate their advertisers or to undermine readers' "buying mood."

Herman and Chomsky (among others) also argue that the news media are biased by their close relationships with their sources. Media outlets depend on their sources—especially those in government and, often, business settings—for access to news and information. Taking too critical a perspective toward these sources may jeopardize their access. Thus, media outlets have incentives to report the views of their sources, even competing sources, rather uncritically. Other media critics have derided this propensity as "false balance" or "opinions differ on shape of earth" reporting: if powerful sources debate whether the earth is round or flat, the media will faithfully report both sides and let readers decide![14] In a context in which the sources are almost entirely on one side—as in the Tonkin Gulf incident we discussed in Chapter 10, for which the US government was inevitably the main source of information—uncritical reporting may convey the impression that these sources are reliable beyond question. Thus the media essentially amplify elite voices instead of illuminating the facts. In all these and other ways, Herman and Chomsky argue, the media serve the interests of the powerful rather than the public interest.

Many observers consider Herman and Chomsky's critique overstated. Arguably Americans have access to a wide variety of media sources, including many that resolutely challenge elites from various perspectives; in the end, any shortcomings of the media may have more to do with what audiences demand than with what the media supply. Regardless of what one thinks about allegations of media bias, it is clear that news media do not simply report "the facts," but are to some extent caught up in attempts to influence public opinion.

THE EFFECTS OF MASS MEDIA ON PUBLIC OPINION

Do these efforts at influence and manipulation through the media work? Is public opinion affected? A succinct answer might rephrase Harold Lasswell: some of the messages carried by some of the media have some effects on some audiences some of the time.[15] Here we consider four broad categories of possible effects on (1) the public agenda for issues; (2) how informed the public is about issues; (3) public opinions, attitudes, and behaviors; and (4) public values and norms.

The Media and the Public Agenda

Many observers neglect the importance of the *public agenda*, that is, how and why people choose to direct their attention to one issue at the expense of another, to spend more time and effort thinking about one problem than another. Some of us may pay great attention to gender discrimination and others to US involvement in international conflicts; some may be concerned over economic policy and still others over global environmental issues. None of us can give equal attention to every issue; rather, we "agendize" and prioritize our concerns. As we have already indicated, the news media appear subtly and consistently to influence the agenda of issues we have opinions about. As succinctly stated by political scientist Bernard Cohen, "The press may not be successful much of the time in telling people what to think, but it is stunningly successful in telling its readers what to think about."[16] A multitude of studies have confirmed this agenda-setting function of the news media. The more play and emphasis newspapers or television news give to particular events or issues, the more likely are audiences of those media to regard them as more salient, more important.

Early work on agenda-setting in the 1970s, primarily by communication scholars Maxwell McCombs and Donald Shaw, found that the extent of news coverage given to issues in the news media strongly predicted public evaluations of their importance.[17] How audiences of specific news media ranked the importance of, say, Vietnam War issues or the economy or race issues generally agreed with how much news coverage those issues had received. News coverage in these studies is typically measured by content analysis of how much space or time is given to each topic. The prominence of the coverage is also considered; for example, when analyzing television news, the lead (first) story is generally considered most important.

In order to conclude that news coverage really is influencing the public agenda, it is important to consider time order: What changes first? Careful research has confirmed that usually greater news attention to an issue precedes a public perception of increased importance; the media tend to lead, rather than follow, the public. Laboratory experiments involving television newscasts across a number of topics have supported this finding.[18] News coverage may also influence governmental policymakers apart from its influence on citizens. This influence can proceed through a *third-person effect*, as described in Chapter 7: policymakers may act on how they expect the public to react to a story, even if the public's actual reaction is smaller or different.[19]

Experimental research confirms that the influence of news media extends beyond what issues people think about, to how people think about the issues. One kind of influence is framing; as we discussed earlier in the chapter, how the media characterize an issue can alter how audiences understand it. Indeed, Shanto Iyengar's research[20] has found that framing effects can extend to the style of reporting. Some stories use what Iyengar calls an "episodic" style based on particular events; other stories are primarily "thematic," providing context and explanation. For example, an episodic story about poverty might focus on the circumstances of a homeless individual coping with a cold snap, whereas a thematic story might focus on statistics about, say, rising poverty rates and cuts in assistance programs. Many news producers believe that episodic stories bring readers and viewers into a story, while thematic stories can leave the audience disengaged. Iyengar was interested in how the choice of approach might affect how people thought about the underlying issue.

In his experiments, Iyengar showed audiences newscasts depicting six issues: crime, international terrorism, poverty, unemployment, racial inequality, and the 1980s Iran-Contra scandal. Some participants saw episodic stories about

---

BOX 11.1

Whose Opinions Sway the Public?

In a pathbreaking study, Benjamin Page, Robert Shapiro, and Glenn Dempsey traced opinion changes on numerous public policy issues between 1969 and 1983. They particularly looked for cases in which support for a policy substantially changed within a few months, as measured by responses to identical survey questions. They then analyzed television news coverage of these issues over the same short time periods. (Major network news programs arguably were the most influential news sources in those years.) For each story, they exhaustively coded the source of each statement—a reporter, the president or administration member, another officeholder, a policy expert, and so forth—and whether the statement was supportive or negative.

Page and his colleagues found that overall, the tone of the statements strongly predicted opinion change: the more positive statements there were about a policy option, the more likely public response was to move in that direction. But it made a difference who made the statement. Statements by television commentators or by "experts" on the particular topic seemed to produce larger opinion shifts than statements by politicians or interest group members. It seems likely that viewers considered the news commentators and experts less biased and therefore more credible sources. The study provided evidence that people routinely judge some sources as more credible than others, as has been found in laboratory experiments.

SOURCE: Benjamin I. Page, Robert Y. Shapiro, and Glenn R. Dempsey, "What Moves Public Opinion?" *American Political Science Review* 81 (1987): 23–43.

---

these issues; others viewed thematic stories. Participants then were asked questions about the causes of the problems, who or what was responsible for them. In most but not all cases, audiences who saw the episodic versions of the stories tended to attribute responsibility more to the individuals involved in them, whereas groups seeing the thematic stories placed more responsibility on societal or policy-related causes. This was particularly true for poverty. After viewing an episodic story that depicted the plight of individual poor people, viewers were more likely to hold the poor responsible for their situations—even though the story was designed to be sympathetic—than those who viewed the thematic story. Iyengar's results were mixed and cannot be generalized to all stories, issues, or media. But they raise the possibility that reporters' (or policy advocates') choices about how to tell a story can have subtle and important impacts on their audiences. Bear in mind that framing is not entirely within the media's control; audiences use frames as they observe and communicate, putting information into the perspective of their own cognitive experience.[21]

A second kind of influence is *priming*, a concept we touched upon in Chapter 3.[22] Priming operates indirectly, by cuing people to consider certain themes. For example, Iyengar and Kinder found that when people watched a news story on national defense and then were asked to rate the president's performance, they placed more weight on how they assessed the president's foreign policy performance than if they had seen a story on some other issue. Notice how this phenomenon differs from framing: the foreign policy prime influences attitudes on a question (presidential performance) that the media story does not even discuss. Most primes are ephemeral; they remain near the top of people's minds until the next few primes come along. However, priming effects can be more enduring if they are reinforced. For example, Jon Krosnick concluded that people's evaluations of former President George H. W. Bush depended more on how people assessed his handling of the 1991 Persian Gulf War than on the other issues that normally dominate these assessments. Krosnick attributed this result to the massive media reporting of the war, which primed people to think of it even after the war ended and the reporting tailed off.[23] Parties and candidates have incentive to prime voters on issues that will give them an advantage. For example, the Republican Party and George W. Bush's reelection campaign primed "terrorism" to their advantage in the 2004 presidential election by holding the Republican National Convention in post-9/11 New York City.

The media's power to shape the public agenda and assessments is limited. Citizens are not helpless recipients of media messages; they react to what they see and hear and even may react against it. For example, in a 2010 poll 87 percent of respondents opined that the media paid too much attention to celebrities, but 84 percent also said that Americans paid too much attention to celebrity news.[24] However one construes this result (Do people suppose that "everybody else" is too obsessed with celebrities, an example of disowning projection?), it suggests that people are willing and able to think critically about media content.

The Media and an Informed Public

As we saw in Chapter 9, Americans are not as well informed about public affairs as most observers think participants in democratic government should be, and there is little sign that they have become more informed even as formal education has spread. Strangely, although many believe that the news media should promote an informed public, there has been less systematic research into how people learn (or do not learn) information from media than on subtler aspects of attitudinal and behavioral change.

We know in the most rudimentary way that citizens gain information about public issues from one another and from institutions such as schools, governmental and political organizations, and mass media. Studies indicate that citizens also learn from election campaigns, not only about candidates and their positions, but also about current issues. We also see that major news events very quickly inform the public (at least to some extent) about issues of consequence, whether war, natural disasters, violent protest, assassinations, major medical discoveries, or economic booms or busts. But we still have little understanding of how information is transferred, from what sources, through which channels, and to which audiences or publics.

We do know that political knowledge varies widely. Some people have greater access to information; but even among those with equal access, some learn far more than others. The pioneering campaign studies of the 1940s and 1950s (see Chapter 9) established that some voters paid much more attention to the campaign than others, presumably learning more as a result. Many studies have found that people with greater education and from higher social classes tend to be both more attentive to politics and better informed. (The reasons are ambiguous: highly educated people may have greater access to information, greater skill in processing it, more motivation to seek it out, greater use for it, or some combination of those factors.[25]) These facts have inspired the knowledge gap hypothesis: as the rate of information flow into a social system increases, groups with higher socioeconomic status acquire the information at a faster rate than lower-status groups, widening the knowledge gap between them.[26] The knowledge gap argument can be extended to young people. Pew studies dating back to 1994 have found that people aged eighteen to twenty-nine spend about one-third less time each day watching, reading, or listening to news. Almost 30 percent of these young respondents said they got no news the previous day.[27] This generation gap appears in part because young people are enthusiastic early adopters of new media channels, so more content is competing for their attention.

The knowledge gap hypothesis challenges common assumptions. Many people have assumed that increasing the flow of information in a democracy would help promote more equal levels of awareness and knowledge across the system, reducing differences between "information rich" and "information poor" segments of society. Attempts to enlist mass media in this project have included childhood television programs such as *Sesame Street* and massive public education efforts aimed at voter participation, public safety, disease prevention, and the like. Presumably such public efforts could help reduce information disparities brought about by circumstances of social class and lack of education. However, the knowledge gap hypothesis predicts that in general, broadcasting information disproportionately benefits those who are already more knowledgeable. This is not to say that all information campaigns do widen the knowledge gap, much less that they necessarily leave some people worse off, but it does counsel caution about naïve efforts to "educate the public" in general.

Research has shown that the more someone already knows about political affairs, the more likely that person is to learn about current news events, consistent with the knowledge gap hypothesis.[28] Across a wide range of topics—from abortion debates to primary elections to celebrity trials—the best predictor of people's knowledge was how much they already knew about politics, regardless of the specific ways in which they used news media. Thus we can speak of a "general news audience," consisting of citizens who are more politically aware, who use news media more, and who gain more information from that use. The limited size of this audience explains why with the advent of new cable and satellite media, and then the Internet and social media, there has been no general increase in the public's political knowledge and attention to public affairs. Rather, as Markus Prior aptly observed, there is a divide in the latest new media use: those interested in politics and world affairs have more opportunity to pursue those interests, and those not interested have new outlets for their nonpolitical pursuits.[29]

Another way that media might inform citizens is through systematic fact-checking to point out misinformation purveyed by political candidates and leaders. Fact-checks arose in part in response to complaints (as we mentioned previously) that the media too often credulously report "both sides" of disputes when one side is objectively wrong. During the 1988 presidential campaign, national newspapers published "truth boxes" that evaluated claims in campaign advertisements. Subsequent campaigns have seen "ad watches" in print, on television news, and increasingly on the Internet.[30] At least two well-known Web sites, FactCheck.org and PolitiFact.com, are dedicated exclusively to fact-checking political claims—and as we write, new "crowdsourced" sites are emerging. Past studies have differed on the effectiveness of ad watches and fact-checks. For example, an early study by Stephen Ansolabehere and Shanto Iyengar found that ad watches were largely ineffectual or even counterproductive, actually increasing support for the candidates whose ads were critiqued.[31] Political communication scholar Kathleen Hall Jamieson has found that ad watches can be effective, and that their design and placement substantially influences their effectiveness.[32]

Media Effects on Change in Public Opinions, Attitudes, and Behaviors

Most studies of what people learn from media and how they process such information have been done only since the 1970s. Earlier research on media effects focused on less subtle questions about whether media were directly altering people's opinions, attitudes, and behaviors. From the early 1900s through the 1940s, it was common to analogize the media to a hypodermic needle, "injecting" members of an increasingly atomized mass public with whatever thoughts and opinions the media manipulators wanted to instill. Fanciful, perhaps, but the *hypodermic model* underscored the media's increasingly immediate access to individuals in their homes, providing information unfiltered by other human interaction or dialogue. Likely adding to the speculative fear was the seeming ease with which the Nazi party gained power in Germany during the 1930s, with extensive and sophisticated use of radio, film, and print media.

Anecdotal evidence of powerful media effects in the United States was fanned by events such as Orson Welles's 1938 radio broadcast of *The War of the Worlds*, a fictional invasion from Mars that reportedly scared countless listeners (see Box 11.2). American involvement in World War II led to heavy investment in wartime propaganda, some of which appeared to succeed in rallying public support for the war and various policies at home.

However, when scholars later reexamined these and other supposedly strong media effects, the evidence became much less clear, and other important mitigating factors became apparent.[33] In this era, survey research and other sophisticated social science tools, including content analysis, focus groups, and field experiments (see Chapter 3), came to the fore. These techniques allowed for more valid and accurate measurement of communication influences. Despite several notable efforts, scholars of that era found nothing like the massive effects of mass communication on public views and actions that the hypodermic model had posited.

A Revised View: Media's Limited Power

Lazarfield's campaign studies, already discussed in this chapter and earlier, provided important evidence against massive media effects.[34] Lazarsfeld's hypothesis was a basically rational, information-based model for voting decisions: people

BOX 11.2

Mars Invades

On October 30, 1938, the night before Halloween, the CBS radio network program Mercury Theatre on the Air broadcast a "virtual journalism" version of H. G. Wells's classic science fiction novel The War of the Worlds. The novel details an invasion of England by Martians, including the mass destruction of major cities and their inhabitants, with national military forces defenseless against the onslaught. The radio program, produced by Orson Welles, began (after brief announcements about the show) as if it were a live orchestra program, popular in those days. The music was interrupted by a mock news bulletin that announced that a "flaming object" had fallen to the earth in the New Jersey countryside. Subsequent bulletins described creatures emerging from the object (and others elsewhere) and wreaking havoc and death. The production of the show was excellent, with top-flight scripting, actors, and special effects.

Perhaps it was too good. Many listeners were drawn into the story enough to flood police and radio station switchboards, call relatives and friends to spread the panic, and flee their homes in areas close to those identified on the program as being under attack. Some were convinced that they had seen signs of the invasion. As reality sank in over the next several hours, the network issued fervent apologies. Press stories over the next several days told countless stories of listeners' sheer terror. Soon the Federal Communications Commission put out guidelines intended to prevent similar panics in the future.

A pioneering group of broadcast researchers at Princeton University (less than ten miles from the purported invasion site) quickly undertook a study. They interviewed people who had been affected and tried to assess the scope of the panic, in an attempt to understand why some people had reacted but others had not.[1] They estimated that perhaps 1.2 million listeners were frightened or disturbed by the program. Many of these people had not heard the introduction to the broadcast that set the stage for the imaginary news coverage and either did not hear or ignored later statements indicating that it was a fictionalized account. To some extent, the lesser educated, the more insecure, and those with stronger religious beliefs were more inclined to panic.

More recent scholars have sharply criticized the Princeton group's findings.[2] Much of the study was based on interviews with 135 people, most of whom were selected because they were known to have been afraid. The extrapolation to over one million frightened listeners was speculative, and

(continues)

(continued)

BOX 11.2

Mars Invades

there was no solid evidence of widespread panic. These scholars argue that the story of the panic was trumped up by newspapers, to sell papers and perhaps in an attempt to undermine radio's credibility as a news source. If so, then the real story of media effects here is not how Orson Welles and his performers created a social panic, but how hundreds of newspapers invented one. Either story is disturbing, in its own way.

---

[1]Hadley Cantril, *The Invasion from Mars: A Study in the Psychology of Panic* (Princeton, NJ: Princeton University Press, 1940).

[2]Jefferson Pooley and Michael J. Socolow, "The Myth of the War of the Worlds Panic," *Slate*, October 28, 2013.

would weigh information they received from the candidates and news media, then make their final electoral decisions as the November election day neared. He suggested that mass media would convert undecided and wavering voters to particular candidates, reinforce voters who had already firmly decided, and activate people to get out and vote. The results surprised him: the vast majority of voters knew all along whom they would vote for, and political party affiliation far overwhelmed direct media effects in those choices. Although most voters followed the campaigns in newspapers and magazines and over radio, they paid most attention to content that supported their own chosen candidates. The small minority of undecided voters appeared to be among the least knowledgeable citizens and the least attentive to the campaign as well.

What of the cases in which individuals did decide to vote for a candidate during the campaign, or even to switch support from one candidate to another? There, interpersonal influence—the opinions of a spouse or a respected, knowledgeable neighbor—appeared to carry more weight than campaign news coverage, candidate speeches, or editorials. Primary reference groups, consisting of family and close friends, and secondary ones (e.g., party, union, church) appeared to be far more influential than media. This finding inspired the popular two-step flow hypothesis of social influence, in which more politically aware and active opinion leaders could (selectively) pass information from the media to other citizens. This hypothesis struck yet another blow against the presumed power of the media to sway political opinions or behaviors.

All in all, these studies supported what came to be known as a model of "indirect" or "minimal effects" of the media on public opinion and behaviors. This view also gained support from several other studies of that time, particularly those of public information programs aimed at promoting social change on a variety of topics. According to sociologist Joseph Klapper, media influence was slight because when people encounter media messages, they are already armed with strong predispositions—personal beliefs, attitudes, and behaviors—that inspire selective exposure, perception, and retention. That is, people tend to hear or read messages they already agree with, to interpret (or distort) messages in keeping with their predispositions, and to remember the parts they find agreeable while forgetting the rest.[35] Herbert Hyman and Paul Sheatsley cited such "psychological barriers" in a famous 1947 article bluntly titled "Some Reasons Why Information Campaigns Fail."[36]

Thus, the media seemed primarily to reinforce the existing views of audience members. The voters exposed to the most campaign media were the most partisan and the least likely to change their minds. Interpersonal interaction was far likelier to change minds than campaign exposure. At most, media might exercise an indirect persuasive effect via opinion leaders, as in the two-step flow model. This perspective was somewhat reassuring—citizens were not so much at the mercy of media propagandists after all—and prevailed for decades, until some of its limitations became apparent. Even then, there was no going back to the hypodermic model: media effects—persuasion—would continue to be seen as limited. However, more recent studies have found evidence for noteworthy media effects. Over time, opinions about racial policy and capital punishment appear to have responded to changes in media coverage of the issues.[37]

RECONSIDERATIONS OF MEDIA EFFECTS

The rise of television raised new questions about media influence. By the 1960s television had become the preeminent news medium, with extended coverage of nominating conventions, candidate debates, the assassination of President Kennedy, and the "living-room war," Vietnam. The growth of television paralleled an array of social changes that might transform public opinion processes. The post–World War II baby boom pushed a proportionally greater number of teens and young adults into the populace than had been seen in decades. They were also more educated and more affluent than their predecessors, with a less constrained, more mobile lifestyle. People in general moved around more, usually toward urban and suburban centers, reducing the pull of traditional family, neighborhood, and community affiliations. Some political attitudes and behaviors became more fluid, as evinced by an increase in "independent" voters, who did not affiliate with a political party, and in "ticket-splitters," who divided their votes among candidates of both major parties.[38] Political communication researchers finally began catching up with these trends in the 1970s, and new perspectives on the relationship between mass media and public opinion emerged.

Cultivating the Public

The *cultivation perspective*, one of these newer views, proposes far-reaching influences of television on virtually all aspects of audience perceptions and attitudes. Developed by George Gerbner and his colleagues at the University of Pennsylvania, this perspective asserts that television has become the "common storyteller of our age," providing our diversified society with consistent and repeated messages and images.[39] This integrated content reaches across all levels of our society, cultivating shared views and conceptions of reality among otherwise diverse social groups.

Extensive analysis of television content, especially in the 1970s and 1980s, found somewhat consistent portrayals of American life and values that often diverged from reality. For example, both entertainment and news programs depicted (and still depict) substantially more crime and violence than actually occurred. Of course, people generally want news to alert them to unusual events, particularly threatening ones, not to represent ordinary daily life. Similarly, entertainment is supposed to provide a break from ordinary routine, not to show the workaday world. Even so, we can wonder how this surfeit of crime and violence affects people's perceptions of reality.

Unfortunately, the evidence of television's effects on audiences is spotty. Gerbner predicts that heavier exposure to television content will cultivate perceptions or beliefs about social reality that diverge from reality toward the "television view." For example, we would expect heavier viewers of television to be more fearful of crime. Some early studies supported this view. However, subsequent surveys have found little evidence that the overall amount of television viewing has any effect on perceptions of or attitudes toward crime, although specifically watching crime news may have some influence.[40]

A refinement of the initial cultivation perspective posits that exceptionally heavy viewing of television—several hours per day—may override other social and cultural differences between people. That is, people who share watching large amounts of television may have more closely shared worldviews than their demographic and other social differences would suggest. This phenomenon is called mainstreaming, and Gerbner and associates found that people who watch more television, regardless of their demographic makeup, see themselves as somewhat more moderate in their political and social beliefs. Gerbner attributed this tendency to network television's attempt to program for the middle ground, balancing countering perspectives and avoiding controversy. The cultivation approach has not been widely applied to other aspects of public opinion, and social scientists have disputed its rationale and analytic methods.[41] In any case, the approach illustrates how television—and, by extension, other media—might influence public opinion, not through discrete messages here and there, but by more subtly and systematically shaping people's assumptions about social reality.

Moving Toward the Active Audience

Partly in reaction to the failure of the hypodermic model, emphasis has turned toward construing individuals as active users of media—considering what people do with media, as opposed to what media do to people—as proposed by communications researchers Wilbur Schramm, Jack Lyle, and Edwin Parker.[42] This view posits that audiences are proactive in their dealings with media, deliberately using them to seek out rewards or gratification, such as reinforcement of opinions, learning new information of value, surveillance of the environment, entertainment, excitement or stimulation, companionship, diversion, and passing time. The approach became known as the *uses and gratifications model* of communication effects—that is, people purposely use certain media content to gratify specific needs. Individuals try to choose media content that they expect will do the best job of meeting those needs, based on previous experience.[43] You may read articles on *Huffington Post* or on the Fox News Web site, but probably not both, because you know that you generally agree with the views expressed by one of them, and you will derive some satisfaction from having a well-known source agree with you. You will also probably get more facts and arguments to buttress your opinions. Or you may always turn on a certain radio station in the morning because you know it will play music you like to hear, and the station gives you a little—but not too much—surveillance of the world through its brief news and weather segments.

Obviously, however, the media chosen do not always provide the rewards people expect them to; moreover, media use may have unintended effects or consequences for the public. You may turn on a television show or visit a Web site expecting escapist fun, but instead you may encounter a news event or a political message that inspires, alarms, annoys, or enrages you. More subtly, media content can help shape our thinking even when we do get from a message much of what we had expected. Few media gratifications come without something extra: the particular spin that a newscaster puts on a point, additional information that slightly alters our expectations, or a broader contextual narrative that expands our horizons.

While most theories of media influence now emphasize an active audience role, clearly sometimes people are passive or reactive in attending to media—or in everyday conversations, for that matter—simply letting words or images wash over them, leaving themselves more open to influence or manipulation.[44] The juxtaposition of more active and more passive audience involvement with media has led researchers to examine media effects on public opinion as a more interactive or transactional process. The relationship between audiences and media likely changes and shifts across different personal traits, moods, contexts, and situations.[45] Generalizing to political communication, Robert Huckfeldt and John Sprague conclude that "the acquisition of political information is the end result of a complex interplay between individual choice and environmental supply,"[46] in which supply partly depends on the strategies adopted by various media content producers.

Media Dependency

How much we rely on media for various gratifications, and how much they influence us, also depend on our alternatives—for information, social support, diversion, and so forth. Some people have more access to alternatives than others, for various reasons of temperament and circumstance.[47] On a broader scale, the overall extent of media dependency may vary with social and political circumstances. Sociologists Sandra Ball-Rokeach and Melvin DeFleur have argued that in times of greater conflict and change, media dependency is apt to rise. When change challenges traditional means for coping with threats to established norms and behaviors, media may provide a coping mechanism.[48]

During the late 1960s, for example, many citizens may have turned more to newspapers and especially television to try to make sense of a seeming explosion of social protest and turmoil. The news media not only kept audiences up to date on the latest expressions of discontent, but also provided a somewhat authoritative and reassuring perspective on those developments and other citizens' reactions. Walter Cronkite, CBS News anchor at that time, became known as "the most trusted man in America." Also, in times of conflict or crisis, when immediate action seems likely, citizens may turn to media for relevant information. Media usage spiked after 9/11 as people sought insight into what had happened, what would happen next, and what the United States should do.

The Interpersonal Factor

Although conversations between citizens are crucial to development and change in opinion, most studies of media influences neglect these interpersonal influences. When people confront a decision or a challenge to their existing views, they seek information and advice from the most available—and the most trusted—sources. Mass media may serve some of these functions some of the time, but social contingencies and interactions remain crucial in opinion formation.[49] The two-step flow model still offers the starting point for most consideration of these influences. However, that model assumed relatively few media channels, mediated through stable primary group relationships, whereby "influentials" could consistently pass along interpretations of media messages to "followers." These assumptions were always problematic and may seem downright obsolescent in an era of social media networks and rapid growth in media channels. The challenge is to improve on the two-step flow model without rendering it unusably complex.

Some scholars have focused on the relationship between "opinion leaders" and other citizens. John Robinson suggested allowing for reciprocal influence, noting that influence is seldom a one-way street: the "followers" are likely to exert some influence on the leaders.[50] Another question is whether opinion leaders in fact use media more or differently than other citizens. In a pathbreaking study of influential individuals in the United States, Germany, and Israel, Gabriel Weimann found that they used media no more often than anyone else, but tended to use higher quality media, such as books and magazines on specialized topics.[51] Weimann also found influential people had political news agendas that were more closely tied to those of news media. This finding suggests that influentials were more susceptible to agenda-setting, or perhaps more able to influence the media agenda themselves.

A more speculative question is whether and how media technologies have influenced interpersonal communications themselves. For example, some observers have suggested that the rise of television has contributed to a diminished sense of civic community—or "sense of place" in Joshua Meyrowitz's term—and a decline in "social capital," or the social networks, discussions of values, and shared participation that move citizens more effectively toward shared objectives.[52] Similarly, James Carey has argued that over most of the twentieth century, mass media became more privatized and less of a public space for democratic discussion.[53] Contrariwise, the Internet and social media provide new opportunities for public discussion and disputation, although it is far from obvious whether these channels tend to enrich or to fragment the public sphere.[54]

Fragmentation and Polarization of Media Audiences

Recognizing the role of the "active audience" in media provides an analytical context for considering the effects of a partial fragmentation of news media—and beyond that, a polarization along partisan and ideological lines. In the heyday of major network news, the three largest networks (CBS, NBC, and ABC) generally presented similar news stories in similar ways. In what Markus Prior calls the postbroadcast era,[55] as cable channels and online news sites have proliferated, there is more evident ideological diversity in how news is presented than during the era of the Big Three. This is not to say that once upon a time all news media were ideologically moderate and nonpartisan. On the contrary, as we saw in Chapter 2, historically many US newspapers have been extremely partisan, not only on their editorial pages but also in their main news content. The expectation that professional journalists should offer unbiased reporting is relatively new. So the rise of such ideologically polarized news networks as the conservative Fox News and the liberal MSNBC can be seen as a return to form: these networks seek competitive advantage by targeting distinct ideological market segments. These networks offer viewers real choice about what news they hear and how they hear it—and many observers are appalled by the results.

One result is that these networks have highly unrepresentative audiences. A 2012 Pew study found, for example, that self-identified conservatives comprised 78 percent of Fox News host Sean Hannity's audience, and 69 percent of Fox colleague Bill O'Reilly's, compared with just 35 percent of the public. (Talk radio host Rush Limbaugh also had a strikingly conservative audience.) Conversely, 57 percent of MSNBC host Rachel Maddow's audience, and 48 percent of the audience for MSNBC's *Hardball with Chris Matthews*, were self-identified liberals, compared with just 22 percent of the public.[56] Overall, 60 percent of self-identified regular Fox News viewers were conservatives, and 40 percent were Republicans; the regular MSNBC audience comprised just 32 percent conservatives and 16 percent Republicans.[57] These differences in viewership correspond to marked differences in the tone of the reporting and commentary on these networks. Both have large audiences: 21 percent of Americans reported that they regularly watched Fox News, and 11 percent that they regularly watched MSNBC. (CNN was in between, at 16 percent.)[58]

Moreover, the disparate audiences of various news sources often (but not always) sharply disagree about what might be construed as factual questions. For example, a 2003 study asked people whether they thought the United States had found "clear evidence in Iraq that Saddam Hussein was working closely with the al Qaeda terrorist organization." Two-thirds (67 percent) of people who got their news primarily from Fox News opined that the United States had found such evidence, compared with just 16 percent of people who primarily used PBS and/or National Public Radio. (MSNBC had not yet taken a liberal direction in 2003.)[59] A similar study in 2010 found that regular Fox News viewers were 40 percentage points more likely than regular MSNBC viewers to deny that most scientists think climate change is occurring. Conversely, MSNBC viewers were far more likely to say that the US Chamber of Commerce had been proven to "spend foreign money to back Republicans." (The researchers considered both these beliefs false.)[60] To some extent, these networks' audiences inhabit different worlds.

But why? Obviously liberals and conservatives, Democrats and Republicans, existed before these networks did, and everything we know about social psychology leads us to expect some differences in these groups' worldviews and their attentiveness to information that might reinforce or challenge those views. Do opinion differences such as these in any way reflect actual media effects, or do they merely reflect the media choices of people who would tend to disagree about these questions regardless of what they see and hear on the news? Media effects are notoriously difficult to assess, but there is evidence that media exposure does exercise some influence on people's beliefs and even their behavior. A 2007 study, based on the geographical availability of Fox News in 2000, found evidence for a substantial persuasion effect: voters being persuaded by Fox News to vote Republican, rather than Democratic, in both presidential and US Senate contests. A 2012 study using a different dataset was inconclusive overall, but found evidence that availability of Fox News led some Republicans, Republican-leaning independents, and pure independents to vote Republican.[61] Thus, there is reason to believe that polarized news media—not only the networks, but also the increasingly popular Internet news sources—may in fact increase polarization in public opinion. This theme is likely to inspire continued research and debate.

CAMPAIGNING AND OPINION CHANGE

We have argued that changing communication styles, formats, and technologies affect public opinion processes. Mass media in particular have significantly altered how people view, think about, and respond to the political world. Now we focus on an important special case: communication campaigns. Here we mean not only election campaigns (our focus later in the chapter), but also publicity campaigns that influence everything from our purchasing habits to health practices to cultural myths. We discuss the purposes and practice of contemporary campaigns and how well they seem to work. We also examine an underlying tension between campaigns' effects on individual attitudes and behaviors and their less obvious but sometimes more consequential impact on society as a whole.

The Campaign Environment

Communication campaigns try to "(1) generate specific outcomes or effects (2) in a relatively large number of individuals, (3) usually within a specified period of time and (4) through an organized set of communication activities."[62] This definition fits a multitude of persuasive situations we are all too familiar with as media consumers.

That Super Bowl television commercial for, say, a new model of sport utility vehicle is likely to be just one component of a carefully planned set of communication activities. These might include ad placements in magazines and on the Internet and social media, promotional displays at automobile dealers, reviews of the vehicle in auto trade publications and newspapers, and perhaps even the use of the vehicle in a new action movie. These components are tied together to distinguish the vehicle from its competition and place it in the most favorable light possible. The specific message may vary depending on the medium and the target audience. The Super Bowl commercial may emphasize virility, power, and economy, whereas an ad in *Outside* magazine may display the model's off-road capabilities in a setting of solitude. The campaign tries to make the target audience aware of the product in a positive way, motivating people to test-drive it and ultimately to buy it.

Similarly, public service advertisements/announcements (PSAs) on television are simply the most visible sightings of other extensive campaigns at work. Appeals to "drink responsibly," warnings against texting while driving, heart health messages, and Smokey Bear's pleas to prevent unwanted human-caused wildfires are products of public policy campaigns to persuade people to change certain behaviors for their own good, for the public good, or for the benefit of the environment (see Figure 11.1). Some campaigns or messages do not directly target behaviors, but instead try to influence people's beliefs and attitudes—for example, to persuade them that a problem exists, to convey optimism that "we can fix it," or to build support for a particular policy change. These social marketing programs attempt to use many of the precepts of commercial marketing to promote social change.[63]

Like other campaigns, these PSAs are designed to match their target audiences and purposes. One AIDS-prevention advertisement, for example, may target gay men as an audience, whereas another—using a very different

FIGURE 11.1. **"Smokey Bear" Wildfire Prevention Advertisement.** Smokey Bear has been featured in hundreds of public service ads. These made the slogan "Only you can prevent forest fires" so familiar that it could be abbreviated, as in this example.
SOURCE: Smokey Bear images used with the permission of the USDA Forest Service.

approach—may focus on heterosexual, at-risk high-school students. The campaigns underlying these ads may contain elements as disparate as press releases, talk show appearances, participation in public meetings, and lobbying efforts in Washington, DC.

Campaign Strategies and Tactics

Many marketing campaigns—including political campaigns—have similar design strategies. First marketing research is used to identify potential audiences and to determine their existing ideas and behaviors regarding the product (perhaps a candidate) or problem. Then potential themes and messages are tested with smaller groups of people. The targeted audiences are segmented by their demographics, awareness, and interest in the topic and by their existing behaviors, and appropriate media are then chosen to reach particular audience groups. Modern polling and statistical analysis techniques help marketers target their strategies toward various groups with considerable precision.

Indeed, polling-based conceptualizations of American lifestyles have found their way into most major communication and marketing campaigns. Statistically derived typologies are used to describe purchasing habits, health practices and disease risks, automobile safety, environmental activities, and of course voting predispositions. Psychological dispositions toward behavior change, as well as media habits, are often tied into these profiles. Marketers use such catchy terms as "Yellowstone Yuppies" to profile, say, fortyish upper-income urbanites with a yen for expensive sport utility vehicles and outdoor gear, backpacking vacations, and gourmet foods, and with socially liberal but economically conservative political leanings. Postal zip codes and US census data are often used to locate concentrations of such groups. The targeted market segments then can be reached by television and radio, newspapers and magazines, billboards and posters, and direct mail. More interactive tactics may include telephone pitches, talks to civic organizations, special-interest clubs and discussion groups, and increasingly, e-mail and the Internet. (The Internet increasingly provides rich information about people's preferences, allowing marketers to target people individually rather than geographically.) Campaigners seek positive news media coverage of their products, services, and promoted behaviors, to increase the reach and legitimacy of the campaigns. Ideally, these multidimensional campaigns are carefully orchestrated for maximum effect.

Campaigns have become notoriously expensive undertakings, with skyrocketing research and media costs. This trend places a greater premium on measuring the effectiveness of various techniques, in order to plan for the next round. However, even for a commercial product with objective sales figures, it is often difficult to assess how various techniques affected the results. Moreover, even very sophisticated campaigns can fall flat. Two of the most heavily market-researched and cleverly promoted "innovative" products of their times were the Edsel automobile in the mid-1950s and the "new Coke" formula of the late 1980s, both of which proved to be abject failures.

Evaluating social marketing campaigns is much more difficult. Often the intended outcomes can only be measured through survey research, at great expense. Most public service campaigns operate on small budgets, especially when compared with the hefty amounts spent by industry to promote consumer goods. Many public service efforts only become possible through the willingness of media outlets—especially television—to donate free time or space. Nonetheless, some studies of public service campaigns have found evidence of their effectiveness. At the same time, researchers have found that some techniques are less effective than advocates might hope or expect. For example, one study tested four messages intended to encourage parents to vaccinate their children against various infectious diseases. It found that none of these messages worked, and some actually backfired.[64] Such results underscore the importance of testing social marketing messages before investing resources in them.

The same mechanisms that influence the media effects we discussed previously apply to campaigns. Think of a campaign as an orchestrated cluster of communication stimuli that may prompt learning, persuasion, reinforcement, agenda-setting, priming, and other mechanisms that lead to social influence and change. In our society, one barrier to large campaign effects is simply that campaigns are typically competing for public attention. The automotive campaign competes against possibly dozens of others with similar goals and persuasive techniques. An AIDS-awareness program competes against countless other health prevention and other social welfare messages. Antismoking ads risk being swamped by tobacco company promotions. Indeed, the US government has acted over time to restrict such promotions. In 2010 the Food and Drug Administration banned tobacco company sponsorship of sporting and entertainment events.

How Campaigns Can Succeed

How successful a campaign is depends a great deal on how effectively it is planned, produced, and disseminated to reach its audience. Reviews of successful campaign strategies and tactics suggest that key factors include the following:

1. Using social science models of public opinion and persuasion in their design rather than relying on "gut feel" or conventional wisdom about social influence. A successful heart-disease prevention campaign at Stanford University in the 1980s drew on the social learning theory that behavioral change can be successfully promoted through modeling the actions of others.[65] Incorporating research on source credibility, fear appeals, and audience learning capabilities can help to avoid common mistakes.

2. Taking into account audiences' existing cognitions, attitudes, and behaviors, as well as their communication patterns and habits. For example, understanding people's information needs and the sources they use to satisfy those needs can avoid wasted effort.

3. Using extensive precampaign research to examine audience perceptions and needs, then pilot-testing possible themes and messages on targeted groups. Appropriate use of audience surveys and focus groups can illuminate reasonable goals and effective means.

4. Having clear and realistic campaign goals; high-quality, professionally produced materials; and a careful, well-executed dissemination strategy. It may sound banal to recommend careful planning and execution, but many campaigns fail this test. Often, campaign producers do not fully think through their objectives for building awareness or behavioral change, subverting their best intentions.[66] Bear in mind that it is far easier to build awareness about an issue than to prompt changes in behavior, especially changes that individuals see as costly or requiring great effort. It may be most effective to focus on this belief and attitudinal change—an agenda-setting effect—in the expectation that interpersonal communication will then promote behavioral changes.

5. Implementing a multimedia campaign that appropriately combines television, radio, print, the Internet, social media, and mobile platforms. Multimedia campaigns generally are more effective, but require careful coordination.

Societal Consequences of Campaigns

Both commercial and public information campaigns may have influences on public opinion other than their directly intended ones. Ford's latest campaign to sell its newest F-Series pickup truck may or may not successfully sway buyers away from Dodge Rams, but all the pickup advertising together is likely (although not certain) to increase public demand for pickups. The societal impacts may include increased fossil fuel consumption and air pollution (these trucks often use 40–50 percent more fuel than efficient midsized cars), as well as safety risks to drivers of smaller, lighter vehicles—and land erosion if drivers emulate the off-road driving in the advertisements.

Based on reasoning about social impacts, tobacco advertising has been restricted in an attempt to reduce overall demand for cigarettes and other tobacco products, especially among the young. Some social critics have extended this argument to conclude that product campaigns, taken together, drive us toward being a society of consumers, more concerned with shopping and material possessions than other pursuits.[67] Other commentators take a similar but more positive view: they see advertising campaigns as tending to strengthen the market economy and thereby increase social well-being, in part by making consumers aware of new products and services.[68] In any case, it seems clear that commercial campaigns help determine what is "in" or "out of" our consumer culture. How such consumer opinions may carry over into the political sphere is far less clear. But if, for example, product advertising builds expectations of goods and services that many individuals are unable to obtain, the consequences may be substantial.

The same can be said for public information campaigns. The tremendous growth in preventive health campaigns since the 1970s, for example, may have strongly contributed to making us a more health aware and responsible society, regardless of any individual gains in fighting cancer, nutritional deficiencies, or substance abuse. The more subtle message of most public health and safety campaigns has been one of citizens taking more individual responsibility for their well-being, moving away from reliance on governmental and quasi-public agencies.

Concerns often arise over which "social good" programs should be promoted, since support for one can lead to neglect of another.[69] If more media time is allocated to a crime prevention program, will that take away from an equally salient program promoting proper infant nutrition practices? And who is to set the agenda to decide which issues win out? A related concern has been that the vast majority of public information campaigns that win media acceptance are uncontroversial. Few citizens would argue for more crime, drug abuse, or cancer. Greater media attention to such "valence issues" may draw attention away from more controversial issues such as economic welfare benefits, government-sponsored abortion, and legalization of drugs.[70]

A broader critique of government information campaigns is that their "top-down" approach to informing or mobilizing "target audiences" bypasses public discussion of problems and solutions and may therefore lessen public acceptance.[71] During a drought, rather than running commercials on the importance of conserving water, it may be more effective to work with citizens to see what conservation approaches work best for them. This emphasis on public participation has succeeded in many settings, including health education and international development programs to promote agricultural productivity and environmental protection.[72]

ELECTION CAMPAIGNS

We turn now to those campaigns that have the most conspicuous consequences for public opinion: those targeted at swaying people's votes on public offices and issues. Election campaigns come in many shapes and sizes, from nationwide presidential campaigns to positions for individual political precincts, as well as issue campaigns (such as for and against statewide initiatives and referenda). Election campaigns are nothing new. From George Washington's day on, candidates for all levels of office have proudly trumpeted their own virtues, roundly disparaged their opponents, and put odd twists on the "facts" regarding their positions and records (see Figure 11.2). Of course campaigns have changed markedly with changes in communication technology, plus many changes in political and social contexts. For example, in the twentieth century there was a shift from "party-centered" to "candidate-centered" campaigns. In 1900 political parties essentially chose their own candidates and managed their campaigns. By the 1970s, new media forms made it easier for candidates to cultivate their public reputations; political reforms allowed more candidates to reach the ballot by winning primary elections, without relying on party leaders.

Major campaigns—presidential campaigns in particular—have a bewildering variety of players. The candidates have campaign committees that manage spending on all campaign activities (advertising, polling, travel, staff, and so on). The major political parties have their own permanent campaign committees, such as the Republican and Democratic National Committees (RNC and DNC). Then there is a welter of political action committees (PACs), which can raise and spend money for their own political purposes. Some PACs are associated with industry groups, unions, advocacy groups, and other organizations that want to influence elections, others with candidates themselves. Yet others are created independently to advance various interests and goals. So-called 527 groups do not expressly advocate for or against candidates, but clearly intend to affect their electoral prospects. (The "527" refers to a section of the US tax code.) The most famous of the 527s, Swift Boat Veterans for Truth, ran advertisements in 2004 arguing that Democratic presidential nominee John Kerry had lied about his war record and was "unfit to serve." These ads and the media attention they attracted may have cost Kerry the presidency. In 2010 the Supreme Court ruling *Citizens United v. Federal Election Commission* struck down restrictions on express advocacy, as unconstitutional constraints upon free speech. Since then, so-called Super PACs have been able to raise and spend unlimited sums to expressly support or oppose candidates, although they cannot directly contribute to candidate campaigns and are not supposed to coordinate directly with candidate or party

FIGURE 11.2. **Barack Obama Speaks at a 2008 Campaign Rally in Ohio.**
SOURCE: © EdStock | iStock.

campaign staffs. And then there are the thousands of volunteers, celebrities, and other people who may participate in or influence campaigns.

Some other aspects of election campaigns set them apart from commercial or social marketing programs. One is the compressed time frame during which two or more campaigns are directly pitted against each other. Of course commercial advertisers such as car companies compete for market share, but they do not face a winner-take-all deadline akin to Election Day. Election campaigns are also distinctive in that usually the "product" being promoted is a living, breathing candidate with human virtues and frailties. Car companies may boast about the careful design and manufacture of their vehicles, but for candidates, careful design usually is far from a selling point. On the contrary, an election campaign strives to convince voters that the candidate spontaneously, authentically has just the personality traits they want for that position—not just the right ideology and issue positions, but the right temperament, the right values, the right "people skills." Indeed, with the rise of candidate-centered politics, election campaigns have increasingly emphasized personality and image aspects of candidates over issue-related appeals. Voters are legitimately interested in candidates' personalities; campaigns seek to satisfy this curiosity in the most flattering way possible, in part using advertising and media strategies inspired by corporate campaigns.[73]

As have other kinds of campaigns, political campaigns have become wildly more expensive. For the 2012 presidential election, the campaigns for the two major candidates (Democratic incumbent Barack Obama and Republican challenger Mitt Romney) spent over $1 billion apiece.[74] These unprecedented totals included funds contributed to campaign- and party-affiliated committees, but did not include independent expenditures by other groups, which were reported to have totaled at least another $524 million.[75] In the 2014 election cycle—which of course did not include a presidential contest—total spending on US House and Senate campaigns has been estimated at about $3.7 billion.[76] The winner-take-all nature of electoral competition lends itself to spending "arms races": What candidate would willingly settle for being outspent?

The upward spiral in campaign spending—and therefore fund-raising—poses a normative dilemma for democratic theory. On the one hand, restricting people's ability to support the candidates and causes of their choice seems intrusive, if not downright oppressive. On the other hand, the money competition inevitably gives some citizens a greater role than others in influencing election outcomes. The more one has, the more one can afford to give. As we saw in Chapter 10, this money gap is unlikely to be politically neutral. In the 2012 presidential contest, wealthy donors were far more likely to contribute to Republican candidates than to Democrats, a major competitive advantage for conservative candidates that is likely to hold for the foreseeable future.[77] Any partisan or ideological advantage aside, the need for contributions provides obvious incentives for all campaigns to attend to the concerns of wealthy contributors, which—again as we saw in Chapter 10—may systematically differ from most citizens' concerns.

Concerns about campaign financing have led to moderate regulation at federal, state, and, in some cases, local levels. The basic worries are twofold: (1) that candidates will be "bought" by dominant contributors, who will expect favors from those elected; and (2) that candidates who cannot afford these expenses will be defeated by richer or better funded candidates, or will be discouraged from even campaigning, even if they are strong candidates in principle. Such concerns date back to the earliest experiments in democracy. In 1931 humorist Will Rogers gibed, "Politics has got so expensive that it takes lots of money to even get beat with nowadays"; one can only imagine what he would say today. Federal campaign finance laws limit exceptionally large contributions to campaigns and political committees by individuals and organizations to single persons or organizations that might bring undue influence to bear on candidates. They also require that campaign contributions and expenditures be carefully documented, and restrict certain kinds of spending—although, as we mentioned above, the Supreme Court in *Citizens United* struck down some of these restrictions.

Campaign Media

The increase in campaign spending has been driven by the costs of mass media campaigns, especially television advertising. The cost of advertising time alone runs from hundreds of dollars a minute in the smallest market areas to hundreds of thousands of dollars nationally. Planning and producing these ads is also expensive. Then there are all the other forms of controlled (paid) media—Internet ads, crafted messages on social media and mobile platforms, radio spots, direct mail, bumper stickers, posters and yard signs, and so on—along with their research and development costs. Campaigns also attempt to influence *uncontrolled* media, especially news coverage (and, increasingly, social media), which can offer wide and credible exposure.

Controlled Media. In well-run campaigns, controlled media messages are carefully designed to influence particular kinds of audiences, and media channels are chosen to maximize impact on those audiences. No doubt some campaigns make these decisions more effectively than others, but bad choices are punished (perhaps not visibly) on Election Day.[78]

Various media are well suited to particular purposes. For example, direct mailings, such as brochures and postcards, are most heavily used in local campaigns, but can be useful in any campaign to reinforce messages in other media. Some people who "tune out" television ads are willing to read their mail. Traditionally, direct mail often has been geographically targeted based on the demographic or lifestyle characteristics of a neighborhood, by zip code or even by block. For example, a neighborhood with a high proportion of retirees might read about a candidate's commitment to protecting Social Security, while one with many Hispanic residents may receive Spanish-language or bilingual mailings about the candidate's support for immigration reform. Increasingly, consumer data files allow campaigns to target individuals. Radio advertisements often provide another way to target groups of voters—often less expensively than television—because various radio formats attract different kinds of listeners.

Television commercials, still the dominant form of controlled political media, offer an interesting mix of advantages and disadvantages for candidates. An obvious advantage is reach: no other medium can connect with tens of millions of viewers around the country at the same time. Television ads also benefit to some extent from a "captive audience"—people who are watching a program have to make some effort not to see the ads—and the medium is more evocative than radio or print. A subtler disadvantage than cost is clutter: television ads usually come one after another in a short period of time, so it can be difficult for one message to stand out. Television ads can be targeted, but only somewhat crudely, and ads on the programs with the largest and most desirable audiences are often far more expensive.

The common fifteen- to thirty-second television spot format offers a wide array of creative possibilities.[79] An ad may evoke the candidate's leadership qualities, old-fashioned hometown values, and picture-perfect family; why the candidate offers the best way to improve the economy, reward hard work, or fight crime; or the comic ineptitude, dangerous ideas, or intolerable corruption of the opponent. The content and approach depend heavily on context. Political newcomers may promote their personal qualities, whereas well-known incumbents emphasize their records in office. Telegenic contenders often favor visuals of themselves in action; others may prefer imagery that focuses less on themselves.

Digital advertising delivered via the Internet and mobile platforms can take several forms: audio, video, text, and/or images. It also can be conveyed through many channels, including advertisements on Web sites and search engines; ads on social media platforms such as Facebook, Twitter, and Instagram; and e-mail. All of these initial channels can link to high-quality video ads and other resources, such as candidate Web sites that provide biographical information, position papers, and invitations to join e-mail lists, become a volunteer, or—you guessed it—donate. Because online advertising is often far cheaper than traditional alternatives, digital advertising has become a valuable alternative for lesser-known candidates. However, targeting voters can be difficult; it often relies on statistical models that analyze people's Web use based on tracking cookies, an inexact approach—especially when users adjust privacy settings to prevent it.[80]

Uncontrolled Media. Uncontrolled media, primarily news coverage and social media, can be crucial in campaigns. Precisely because the medium is not controlled by the candidates, it is often seen as more credible—and the media exposure itself is free, although candidates may spend considerable amounts trying to obtain favorable exposure.

Major political campaigns, like other campaigns, actively solicit news coverage of their "product," preferably on their terms. Media relations specialists provide reporters with reams of press releases, position papers, and other documentation supporting the candidate's alleged virtues. Campaign events are often timed to coincide with the schedules of evening network television programs and morning newspapers. Journalists are accorded preferential treatment in the campaign entourage and are privy to behind-the-scenes comings and goings and the occasional exclusive interview, all intended to foster good will while avoiding embarrassment. In this battle of wits, journalists balance their mandate as independent arbiters of the news with their need for access to the candidates. Of course, matters may be far different for local campaigns: a city council candidate might be thrilled to get one newspaper interview during the campaign—if there still is a local newspaper. In 2011 there were about one-quarter fewer newspapers than in the 1970s, and circulation was down about 30 percent despite the increase in population.[81] (A 2014 study found that newspaper closings in Denver and Seattle were associated with declines in people's civic engagement, although it cannot be proven that the former caused the latter).[82]

The pace of news coverage has quickened considerably, with the coming of around-the-clock news coverage on CNN (created in 1980) and its competitors, instantaneous satellite transmission to local broadcast stations and newspapers, and continuous news coverage on the Internet. Also, with the proliferation of camcorders and smartphones, statements by politicians that would have gone unreported in the past can end up as new stories, Internet viral videos, or both. Marion R. Just argues that "the audience has invaded the newsroom and is shaping the definition of news," not only by "contributing news content and comments," but also by "taking on the roles of distribution and editorial signaling via social network computing."[83] Social networks both draw audiences to news stories and provide continuous information to editors about what topics and approaches are catching on.

Despite the rise of online and mobile news sources, television remains the most broadly used news source. In a 2012 Pew study, 55 percent of respondents said they got news on television the day before, compared with 39 percent for online/mobile, 33 percent for radio, and 23 percent for print newspapers.[84] The approach of television news to campaign news has changed dramatically, as epitomized by the sharp decline in the length of "sound bites," or quotations from the candidates. In the 1968 campaign the average candidate sound bite was 43.1 seconds long. By 1988 it was down to 9 seconds, and it has been slightly shorter in recent campaigns.[85] This change does not necessarily mean that coverage has become more superficial; as Craig Fehrman points out, "Letting politicians ramble doesn't necessarily produce a better or more informative political discourse."[86] But surely it alters how candidates try to "get their message out" on the news.

Beyond the news, candidates often appear on—and are discussed or depicted on—other programs, such as talk shows and contemporary political comedy shows. In 1992 Democratic presidential candidate Bill Clinton played the saxophone on the *Arsenio Hall Show*, a late-night variety program, in part to increase his appeal to its relatively young audience. In twenty-first-century campaigns, comedy programs such as Comedy Central's *The Daily Show* and *The Colbert Report* (2005–2014) and HBO's *This Week Tonight* all provide a venue for candidates to be viewed in a positive or negative light. A 2009 study found that *The Daily Show* appeared to significantly worsen viewers'—especially nonpartisan viewers'—assessment of conservative candidates covered on the show during the 2004 primary season. Many conservative candidates, as well as liberal ones, appear on these programs hoping to appear in a positive light. However, appearing on a satirical program, or even playing the saxophone, is not without reputational risk.[87] Uncontrolled media may be free, but they rarely offer a free lunch.

Critics often complain that news media focus on "horse race" aspects of campaigns—who is behind and by how much, who is gaining, what strategies the candidates are using—at the expense of more substantive reporting about the candidates' policy proposals and qualifications. "Horse race" coverage may appeal to journalists for at least three reasons. First, it seems in fact to be popular; many people are more interested in knowing how the race stands than in learning more about candidates' competing visions of education reform. Second, it may be easier to sound objective in horse race coverage. Issue coverage poses awkward choices: either uncritically report what candidates have to say or risk being seen as taking a partisan stance by reporting, for example, that one candidate's education proposal is widely ridiculed by experts. As Jay Rosen puts it, "Focusing on the race advertises the political innocence of the press because 'who's gonna win?' is not an ideological question. By asking it you reaffirm that yours is not an ideological profession."[88] (Granted, horse race coverage has its own pitfalls; a candidate's supporters are unlikely to construe as objective a story that savages the candidate's electoral prospects.) Finally, actually locating, interviewing, and understanding experts on substantive issues—and then communicating what they have to say—may be far more difficult than "horse race" reporting, and most reporters are spread thin. Nevertheless, often ample issue coverage—at least straightforward reporting of candidates' stated positions—is available in some media sources. Issue coverage may be more prominent in smaller campaigns where polling data about the "horse race" is scanty or nonexistent.

The Emergence of Digital Politics

The 2008 presidential election was a watershed in citizens' use of digital media. In 2000 just 11 percent of adults relied on the Internet for most of their election news, far behind television, newspapers, and even radio. (Adults could mention one or two sources.) By 2008 that share had more than doubled, to 26 percent, surpassing radio and almost matching newspapers (28 percent)—although television remained far ahead, used by more than three-quarters of adults.[89] Nearly three-quarters of US Internet users—or 55 percent of adults—got some election news and information from the Internet. Over half (59 percent) of Internet users used e-mail, instant messaging, text messaging, or Twitter to send or receive political messages during the campaign.[90]

The 2008 election also saw greater polarization in the use of news sources. In 2004 only 26 percent of Internet political users said that most of the sites they visited shared their point of view; in 2008 that figure rose to 33 percent. The increase was even starker among young respondents aged eighteen to twenty-four: from 22 percent in 2004 to 43 percent in 2008. These changes parallel some critics' concerns that digital media contribute to a fragmentation and polarization of public discourse, as people confine themselves to ideologically homogeneous silos and seldom encounter opposing views.[91] Indeed, a highly polarized blogosphere of writers and readers—split between left and right—has emerged.[92] This polarization may be exacerbated by the knowledge gap phenomenon we described earlier in the chapter. Markus Prior argues that the massive information flow via cable television and the Internet has allowed motivated partisans to eclipse their less interested peers in political knowledge, leaving moderates with relatively little to say.[93]

Some elements of the digital campaign used in the 2008 election were used in earlier campaigns. In 1996 President Bill Clinton and at least six of his Republican challengers had candidate Web sites, though they were rather rustic by today's standards.[94] During the 2000 presidential primary campaign Republican John McCain pioneered online fund-raising. In 2004 Democratic candidate Howard Dean used online meeting technologies and blogging to increase voter engagement.

But Barack Obama's 2008 campaign set a new standard for digital campaigning. He offered supporters a wide range of digital tools, including donation boxes, sign-up sheets for volunteer opportunities, message boards, and political communications via e-mail and text message.[95] The MyBO.com (My Barack Obama) Web site served as the central hub for volunteers and was used to assign them tasks best suited to their location. The Web site allowed financial contributors to set giving targets, start fund-raisers, and even sign up to make donations at regular intervals. In addition, the campaign disseminated unfiltered promotional videos via You-Tube; regularly sent text messages to supporters; and aggressively used Twitter, Facebook, and MySpace. Obama campaign videos often went "viral," getting for-warded user-to-user via e-mail, social media platforms, and mobile phones. More than two-thirds of Internet users aged eighteen to twenty-nine watched one or more online campaign videos during the election season,[96] and this age group broke sharply for Obama. The campaign's skillful use of digital media is widely credited with contributing to his victories in both primary and general campaigns, particularly by motivating young people to vote. However, the impact of these media is difficult to assess. For example, according to exit polls, young voters (aged eighteen to twenty-nine) comprised 17 percent of the electorate in 2004 and 18 percent in 2008, hardly an epochal increase.[97]

By 2012, for the first time half the American public, and 71 percent of Amer-icans aged eighteen to twenty-nine, identified the Internet as a "main source of national and international news"—and nearly as many (47 percent of the public) turned to the Internet for campaign news.[98] And while digital news consumption increased significantly from 2008 and 2010, mobile and social media-based news consumption grew by leaps and bounds during the same period.[99] The Obama campaign redoubled its efforts in the digital sphere, making substantial use of social media and data-mining capabilities, particularly to increase voter registra-tion and turnout in key districts.[100] These campaign strategies were particularly appealing and engaging for younger voters, who arguably accounted for Obama's margin over Republican challenger Mitt Romney.[101] Undoubtedly political con-sultants will urge candidates to keep up with emerging forms and styles of digital media.

Impact of Election Campaigns on Public Opinion and Voting

We now examine three aspects of the impact of election campaign strategies and tactics on voters: what voters learn from such campaigns, the degree to which campaigns can influence voters' decisions, and the effect of campaigns on citizen interest in voting.

Learning from Campaigns. Voters can learn a lot from news coverage of candi-dates. Both newspaper and television news play significant roles in informing the public about campaign issues, and usually about candidate positions on them.[102] Some studies indicate that newspapers do a far better job than television of in-forming voters, presumably because of how they are used.[103] (Less is known about the effects of long-form journalism in magazines and some Internet sites, which may do even more to inform voters who use them.) But learning can vary for many other reasons, some of which are not well understood. For example, one study of the 1992 presidential election, in which Bill Clinton defeated Republican incumbent George H. W. Bush and third-party challenger Ross Perot, found very low levels of learning about the candidates' positions from either newspaper or television news, possibly due to a relative lack of substantive coverage.[104] As for differences in citizen response, politically interested people may learn more about candidates from newspapers than from television, but television and newspapers appear about even in informing the less involved.[105]

Well-publicized events such as debates provide a wellspring for issue learning and impression formation and may be especially effective in informing citizens who are less attuned to other aspects of the campaign.[106] Some individuals may also learn from the much-maligned television commercials. Political scientists Thomas Patterson and Robert McClure were the first to suggest that the ubiquitous spot ads contained enough nuggets of basic information—and were repeated often enough—to enlighten otherwise inattentive viewers about candidates' basic policy stances.[107] Indeed, the same study that found limited learning from television and newspaper coverage in 1992 found that watching campaign spot ads—both positive and negative—was highly associated with learning more about candidates' positions on issues.[108]

How Persuasive Are Campaigns? Election campaigns influence public opinion in several ways. "Strong" effects, such as dramatic changes in voter moods or preferences, are unlikely, but "weaker" influences on citizen perceptions and opinions are probable in major campaigns, given the effort expended.

One significant impact that campaigns are often assumed to have, but that is actually fairly rare, is convincing voters to switch from one candidate to another. Later research[109] has supported Paul Lazarsfeld's early finding: in most contests, a small percentage of voters actually change their minds. We need to keep in mind, however, that even small rates of vote switching may be decisive in close races. A shift of 1 percentage point in voting preferences may be "statistically insignificant" in a survey sample, yet decisive in an election.

Campaigns are more likely to keep already decided supporters of a candidate on track, reinforcing their decisions and motivating them to go to the polls.[110] As long as "my" candidates keep providing reasons that I should vote for them, it is unlikely, short of a major blunder or scandal, that I will turn to other candidates. But faced with a flood of messages from opposing politicians and little or no communication from my initial choices, I could begin to at least waver in my support. Even if I did not switch sides, I might simply not bother to vote. A second persuasive influence involves converting undecided voters, who often hold the balance of power in close elections. More difficult is to reach out to less involved citizens, who may appear as "undecided" in polls but are most likely not to vote at all. In recent years the question of how to persuade potential voters to turn out has inspired substantial research. For example, direct contact with campaign volunteers has been demonstrated to be more effective than outreach through the mail, although some mail formats work far better than others.[111]

People's level of involvement in a particular election is likely to influence their process of deciding how (or whether) to vote. Recall the discussion in Chapter 5 of information processing models. Studies have found that people with higher involvement in a problem or issue—or an election—generally make decisions more "logically," seeking and carefully processing relevant information.[112] In choosing a candidate, for example, the more involved voter may closely compare contenders' issue positions, voting records, administrative abilities, and so on. (Of course, highly involved partisans may already know for whom they will vote, so they really have no decision to make. They may learn about candidates for other reasons.) People with lower involvement are likely to base their decisions on peripheral cues that are readily accessible but less relevant to evaluating the candidates. These people might be swayed by the looks of a candidate, the offhand advice of a friend, a celebrity endorsement, the cleverness of a political ad, or hearing about some campaign gaffe.

Citizens vary greatly in our willingness to be involved in election decisions. These differences are partly personal (some people are more interested in politics than others) and partly situational (some elections and contests are more interesting than others). Some of us may spend weeks agonizing over a vote for president or US Senate, but may cast a ballot on the same election day for a city councilperson based on whose name is first on the ballot. Campaigners recognize such differences, particularly in their efforts to reach less involved potential voters. Television commercials that may seem repetitive and senseless to a politically astute voter might provide the only salient message that occurs to a far less interested person on Election Day.

Building Citizen Interest. Campaigns can build citizen interest in the election, alerting potential voters that a consequential event is coming up. Even the most politically disenfranchised and uninterested people find major campaigns difficult to ignore, especially given their exposure on television. Skipping the news is easy, but commercials on popular programs are difficult to avoid, even when they are spiritedly disliked. Studies of presidential campaigns have found that campaign coverage (on television and elsewhere) appears to heighten early interest among citizens during the primaries, with subsequent spikes of attentiveness during the nominating conventions and candidate debates.[113] The visual spectacles of the conventions and debates can draw in less involved voters. (The conventions often produce significant, although usually short-lived, shifts in candidate support as measured in polls.)

Election campaigns could also have broader effects on people's attitudes. On the one hand, campaigns could evoke a sense of public-spiritedness, perhaps reinforcing the legitimacy of the political system. After all, electing our political leaders is at the heart of American democratic governance. On the other hand, campaigns might evoke more cynicism than enthusiasm. If citizens are exposed to large doses of negative advertising, they may conclude that the candidates are all pretty poor—or at least that the system is poor—and lose interest in voting and other forms of participation.[114] Ansolabehere and Iyengar found citizen exposure to attack ads partially related to lower voter turnout in their 1992 California study, especially among independent, less-partisan potential voters.[115] Other evidence suggests that media "horse race" coverage may heighten cynicism; focusing on candidate strategies, rather than substantive disagreements on issues, may induce citizens to see election campaigns as empty games.[116] Despite all these concerns, evidence is scarce that election campaigns systematically demoralize citizens. The "honeymoon" of high approval ratings that Americans typically grant incoming presidents suggests that however skeptical or polarized people may be, most are willing to give a new president the benefit of the doubt.

What We Do Not Know about Election Campaign Influences

We still do not know very much about how political campaigns as *campaigns*—in the sense defined at the beginning of this chapter—affect voting decisions. This is true despite the seemingly endless outpouring of articles, books, and documentaries analyzing election outcomes. Although such analyses sometimes offer reasoned, plausible, and even well-supported speculation about voting behavior, many questions remain unanswered.

Part of the problem here is our inevitably limited information about potential voters. Despite all the questions that (for example) the National Election Studies ask a random sample of voters before and after presidential elections, it is impossible to tease out how all the campaign activities and events over the course of months influenced people's thinking. Shifts in preelection poll results often provide clues about the impact of events, but generally cannot measure the effects of most campaign activities. (Many past elections have few preelection polls to draw on; recent elections have more poll results, but combining data from many different sources is fraught with its own complications.) As we noted before, the sorts of small changes that determine the outcomes of close elections often are near or below the threshold of measurement error, too tiny for most surveys and other studies to detect.

In practice we often cannot separate the effects of the campaign operation itself from the impact of the candidate, of dramatic events beyond the candidate's control, or even of gradual economic trends. Many accounts have pointed to John F. Kennedy's handsome appearance in the first 1960 presidential debate—in contrast to Richard Nixon's beard stubble and generally unattractive demeanor—as a turning point, but the evidence for this is sparse. Similarly, despite all the praise for Barack Obama's 2008 Internet and social media campaign, it can be argued that he won because of the economic crisis in the early fall, and that his campaign made little difference. It further can be debated whether the crisis benefited him because his response to it was seen as more presidential than his opponent, John McCain's, or simply because he was a Democrat and the current president was a Republican. Much of what happens during and around election campaign periods is out of the hands of the planners and strategists. "Real life" goes on, with war, scandal, economic ups and downs, disasters, and similar events being quite beyond the control of the candidates, yet often dramatically affecting how voters respond to them.

A final difficulty worth mentioning is that in a close election, both candidates generally are campaigning hard. The net effect of those efforts often is close to a stalemate: a tug of war between two closely matched opponents. How can anyone tell whether a particular campaign initiative is useless, or on the contrary is crucial to maintaining that balance? Indeed, how can anyone tell how different things would be if one campaign took a week off?

For all these reasons, we should not expect comprehensive and definitive answers about campaign effectiveness. Even so, some learning is possible. For example, by looking at poll trends in past election seasons, we can learn to be skeptical about many accounts of "turning points" or "game-changers" that appear not to have made much difference at all. (A reporter found almost 20,000 media references to sixty-eight distinct "game-changers" in the 2012 presidential campaign, most of which seem not to have mattered.[117]) Internet-based panel surveys, in which the same people participate repeatedly over the course of a campaign, provide new insights into campaign dynamics, although we can be skeptical about their generalizability to citizens who are not repeatedly asked the same questions. Drawing, in part, on evidence from a YouGov panel survey, political scientists John Sides and Lynn Vavreck conclude that campaign advertisements had measurable but short-term effects. Analyzing the election results, Sides and Vavreck also conclude that Obama's field operation (direct contacts to potential voters) outperformed Romney's but was not decisive in any state. Thus, field operations may have a substantial impact on turnout even without influencing election outcomes.[118] Many experiments shed light on forms of campaign advertising and fieldwork that are more or less likely to work as intended. And it should be borne in mind that even a technically perfect campaign operation is unlikely to save a poor candidate who faces a strong opponent.

Emerging media channels will continue to give rise to new questions. Consider the relatively new phenomenon of "following" political candidates on social media such as Facebook, Twitter, and Instagram. One study found that by 2014, 16 percent of Americans followed at least one political figure on social media—up from just 6 percent in 2010.[119] This behavior may be utterly inconsequential—for example, if only the most committed partisans engage in it. Alternatively, it might provide new means for politicians to promote their policy views as well as their own candidacies. Similarly, by 2014, 28 percent of registered voters followed politics on their cell phones, up from 13 percent in 2010.[120] Could this trend increase public engagement and influence in politics, as people become increasingly able to react to political events and express their opinions during all waking hours? Will it widen the knowledge gap, and if so, with what consequences? On a related note, one Facebook experimental study during the 2010 general election found that posting a "social message" tagged with the names of friends who had voted increased turnout by about 0.4 percent—a small change, but noteworthy for a single message.[121] This study provides an intriguing glimpse into not only how campaigns may try to use social media, but also how social media may become a crucial venue for social persuasion processes such as those considered by the Columbia school (see Chapter 9). Even if, as one meta-analysis of relevant research suggests, social media use has "minimal impact on participation in political campaigns," including voting,[122] social media will provide a new window into people's attitudes and behaviors during campaigns.

How Well Is the Public Served by Press Coverage of Campaigns?

We have noted the complaint that news media show excessive concern with the "horse race" aspects of campaigns—and, some critics add, with negative depictions of candidates' personal attributes. As Todd Gitlin has put it, coverage of presidential campaigns is "shallow, trivial, preoccupied with the evanescent ups and the electrifying downs, the insiders' moods, the rumors and gaffes, and incurious about the candidates' records, and the weight or weightlessness of their arguments, the truth and untruth of their claims, and seemingly indifferent to the stakes of the most consequential election on earth."[123] Would not the public interest be far better served by more substantive reporting?[124] Many of these debates arguably pivot on the distinction, made in Chapter 4, between normative and empirical theory. Media critics present normative arguments about the kinds of information that voters should rely on in making their decisions. They argue that the media should provide that information, rather than resorting to cheap horse race coverage, "gotcha" reporting of trivial gaffes, and even invasions of personal privacy. Journalists often have a twofold response: that they offer more substantive information than the critics give them credit for, but crucially, that their decisions are—and must be—guided by what their audiences actually want and are willing to pay for. As Patterson notes:

> The problem is that the press is not a political institution. Its business is news, and the values of news are not those of politics. . . . Election news emphasizes what is controversial about events of the previous twenty-four hours rather than that which is stable and enduring. The coverage is framed within the context of a competitive game rather than being concerned with basic issues of policy and leadership. It projects images that fit story lines rather than political lines. Election news highlights what is unappetizing about politics rather than providing a well-rounded picture of the political scene.[125]

Crucially, for Patterson, these characteristics are not best understood as shortcomings of the news media: they are inherent in the news business, and they fulfill expectations of the audience. To wish for news to focus on "that which is stable and enduring" is to ignore the meaning of "news." Patterson does think that reporting can be better than it is—as is made quite apparent in his 2013 book *Informing the News*—for example, at identifying outright misinformation.[126] Nevertheless, we should not expect the news media to conform to idealized images of what a democratic public ought to want.

CONCLUSION: HOW WELL DO THE MEDIA SERVE PUBLIC OPINION?

It may have occurred to you that with a few adjustments, the previous discussion of election news is applicable to the news in general. Many media critics have complained that the news media fall far short of giving citizens the knowledge and understanding they need to form reasonable opinions about major social and political issues. The media's defenders reply that it is unrealistic to expect media outlets to play this educational role. Walter Lippmann observed in his 1922 book *Public Opinion*:

> We expect the newspaper to serve us with truth however unprofitable the truth may be. For this difficult and often dangerous service, which we recognize as fundamental, we expected to pay until recently the smallest coin turned out by the mint. . . . Nobody thinks for a moment that he ought to pay for his newspaper. . . . He will pay a nominal price when it suits him, will stop paying whenever it suits him, will turn to another newspaper when that suits him. . . . A free press, if you judge by the attitude of the readers, means newspapers that are virtually given away.[127]

Almost a century later, many readers expect news stories to be available for free online. Lippmann further noted that few newspapers could rely on readers' interest in political and social news, and so they resort to publishing "scandal and crime . . . , sports, pictures, actresses, advice to the lovelorn . . . , gardening, comic strips," and whatever else will draw readers.[128]

The underlying problem, Lippmann argued, is that critics unrealistically want the media to act as "the umpire in the unscored baseball game," adjudicating the truth of political disputes and a wide array of other questions.[129] Not only is this task wildly difficult, but most readers place little value on it. Reporters face both "a practical difficulty in uncovering the news, and the emotional difficulty of making distant facts interesting."[130] It is far easier, and for most readers more compelling, to report how an industrial strike will affect the readers than to investigate and report the underlying issues. It also poses less risk of alienating some readers by reaching conclusions they dislike. Lippmann concluded that we should not expect the press to overcome the limitations of our institutions—which rarely, if ever, provide answers to social questions in unambiguous, factual form—and our own limited taste for "uninteresting truths."[131]

We find Lippmann's analysis persuasive even now, but it is not the end of the story. The quality of journalism—the extent to which it serves the public's need for accurate information and insight into various important issues—can get better or worse over time. Many say it is getting worse; in the words of a 2006 Carnegie Corporation report, "the quality of journalism is losing ground in the drive for profit, diminished objectivity, and the spread of the 'entertainment virus.'"[132] Arguably the Internet provides access to some of the best journalism in history, if one knows where to find it, but for casual news consumers, the quality of information may well have declined. Local news seems especially under threat, as many newspapers have closed or sharply reduced their reporting.

We venture no predictions, but we reason that journalism is not foreordained to get worse. Patterson, in *Informing the News*, cites some encouraging evidence that media can improve. One promising sign is that although most people do not crave the healthy diet of policy analysis that some media critics might wish upon them, they do place real value on meaningful news. Patterson cites political scientist Michael Robinson's study of the headline news stories that Americans followed most closely over the period from 1986 to 2007. Some of the most closely followed categories are relatively "lowbrow": bad weather (short of disasters) ranked second, just behind war and terrorism. And as you might expect, foreign policy and international affairs ranked near the bottom. However, a variety of social problems and policy issues—pertaining to the economy, crime, health and safety, and other topics—all outranked "Inside Washington" politics, political scandals and other strictly political coverage, and celebrity stories. Celebrity scandals ranked lowest of all.[133]

Patterson argues that insider political coverage is oversupplied, due to journalists' preferences—"[m]ost journalists know a lot more about politics than they do about policy, and they like to cover what they know best"—and because it is faster and therefore cheaper.[134] But, he adds, reporting that better suits people's interests can succeed in the marketplace. Studies of local newscasts and newspapers have found that longer stories and stronger content tend to yield larger and more loyal audiences. Similarly, National Public Radio's in-depth reporting has attracted a growing audience, more than six times as large in the 1980s, while other broadcast news outlets have seen large declines in their audiences.[135] On the Internet, too, long-form journalism can draw substantial audiences.[136]

The social impact of this reporting is difficult to gauge and impossible to predict. It is manifestly unlikely that most citizens will turn to in-depth reporting, but it is surely possible that enough people will find enough quality information to sustain vibrant public debate. Policy interventions may help. Some observers argue, for example, that government subsidies to public television and radio networks (and their Internet portals) can help to sustain a healthy competition for quality news, or that providing free airtime to political candidates while restricting the torrents of campaign advertisements can improve the information quality of campaigns.[137] The increasing popularity of the Internet and social media further confounds any efforts to predict the trajectory of American mass media and democracy. We are at least confident that it will be interesting to watch.

NOTES

1. Harold Lasswell, "The Structure and Function of Communication in Society," in Lyman Bryson, ed., *The Communication of Ideas* (New York: Harper, 1948), 32–51.

2. Charles Wright, "Functional Analysis and Mass Communication," *Public Opinion Quarterly* 24 (1960): 606–620.

3. For example, see Herbert Blumer, "The Mass, the Public and Public Opinion," in Bernard Berelson and Morris Janowitz, eds., *Reader in Public Opinion and Communication* (New York: Free Press, 1960), 43–50.

4. US Census Bureau, *Statistical Abstract of the United States: 1999*, Table No. 1440, https://www.census.gov/prod/99pubs/99statab/sec31.pdf.

5. Lawrence R. Jacobs and Robert Y. Shapiro, "Informational Interdependence: Public Opinion and the Media in the New Communications Era," in Robert Y. Shapiro and Lawrence R. Jacobs, (eds.), *The Oxford Handbook of American Public Opinion and the Media* (New York: Oxford University Press, 2011), 1.

6. Walter Lippmann, *Public Opinion* (1922; New York: Free Press, 1965), ch. 1.

7. A classic study is Maxwell E. McCombs and Donald L. Shaw, "The Agenda-Setting Function of the Press," *Public Opinion Quarterly* 36 (1972): 176–187.

8. Oscar Gandy, *Beyond Agenda Setting* (Norwood, NJ: Ablex, 1982).

9. Michael B. Grossman and Martha J. Kumar, *Portraying the President: The White House and the News Media* (Baltimore, MD: Johns Hopkins University Press, 1981).

10. Benjamin I. Page, Robert Y. Shapiro, and Gregory R. Dempsey, "What Moves Public Opinion?," *American Political Science Review* 81 (1987): 23–43.

11. John R. Zaller, *The Nature and Origins of Mass Opinion* (Cambridge, UK: Cambridge University Press, 1992); Robert M. Entman, "Framing: Toward Clarification of a Fractured Paradigm," *Journal of Communication* 43 (1993): 293–300.

12. Clarice N. Olien, George A. Donohue, and Phillip J. Tichenor, "Conflict, Consensus and Public Opinion," in Theodore L. Glasser and Charles T. Salmon, eds., *Public Opinion and the Communication of Consent* (New York: Guilford Press, 1995), 301–323.

13. Edward Herman and Noam Chomsky, *Manufacturing Consent: The Political Economy of the Mass Media*, with new introduction (New York: Pantheon, 2002). A somewhat parallel critique, which also considers the campaign spending issues treated below, is John Nichols and Robert W. McChesney, *Dollarocracy: How the Money and Media Election Complex Is Destroying America* (New York: Nation Books, 2013).

14. On false balance, see David T. Z. Mindich, *Just the Facts: How "Objectivity" Came to Define American Journalism* (New York: New York University Press, 1998). The "opinions" language is inspired by economist Paul Krugman, who originally wrote— ironically, in the *New York Times*—that "If a presidential candidate were to declare that the earth is flat, you would be sure to see a news analysis under the headline 'Shape of the Planet: Both Sides Have a Point.'" Paul Krugman, "Reckonings: Bait and Switch," *New York Times*, November 1, 2000.

15. Lasswell, "Structure and Function of Communication in Society."

16. Bernard Cohen, *The Press and Foreign Policy* (Princeton, NJ: Princeton University Press, 1963), 13.

17. McCombs and Shaw, "Agenda-Setting Function of the Press."

18. Shanto Iyengar and Donald R. Kinder, *News That Matters: Television and American Opinion* (Chicago: University of Chicago Press, 1987).

19. David L. Protess et al., *The Journalism of Outrage: Investigative Reporting and Agenda Building in America* (New York: Guilford Press, 1991); Klaus Schoenbach and Lee B. Becker, "Origins and Consequences of Mediated Public Opinion," in Glasser and Salmon, eds., *Public Opinion and the Communication of Consent*, 301–323.

20. Shanto Iyengar, *Is Anyone Responsible? How Television Frames Political Issues* (Chicago: University of Chicago Press, 1991).

21. Jack M. McLeod, Gerald M. Kosicki, and Douglas M. McLeod, "The Expanding Boundaries of Political Communication Effects," in Jennings Bryant and Dolf Zillman, eds., *Media Effects: Advances in Theory and Research* (Hillsdale, NJ: Lawrence Erlbaum, 1994), 123–162.

22. Iyengar and Kinder, *News That Matters*; Dietram A. Scheufele and David Tewksbury, "Framing, Agenda Setting, and Priming: The Evolution of Three Media Effects Models," *Journal of Communication* 57 (2007): 9–20.

23. Jon A. Krosnick, "The Media and the Foundations of Presidential Support: George Bush and the Persian Gulf Conflict," *Journal of Social Issues* 49, no. 4 (1993): 167–182.

24. Rasmussen Reports, "87% Feel Media Covers Celebrities Too Much." July 18, 2010. http://www.rasmussenreports.com/public_content/lifestyle/people/july_2010/87_feel_media_covers_celebrities_too_much.

25. K. Viswanath and John R. Finnegan Jr., "The Knowledge Gap: Twenty-Five Years Later," in *Communication Yearbook 19*, ed. Bryant R. Burelson (Thousand Oaks, CA: Sage Publications, 1996), 187–228.

26. Phillip J. Tichenor, George A. Donohue, and Clarice N. Olien, "Mass Media and the Differential Growth in Knowledge," *Public Opinion Quarterly* 54 (1970): 158–170.

27. Pew Research Center, "Trends in News Consumption: 1991–2012; In Changing News Landscape, Even Television Is Vulnerable," September 27, 2012, 11. http://www.people-press.org/files/legacy-pdf/2012%20News%20Consumption%20Report.pdf.

28. Vincent Price and John Zaller, "Who Gets the News: Alternative Measures of News Reception and Their Implications for Research," *Public Opinion Quarterly* 57 (1993): 133–164.

29. Markus Prior, *Post-Broadcast Democracy* (New York: Cambridge University Press, 2007).

30. Darrell M. West, *Air Wars: Television Advertising and Social Media in Election Campaigns, 1952–2012*, 6th ed. (Washington, DC: CQ Press, 2013), esp. 152–154.

31. Stephen Ansolabehere and Shanto Iyengar, *Going Negative: How Political Advertisements Shrink and Polarize the Electorate* (New York: Free Press, 1995), 139–142.

32. Kathleen Hall Jamieson and Joseph N. Cappella, "Setting the Record Straight: Do Ad Watches Help or Hurt?," *International Journal of Press/Politics* 2 (1997): 13–22. For

further discussion, see Prior, *Post-Broadcast Democracy*; Glenn W. Richardson Jr., *Pulp Politics: How Political Advertising Tells the Story of American Politics* (Lanham, MD: Rowman & Littlefield, 2008), ch. 4.

33. Hadley Cantril, Hazel Gaudet, and Herta Hertzog, *The Invasion from Mars* (Princeton, NJ: Princeton University Press, 1940); Carl I. Hovland, Arthur A. Lumsdaine, and Fred D. Sheffield, *Experiments in Mass Communication* (Princeton, NJ: Princeton University Press, 1949).

34. Paul F. Lazarsfeld, Bernard Berelson, and Hazel Gaudet, *The People's Choice* (New York: Duell, Sloan and Pearce, 1944); Bernard Berelson, Paul. F. Lazarsfeld, and William N. McPhee, *Voting: A Study of Opinion Formation in a Presidential Campaign* (Chicago: University of Chicago Press, 1954).

35. Joseph Klapper, *The Effects of Mass Communication* (New York: Free Press, 1960).

36. Herbert H. Hyman and Paul B. Sheatsley, "Some Reasons Why Information Campaigns Fail," *Public Opinion Quarterly* 11 (1947): 412–423. This article eventually inspired a counterpoint: Harold Mendelsohn, "Some Reasons Why Information Campaigns Can Succeed," *Public Opinion Quarterly* 37 (1973): 50–61.

37. Paul M. Kellstedt, *The Mass Media and the Dynamics of Racial Attitudes* (New York: Columbia University Press, 2003); Frank R. Baumgartner, Suzanna L. De Boef, and Amber E. Boydstun, *The Decline of the Death Penalty and the Discovery of Innocence* (New York: Cambridge University Press, 2008).

38. The breadth of these changes was disputed. One group of political scientists, in *The Changing American Voter*, posited that American voters were becoming more politically sophisticated. A rebuttal was pointedly titled *The Unchanging American Voter*. Norman Nie, Sidney Verba, and John R. Petrocik, *The Changing American Voter* (Cambridge, MA: Harvard University Press, 1976); Eric R. A. N. Smith, *The Unchanging American Voter* (Chicago: University of Chicago Press, 1989).

39. See, e.g., George Gerbner, Larry Gross, Michael Morgan, and Nancy Signorelli, "Living with Television: The Dynamics of the Cultivation Process," in Jennings Bryant and Dolf Zillman, eds., *Perspectives on Media Effects* (Hillsdale, NJ: Lawrence Erlbaum, 1986), 17–40.

40. Paul M. Hirsch, "The 'Scary World' of the Non-viewer and Other Anomalies—A Reanalysis of Gerbner et al.'s Findings in Cultivation Analysis, Part 1," *Communication Research* 7 (1980): 403–456; Anthony Doob and Glenn E. MacDonald, "Television Viewing and the Fear of Victimization: Is the Relationship Causal?," *Journal of Personality and Social Psychology* 37 (1979): 170–179; Garrett J. O'Keefe, "Television Exposure, Credibility and Public Views on Crime," in Robert Bostrum, ed., *Communication Yearbook 8* (Newbury Park, CA: Sage Publications, 1984), 513–536.

41. See W. James Potter, "Cultivation Theory and Research: A Conceptual Perspective," *Human Communication Research* 19 (1993): 564–601.

42. Wilbur Schramm, Jack Lyle, and Edwin Parker, *Television in the Lives of Our Children* (Palo Alto, CA: Stanford University Press, 1961).

43. Elihu Katz, Jay G. Blumer, and Michael Gurevitch, "Utilization of Mass Media by the Individual," in Jay G. Blumer and Elihu Katz, eds., *The Uses of Mass Communication* (Beverly Hills, CA: Sage Publications, 1974), 9–32.

44. Alan M. Rubin, "The Effect of Locus of Control on Communication Motivation, Anxiety and Satisfaction," *Communication Quarterly* 41 (1993): 161–172.

45. Jack M. McLeod and Lee B. Becker, "Testing the Validity of Gratification Measures Through Political Effects Analysis," in Blumer and Katz, eds., *The Uses of Mass Communication*, 137–164.

46. Robert Huckfeldt and John Sprague, *Citizens, Politics, and Social Communication* (New York: Cambridge University Press, 1995), 292.

47. Karl E. Rosengren and Sven Windahl, "Mass Media Consumption as a Functional Alternative," in Dennis McQuail, ed., *Sociology of Mass Communication* (Hammondsworth, England: Penguin Books, 1972), 166–194.

48. Sandra J. Ball-Rokeach and Melvin DeFleur, "A Dependency Model of Mass Media Effects," *Communication Research* 3 (1976): 3–21.

49. Huckfeldt and Sprague, *Citizens, Politics, and Social Communication*.

50. John P. Robinson, "Interpersonal Influence in Election Campaigns: Two-Step Flow Hypotheses," *Public Opinion Quarterly* 40 (1976): 304–319.

51. Gabriel Weimann, *The Influentials: People Who Influence People* (Albany: State University of New York Press, 1994).

52. Joshua Meyrowitz, *No Sense of Place* (New York: Oxford University Press, 1985); Robert D. Putnam, *Bowling Alone: The Collapse and Revival of American Community* (New York: Simon and Schuster, 2001).

53. James W. Carey, "The Press, Public Opinion and Public Discourse," in Glasser and Salmon, eds., *Public Opinion and the Communication of Consent*, 373–402.

54. Contrast, e.g., Yochai Benkler, *The Wealth of Networks: How Social Production Transforms Markets and Freedom* (New Haven, CT: Yale University Press, 2006), and Cass R. Sunstein, *Republic.com 2.0* (Princeton, NJ: Princeton University Press, 2009).

55. Prior, *Post-Broadcast Democracy*.

56. Pew Research Center, "Trends in News Consumption," 16.

57. Ibid., 39.

58. Ibid., 4.

59. Steven Kull (principal investigator), "Misperceptions, The Media and the Iraq War," Program on International Policy Attitudes and Knowledge Networks, October 2, 2003, http://www.pipa.org/OnlineReports/Iraq/IraqMedia_Oct03/IraqMedia_Oct03_rpt.pdf.

60. Clay Ramsay et al., "Misinformation and the 2010 Election: A Study of the US Electorate," conducted by WorldPublicOpinion.org and Knowledge Networks, December 10, 2010, http://www.worldpublicopinion.org/pipa/pdf/dec10/Misinformation_Dec10_rpt.pdf.

61. Stefano DellaVigna and Ethan Kaplan, "The Political Impact of Media Bias" (working paper, June 26, 2007), http://eml.berkeley.edu/~ekaplan/wbpaper.pdf; Daniel

J. Hopkins and Jonathan M. Ladd, "The Reinforcing Effects of Fox News" (working paper, February 13, 2012), http://people.iq.harvard.edu/~dhopkins/FoxPersuasion 021212.pdf.

62. Everett M. Rogers and J. Douglas Storey, "Communication Campaigns," in Charles R. Berger and Steven H. Chaffee, eds., *Handbook of Communication Science* (Newbury Park, CA: Sage Publications, 1987), 821.

63. Philip Kotler and Eduardo L. Roberto, *Social Marketing: Strategies for Changing Public Behavior* (New York: Free Press, 1989).

64. Brendan Nyhan, Jason Reifler, Sean Richey, and Gary L. Freed, "Effective Messages in Vaccine Promotion: A Randomized Trial," *Pediatrics* 133 (2014): 835–842.

65. June A. Flora, Nathan Maccoby, and John W. Farquhar, "Communication Campaigns to Prevent Cardiovascular Disease: The Stanford Community Studies," in Ronald Rice and Charles Atkin, eds., *Public Communication Campaigns*, 2nd ed. (Newbury Park, CA: Sage Publications, 1989), 233–252.

66. Rogers and Storey, "Communication Campaigns"; Garrett J. O'Keefe and Kathaleen Reid, "The Uses and Effects of Public Service Advertising," in James Grunig and Larissa Grunig, eds., *Public Relations Research Annual* (Hillsdale, NJ: Lawrence Erlbaum, 1990), 2:67–94.

67. Jean Baudrillard, "Consumer Society," in Jean Baudrillard, *Selected Writings* (Stanford, CA: Stanford University Press, 1988), 29–56.

68. Leo Bogart, *Commercial Culture: The Media System and the Public Interest* (New York: Oxford University Press, 1995).

69. Charles T. Salmon, "Campaigns and Social 'Improvement': An Overview of Values, Rationales, and Impacts," in Charles T. Salmon, ed., *Information Campaigns: Balancing Social Values and Social Change* (Newbury Park, CA: Sage Publications, 1989), 19–53.

70. David Paletz, Roberta Pearson, and David Willis, *Politics in Public Service Advertising on Television* (New York: Springer, 1977).

71. Lana F. Rakow, "Information and Power: Toward a Critical Theory of Information Campaigns," in Salmon, ed., *Information Campaigns*, 164–184.

72. Shirley A. White, with K. Sadanandan Nair and Joseph Ascroft, eds., *Participatory Communication* (Thousand Oaks, CA: Sage Publications, 1994); Jan Servaes, ed., *Communication for Development and Social Change* (Thousand Oaks, CA: Sage Publications, 2007).

73. A classic description of the rise of these techniques is Joe McGinnis, *The Selling of the President 1968* (New York: Simon & Schuster, 1969).

74. Aaron Blake, "Both Romney and Obama Ran $1 Billion Campaigns," *Washington Post*, December 7, 2012, http://www.washingtonpost.com/blogs/the-fix /wp/2012/12/07/both-romney-and-obama-ran-1-billion-campaigns/.

75. "Election 2012: Independent Spending Totals," Politics, *New York Times*, http:// elections.nytimes.com/2012/campaign-finance/independent-expenditures/totals.

76. "Overall Spending Inches Up in 2014: Megadonors Equip Outside Groups to Capture a Bigger Share of the Pie," Center for Responsive Politics, October 29, 2014,

http://www.opensecrets.org/news/2014/10/overall-spending-inches-up-in-2014
-megadonors-equip-outside-groups-to-capture-a-bigger-share-of-the-pie/.

77. Darrell M. West, "Can Billionaires Buy Elections?" *FixGov* (blog), Brookings Institution, January 27, 2015, http://www.brookings.edu/blogs/fixgov/posts/2015/01/27
-can-billionaires-buy-elections-west.

78. An informative discussion of how campaigns assess the impact of controlled media and other campaign activities is Sasha Issenberg, *The Victory Lab: The Secret Science of Winning Campaigns* (New York: Broadway Books, 2013).

79. An excellent history of early televised campaign advertisements is Edward Diamond and Steven Bates, *The Spot: The Rise of Political Advertising on Television* (Cambridge, MA: MIT Press, 1984).

80. Derek Willis, "Online Political Ads Have Been Slow to Catch On as TV Reigns," *The Upshot* (blog), *New York Times*, January 29, 2015, http://www.nytimes
.com/2015/01/30/upshot/why-online-political-ads-have-been-slow-to-catch-on.html.

81. Newspaper Association of America, "Newspaper Circulation Volume," September 4, 2012, http://www.naa.org/Trends-and-Numbers/Circulation-Volume/Newspaper-Circulation-Volume.aspx.

82. Lee Shaker, "Dead Newspapers and Citizens' Civic Engagement," *Political Communication* 31 (2014): 131–148.

83. Marion R. Just, "What's News: A View from the Twenty-First Century," in Shapiro and Jacobs, eds., *The Oxford Handbook of American Public Opinion and the Media*, ch. 7, 106.

84. Pew Research Center, "Trends in News Consumption," 12.

85. Daniel C. Hallin, "Soundbite News: Television Coverage of Elections, 1968–1988," in *We Keep America on Top of the World: Television Journalism and the Public Sphere*, ch. 7 (New York: Routledge, 1993); Eric Bucy and Maria E. Grabe, "Taking Television Seriously: A Sound and Image Bite Analysis of Presidential Campaign Coverage, 1992–2004," *Journal of Communication* 57 (2007): 652–675.

86. Craig Fehrman, "The Incredible Shrinking Sound Bite," *Boston Globe*, January 2, 2011, http://www.boston.com/bostonglobe/ideas/articles/2011/01/02/the_incredible
_shrinking_sound_bite.

87. Jonathan S. Morris, "*The Daily Show with Jon Stewart* and Audience Attitude Change during the 2004 Party Conventions," *Political Behavior* 31 (2009): 79–102.

88. Jay Rosen, "The Beast Without a Brain: Why Horse Race Journalism Works for Journalists and Fails Us," *TomDispatch.com*, January 20, 2008, http://www.tomdispatch.com/post/174883/.

89. Aaron Smith, "The Internet's Role in Campaign 2008," Pew Internet & American Life Project, April 2009, 51–52, http://www.pewinternet.org/files/old-media/Files
/Reports/2009/The_Internets_Role_in_Campaign_2008.pdf

90. Ibid., 3.

91. W. Lance Bennett and Shanto Iyengar, "The Shifting Foundations of Political Communication," *Journal of Communication* 60 (2010): 35–39; Sunstein, *Republic.com 2.0*.

92. Eric Lawrence, John Sides, and Henry Farrell, "Self-Segregation or Deliberation? Blog Readership, Participation, and Polarization in American Politics," *Perspectives on Politics* 8 (2010): 141–157.

93. Markus Prior, *Post-Broadcast Democracy* (New York: Cambridge University Press, 2007).

94. Captures of these and other presidential campaign Web sites can be found at http://www.4president.us.

95. Smith, "The Internet's Role in Campaign 2008," 11–12; David Talbot, "How Obama *Really* Did It," *MIT Technology Review*, August 19, 2008, http://www.tech nologyreview.com/featuredstory/410644/how-obama-really-did-it/.

96. Smith, "The Internet's Role in Campaign 2008," 31–32.

97. Scott Keeter, Juliana Horowitz, and Alec Tyson, "Young Voters in the 2008 Election," Pew Research Center, November 13, 2008, http://www.pewresearch.org/2008 /11/13/young-voters-in-the-2008-election/.

98. Andrea Caumont, "12 Trends Shaping Digital News," *Fact Tank* (blog), Pew Research Center, October 16, 2013, http://www.pewresearch.org/fact-tank/2013/10/16/12 -trends-shaping-digital-news/.

99. Pew Research Center, "Trends in News Consumption," 6–7.

100. Joe Murphy et al., "Social Media in Public Opinion Research: Report of the AAPOR Task Force on Emerging Technologies in Public Opinion Research," American Association for Public Opinion Research, May 28, 2014, 44, http://www.aapor.org /AAPORKentico/AAPOR_Main/media/MainSiteFiles/AAPOR_Social_Media_Re-port_FNL.pdf; Richard M. Perloff, *The Dynamics of Political Communication: Media Politics in a Digital Age*, 3rd ed. (New York: Routledge, 2014), 334–335; Issenberg, *The Victory Lab*.

101. CIRCLE (The Center for Information and Research on Civic Learning and Engagement), "At Least 80 Electoral Votes Depended on Youth," November 7, 2012, http://www.civicyouth.org/at-least-80-electoral-votes-depended-on-youth/.

102. Steven H. Chaffee, Xinsho Zhao, and Glenn Leshner, "Political Knowledge and the Campaign Media of 1992," *Communication Research* 21 (1994): 305–324.

103. John P. Robinson and Dennis K. Davis, "Television News and the Informed Public: An Information-Processing Approach," *Journal of Communication* 40 (1990): 106–119.

104. Craig Leonard Brians and Martin P. Wattenberg, "Campaign Issue Knowledge and Salience: Comparing Reception from TV Commercials, TV News, and Newspapers," *American Journal of Political Science* 40 (1996): 172–193.

105. Thomas E. Patterson, *The Mass Media Election: How Americans Choose Their President* (New York: Praeger, 1980).

106. Stanley Kaus, *The Great Debates: Carter vs. Ford* (Bloomington: Indiana University Press, 1979); Kathleen Hall Jamieson and David S. Birdsell, *Presidential Debates: The Challenge of Creating an Informed Electorate* (New York: Oxford University Press, 1988).

107. Thomas E. Patterson and Robert D. McClure, *The Unseeing Eye: The Myth of Television Power in National Politics* (New York: G. P. Putnam's Sons, 1976).

108. Brians and Wattenberg, "Campaign Issue Knowledge."

109. See, e.g., Diana C. Mutz, Paul Sniderman, and Richard Brody, eds., *Political Persuasion and Attitude Change* (New York: Springer, 1986).

110. For example, Ansolabehere and Iyengar, in a study of 1992 California elections, found that television ads were far more effective in reinforcing existing partisan sentiments among voters than in manipulating or causing changes in candidate predispositions. Steven Ansolabehere and Shanto Iyengar, *Going Negative: How Attack Ads Shrink and Polarize the Electorate* (New York: Free Press, 1993).

111. Perloff, *Dynamics of Political Communication*, 335; Donald P. Green and Alan S. Gerber, *Get Out the Vote: How to Increase Voter Turnout*, 2nd ed. (Washington, DC: Brookings Institution Press, 2008). For other examples, see Issenberg, *The Victory Lab*.

112. Richard E. Petty and John T. Cacioppo, *Communication and Persuasion: Central and Peripheral Route to Attitude Change* (New York: Springer, 1986).

113. Thomas E. Patterson, *The Mass Media Election: How Americans Choose Their President* (New York: Praeger, 1980).

114. Kathleen Hall Jamieson, *Dirty Politics: Deception, Distraction, and Democracy* (New York: Oxford University Press, 1992).

115. Ansolabehere and Iyengar, *Going Negative*.

116. Joseph N. Cappella and Kathleen Hall Jamieson, *Spiral of Cynicism: The Press and the Public Good* (New York: Oxford University Press, 1997).

117. Tim Murphy, "Every Single Political Game-Changer of the 2012 Election," *Mother Jones*, November 4, 2012; John Sides and Lynn Vavreck, *The Gamble: Choice and Chance in the 2012 Presidential Election* (Princeton, NJ: Princeton University Press, 2013).

118. Sides and Vavreck, *The Gamble*.

119. Aaron Smith, "Cell Phones, Social Media and Campaign 2014," Pew Research Center, November 3, 2014, 3–5, http://www.pewinternet.org/files/2014/10/PI_Cell PhonesSocialMediaCampaign2014_110314.pdf.

120. Ibid., 2.

121. Robert M. Bond et al., "A 61-Million-Person Experiment in Social Influence and Political Mobilization," *Nature* 489 (September 13,2012): 295–298.

122. Shelley Boulianne, "Social Media Use and Participation: A Meta-Analysis of Recent Research," *Information, Communication & Society* 18 (2015): 524–538.

123. Gitlin wrote this in 2008 as his recollection of his comments to a CBS News *60 Minutes* producer on coverage of the 1980 election. Todd Gitlin, "A Pause for a Meta Moment," *TPMCafe* (blog), January 20, 2008, http://www.tpmcafe.com/blog/coffee-house/2008/jan/20/a_pause_for_a_meta_moment (via archive.org).

124. Larry Sabato, *Feeding Frenzy: How Attack Journalism Has Transformed American Politics* (New York: Free Press, 1993); Twentieth Century Fund, *The Report of the Twentieth Century Fund Task Force on Television and the Campaign of 1992:*

1-800-PRESIDENT (New York: Twentieth Century Fund Press, 1993); S. Robert Lichter and Richard E. Noyes, *Good Intentions Make Bad News: Why Americans Hate Campaign Journalism* (Lanham, MD: Rowman and Littlefield, 1995); Jay Rosen, "The Beast Without a Brain," http://www.tomdispatch.com/post/174883/.

125. Thomas E. Patterson, *Out of Order* (New York: Vintage Books, 1994).

126. Thomas E. Patterson, *Informing the News: The Need for Knowledge-Based Journalism* (New York: Vintage Books, 2013).

127. Lippmann, *Public Opinion*, 203–204.

128. Ibid., 211.

129. Ibid., 217.

130. Ibid., 221.

131. Ibid., 228.

132. Christopher Connell, *Journalism's Crisis of Confidence* (New York: Carnegie Corporation of New York, 2006), 3, quoted in Patterson, *Informing the News*, 6.

133. Patterson, *Informing the News*, 109–114; Michael J. Robinson, "Two Decades of American News Preferences," parts 1 and 2, Pew Research Center, 2007, http://www.pewresearch.org/2007/08/15/two-decades-of-american-news-preferences/.

134. Ibid., 115–116.

135. Ibid., 121–122.

136. Ibid., 123–124.

137. See, e.g., Nichols and McChesney, *Dollarocracy*.

12

CHAPTER

Looking Ahead

This text has covered enormous ground, because public opinion is such an interesting and complex phenomenon. The continuing growth in opinion polling and the rise of new media, social media, and communication technology intensify this complexity. With so much varied research in the area, it is difficult to wrap things up, to come to a clean and decisive endpoint in our analysis of public opinion. Early on in this book, we argued that the meaning of "public opinion" is always shifting. How we think about the concept depends on historical circumstance as well as on our research hypotheses and, more than ever today, the technologies we have on hand to assess public opinion and the influences on it. As sophisticated as our present techniques for opinion expression and measurement may seem, there will always be new developments because so many agents—including political candidates and leaders, journalists, market researchers, and citizens—will always have a stake in the effective evaluation of the popular mood. From a scholarly perspective, one thing about public opinion is clear: it must be studied from an interdisciplinary viewpoint. As you saw in this book, public opinion is a psychological, sociological, economic, and political phenomenon all at the same time. Public opinion formation takes place constantly as people react to the world around them. We are all bombarded with persuasive communications daily, from the mass media, online, through social media, from local political leaders, and from our friends and our families. This flood of incoming information—often symbolic in nature—shapes how people think about particular political events, actors, and policy. We have studied the way individuals' opinions are shaped, but we have also looked at those who do the shaping, the mass media in particular. And we have spent some time on the relationship between public opinion and the nature of American government and policymaking in different areas. All of these linkages—between people and media, among people, and between people and their leaders—are critical to understanding the role of public opinion in American democracy. It is a challenge to think about the nature of public opinion and how it changes, but it is also one of the most important and exciting phenomena in democratic theory to study. We can only improve our democracy by paying attention to public opinion, since the voice of the people is the foundation for self-rule.

We can detect some clear trends in public opinion research, in particular that an ever-growing community of researchers across fields, in public and private sectors, is interested in studying public opinion. Yet what about public opinion itself? How will citizen expression alter in the future? What public opinion becomes, what the channels for expression will be, and how much attention will be paid to it all depend on general social conditions and trends, events, the behavior (and misbehavior) of the nation's leaders at all levels, and developments in our political institutions. For example, if the American political parties continue to engage in a high level of conservative versus liberal ideological conflict, will this conflict penetrate throughout the public at large? Will moderates in the public disappear as people take sides—creating the "50–50 nation" referred to in Chapter 9—or will they remain substantial but increasingly alienated from politics? Will interest groups fall in line on one side or the other in this political configuration, or will they remain important as a fully separate means of articulation of public opinion? Or will events upend what we think we know about partisan polarization? For example, will a third major party somehow emerge, drawing support from both major parties? Or will changes in the communication environment compel the parties to become less ideologically distinct and more likely to engage in compromise to deal with pressing national problems and issues? If this were to happen—or in order for this to happen—parties might develop different means of understanding and articulating public opinion, or of leading and educating the citizenry of the nation.

As shown in this book, technologies for public-opinion-related processes and expression matter very much in any historical period. For at least the last forty years, television has dominated the scene as the shaper of public attitudes. Before television, there was radio, and before that, the heyday of newspapers. The Internet and now also social media have become places to find news and information, to express opinions and to learn about the opinions of our fellow citizens. Politicians have also found ways to keep in touch with constituents and persuade them through this new medium. The possibilities for public opinion expression and evaluation over the Internet and social media are astounding today, and we look forward to seeing how this plays out further in the years ahead. But it is important to keep in mind that technology has ultimately been controlled by people. Political culture will always determine how and when the Internet and social media are used for the expression or manipulation of public opinion, since technologies do not act—people do.

As computer-mediated social environments continue to grow, how will public opinion research change? It is likely that many of the theories and research findings in this book that deal with public opinion change may be replicated in computer-mediated environments. A persuasive speech may be persuasive in the same ways whether it is received in person at a town meeting, in one's living room via television, over the Internet, or on a handheld device. Some theories will receive support across media environments, but we will also have to develop new ideas about public opinion that are tied specifically to new technologies like the Internet and social media. Interpersonal communication appears to be very different over the Internet and through social media than in face-to-face interactions, as many communication scholars have argued. If this is the case, an entirely new style of political conversation has developed, and we are only now figuring out how best to study such dialogue among citizens and their leaders.

When we think about the future, we must always think about the past. A historical perspective is crucial if we are to consider the shape of public opinion—and indeed democracy—in the next few decades. Our older theories and ideas are of enormous value because they tell us what to look for and what might be important as we describe and analyze the political world. It is a certainty that as long as we live in a democracy, public opinion will be the focus of great efforts. People will always want to express their opinions, and politicians will always want to hear those opinions, whether to serve citizens better, to manipulate them more effectively, or perhaps just to stay in office.

As we think about the often troubled but crucial relationship between the public and its leaders, perhaps it is best not to end on a cynical note, but on a hopeful and historical one. Abraham Lincoln, one of the most impressive democratic leaders of all time, was also—not surprisingly—very attentive to public opinion, and thoughtful about it. In many ways, Lincoln anticipated the problems of mass democracy and how difficult it would be for American presidents to hear all the citizens all the time. But Lincoln did his best, creating forums for public expression and listening as hard as he could, given the pressures of his office. As the Civil War raged in 1863, Lincoln explained to a journalist why he had common citizens visit him at the White House:

I feel—though the tax on my time is heavy—that no hours of my day are better employed than those which thus bring me again within the direct contact and atmosphere of the average of our whole people. Men moving only in an official circle are apt to become merely official—not to say arbitrary—in their ideas, and are apter and apter, with each passing day, to forget that they only hold power in a representative capacity. Now this is all wrong. I go into these promiscuous receptions of all who claim to have business with me twice a week, and every applicant for audience has to take his turn, as if waiting to be shaved in a barber's shop. Many of the matters brought to my notice are utterly frivolous, but others are of more or less importance, and all serve to renew in me a clearer and more vivid image of that great popular assemblage out of which I sprung, and to which at the end of two years I must return. I tell you that I call these receptions my *"public opinion baths,"* for I have but little time to read the papers and gather public opinion that way; and though they may not be pleasant in all their particulars, the effect, as a whole, is renovating and invigorating to my perceptions of responsibility and duty [1] (emphasis in original).

Do our own leaders do as well as Lincoln in taking public opinion seriously? Might new media, social media, and advances in communication technology be used to this effect? How will people go about forming and expressing their opinions on major political and social issues? The future of public opinion remains to be written.

NOTES

1. Abraham Lincoln, introduction to "My 'Public Opinion Baths,'" in Mario Cuomo and Harold Holzer, eds., *Lincoln and Democracy* (New York: HarperCollins, 1990), 284–285.

INDEX

CPSIA information can be obtained at www.ICGtesting.com
Printed in the USA
LVOW10s2041250516

489709LV00008B/11/P